TRACKING
AMERICA'S
ECONOMY

Third Edition

TRACKING
AMERICA'S
ECONOMY

Third Edition

Norman Frumkin

M.E. Sharpe
Armonk, New York
London, England

Library of Congress Cataloging-in-Publication Data

Frumkin, Norman.
Tracking America's economy / Norman Frumkin.—3rd ed.
p. cm.
Includes bibliographical references and index.
ISBN 0-7656-0001-3 (hardcover : alk. paper).—ISBN 0-7656-0002-1 (pbk. : alk. paper)
1. Economic forecasting—United States.
2. Economic indicators—United States.
3. United States—Economic policy—1981–1993.
4. United States—Economic policy—1993–. I. Title
HC106.8.F78   1997
338.5′44′0973—dc21
97–38468
CIP

Printed in the United States of America

The paper used in this publication meets the minimum requirements of the
American National Standard for Information Sciences—
Permanence of Paper for Printed Library Materials,
ANSI Z 39.48-1984.

♾

BM (c)   10   9   8   7   6   5   4   3   2   1
BM (p)   10   9   8   7   6   5   4   3   2   1

To Sarah, Jacob, and Samuel

In memory of Anne Frances Frumkin and Joseph Harry Frumkin

CONTENTS

13 • Leading Indicator System

TABLES

FIGURES

PREFACE

What is meant by "the economy"? It is a way of grasping a basic aspect of human existence—how people earn a living and what affects their living conditions. It is tangible in that we continuously experience it and intangible because we cannot touch or see it.

Since ancient times, people have grappled with the question of what drives the economy. But understanding continues to be elusive. Success as an entrepreneur or executive, as a worker, or as a public official brings insights into particular aspects of the economy, but these are limited. Economists build constructs of the economy to monitor and evaluate such phenomena as economic growth, business cycle fluctuations, incomes, inflation, and productivity. Analyses of how the economy is performing and how to affect its performance center on the interrelationships of various economic indicators that record statistical movements on a daily, weekly, monthly, quarterly, annual, and multiyear basis. These are helpful, but the economy is too complex to be reduced to particular theories and how the theories conform to statistical experience.

Despite this incomplete understanding, the economy's importance in the private and public lives of a nation makes it essential that we continue to study it to elucidate private and public actions that are likely to improve the material well-being of the population. Economic history is made every day. The economy is a living field that continuously brings new conditions, new data, and new understanding. Its study is never finished. It is in this spirit that I have written this third edition of *Tracking America's Economy*.

The book provides a pragmatic approach for viewing the domestic and international dimensions of the ever-new economic landscape of the United States, for gauging its strengths and weaknesses, and for anticipating where it is headed. This edition broadens the focus of the earlier ones. The previous editions highlighted the use of several economic indicators in measuring and evaluating business cycles and economic growth, employment, inflation, and finance. In contrast, the current volume emphasizes broad economic topics, each of which includes several economic indicators used in quantifying and analyzing the overall topic. For example, the chapter on economic growth encompasses the gross domestic product as the basic measure of economic growth, the sources of economic growth, and a technique for anticipating when economic growth will turn negative into a cyclical recession. Thus, this edition shows more of the interrelationships that drive the American economy.

As previously, two guiding principles are followed in this edition. First, because it is important that the content and meaning of the statistical data underlying the economic indicators be understood, the data methodology as well as interpretation of the indicators are basic ingredients of the book. Second, every effort is made to write the book clearly so that it is accessible to persons with no special training in economics as well as to economists.

Tracking America's Economy concentrates on the macro economy, although it includes qualitative influences of microeconomic factors on macro developments. The macro economy summarizes the myriad transactions occurring every moment among individual buyers and sellers, employers and employees, lenders and borrowers, private parties and governments, and U.S. individuals and businesses and those of other countries. It is real in that it systematizes what actually occurs in daily economic life. It is also an abstraction in that while it reflects the results of the motivations and decisions made by individuals, companies, unions, governments, and other parties, it does not identify or quantify the underlying motivations and decisions. These motivations and decisions constitute the micro economy. In short, the micro economy represents the causes of individual economic actions and the macro economy represents their effects. But there are also feedback effects of the macro economy on the micro economy, such as changes in interest rates through the monetary policies of the Federal Reserve and the fiscal tax and spending programs of federal, state, and local governments.

The book has these new and expanded features:

- New framework for macroeconomic analysis, policies, and forecasting
- Expanded analyses of economic growth, inflation, and finance
- Expanded conceptual and statistical aspects of economic indicators
- Data and analyses are updated to 1996 and the first quarter of 1997

Chapter 1 discusses several conceptual and statistical aspects of the data used in the book, an important but often neglected topic in economic analysis. Chapter 2 provides a framework for analyzing and forecasting the economy; it also introduces and places the individual topics in chapters 3 through 13 in an overall perspective. Chapter 3 covers the aggregate dimensions of economic growth. Chapters 4 through 7 cover the household, business, international, and investment and saving components of economic growth. Chapters 8 through 10 cover the labor indicators of employment, unemployment, and productivity. Chapter 11 discusses inflation. Chapter 12 focuses on finance. Chapter 13 covers the leading indicator system.

The chapters include short statements in italics following the analytic discussions of what the analyst should focus on in evaluating recent movements of the data. Review questions at the end of each chapter are useful for solidifying the understanding of main topics in the chapter.

The manuscript was completed in the spring of 1997. The bulk of the data is produced by U.S. government agencies: Bureau of the Census and Bureau of Economic Analysis in the Department of Commerce, Bureau of Labor Statistics in the Department of Labor, Federal Reserve Board, Department of the Treasury, and Office of Management and Budget. Main publications for the primary data of these agencies are the *Survey of Current Business, Monthly Labor Review, Federal Reserve Bulletin, Treasury Bulletin,* and *Budget of the United States Government.* Selected data series are also produced by private organizations. The specific data sources are noted in the chapters where they are used. Much of the data used in the book are compiled monthly in *Economic Indicators,* a handy secondary publication prepared by the U.S. Council of Economic Advisers for the Joint Economic Committee of Congress. The appendix tables to the annual *Economic Report of the President,* also prepared by the Council of Economic Advisers, are the most convenient source for historical data.

Stephen Dalphin of M.E. Sharpe encouraged me to write this edition. Edward Steinberg reviewed the entire manuscript and provided the "extra credit" review questions. His incisiveness and sophistication were a unique contribution to the ideas and clarity of the book. Others who gave important comments on various sections are: James August, Dean Baker, Michael Boldin, William Dickens, Gerald Donahoe, Stanley Duobinis, Jacob Frumkin, Steven Haugen, David Hirschberg, Patrick Jackman, William Lang, David Laster, Robert McIntire, Stephen McNees, Thomas Nardone, Lois Plunkert, Howard Rosen, Larry Rosenblum, Stuart Scott, John Stinson, and Victor Zarnowitz. I had helpful discussions with Robert Arnold, Edward Cowan, Seth Elan, David Findley, Robert Parker, Richard Peach, and Geoffrey Tootell. Samuel Frumkin retrieved and converted data and texts between different computer systems. And I benefited from classes I gave to U.S. Census Bureau employees on the use and preparation of economic indicators. The editorial staff of M. E. Sharpe produced the book with the highest professionalism: Esther Clark prepared the manuscript for production; Wendy Muto was the production editor; Irene Glynn was the copyeditor; Arden Kuhlman was the typesetter.

I thank all of the above for their help. They made the book much better. But they do not necessarily agree with all the statements here. I am responsible for everything in the book.

I worked on the book over the course of a year at home in Washington, D.C., and during a winter in Hollywood, Florida, in the companionship of my wife, Sarah.

TRACKING
AMERICA'S
ECONOMY

Third Edition

1
CONCEPTUAL AND STATISTICAL
ASPECTS OF ECONOMIC INDICATORS

The statistics central to evaluating and forecasting the macro economy of the United States are often referred to as economic indicators. This chapter discusses several conceptual and statistical topics that underlie the indicators. The topics are business cycles, economic growth and growth cycles; seasonality; index numbers; data accuracy; calculating and presenting growth rates; inflation-adjusted dollars; the underground economy; distinctions among "goods," "services," and "structures"; the production of economic statistics; and data integrity.

BUSINESS CYCLES, ECONOMIC GROWTH, AND GROWTH CYCLES

Business cycles are the recurring rises and falls in the overall economy as reflected in production, employment, profits, and prices. They are associated with capitalistic societies in which production, employment, prices, wages, and interest rates are largely determined in the marketplace. They are primarily associated with industrially advanced nations that have highly developed business and financial structures, in contrast to developing nations that have a large agricultural component that is subject to the vagaries of weather and the consequent abundant or poor harvests. Business cycles reflect the inability of the marketplace to accommodate smoothly such factors as new technologies, shifting markets for new and substitute products, uncertainties and risks in business investments, intensified worldwide competition, and shortages and gluts created by wars, weather-dependent harvests, and cartels.

Economists have offered various theories to explain the causes of business cycles in the past, and they continue to provide varying explanations today. The theories are tested empirically against the movements of the relevant economic indicators to determine how well the theories conform to the data. This is a continuing task of the economics profession in its pursuit of better insights into the workings of the economy. A basic purpose of the profession is to provide ever-better guides for government policies to foster maximum and stable economic growth, contain price inflation, and raise living conditions among all income groups, and to provide better guides for households and businesses to consider their spending, saving, and investment decisions in the light of prospects for the overall economy.

While business cycles do not recur on a periodic basis, and each cycle has unique characteristics, there are discernible regularities in the behavior of business cycles over time, as Victor Zarnowitz, the foremost student of business cycles, points out.[1] Examples of regularities are that business cycles are national and even international in scope, they last several years, and they often show repetitive patterns from cycle to cycle in the statistical movements of production, employment, various industries, household expenditures, business investment, prices, and interest rates.

The overall thrust of the American economy fits the competitive model, even though the federal, state, and local governments provide public services and intervene in the economy in other ways, and though there are monopolistic aspects in the private sector that are insulated from fully competitive markets. While the American economy has changed considerably over the past two centuries because of new technologies and the growing population, business cycles are not new. They have occurred repeatedly in the nineteenth and twentieth centuries.

The rising phase of a business cycle is typically referred to as expansion and the falling phase as recession. Although business cycle analysis focuses on the overall economy, it recognizes that particular sectors may be moving against the overall trend—a stagnant or declining industry may not participate in the prosperity of a general expansion, and a growth industry may be insulated from a general recession.

Determining Business Cycle Phases

What is a recession? Generally speaking, we know there is a recession when we see slack business activity and high unemployment. But there is also an observable measure of a recession period. The National Bureau of Economic Research, Inc. (NBER), a private nonprofit organization in Cambridge, Massachusetts, officially designates such periods.

Under the auspices of the NBER, a committee of economists determines the beginning and ending points of expansions and recessions by assessing the preponderant direction of a wide range of economic indicators. The NBER Business Cycle Dating Committee has established a reputation for objectivity, and its designations are accepted by many liberal and conservative economists and politicians.

The advantage of having a nongovernmental body such as the NBER designate expansions and recessions is clear. It reduces the possibility that the administration in office will politicize the designations to put its own policies in the most favorable light, or even revise designations for previous periods to make the opposition party look worse, as the executive branch of the federal government runs the government's statistical programs.

The NBER Dating Committee designates a recession as beginning in the month in which the overall direction of a broad spectrum of economic indicators turns downward; similarly, an expansion is designated as beginning in the month in which the overall direction turns upward.[2] While various numerical tests are applied to the indicators to assess their direction, ultimately the decision is based on the judgment of the NBER committee. For example, while a recession is popularly defined as occurring when the real gross domestic product (i.e., the inflation-adjusted GDP) declines for two quarters in a row, the NBER actually considers a variety of monthly and quarterly data before making a determination, including the GDP in current and inflation-adjusted dollars, business sales, bank debits outside New York City, industrial production, unemployment rate, nonfarm employment and hours worked, and personal income.

In fact, before the benchmark GDP revisions were published in 1996, Edward Renshaw noted that if the two-quarter real GDP guide were the criterion, no short recessions would have been recorded in 1960 and 1980, and the 1973–75 recession, which is shown as beginning at the end of 1973, would appear as beginning a year later, at the end of 1974.[3] But as an example of how revised data sometimes give a different slant on economic movements, the 1996 revision shows a three-quarter GDP decline in 1960 and a two-quarter decline in 1980, both of which meet the popular criterion for a recession of a consecutive-two-quarter decline in the real GDP. However, the 1996 revision, like the previous data, show that the decline in the real GDP during the 1973–75 recession began in late 1974.

A notable exception to the typical designations occurred after World War II. There was a short recession in 1945 from February to October (the war ended in August). It turned out to be a surprisingly modest transition to a peacetime economy. Unemployment rose substantially in the postwar period from 670,000 workers in 1944 to 1.04 million in 1945, and to 2.27 million in 1946. However, forecasts for unemployment increases of about 8 million did not materialize.[4] In 1946 and 1947, the real GDP declined by 11 percent and 1 percent, respectively. The sharp drop was due entirely to the demobilization and concomitant plunge in defense outlays. In contrast, the private-sector and civilian government components of the GDP rose during the demobilization. Because the "recession" in 1946 was *sui generis* due to the conversion from war to a peacetime economy, it was not considered a recession period by the NBER Business Cycle Dating Committee.

While "expansion" is the general term for the upward phase of the cycle, the upturn immediately following a recession, until the economy regains its previous peak level of activity, is often referred to as "recovery." When economic activity in the recovery exceeds the highest levels attained in the previous expansion, this higher-growth period is traditionally called "expansion." An analogous designation that the author makes with respect to the downward phase is the transition from recession to contraction. The immediate downturn is called "recession"; and if overall activity falls below the lowest level of the previous recession, the depressed period is called "contraction." Such a contraction has not occurred since the depression of the early 1930s, however, when economic activity at the low point of the depression in March 1933 was below that at the low point of the previous recession in November 1927, and so "recession" and "contraction" are used interchangeably in current terminology.

The high point of an expansion before it turns downward to recession is called the "peak," and the low point of a recession before it turns upward to recovery is the "trough." A complete cycle is composed of both the expansion and recession phases and is typically viewed from the peak of one expansion to the peak of the following expansion. This way of looking at the cycle emphasizes the long-term growth of the economy independent of short-term cyclical movements, although for some analyses it may be useful to measure the cycle from the trough of one recession to the trough of the next recession, which is also a complete cycle.

The last term used in this categorization is "depression." A depression is a collapse of the economy such as last occurred in the 1930s. It involves a general breakdown of economic life affecting people in all social and economic strata, including mass unemployment, widespread loss of assets such as homes and life savings, the disappearance of established businesses through bankruptcy, and an overall undermining of the financial system through failures of the banking, securities, and insurance industries. A depression is far more devastating than a recession. For example, unemployment reached a high of about 25 percent in the 1930s, compared with peaks of 9 percent and 11 percent during the severe recessions of 1973–75 and 1981–82, respectively.

Figure 1.1 shows business cycle recessions, recoveries and expansions from 1979 to 1996. The recession periods are designated by the NBER Business Cycle Dating Committee. The coincident index of the leading indicator system represents actual production (Chapter 13 covers the system). The cyclical turning points of the coincident index approximate, and sometimes are the same as, the NBER business cycle turning points. As noted above, the committee bases its designation of cyclical turning points on a judgment of the movements of a variety of economic indicators, not on any single indicator such as the coincident index.

Since the end of World War II, the closest a recovery has come to falling below the peak of the previous expansion was the 1980–81 upturn. The July

Figure 1.1 **Business Cycle Phases and Indicators: 1979–97**

Index: 1992=100

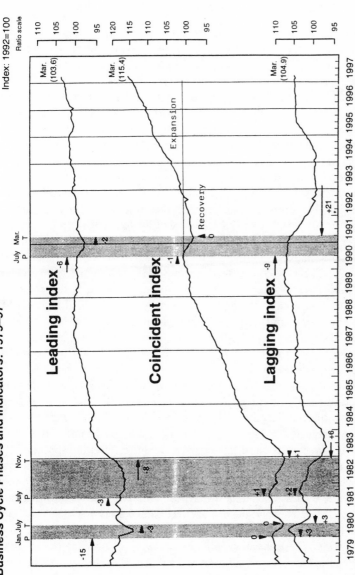

Note: P (peak) indicates the end of general business expansion and the beginning of recession; T (trough) indicates the end of general business recession and the beginning of expansion (as designated by the NBER). Thus, shaded areas represent recessions. Arrows indicate leads (−) and lags (+) in months from business cycle turning dates.
Source: The Conference Board.

1981 peak barely exceeded the peak of the previous expansion in January 1980. Had the NBER Dating Committee determined that the 1980–81 upturn at its high point in July 1981 did not exceed the previous expansion's high point in January 1980, however slightly, the committee probably would not have identified it as a separate business cycle phase.[5] This absence of recoveries turning into recessions reflects the twentieth-century pattern, but particularly that since the end of World War II, in which recovery and expansion are typical of the United States' long-term growing economy, with periods of rising economic activity being much longer than declining periods. The closest a recession has come to worsening into a contraction since World War II was the 1981–82 recession, when the coincident index in November 1982 was minimally below the trough of the previous recession in July 1980. But that did not have the properties of a contraction, which is characterized by an unambiguously lower level of output than the low point of the previous recession.

The process of determining when a turning point in the business cycle occurs is a protracted one that often is made long after the actual recession or recovery began. For example, the recession that ultimately was determined to have started in July 1990 was first announced by the NBER committee nine months later in April 1991, and the subsequent recovery that began in April 1991 was first announced by the committee twenty-one months later, in December 1992.[6] These delays reflect the fact that movements in the various economic indicators around the cyclical turning points that the committee monitors often give ambiguous and contradictory signs of the direction of the economy. This uncertainty in the contemporaneous data is heightened by revisions to the preliminary indicators that come out every month. Thus, before reaching agreement on the timing of a turning point, the committee waits for clear confirmation of the change in direction of the business cycle. This delay has its tradeoffs: economic analysts, policymakers, and the public are deprived of timely intelligence on the business cycle, but once the designations are announced they are unlikely to be revised.

All told, as indicated in Table 1.1, in the nine complete business cycles since World War II (the expansion of the tenth cycle beginning in the spring of 1991 was still in progress at the time of this writing in the spring of 1997), the average expansion was 50 months and the average recession was 11 months. For the seven peacetime cycles (excluding the Korean and Vietnam wars), the average expansion was 43 months and the average recession was 11 months. Thus, since World War II, the average expansion has lasted 4 to $4^1/_2$ times as long as the average recession. These durations are an improvement over the experience of the 1919–45 period and even more so over the previous century, when the length of expansions was only slightly longer than the length of recessions. This improvement is most telling for peacetime cycles, which do not have the stimulus of wartime production (detailed below in Changing Characteristics of Business Cycles Since the Nineteenth Century).

Table 1.1

Average Duration of U.S. Business Cycles (in months)

	Expansion	Recession
All Cycles		
1854–1919 (16 cycles)	27	22
1919–1945 (6 cycles)	35	18
1945–1990 (9 cycles)	50	11
Peacetime Cycles		
1854–1919 (14 cycles)	24	22
1919–1945 (5 cycles)	26	20
1945–1991 (7 cycles)	43	11

Source: *Survey of Current Business,* October 1994, p. C1.

Business Cycles and Economic Growth

A question is often raised about the relationship between cyclical stability and economic growth. Specifically, does the economy grow faster during periods of cyclical stability, that is, when there are relatively few recessions, or when there are more instability and more frequent recessions? The short answer is that the experience is inconclusive over the 50 years since World War II, and for a 100-year period ending in 1980 there is at best a hint of a direct relationship between economic growth and cyclical stability.

The cyclical expansion beginning in the spring of 1991 and still in progress in the spring of 1997 (the time of his writing) is the start of the tenth postwar business cycle. Table 1.2 shows the annual economic growth rates approximately by decade since the late 1940s and the number of recessions in each period. Following the increase of economic growth from 3.6 percent in the 1950s to 4.4 percent in the 1960s, the rate declined steadily in subsequent decades to a low of 1.9 percent in the first two-thirds of the 1990s. But there is little relationship between this pattern of growth rates and the number of business cycles in each period. Thus, the 1950s had the most recessions and also the highest growth rate except for the 1960s, while the 1960s and the 1990s both have only one recession but also the highest and lowest growth rates respectively.

In a highly sophisticated analysis of this question for the period from 1882 to 1980, Victor Zarnowitz finds that while there is a suggestion that economic growth is faster during periods of greater stability, this is far from conclusive. He has reservations on statistical grounds and because equally competing arguments can be made for faster growth being related to more stable and less stable

Table 1.2

Economic Growth and Cyclical Stability

	Annual growth rate	Number of recessions
1948–59	3.6%	3
1959–69	4.4	1
1969–79	3.2	2
1979–89	2.7	2
1989–96	1.9	1

Note: Growth rates are based on the gross domestic product in 1992 dollars. Recessions are based on the business cycle designations of the National Bureau of Economic Research.

cyclical environments.[7] But he does conclude that economic growth is impeded by periods of severe economic depression.

Changing Characteristics of Business Cycles
Since the Nineteenth Century

In an assessment of how the durations of expansions and recessions change over time, peacetime cycles are the best indicator, since peacetime economic activity excludes the temporary but significant stimulus of military wartime production. Table 1.1 shows that on average peacetime expansions became progressively longer and peacetime recessions progressively shorter over the 137-year period from 1854 to 1991. But most of this improvement occurred after World War II. During 1854–1919, expansions and recessions were almost equally long (24 months for expansions and 22 months for recessions); during 1919–45, expansions were 6 months longer than recessions (26 months and 20 months, respectively); and during 1945–91, expansions were 32 months longer than recessions (43 and 11 months, respectively).

In the author's view, there are three broad categories of reasons why the economy has performed better since World War II. First, Keynesian economics fostered a greater understanding of the economy as well as more widespread recognition of the importance of federal government budgets. The government's more active role in influencing the economy resulted from this triumph of Keynesianism over the classical belief that full employment would occur automatically. The Keynesian perspective was in turn critiqued and modified by several developments: the greater recognition of interest rates as a key factor affecting economic activity; the importance given by monetarists to the money supply; the Phillips curve analysis of the tradeoff between unemployment and inflation; the integration of potential output and inflation with unemployment in Okun's Law; the rational expectations theory that the market adjusts to and frustrates government intervention in the economy; and the NAIRU concept of the nonaccelerating inflation rate of unemployment.

The second reason the economy has done better is that this greater understanding is applied to economic policies. Thus, the federal government actively stabilizes the economy through tax and spending fiscal policies. The active role of the government was encouraged by the Employment Act of 1946, which enunciated the pursuit of national goals for maximum employment and purchasing power. This was heightened by the monetary policy change of 1951 (i.e., the Treasury Department–Federal Reserve accord), which allowed the Federal Reserve to pursue interest policies to benefit the economy independent of their effect on interest rates of government securities used in financing the federal debt.

Third, there is a general category of institutional factors contributing to the economy's improved performance. These include the cushioning effect of unemployment insurance and other income maintenance programs that provide an income floor during recessions; bank deposit insurance and actions taken by the federal government and the Federal Reserve to prevent a widespread financial collapse of failing banks; and the increasing sophistication of companies using greater amounts of economic information to balance sales and production. This last factor may also result in better inventory control and thus moderate production fluctuations.

Christina Romer has challenged the impression given by the official statistics that the economy has become more stable since World War II, while David Weir, Stanley Lebergott, and Victor Zarnowitz have objected to her thesis.[8] She argues that statistics on unemployment, the gross national product (GNP), and industrial production are misleading because the underlying data on which they are based changed considerably after World War II. The prewar statistics use far more fragmentary and less reliable underlying data than the postwar statistics. When historical statistics are reconstructed to simulate a consistent methodology over the prewar and postwar periods, Romer's argument continues, the prewar economy appears to be similar to the postwar economy in terms of both the severity of economic declines and the volatility of output and unemployment as measured by yearly deviations from long-term trends. Weir, Lebergott, and Zarnowitz maintain that Romer's methodology of superimposing post-1948 data characteristics on the pre-1930 period, but without providing fresh underlying data, is based on the faulty assumption that sectoral output-employment relationships, cyclicality of labor force participation rates, sectoral composition of employment, and GNP-commodity output relationships have not changed over the entire time period. In short, this rebuttal states that Romer's methodology is based on a synthetic estimation procedure that prejudges the question and thus ensures the outcome.

Whatever the merits of Romer's argument, her reconstructed measures do not refute the assertion that the relative duration of expansions and recessions has improved. Because the methodology does not alter the dates for the turning points of business cycles, the reconstructed statistics do not contradict the traditional measures that indicate an improvement over time toward longer expansions and shorter recessions.

Differences between Growth Cycles and Business Cycles

Business cycles are affected by growth cycles, and vice versa, but these two cyclical phenomena are quite different. Before highlighting the differences, it is helpful to summarize the definitional characteristics of growth cycles as distinguished from business cycles. The appendix to this section provides a more technical description of the growth cycle methodology.

Business cycles record expansion periods when the direction of economic activity continues upward from the trough of the previous recession's low point, and recession periods when the direction of economic activity continues downward from the peak of the previous expansion's high point, as noted above. By contrast, growth cycles record the upward and downward variations in business activity from the long-term average rate of growth that spans several business cycles. The peak of the growth cycle occurs when the growth rate is furthest above its long-term trend and the trough occurs when the growth rate is furthest below the long-term trend. Figure 1.2 shows growth cycles from 1973 to 1996.

When the growth in economic production during a business cycle expansion exceeds the long-term growth rate for a sustained period, which is defined as six months or more, the period is referred to as a "growth expansion." Analogously, when the growth rate of overall economic activity remains below the long-term growth rate for six months or more, the period is referred to as a "growth recession." A growth recession can occur when production and employment are both rising. Production in such cases is not keeping pace with the labor force growth resulting from the influx of young people just out of school and people with job experience coming back into the labor force.

This results in the following interrelationships between growth cycles and business cycles:

- Growth cycle recessions include major slowdowns that occur during business cycle expansions; they also coincide with absolute declines in business cycle recessions. The result is that growth cycle recessions are longer in duration than business cycle recessions and growth cycle expansions are shorter in duration than business cycle expansions. These differences are apparent in comparisons of Figures 1.1 and 1.2.
- A growth cycle recession may signal an oncoming business cycle recession, or it may indicate a less serious slowdown in economic growth.
- A growth cycle expansion signifies a general period of robust economic growth, even though it may be below the rate of increase in the concurrent business cycle expansion.

Figure 1.2 **Growth Cycle Phases and Indicators: 1950—97** (six-month smoothed annualized rate)

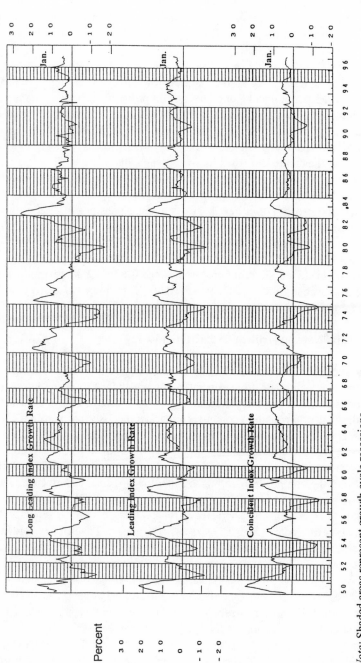

Note: Shaded areas represent growth cycle recessions.
Source: Center for International Business Cycle Research at Columbia University.

- There are more growth cycles than business cycles because (a) some growth cycle recessions do not turn into business cycle recessions, and (b) business cycle recessions by definition involve growth cycle recessions.

The coincident index is the measure of current economic production in growth cycles. Leading and long-leading composite indexes are also prepared for growth cycles. The leading indexes change direction before a significant change occurs in the sustained growth rate of the coincident index. On average, the leading index leads the coincident index by four months, and the long-leading index leads the coincident index by six to twelve months.

Growth cycles aid in the interpretation of business cycle movements by providing a broader setting for business cycle movements. Thus, growth cycles elucidate the strength of current business cycle expansions in light of the underlying rate of long-term growth. This focuses attention on prospects for faster economic growth, for a cyclical recession, or only for a slowdown in the current cyclical expansion.

Growth cycle measures are prepared by the Center for International Business Cycle Research at Columbia University. The Center prepares growth cycle measures for ten other countries in addition to the United States.

Appendix: Note on Growth Cycle Methodology

Economic growth in growth cycles is measured by a composite coincident index. The index is combined from several economic indicators that represent actual production in the current period and thus are considered to "coincide" with overall production in the economy contemporaneously as it occurs. The data elements of the composite coincident index are industrial production, real gross domestic product (GDP), manufacturing and trade sales in constant dollars, employment, and unemployment. The elements of the coincident index are combined into the composite by a method that gives the same influence to all data series regardless of whether they typically show small or large month-to-month changes. This prevents data series with typically large monthly movements from dominating the index. Other adjustments are made to have the coincident index and the leading and long-leading indexes consistent with each other in terms of the cyclical amplitude and the long-term trend. This is done by superimposing the monthly movement of the industrial production index for the amplitude (the amplitude is the amount of the rise during a cyclical expansion and the amount of the decline during a cyclical recession) and the long-term growth of the GDP for the trend on the coincident and the leading indexes.

The peaks and troughs in the deviations from the long-term trend in the coincident index and its component indicators are the reference criteria for dating the peaks and troughs of growth cycles. The general rule is that the peak is reached when the index is furthest above the long-term trend for a sustained period of at least six months, and the trough is reached when the index is furthest below the long-term trend for at least six months. This is modified by a visual inspection of the data to avoid the situation when strict adherence to the rule would result in cycles with relatively small amplitudes or when atypical events such as strikes or lockouts create the appearance of a cycle.

The data elements of the composite leading index are unemployment insurance initial claims, net business formation (business incorporations and business failures), consumer goods and materials new orders, plant and equipment contracts and orders, housing building permits, business inventories changes, industrial materials price change, stock market prices, corporate profits after taxes, price/labor cost ratio in the nonfarm business economy, and consumer installment credit change. The data elements of the composite long-leading index are bond prices, price to unit labor cost ratio in manufacturing, money supply (M2) in constant dollars, housing building permits, output per hour in manufacturing, and consumer price index for services. The methodology for combining the elements of the leading indexes into the composites is the same as that noted above for the coincident index.

SEASONALITY

Economic activity is bumpy not only on a daily, weekly, monthly, and quarterly basis but also minute-by-minute as reflected in price quotations in commodity and financial markets. Even when cyclical movements continue in the same direction over several periods (rising during an expansion and declining during a recession), there are continuing deviations from the general upward or downward movement as households, businesses, and governments speed up or slow down their rate of spending. These short-term fits and starts have many causes: the intrinsic tempo of economic life with its bursts and lulls in activity followed by a return to the routine pace; quick response to changes or perceived changes in the economic environment; surprise shocks of nature such as hurricanes, severe snowstorms, floods, droughts, and earthquakes; surprise shocks of human origins such as oil spills, strikes, lockouts, government shutdowns and terrorist attacks; and expected repetitive seasonal variations within every twelve-month period resulting from such factors as farm crop planting and harvesting seasons, school vacations, holidays, Christmas shopping, less outside construction during winter months, automobile plant shutdowns for model year changes during the summer, the payment and reimbursement of annual individual income taxes in the first four calendar months of the year, and federal, state, and local government fiscal year budgets that affect their year-end spending patterns.

Such inherent bumpiness in the real world presents problems for analyzing short-term movements in economic indicators because the gyrations may give misleading appearances of sharp changes in the direction of economic activity when in fact they are only temporary. For example, in construction the normal pattern is that much of the drop in work on buildings and roads in the winter months stems from the cold weather, but this is reversed in the spring when construction activity increases greatly. Thus, unless it is recognized that when the weather becomes warmer, construction will likely pick up, someone just observing the the winter decline may conclude that construction is in a longer-term doldrum. Because of the intense interest in short-term economic movements, many economic data obtained from weekly, monthly, and quarterly surveys of households and businesses are routinely adjusted by statistical methods to approximate what their movements would be if there were no repetitive changes within every twelve-month period due to such factors as the weather, vacations, holidays, model changeovers, government fiscal year budgets, and tax payment dates.

Estimates of seasonal adjustment are based on the economic experience of previous years. When consistent seasonal patterns for particular months (or quarters in the case of quarterly data) show on average that the indicator is a certain amount higher or lower, or is the same as the monthly (quarterly) average based on the entire year, then the indicator is adjusted accordingly that month. For example, if sales of women's shoes typically are 5 percent below the monthly average for the year in January and 7 percent above the monthly average for the year in April, actual January sales are increased by 5 percent and actual April sales are reduced 7 percent. And if sales in June typically are the same as the monthly average for the year, no change is made to the actual June data.

Extraordinary Events

The economic effects of extraordinary events such as strikes, lockouts, floods, hurricanes, and earthquakes are not included in the development of seasonal factors. For example, sharp declines in sales and employment in months when the extraordinary events occur show up as "outliers" in the computer programs, and these sharp declines are excluded from the calculation of the seasonal factors for that year. This is done because the purpose of seasonal adjustment is to capture the repetitive seasonal changes from year to year. For that reason, cold and hot weather extremes in a particular year that have atypical seasonal effects on business activity may also appear as outliers that are excluded from the calculation of seasonal factors. The outliers arising from the computer programs are not used mechanically, but are reviewed by analysts to ensure that they reflect extraordinary or extreme events. To include the effect of the extraordinary events and extreme weather changes in the calculation of the seasonal factors would distort the meaning of seasonally adjusted data.

However, the actual economic activity levels of the various monthly and quarterly economic indicators include the effects of the extraordinary or extreme events in the periods when they occur, and thus are included in the seasonally

Figure 1.3 **Seasonal Patterns of Retail Sales: 1996**

Billions of dollars

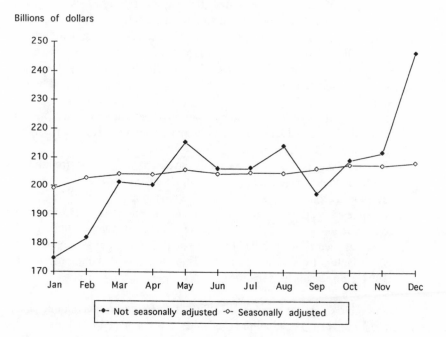

Note: Based on U.S. Bureau of the Census data.

adjusted data. The only effect of excluding outliers in the seasonal adjustment process is that the outliers are not used in developing the seasonal factors, which in turn are used to modify the actual activity levels to obtain seasonally adjusted levels.

Figure 1.3 shows total retail sales of all products in 1996 both "seasonally adjusted" and "not seasonally adjusted." Seasonally adjusted sales are far less volatile than the actual, not seasonally adjusted, sales. Thus, given the normal buying patterns before and after Christmas, actual sales are much higher in December and much lower in January and February than the seasonally adjusted sales data.

Sophisticated techniques are used to adjust economic data seasonally. The procedures are too technical to detail here, but the following usages illustrate the general method:

- At least six to ten years of historical experience are usually used to develop seasonal factors.
- Seasonal patterns of recent years receive greater weight than those in earlier years.

- Revisions of the last few years' seasonal factors are made every year. The time span of years used to compute the seasonal factors is usually updated each year by adding the data for the most recent year and dropping the data for the earliest year used in the previous year's computations. That is, a rolling fixed period of years is used. For example, in a series for which fifteen years of data from 1982 to 1996 were used to compute seasonal factors at the end of 1996, data for 1983 to 1997 would be used at the end of 1997.
- Extreme values of the indicator in particular months or quarters, such as those due to an earthquake or government shutdown, are downweighted or excluded as an aberration.
- An increasing number of data series have adopted a "concurrent adjustment" method, which uses actual data from the most recent period to develop seasonal factors for the most recent month.
- In some cases, the trend of seasonal factors in previous years is projected one year ahead for use in the current year. For example, during 1997 seasonal factors are available only through 1996. In order to apply seasonal factors to current data in 1997 that are considered appropriate for 1997, a forecast is made of the expected 1997 seasonal factors.

It is desirable to prepare seasonally adjusted data for use in economic analysis. But regardless of the technique used, seasonally adjusted economic indicators are a statistical artifact. Thus, seasonally adjusted data reflect a type of measurement that, while usually adequate for its intended purpose, is inevitably less than perfect. Although seasonally adjusted data are based on the average experience of past years, seasonal variations may be atypical in any particular year. For example, the winter may be colder or warmer than normal, or automobile model year changeovers may be more or less extensive than average. On the other hand, movements that appear to be merely seasonal, such as a decline in business from December to January, may in fact reflect an actual deterioration in the health of the economy that will become apparent only when the data for subsequent months appear. Also, seasonally adjusted data contain an unknown amount of random movements that ideally should be eliminated but cannot be quantified; this has been a long-standing limitation in the methodology of seasonal adjustment. These factors should be considered in analyzing monthly or quarterly movements of the indicator.

The majority of economic data are seasonally adjusted. But some are not. The reasons for no seasonal adjustment vary: the monthly or quarterly data may be too erratic to establish a seasonal pattern; in the case of new data series, there may be insufficient historical experience; or the organization providing the data may not think a seasonal pattern is relevant, as in the case of interest rates and stock market price indexes. When an indicator is not seasonally adjusted, one indirect means of understanding the seasonally adjusted movement is to compare percent changes between the current period (month or quarter) and the same period (month or quarter) of a year earlier for several consecutive periods. While this indirect approach provides a broad magnitude of the current seasonally adjusted movement, it cannot indicate cyclical turning points. The result also may be misleading if differences in the calendar are significant from year to year. For example, in one year, March could have more weekends than in the next year; this fact could affect the amount of business activity in the month.

INDEX NUMBERS

Economic data represent the myriad of transactions between buyers and sellers in consumer, industrial, labor, and financial markets involving both private parties and governments. In order to analyze this vast amount of detail, the individual transactions are combined and summarized into subgroupings and overall totals. One method of summarizing is through index numbers, which are a convenient way of quickly assessing the direction and amount of change in economic activity. Index numbers are used for various types of economic activity, such as production, prices, wages, productivity, and leading and lagging indicators.

An index number starts with a base period, usually a single year or the average of a few consecutive years. The base period is typically, but not always, defined as equivalent to 100, and all movements of the indicator before and after the base period are represented as percentage differences from the base. For example, using the base of 100, an index of 95 means that the indicator for that period (month, quarter, year) is 5 percent below the base period, and an index of 128 means the indicator is 28 percent above the base period. The formula for calculating the percentage change between two periods is:

$$\frac{\text{Period 2}}{\text{Period 1}} - 1.0 \times 100$$

Thus, in the text example of the index numbers for periods 1 and 2,

$$\frac{128}{95} = 1.347 - 1.0 \times 100 = 0.347 \times 100 = 34.7\%$$

Assuming 95 is the period 1 index and 128 is the period 2 index, the change between the two periods is 34.7 percent.

The base period of an indicator may represent a single year, such as the industrial production index where 1992 = 100, or a few consecutive years, such as the consumer price index where the current 1982–84 = 100 will be updated to 1993–95 in 1998. The base period is selected according to a schedule that is linked to the availability of the most recent comprehensive and detailed survey

Table 1.3

Index Number Weights and Price Change (illustrative only)

| | 1987 Price Weights | | |
	1 1987 expenditures (% distribution)	2 Ratio of 1997 price to 1987 price	3 1996 price index (1 x 2)
Bananas	50	1.10	55
Airline flights	40	1.20	48
Computers	10	0.60	6
	100		109

| | 1992 Price Weights | | |
	1 1992 expenditures (% distribution)	2 Ratio of 1996 price to 1987 price	3 1996 price index (1 x 2)
Bananas	40	1.10	44
Airline flights	30	1.20	36
Computers	30	0.60	18
	100		98

data. For example, the base period for the producer price indexes (PPI) is governed by the year of the most recent five-year economic censuses, which provide the most detailed itemization of manufactured goods produced and minerals extracted from the ground. By contrast, the base period for the consumer price index (CPI) reflects the current practice of updating the index approximately every ten years and using a three-year span to avoid the possibility that a single year may not adequately reflect consumer purchasing patterns of specific goods and service items. Because detailed consumer expenditure information is collected every year, there is greater flexibility in determining the base period for the CPI than that for the PPI. Ideally, the base period would be one when the economy is relatively balanced with no excesses, rather than one that is booming with high inflation, depressed with high unemployment, or in which external shocks such as an oil embargo or flood may have a large temporary impact on supplies and prices.

Indexes are calculated by multiplying each item's relative importance in the base period, referred to as the item's weight, by the percentage change in the item's value since the base period; the sum of these calculations for all items is the index for the current period. The combination of several items into an overall index also causes a problem, however, because the relative importance of the various items in the index will have changed since the base period. Table 1.3 illustrates this in a hypothetical price index that compares two different price movements that are due simply to differences in weights from a previous period to a more recent one. This example calculates two price changes from 1987 to 1997 for a price index composed of bananas, airline flights, and computers, one using 1987 weights and one using 1992 weights. The actual price changes for the three individual product items are the same in both weighting structures. The index with 1987 weights *increases* 9 percent over the 1987–97 period, while the index with 1992 weights *decreases* 2 percent over the same period. The difference is due to the greater weight for computers based on 1992 expenditures than based on 1987 expenditures.

Some index numbers are based on the same fixed weights that add up to 100 percent in the base period for long periods of time (e.g., five, ten, or more years). Other index numbers allow these proportions to change more frequently, such as every year, to reflect more current production or consumption patterns. The weights change because on a relative basis some items increase in use and others become less important due to changing buyer preferences, competition from substitute products, and differential price movements. Because the relative importance of individual items in the index changes over time—for example, housing may rise faster than food prices, or a new product with rapidly growing sales often has a high price when first introduced and the price subsequently declines as output expands—the overall index will show a differential rate of change depending on whether earlier or later proportionate weights are used. This "product mix" problem is a continuing issue in the construction of index numbers. Use of a weighting scheme that incorporates the geometric mean of the weights between two periods gives a still different view of price change. Research is under way in 1997 on the possible use of this alternative for the consumer price index (Chapter 11).

For example, in the case of price indexes, one that maintains the same relative *quantities* of the various items purchased as in the base period is likely to show a higher rate of price increase (or lower rate of decline) than when the index represents the actual items bought in each period. This occurs because on average buyers tend to switch to substitutes that have more slowly rising prices, and to new products after the new product price declines. Analogously, a production index that holds the relative *prices* of the various items produced constant at their base-period relationship tends to show a higher rate of production growth (or lower rate of decline) than when the index represents the actual prices paid in each period, because the introductory high price of a new product usually declines with the growth in production.

Index numbers do not require that the years used to develop the weights are the same as the years used for the base period. Thus, revisions to index numbers associated with re-weighting (changing the weights) and re-basing (changing the base period) are entirely different. In fact, the weights and the base period often represent different years.

There is no right or wrong way to construct index numbers. Usually the choice of which period weights to use is based on a judgment concerning the use of the index. For example, when the goal is to measure price change for the same items over time, the base-period weights of the items purchased are held constant for several years. But when interest is in measuring price change to reflect the continuing change in the types of items purchased, the proportions of items purchased are changed in every period to reflect actual buying patterns. Even including another index number method based on the geometric mean of the weights between two periods noted above is obviously a case where one size does not fit all.

DATA ACCURACY

Several types of questions can be raised about the accuracy of economic indicators. Conceptual issues, such as whether the indicators measure what they purport—for example, if the unemployment rate truly represents the proportion of people out of work or if the consumer price index truly represents inflation to the consumer—are beyond the scope of this book. More practical considerations, such as how closely the underlying data represent the definitions of the indicator, are also incapable of being measured. Thus, data based on income tax returns that were originally developed for assessing the economic effects of income tax laws and of proposed changes in tax laws, are also used for estimating certain components of the gross domestic product and for obtaining information on small firms for the economic censuses. Even though some data sources may not exactly correspond to the definitional concepts of certain indicators, secondary sources are used in preparing economic indicators to hold down the costs of data collection and to limit the reporting burden on the public.

There are two fairly simple ways to evaluate the accuracy of economic indicators, however. The effect of data errors and the relative accuracy of an indicator can be estimated by taking into account the extent of revisions to preliminary data and, in the case of indicators based on information from surveys obtained from household, business, and government respondents, the sampling reliability of the surveys. Quantitative measures of the effect of these errors have been developed in some cases.

Error due to revision reflects changes in the indicators from when they are initially provided to the later, more accurate information. The size of revision error is based on the past experience of these changes. For example, in the case of the real gross domestic product, during 1981–92 two-thirds of the revisions between the advance estimates published twenty-five days after the quarter and the latest estimates based on the most recent annual and five-year benchmark revisions have been within a range of −1.2 to 1.7 percentage points. Thus, at a 67 percent confidence, it is likely that an advance quarterly estimate of real GDP growth at an annual rate of 3 percent will be revised within a range of 1.8 to 4.7

percent. Raising the confidence level to 90 percent increases the likely revision to a range of –3 to 3 percentage points.

Error due to sampling results from the likelihood that data obtained from a sample of a population differ from what they would be if the entire population were surveyed. Estimates of sampling error are developed from mathematical formulas of probability, and there is a predetermined direct relationship between error size and its chances of occurring. For example, the sampling error for housing starts based on a 67 percent confidence is plus or minus 3 percent. Thus at a confidence of 67 percent, it is likely that a monthly figure of housing starts at an annual rate of 1.5 million units ranges within 1.455 and 1.545 million if all starts were surveyed. Raising the confidence level to 95 percent approximately doubles the sampling error to a range of 1.41 to 1.59 million.

When such estimates are available, it is important to take them into account. Whether error estimates are available or not, however, it is clear in all cases that any single number provided by an indicator cannot always exactly represent reality. Because of the various sources of error inherent in economic data, in general an indicator should be considered as representing a range rather than a single number. Analysis of the actual or related data, as well as estimates of the size of revisions or sampling errors available, can sometimes suggest whether actual measurements fall closer to upper or lower bounds of that range.

Revisions

Economic indicators are developed from data gathered in surveys of households, businesses, and governments, and from tax and regulatory reports submitted to the federal and state governments. The indicators are available weekly, monthly, quarterly, or annually depending on the data series on which they are based. Because policymakers in the Presidential administration, Congress, and the Federal Reserve System want the indicators as soon as possible following the month or quarter to which they refer, the data are initially provided on a preliminary basis and are subsequently revised as more complete and accurate survey information is received. The use of preliminary and revised information results from the tension between the need for both timely and accurate data. Revisions are sometimes substantial, and therefore it is important that preliminary information be treated as tentative.

Contemporaneous Revisions

Economic activity over short spells of three to six months moves in fits and starts with varying rates of growth, and sometimes temporarily reverses the dominant upward or downward direction before resuming the dominant pattern (see Seasonality above for causes of these short-term interruptions). At the time these movements are occurring, however, it is not clear if they signal a basic change in the tempo of economic life or a limited interruption of the underlying momen-tum. Because of these continuous wiggles in marketplace activity and because data revisions become available shortly after the preliminary numbers are pub-lished, it is important not to be swayed by the most recent blip in the indicators. A changed movement of at least six months should be identified before deter-mining that the overall tempo or direction is occurring.

Nevertheless, data revisions within a somewhat longer, twelve-month period have occasionally shown that the earlier information gave misleading movements of current economic activity. For example, the initial real gross national product estimates for the last three quarters of 1989 were revised significantly downward in the annual GNP revisions published in July 1990, which was also the eve of the 1990–91 recession. Had economic policymakers been aware early in 1990 of this weak economic growth, they might have adopted policies to stimulate growth in the six months preceding the onset of the recession in place of the neutral eco-nomic policies (neither stimulative nor restraining) actually in existence.

Revisions play a fundamental role in the system of leading, coincident and lagging indexes that are used to forecast economic activity (Chapter 13). With the exception of the 1980 recession, the preliminary contemporaneous data of these indexes have not given advance signs that the economy was heading for a recession. Clear signals of an impending recession become apparent only long after the fact, when the much later revised data were incorporated in the indexes in subsequent years. This is an inherent weakness in the forecasting record of the leading and lagging system.

Some economic indicators are accompanied by an estimate of the probable range of revisions. Typically, these are indicators prepared from more than one data source, such as the gross domestic product and the industrial production index, or from surveys using nonprobability samples of respondents for which a sampling error cannot be calculated (see Sampling Reliability below).

Benchmark Revisions

In addition to revisions that are made on a current basis, revisions based on a comprehensive set of data that typically undergo no further improvements are called "benchmarks." They are made at annual, five-year, ten-year, or other long-term intervals depending on the indicator. Benchmark numbers include survey data from the most representative samples including in some cases the universe of survey respondents, better methodologies for statistical estimating, and new definitions for components of the indicator. These more accurate and detailed data also improve the quality of the preliminary indicators in later peri-ods. Due to the completion of a benchmark long after the period to which it refers, analytic use of benchmark data concentrates on reformulating and refin-ing theoretical relationships among various indicators and in updating economic forecasting models.

For particular indicators, benchmarks result in a revision of all historical data, as in the case of the gross domestic product; in other cases, application of the new definitions and data-estimating methodologies is limited to future estimates of the indicator, as for the consumer price index. The decision about whether to revise historical data is based on a consideration of several factors—the need to have a consistent series over time balanced against the lack or weakness of comparable data for earlier time periods, the theoretical question of whether to "rewrite history" by including factors that previously were not considered in economic analysis and policymaking and the additional costs for statistical programs to make the more extensive revisions. When the historical data are not revised, there is a break in the series where the previous data are not fully consistent with the new data. These data inconsistencies should be recognized when analyzing long-term trends.

Sampling Reliability

A survey is typically based on a sample of respondents from the universe of the entire population. Many indicators are derived from data collected from a probability sample survey, which represents all groups of the universe in proportion to the size of each group. It is unlikely, however, that any single sample corresponds precisely to the distribution of the groups in the universe. Therefore, a sampling error is calculated to indicate the possible range of error in the survey data. Sampling errors can be calculated only for surveys based on probability samples. The unemployment rate and housing starts are examples of economic indicators for which a sampling error is provided.

Some indicators are published with numerical ranges of error due to sampling of survey respondents (e.g., there may be an error in the data in 19 of 20 cases of plus or minus 3 percent). In such instances, one should allow for a lower and upper range of the number in assessing movements over time. When the error range is larger than the movement in the current indicator (say, the error is plus or minus 3 percent and the monthly movement in the indicator is only 1 percent), the single-period movement is highly tentative. But if such small movements cumulate in one direction over several periods, that trend is more significant. For example, an unemployment rate change of 0.1 percentage point in one month is not statistically significant in two of three cases because it is within the likely sampling error of 0.13 percentage point. If the unemployment rate rises or falls by 0.1 percentage point in the same direction for two or more months, however, the cumulative change is significant.

If a sample does not fully represent the components of the universe in accordance with the relative importance of each component, the survey is not based on a probability sample. For indicators based on nonprobability samples, only revision errors can be calculated. The establishment-based employment survey and the survey of manufacturers' shipments, orders, and inventories are examples of economic indicators for which a revision error, but not a sampling error, is provided.

Even for probability samples, however, the present state of statistical methodology does not allow an estimate of the accuracy with which respondents answer survey questions. Error attributable to inaccurate answers is known as nonsampling or reporting error, and all survey data, including those obtained from the universe as well as from a sample of respondents, contain an unknown amount of such inaccuracy.

Also, with the present state of statistical methodology, sampling errors for probability samples of surveys on different topics cannot be added to arrive at an overall sampling error for all of the surveys combined. For example, the gross domestic product is prepared from a variegated database of many different topics for its household, business, government, and international components that include both probability and nonprobability sample surveys. Even if all the surveys were based on probability samples, the various sampling errors could not be added to get an overall sampling error for the GDP. Because of this methodological limitation, the GDP includes a revision error but not a sampling error (see Revisions above).

Some research is being done on combining the sampling errors from independent surveys done on the same topic, such as in diagnostic or therapeutic studies of the same medical disease; this is known as meta analysis. But meta analysis is not relevant for combining sampling errors from surveys of different topics such as the database underlying the GDP.

CALCULATING AND PRESENTING GROWTH RATES

The public's perception of economic growth rates is affected by how the trends of economic indicators are calculated and how the data are presented. This section highlights three aspects of preparing and presenting growth rates: annualized and annual movements, beginning and ending dates, and charting data graphically.

Annualized and Annual Movements

Three measures are used in gauging various types of annual movements of economic indicators: the seasonally adjusted annual rate, annual change, and December to December or fourth-quarter to fourth-quarter change.

Seasonally Adjusted Annual Rate (SAAR)

The SAAR reflects what the yearly movement of the indicator would be if the same rate of change (adjusted for seasonal variation) were to continue for the next eleven months (monthly indicator) or for the next three quarters (quarterly indicator). This number extends the same rate of change for the current month or quarter compounded to the rest of the year. The SAAR provides a quick view of how a subannual movement looks over a twelve-month period. It also facilitates comparisons of growth rates for periods of different lengths. It is important to recognize, however, that the SAAR number assumes a constant rate of change for comparative purposes only; it is not a forecast of what is expected to happen.

Annual Change

This compares the average level of the indicator in one year with the average level of the next year. The annual averages are computed for the twelve months or four quarters of the indicator. The yearly averages smooth out the effects of unusually high or low levels in particular months or quarters.

December to December or Fourth-quarter-to-fourth-quarter Change

These focus on the movement of the indicator from the end of one calendar year to the end of the next calendar year. This kind of change is often used in economic reports at the beginning of the calendar year to provide a more current assessment of the most recent twelve-month or four-quarter period than the annual change numbers mentioned above. The caveat is that any single period within the year may have abnormally high or low rates of economic growth or inflation. Because these data are not averaged over an annual period, they can distort the view of annual change.

Beginning and Ending Dates

The magnitude of economic change over a particular time period is influenced by the economic conditions at the beginning and ending dates of the period. Average rates of growth for approximately the same period differ somewhat if the end points are changed slightly. Table 1.4 illustrates this in the case of the real gross domestic product during 1990–96. It shows two annual growth rates compounded over the period that vary noticeably with small changes in the initial year, one using 1990:2nd quarter and one using 1991:1st quarter. The end period in both instances is 1996:4th quarter. The growth rate of 1.9 percent for 1990–96 rises to 2.6 percent for 1991–96. The variation reflects different economic environments—1990:2nd quarter was the high point (peak) of the 1981–90 expansion, and 1991:1st quarter was the low point (trough) of the 1990–91 recession.

Long-term growth rates are calculated by using end years that represent similar phases of the business cycle in order not to distort average growth rates for the entire period. In the above example, the 1990–96 end years meet this crite-

Table 1.4

Real Gross Domestic Product (billions of 1992 dollars, seasonally adjusted annual rate)

1990:2	6,174.4
1991:1	6,047.9
1996:4	6,993.6

Average annual growth

1990:2–1996:4	1.9%
1990:1–1996:4	2.6%

Note: Number after colon is quarter of year.

rion, since they both are high points of expansion periods including the ongoing current expansion. It is equally valid to measure long-term growth rates from the low points of recession periods.

By contrast, the 1991–96 end years have a higher growth rate because they start with the low point of a recession and end with a rising expansion. The movement from a cyclical low point to a cyclical high point (or analogously from a cyclical high point to a cyclical low point) is referred to as the amplitude of the business cycle. The amplitude is the size of the rise in cyclical recoveries and expansions and the size of the decline in cyclical recessions and contractions.

In sum, long-term growth rates and cyclical amplitudes are very different. Long-term growth rates measure economic movements that abstract from cyclical fluctuations and span at least one complete cycle of rising and falling economic activity, and sometimes several complete cycles. By contrast, cyclical amplitudes measure the fluctuation separately in the rising and declining phases of a single business cycle.

Charting Data Graphically

Data are depicted visually on charts to convey the main points of the statistics, while requiring a minimum effort by the viewer. Use of such graphics is related to the adage that "a picture is worth a thousand words." Different types of scales are used on the axes of charts to highlight absolute or relative (percentage) changes in the data: arithmetic scales are used to illustrate absolute changes, and ratio scales are used to illustrate relative changes. These are different measures, and the viewer of graphic data should know which type of scale is used on the chart.

Arithmetic scales have the same distance (for example, as measured in inches) between points when the absolute difference between one set of numeric values is the same as the difference between another set of numeric values, regardless of the size of the numbers. Thus, on an arithmetic scale, the distance between 10 and 100 is the same as the distance between 100 and 190. The absolute difference in both cases is 90. On an arithmetic scale, if the absolute differences from point to point are the same all along the line (for example, each point is ten units higher than the previous point), then the slope of the line is the same between all points. When the absolute differences between two sets of two points are not the same, the slope of the line changes accordingly by becoming more or less steep.

By contrast, ratio (or logarithmic) scales have equal distances when the ratio between one set of two numbers is the same as the ratio between another set of two numbers, regardless of the size of the numbers. For example, on a ratio scale, the distance between 10 and 100 is the same as the distance between 100 and 1,000, since the ratio is ten to one in both cases. Thus, on a ratio scale, the slope of the line between 10 and 100 is the same as the slope between 100 and 1,000. When the ratios between two sets of two points are not the same, the slope of the line also changes by becoming more or less steep.

Conventionally, time is shown on the horizontal (X) axis and data values are shown on the vertical (Y) axis of the chart. Time—weeks, months, years, and so on—is always on an arithmetic scale because there is no reason to vary distances for periods of the same time segments. On the other hand, data values are shown on an arithmetic scale when the analysis emphasizes absolute change, but on a ratio scale when relative change is the primary interest. Because a ratio scale is based on logarithms of the data, a chart in which the horizontal axis of time is an arithmetic scale and the vertical axis of data values is a ratio scale is also called a semilogarithmic (or semilog) chart.

Figures 1.4a and 1.4b illustrate the difference between arithmetic and ratio scales. They both use the same merchandise exports data from 1970 to 1996; exports rose from $42 billion in 1970 to $615 billion in 1996. Although they use the same data, the two graphs are not comparable. The year-to-year changes in Figure 1.4a represent the absolute change, while the year-to-year changes in Figure 1.4b represent the relative change.

INFLATION-ADJUSTED DOLLARS

Many economic indicators are measured in current and inflation-adjusted dollars. Current dollars include the combined effect of changes in quantity and price over time and thus represent the *dollar value* of economic activity. For example, the value of retail sales of shoes includes the number of pairs of shoes sold multiplied by their unit prices. By contrast, constant dollars include only the effect of changes in quantity over time, which is the *physical volume* of economic activity. Inflation-adjusted dollar measures, sometimes referred to as constant dollars, are stated in prices of a particular base period such as 1992 dollars, and are not affected by increases or decreases in prices. Because inflation-adjusted dollars

Figure 1.4a **Exports of Goods, 1970–96: Arithmetic Scale**

Billions of dollars

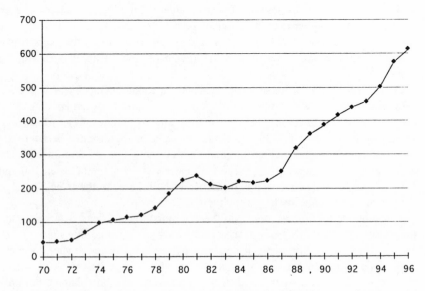

Note: Slope of line indicates yearly absolute changes. Periods with same slope have the same dollar change.

are based on what the value would be if prices were the same as in the base period, they are a measure of quantity.

In the above example, retail shoe sales in 1992 constant dollars for all years are calculated by dividing the dollar value for each year by the ratio change in prices between 1992 and the actual year. To illustrate, in estimating shoe sales in 1996 in 1992 dollars, if shoe prices rose by 9 percent between 1992 and 1996, the actual dollar value of sales in 1996 is divided by 1.09 to arrive at sales in 1992 dollars. In a year when shoe prices were lower than they were in 1992, say by 4 percent, the dollar value of sales in that year is divided by 0.96 for the constant-dollar number. Of course, the current and inflation-adjusted dollar numbers for 1992 are the same. In actual practice, these calculations are done separately for various categories of shoe sales, such as distinguishing among women's, men's, and children's shoes.

Inflation-adjusted dollar numbers are difficult to relate to in everyday terms because of price changes since the base period. Thus, in the late 1990s, it is difficult to think of wages or prices in 1992 dollars. But inflation-adjusted dollars are highly relevant for gauging relative movements over time. In such analyses as rates of economic growth or changes in workers' purchasing power, a measure of quantity (in inflation-adjusted dollars), rather than a measure of value (in

Figure 1.4b **Exports of Goods, 1970–96: Ratio Scale**

Billions of dollars

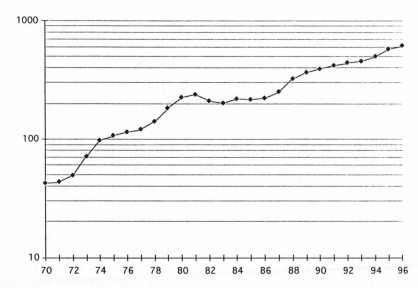

Note: Slope of line indicates yearly relative changes. Periods with the same slope have the same percentage change.

current dollars), is the relevant number. It is far more meaningful to evaluate the percentage change in weekly wages in inflation-adjusted dollars than in current dollars because of the effect of inflation on purchasing power. While wages in current dollars may have risen from one period to the next, wages in inflation-adjusted dollars may have declined because prices of goods and services that workers buy rose more than wages, and consequently workers' purchasing power (i.e., real income) declined.

THE UNDERGROUND ECONOMY

The underground economy (UE) refers to income derived from both legal and illegal activities not reported or understated on tax returns and in economic surveys. In addition to raising the federal government budget deficit, the UE raises questions about the accuracy of various economic indicators. Thus, while UE activity is not directly included in economic indicators, it is indirectly included when the derived UE incomes are respent in the measured economy.

Legal sources of income include employment, investments, and income-support programs that are consistent with national and state laws. Illegal income is associated with street drugs, unauthorized gambling and prostitution, theft, fraud, illegal firearms sales, loansharking, and many other activities. Economic indicators typically do not reflect illegal activity, either because it is excluded from the definitions used or because, as a matter of reality, it is unlikely to be reported on tax returns and surveys. The exclusion of illegal activity should be remembered when making economic comparisons with other countries in which certain activities banned in the United States are not banned abroad.

Two different methodologies are used to estimate the UE. One uses "direct" measurements—for example, studies of compliance with the income tax laws in reporting business incomes. The "indirect" approach uses information that suggests attempts to hide income, such as the tendency to use cash rather than checks in business transactions. The direct approach is more appealing, although it involves considerable estimating. Estimates of the UE based on the direct method tend to be lower than those based on the indirect technique.

There was a spate of studies on the effect of the UE on economic indicators in the late 1970s and the 1980s.[9] Estimates of how much the UE cause the overall economy to be understated ranged from 1 to 33 percent of the gross national product in these studies. Some observers also concluded that the UE grew faster than what is shown in the published indicators. They raise the question that if the economy was in fact substantially stronger than was apparent in the indicators, fiscal and monetary policies adopted to guide the economy on a path of low unemployment and low inflation were more expansionary than they would have been otherwise, and possibly inflationary.

A basic question in these measures is whether the UE has worsened over time by rising as a proportion of the measured economy. The above scenario of overstimulating the economy would be more likely if the UE has worsened. But if it has not worsened, there is less of a chance of overstimulating the economy because period-to-period movements of economic indicators, which are the basis for formulating economic policies, would at most be only minimally affected by the UE.

The gross domestic product, prepared by the U.S. Bureau of Economic Analysis, is the only economic indicator that includes at least partial statistical adjustments for UE activity. The adjustments are based on Internal Revenue Service estimates of noncompliance with federal income tax laws by nonfilers of income tax returns and misreporting on income tax returns.[10]

The unemployment rate, prepared by the U.S. Bureau of Labor Statistics, is another major indicator affected by the UE. Respondents to household surveys on employment and unemployment may report they are not working, when in fact they do have jobs, either in legal or illegal activities. The effect of this misreporting, which is probably most serious among those whose sole job is in the underground economy and among undocumented alien workers, is to lower the employment and raise the unemployment measures.

In a review of the literature on the problem in 1984, the U.S. Bureau of Labor Statistics concluded that there are no sound estimates of the effect of the underground economy on the unemployment rate.[11] The BLS did not estimate the effect of misreporting on the official labor force numbers, but it questioned the validity of other analysts' estimates, such as that the 1978 official unemployment rate was overstated by 1.5 percentage points. The BLS analysis of the household survey data did not substantiate the claims of a significant effect on the unemployment rate.

The effects of the UE on the federal government budget deficit, however, are clearly substantial. The Internal Revenue Service estimated for 1992 that unpaid individual income taxes associated with legal activities (due to unreported and underreported income, overstated deductions and exemptions, calculation errors, and other factors) was $80 billion, compared to the federal budget deficit of $290 billion.[12]

Incorporating the effects of the UE in economic indicators is exceptionally difficult. The UE is a disturbing problem that refuses to go away and adds one more uncertainty to interpreting the movements of economic indicators.

DISTINCTIONS AMONG "GOODS," "SERVICES," AND "STRUCTURES"

Economic output produced in various industries is classified as goods or services. In some cases the definition is obvious, although the distinctions are sometimes ambiguous. The various industries are coded by number in the North American Industry Classification System.[13]

Goods are three-dimensional products as well as liquid and gas products that may be transported from one location to another. All goods are materials that have a mass. Gases are invisible but they may be stored in a container. Goods are commodities that are produced in the agriculture, mining, and manufacturing industries.

Services are outputs produced in all of the nongoods industries except construction. They are summarized in this negative manner because their heterogeneous nature makes it difficult to describe them with uniform characteristics. While service industries interact with goods industries, services are characterized by something other than goods. Personal, business, finance, insurance, real estate, and professional services industries may facilitate, enhance, or otherwise affect goods production, but they do not directly produce goods. Communication, electric and gas utilities, transportation, and wholesale and retail trade industries are more closely associated with goods products. They are not defined as goods industries, however, for the following reasons: communication and utilities industries are dependent on invisible forms of energy such as radio waves and kilowatts of electric power; truck, rail, air, ship, and pipeline transportation industries move goods that are produced in agricultural, mining, and manufacturing industries; and wholesale and retail trade industries distribute and market goods that are produced in agricultural, mining, and manufacturing industries.

Structures are residential, commercial, school, hospital, and other buildings, as well as nonbuilding facilities such as roads, bridges, dams, and power plants. Structures are produced in the construction industries. While structures are three-dimensional products, they are not classified as goods because they are built as an integral part of the land and consequently are not moved from place to place.

The three-way classification is governed by the primary activity of the enterprise producing the item or the primary mode of production, rather than by the ultimate use of the item. For example, a bakery that makes bread and sells it to stores for sale to the public is classified as a manufacturing industry, while a bakery that makes bread on the same premises as the store that sells it to the public is classified as a retail trade industry. To take another example, mobile homes are made in factories and thus are classified as manufacturing industry products; although a mobile home is subsequently attached to the ground when it is bought for housing, it nevertheless is defined as a manufactured product rather than as a structure.

THE PRODUCTION OF ECONOMIC STATISTICS

This book describes how macroeconomic indicators are used to analyze movements in the U.S. economy and formulate fiscal and monetary policies to foster economic growth and lower unemployment and inflation. The lifeblood of such analyses is the weekly, monthly, quarterly, annual, and less frequently provided statistical data such as the five-year economic censuses and the ten-year population census. Most of these statistics are produced by a small group of federal government agencies: Bureau of Labor Statistics in the U.S. Department of Labor, Bureau of the Census and the Bureau of Economic Analysis in the U.S. Department of Commerce, National Agricultural Statistics Service and the Economic Research Service in the U.S. Department of Agriculture, Internal Revenue Service in the U.S. Department of the Treasury, and the Federal Reserve. Spending for the statistical programs of these agencies (excluding the year 2000 population census and the Federal Reserve programs) totaled $800 million in fiscal year 1996.[14]

Many private organizations also provide macroeconomic indicators. Examples are Business Cycle Dating Committee of the National Bureau of Economic Research, The Conference Board, The Dun & Bradstreet Corporation, Center for International Business Cycle Research at Columbia University, Stock and Watson Indicator Report, and various financial firms and trade associations.

The $900 million total for the federal government's statistical programs may seem costly, but the expense cannot be evaluated without considering the importance of quality economic data to successful economic analysis. The most sophisticated analytic techniques are only as good as the data they rely on. Economic data are central in formulating fiscal and monetary policies that affect trillions of dollars of economic output and the lives of hundreds of millions of people.

Relevant, credible, and timely economic data that are readily available to the public are essential to the well-being of a democratic nation. Indeed, one may reasonably conclude that the government invests too little, rather than too much, in economic data programs, when the cost of producing economic data is compared to their importance.

In actions taken to reduce the federal budget deficit, statistical activities along with most federal programs have had real budget reductions (after accounting for inflation) in the 1980s and 1990s. A few examples of the effect of these reductions are that data series have been discontinued for the natural resources and research and development satellite supplements to the national income and product accounts, the survey of plant and equipment expenditures, and the foreign exchange pass-through elements of export and import price indexes; and small-scale research projects in various agencies to improve the methodological procedures in producing more reliable economic statistics have been cut back.

Obtaining increased funding to vitalize statistical data programs in the 1990s is difficult. In fact, the main focus of statistical agencies is to defend the core programs against additional cutbacks in preparing their annual budget requests to the President and Congress. This situation reflects the fact that elected officials are generally reluctant to spend money for intangibles that are not readily perceived as making a difference in people's lives. Unlike spending for income maintenance, housing, education, health, environmental, and defense programs, the payback from increased spending for better economic data is not visible. Even though the costs of statistical programs are relatively small and even though quality statistical data are necessary for effective implementation of civilian and defense programs, neither the public nor elected officials are generally convinced of the need to spend money to maintain, let alone improve, economic statistics. Such resistance is heightened by objections to the reporting and paperwork burden imposed by surveys, and by the increasing tendency among households and businesses not to respond to surveys.

Making the case for strengthening economic statistics is not easy.[15] The difficulty is intensified by a complaint of economic policymakers that when a new issue arises, relevant data to address it are not readily available. Thus, despite the existing stock of mountains of data, unique problems come up that find the stockpile wanting. This may result from the surprise nature of the problem that was not anticipated or from a previous awareness of the possibility of the "surprise" event but which was not considered likely to happen.

One way to develop a greater grasp of the importance of economic statistics is to give elected officials a sense of priorities among the vast array of existing and needed new data. In their book, *Statistics for the 21st Century,* Joseph Duncan and Andrew Gross recommend improvements in basic areas of macroeconomic indicators that are prepared in several statistical agencies and in the interagency coordination role of the Office of Management and Budget.[16] Such perspectives should be followed up by statistical agencies and economic policymakers by working in concert to convey the message in presidential and congressional budget hearings that economic data are not a luxury, but a necessary investment for social and economic well-being.

DATA INTEGRITY

Economic indicators are more than "statistics." They are the factual base for public policies and actions that affect the economic well-being of all Americans. It is essential for the vitality of a democracy that these data be impeccably objective, that they be prepared with the highest professional standards, and that they have no hint of political interference. Only with such integrity will the people have confidence in the data.

The indicators are produced mainly by agencies in the executive branch of the U.S. government, such as the Bureau of the Census, Bureau of Labor Statistics, Bureau of Economic Analysis, National Agricultural Statistics Service, and the Internal Revenue Service. From the 1970s to the early 1990s, there were occasional allegations that the indicators were politicized by "cooking" the preparation of the statistics to make the President who was in office at the time look better. On further examination, these allegations of tampering with the data were shown to be unfounded. Although this is comforting, it still leaves the possibility of future tainting, which must be guarded against. While some data may be more vulnerable to "cooking" than others—for example, the estimation of the gross domestic product is based on more statistical judgments that conceivably could be shaded than is the unemployment rate, which is based on household survey information—the possibility of tampering exists with all data.

One institutional device for insulating statistical agencies from political pressure is for the head of the agency to be appointed by the President and confirmed by the Senate, as is done for the Director of the Census, Commissioner of Labor Statistics, and Commissioner of Internal Revenue. This may give the agency heads the appearance, if not the reality, of heightened stature for resisting pressures from their political superiors, which in these cases are the Secretary of Commerce, Secretary of Labor, and Secretary of the Treasury, respectively. Senate confirmation probably has greater weight when it is specified for a period of time that does not coincide with the presidential term, as is the case of the four-year term for the Commissioner of Labor Statistics. At the same time, a career civil service employee probably has more independence than a political official. Thus, to the extent that an agency head who is confirmed by the Senate is a political official, the "independence effect" of the confirmation is diminished. There obviously are no tidy answers.

A second institutional device that may lessen political interference with the data is the Office of Management and Budget's directive, which requires statistical agencies of the federal government to limit access to their facilities where the data for major economic indicators are being prepared preceding the day when they are released to the public (referred to as a "lockup").[17] During the lockup, which may last several days, only certain employees of the statistical agency have access to the data. The lockup was originally instituted to prevent leaks of unpublished data that give recipients of leaks an unfair advantage in financial markets, but it could have a secondary benefit of fending off attempts to interfere with the data preparation. On the other hand, the argument can be made that if many people know a number ahead of time, a political appointee could not have the number changed without causing a scandal; but if only a few people know the number, the political appointee could conceivably use some leverage (for example, the threat of funding cuts) to get them to change the number. Again, there are no tidy answers.

On balance, I believe the above mechanisms of Senate confirmation of statistical agency heads and of limiting access to the data preparation through the lockup procedure lessen the chances that economic indicators can be compromised. But no system is foolproof when there is a determination to violate it. Thus, these and future measures to protect the integrity of data will reduce, but not eliminate, attempts to contaminate the data for political gain. Therefore, it is essential that the press and analysts be vigilant in safeguarding the integrity of the numbers and sound the alarm when they believe the data may be suspect. This is added insurance for maintaining accurate information, which is a bulwark of a free society.

Another dimension of the integrity of economic data emerged in 1996 in respect to a specific economic indicator, the consumer price index (CPI). As a way of reducing the federal government budget deficit, there have been proposals to lower government spending by lowering the inflation rate of the CPI based on a view that the CPI overstates inflation. A lower inflation rate would reduce the entitlement benefits paid on Social Security and other income maintenance programs. Chapter 11 discusses the substantive issues of measuring inflation through the CPI and the danger of politicizing the CPI.

REVIEW QUESTIONS

- How does the United States depoliticize the determination of when a recession begins and ends?
- Can the designation of a recession period be objective if no fixed formulas are used for determining the beginning and ending points of a recession?
- How do growth cycles supplement business cycles in analyzing current economic movements?
- If monthly or quarterly data are not seasonally adjusted,"seasonal" comparisons are sometimes made between the current month or quarter and the corresponding year-earlier period. What are the limitations of this approach?

- Index numbers are a convenient way to summarize masses of data, but they also have an inherent "product mix" problem. Explain the problem.
- What is a sound way of accounting for upcoming data revisions in analyzing current economic movements?
- What is the problem with a statistical survey on which an economic indicator is based for which a sampling error cannot be calculated?
- How can the phase of a business cycle distort the calculation of long-term growth rates?
- Is the divergence between the current-dollar and inflation-adjusted dollar measures of an economic indicator greater during periods of stable or rising prices?
- Why is the underground economy an issue in analyzing economic indicators?
- Which industries have a more heterogeneous characterization of their products, those classified as "goods" or those classified as "services"?
- Why is the production of economic indicators an issue for economic analysis?
- If there is no foolproof way of preventing the preparation of economic indicators from being politicized, what recourse does the public have?

NOTES

1. Victor Zarnowitz, *Business Cycles: Theory, History, Indicators, and Forecasting* (University of Chicago Press, 1992), chs. 2 and 8.
2. Geoffrey H. Moore, *Business Cycles, Inflation and Forecasting*, 2d ed. (Ballinger, 1983), pp. 3–9.
3. Edward Renshaw, "On Measuring Economic Recessions," *Challenge*, March/April, 1991, pp. 58–59.
4. Michael P. Niemira and Philip A. Klein, *Forecasting Financial and Economic Cycles* (Wiley, 1994), p. 262.
5. In a conversation with the author, Victor Zarnowitz, who is a member of the NBER business cycle dating committee, said this was his recollection of the committee's deliberations. He also noted that the dating of the pre–World War II recovery from the depression trough in March 1933 to the peak in May 1937 as a separate business cycle phase was an exception to this guideline because economic activity at the May 1937 peak was below that at the peak of the previous expansion in August 1929. Following the May 1937 peak, the economy turned down into a recession in June 1937 that culminated at the trough in June 1938.
6. Robert D. Hershey, Jr., "This Just In: Recession Ended 21 Months Ago," *New York Times*, December 23, 1992, p. D1.
7. Zarnowitz, *Business Cycles*, ch. 7.
8. Christina D. Romer, "Spurious Volatility in Historical Unemployment Data," *Journal of Political Economy*, February 1986; idem, "Is the Stabilization of the Postwar Economy a Figment of the Data?" *American Economic Review*, June 1986; idem, "New Estimates of Prewar Gross National Product and Unemployment," *Journal of Economic History*, June 1986. See also David R. Weir, "The Reliability of Historical Macroeconomic Data for Comparing Cyclical Stability," *Journal of Economic History*, June 1986;

Stanley Lebergott, "Discussion," *Journal of Economic History,* June 1986. The Weir and Lebergott articles are rejoinders to Romer, all three being in the *JEH.* See also Zarnowitz, *Business Cycles,* pp. 77–79, 89, 91, 363.

9. Bureau of International Labor Affairs, U.S. Department of Labor, *The Underground Economy in the United States,* September 1992.

10. Bureau of Economic Analysis, U.S. Department of Commerce, "Improved Estimates of the National Income and Product Accounts for 1959–95: Results of the Comprehensive Revision," *Survey of Current Business,* January/February 1996, pp. 24–25. See also Internal Revenue Service, U.S. Department of the Treasury, *Federal Compliance Research: Individual Income Tax Gap Estimates for 1985, 1988, and 1992,* April 1996.

11. Richard J. McDonald, "The 'Underground Economy' and BLS Statistical Data," *Monthly Labor Review,* January 1984.

12. Internal Revenue Service, *Federal Compliance Research.*

13. Office of Management and Budget, Executive Office of the President, "1997 North American Industry Classification System—1987 Standard Industrial Classification Replacement," *Federal Register,* April 9, 1997.

14. Office of Management and Budget, Executive Office of the President, *Statistical Programs of the United States Government: Fiscal Year 1997,* 1996.

15. An analogy can be made with the difficulty of making a convincing case for funding scientific research, which also is often seen to have limited practical application.

16. Joseph W. Duncan and Andrew C. Gross, *Statistics for the 21st Century: Proposals for Improving Statistics for Better Decision Making* (Irwin Professional Publishing, 1995), chs. 9 and 10.

17. Office of Management and Budget, Executive Office of the President, "Statistical Policy Directive No. 3: Compilation, Release, and Evaluation of Principal Economic Indicators," *Federal Register,* September 25, 1985.

2
FRAMEWORK FOR MACROECONOMIC
ANALYSIS, POLICIES, AND FORECASTING

This chapter provides an overview of how the economic indicators in the following chapters are interrelated for use in analyzing and forecasting the economy. The relationships are limited to the most "macro" indicators. This has the virtue of giving a concise view of the forest from the trees, with fairly extensive explanations of the interrelationships between indicators. The chapter briefly notes the substance of each indicator. Subsequent chapters explain the meaning of these and other indicators and how their movements shed light on the strengths and weaknesses of the economy. These give a more complete view of how economists analyze and forecast the economy. Thus, the reader starts in this chapter with a top-down orientation to the indicators as a group, which gives a context for proceeding through the entire book.

Statistical relationships between certain economic indicators are generally consistent with theoretical notions of what the relationships are thought to be, such as between economic growth and unemployment, inflation and unemployment, and interest rates and economic growth. These relationships are attempts to summarize the effect of underlying factors that drive the economy but that are not fully understood. They are proxies for complex interrelationships affecting domestic and international commodity, service, labor, and financial markets; impacts of economic and political actions of governments on the economy; and the intangible but important psychological moods of optimism and pessimism among households and businesses.

The chapter has three main components. The analytic section provides a system for assessing the direction and momentum of the economy. The policy section covers the role of fiscal, monetary, and incomes policies. The forecasting section discusses basic aspects of economic forecasts.

ANALYTIC SYSTEM

The system for evaluating recent and long-term economic movements is based on analyzing the following interrelationships of economic indicators and policies: economic growth versus unemployment; unemployment versus inflation; interest rates versus economic growth; growth cycles; and fiscal, monetary, and incomes policies.

Economic Growth and Unemployment

Economic growth is a key factor affecting unemployment: rapid economic growth lowers unemployment, and slow or declining growth raises unemployment. The relationship between economic growth and unemployment compares economic growth, as reflected by movements in the real gross domestic product, to changes in the unemployment rate. The relationship is referred to as "Okun's Law," after Arthur Okun, who developed it in the 1960s.[1]

Okun's Law and NAIRU

There are two critical aspects to Okun's Law: (1) the break-even point, which indicates the economic growth rate required for maintaining a stable unemployment rate, and (2) the unemployment effects of growth rates above and below the break-even point. Economic growth is represented by the inflation-adjusted gross domestic product (real GDP). Unemployment is defined as the number of persons without jobs who are available for and actively seeking work. The unemployment rate (UR) is the percentage that unemployed persons are of the labor force; the labor force is the sum of employed and unemployed persons. Chapters 3 and 9 detail the GDP and UR concepts and measures, respectively.

The break-even point can be understood with the following example: Assume the UR is 5 percent, the labor force grows by 1 percent per year, and labor productivity (output per worker) increases 1.5 percent annually. Then the real GDP must grow by at least 2.5 percent annually to absorb 95 percent of the labor force growth and thus maintain the UR of 5 percent.

Okun's Law is based on the concept of the gap between actual output and potential output. This recognizes the need to include price inflation in the analysis. Potential output is the maximum level of activity the economy can sustain without causing inflation to accelerate, which stated differently is a steady rate of inflation. It is called NAIRU, the nonaccelerating inflation rate of unemployment. The NAIRU is based on the expected future rate of inflation and is not tied to any specific rate of inflation. This means the same NAIRU can exist at different rates of inflation, depending on the economic environment at a particular time. The corollary is that when unemployment exceeds the NAIRU, the rate of inflation tends to decrease, and when unemployment drops below the NAIRU, the rate of inflation tends to increase.

Changing economic environments have resulted in changing NAIRU estimates over time. While analysts differ on the specific NAIRU for any particular time period, these variations typically are within a range of one percentage point, and the changes estimated by the various analysts in the NAIRU from one period to the next are typically in the same direction. Thus, estimates of the NAIRU rose from 3 to 4 percent in the 1960s to 6 to 7 percent in the 1970s, and by the mid-1990s the NAIRU estimates declined to the 5.2 to 6.3 percent range. These fluctuations are ascribed mainly to the rising teenage share of the labor force until the late 1970s and the subsequent decline in the teenager share into the 1990s. Because teenagers have a higher unemployment rate (UR) than other workers, a rising teenage share of the labor force tends to raise the NAIRU, while a declining teenage share of the labor force tends to lower the NAIRU. In 1996, the UR for all workers was 5.4 percent, for adult workers aged 20 years and older it was 4.7 percent, and for teenage workers aged 16 to 19 years it was 16.7 percent. The teenage share of the labor force declined from 8.8 percent in 1980 to 5.8 percent in 1996.

A much smaller effect has been attributed to the increase in working women, whose URs before the 1980s were slightly higher than those for men; but in the 1980s and 1990s the differential disappeared, with men having higher URs in some years and women having higher URs in other years. For example, in 1996 the UR for men aged 20 years and over was 4.6 percent and the UR for women aged 20 years and older was 4.8 percent. This depiction of the dominance of demographic shifts in the labor force on the NAIRU is a widely accepted view, although Geoffrey Tootell finds that the demographic labor force changes had little effect.[2] (NAIRU estimates are discussed further below under Fiscal Policy: Structural Budget and under Monetary Policy.)

The economy's potential is determined by the size of the labor force; the abilities of workers, managers, executives, and entrepreneurs; the quantity of capital equipment and structures used in production; and the level of technology of the capital facilities. When the economy is operating below its potential, unemployment can go lower without leading to higher inflation. When the economy is operating above its potential, the low unemployment rate leads to higher inflation.

A central task in studying Okun's law is to estimate the break-even point. The break-even point in 1996 is approximated at an annual real GDP growth rate of 2 percent. At the 2 percent rate, the UR tends to be stable. And for every percentage point of annual GDP growth above or below 2 percent, the UR tends to decrease (increase) by 0.6 of a percentage point over the year.

Figure 2.1 shows the GDP/UR relationship from 1960 to 1996. Each black diamond represents the intersection of the GDP growth rate and the UR for a year, and the line of white diamonds is the long-term average relationship. The long-term average indicates the typical inverse relationship: as the GDP increases, the UR falls, and vice versa. Graphically, this appears in the direction of the straight line that slopes downward to the right. This general relationship is expected from economic theory. An exception to this general relationship occurs when the GDP increases, but at a lower rate than the break-even point associated

Figure 2.1 **Okun's Law: 1960–96**

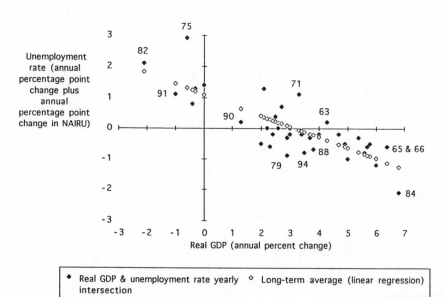

Note: Based on U.S. Bureau of Economic Analysis, U.S. Bureau of Labor Statistics, and Congressional Budget Office data.

with a stable UR, in which case both the GDP and the UR increase.

Several caveats are in order when using Okun's Law to analyze the current economy. First, the law changes over time. For example, the break-even point in the early 1980s was a real GDP growth rate of about 3 percent annually, compared with 2 percent in the 1990s; and the change in the annual UR for every percentage point of annual real GDP growth above or below the break-even point was 0.4 percentage point per year in the early 1980s, compared with 0.6 percentage point in the 1990s. The decline in the break-even point resulted in large part from the declining proportion of teenagers in the labor force, who have very high unemployment rates. In turn, the decline in working teenagers was due to the lower birthrates starting in the 1960s, which have not been substantially offset by increasing numbers of immigrant children who enter the labor force as teenagers. Based on these demographic trends, it is likely that the 2 percent break-even point of the 1990s will rise early in the twenty-first century only if there is a substantial increase in the proportion of teenagers who enter the labor force.

Second, the break-even numbers are multiyear average relationships that typically do not hold in any single year. This is apparent in Figure 2.1, which shows that most years diverge from the long-term average relationship, being either above or below the downward sloping line. For example, GDP growth was 2 percent in 1995, but the UR declined from 6.1 to 5.6 percent in the same period. According to Okun's Law, however, the UR in 1995 should have remained at the 1994 level, since the 2 percent GDP growth was at the break-even point. This divergence results from the fact that GDP growth is driven by employment, hours worked and productivity, none of which necessarily moves in tandem with URs. Third, the break-even estimates are only approximations that have an un-specified error range.

With these caveats, Okun's Law provides an overall perspective for linking economic growth and unemployment. In assessing these trends, the analyst should observe special conditions that may cause large divergences from the long-term trend for particular years. In addition, the break-even point should be reviewed every few years to determine if there are significant changes that should be brought into the analysis.

Unemployment versus Inflation: Phillips Curve

The most direct measure of the relationship between unemployment and inflation is the Phillips Curve. It is named for A.W. Phillips, who in the 1950s assessed the relationship between unemployment and wage rates in England over a 100-year period.[3] In today's analyses, the wage-rate component has been replaced by prices, but it encompasses the same concept as the original formulation.

The Phillips Curve is a graph that depicts the idea of an inverse relationship between unemployment and inflation: as unemployment decreases, inflation in-creases, and vice versa. The reason is that declining unemployment leads to higher production costs, as more outmoded and inefficient machinery is used and less-productive workers are employed. Also, when unemployment is low or de-clining, unions tend to get higher wage increases because they are in a stronger bargaining position. Conversely, when unemployment is high or rising, produc-tion costs and wages increase more slowly or may even decline. In addition, changes in the position of the Phillips Curve indicate if the unemployment-infla-tion long-term tradeoff has improved or worsened between two periods. The tradeoff improves when unemployment in both the past and current periods is unchanged and inflation lessens in the current period. The tradeoff worsens when unemployment is unchanged in both periods and inflation increases in the cur-rent period. Chapters 9 and 11 focus on unemployment and inflation, respec-tively.

Figures 2.2a through 2.2e show Phillips Curve trends for approximate de-cades of the 1950s through most of the 1990s. The unemployment rate (UR) is shown one year before the change in the consumer price index (CPI) on the premise that changes in the UR do not immediately affect prices—for example, changes in the UR in 1995 affect the CPI in 1996.

Figure 2.2a **Phillips Curve: 1950–59**

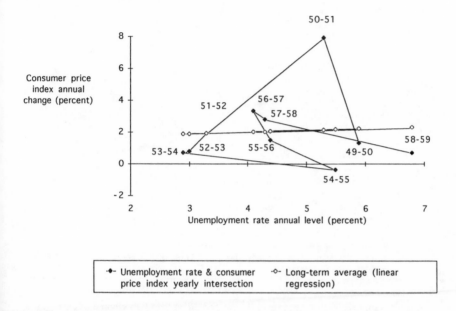

Note: Unemployment rate of previous year corresponds to CPI change of current year (e.g., UR 1958 and CPI 1959).

The figures differ from other formulations of the Phillips Curve in two ways. First, earlier depictions of the Phillips Curve consolidate longer periods of several decades in one time frame. The breakdown by decade is used here because distinct differences appear in the decade-by-decade relationships. Second, a commonly used version in the 1990s is referred to as the "expectations-augmented Phillips Curve."[4] It assumes a shifting Phillips Curve that links different rates of economic growth based on the inflation-adjusted gross domestic product to the "short-run expected change in the rate of inflation," and compares that with the "long-run correct expectations of inflation." By contrast, Figures 2.2a through 2.2e show the actual year-to-year changes in the unemployment-inflation relationship.

The figures conform to the concept of a tradeoff between unemployment and inflation when the long-term average line through the yearly dots slopes downward to the right. This theoretical inverse relationship was most evident in the 1960s when both unemployment and inflation were relatively low. Experience was contrary to the theory in the 1950s and the 1970s, when there was a slight direct relationship (upward-sloping line). In addition, as the 1970s progressed, the unemployment-inflation tradeoff worsened, as the Phillips Curve continually moved to the right from the early 1970s to the late 1970s. For example, the UR

Figure 2.2b **Phillips Curve: 1960–69**

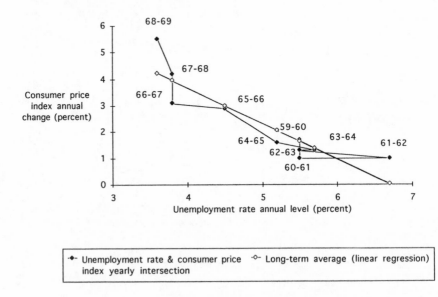

Note: Unemployment rate of previous year corresponds to CPI change of current year (e.g., UR 1968 and CPI 1969).

averaged 6.7 percent and the CPI averaged 4.9 percent during 1970–73, while the UR averaged 6.9 percent and the CPI averaged 7.8 percent during 1976–79. In the 1980s, the average experience was consistent with the theory, except for the 1984–86 period, when both unemployment and inflation declined. The inverse relationship continued in the early years of the 1990s, but then an improvement in the unemployment-inflation tradeoff seemed to occur during the mid-1990s, when the curve shifted to the left. Thus, from an average UR of 6.5 percent and average CPI of 4.2 percent in 1990–92, the UR averaged 5.7 percent and the CPI averaged 2.8 during 1994–96.[5] It is too soon to conclude that this is a permanent improvement at the time of this writing in the spring of 1997.

The Phillips Curve theoretically provides approximations of the NAIRU, and of the implications of a zero inflation rate for unemployment and of a zero unemployment rate for inflation. The NAIRU is implicit in the long-term trend line for each time period in the figures. The NAIRU is obtained from any point on the trend line by comparing the intersection of the unemployment rate on the horizontal (X) axis with the corresponding inflation rate on the vertical (Y) axis at that point. Thus, unemployment at any point on the long-term average line is associated with a nonaccelerating inflation rate at that point.

The implications of zero inflation or of zero unemployment appear by extending the trend line in the figures to the X and Y axes. Zero inflation is reached

Figure 2.2c **Phillips Curve: 1970–79**

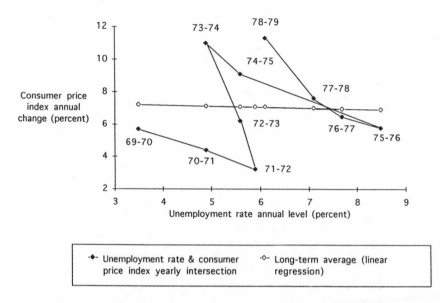

Note: Unemployment rate of previous year corresponds to CPI change of current year (e.g., UR 1978 and CPI 1979).

where the long-term average line touches the X axis, and the corresponding unemployment rate at zero inflation is read at that point on the X axis. Analogously, zero unemployment is reached when the long-term average line touches the Y axis, and the corresponding inflation rate is read at that point on the Y axis. The extension of the long-term line in this manner results in very high unemployment rates at zero inflation, and in very high inflation rates at zero unemployment. Even if this oversimplified technique were valid analytically, the results are too extreme to be sustained politically as a matter of public policy. Also, this simplistic application of the trend line to zero inflation and unemployment rates gives potentially reasonable estimates only when there is a long-term average inverse relationship between unemployment and inflation, such as in the 1960s, 1980s, and 1990s. The application gives nonsense estimates when there is a direct relationship between unemployment and inflation, negative unemployment rates at zero inflation, and accelerating inflation with rising unemployment, such as in the 1950s and 1970s.

The divergence between the theory and experience indicates that, for the most part, the economy is too complex for simple Philips Curve relationships. Most obvious is that there was a direct, rather than an inverse, relationship between unemployment and inflation in the 1950s and 1970s. This was aggravated in the 1970s when both inflation and unemployment were relatively high; in part this

Figure 2.2d **Phillips Curve 1980–89**

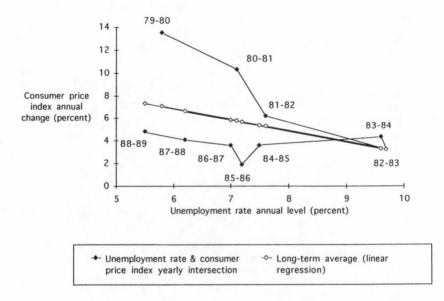

Note: Unemployment rate of previous year corresponds to CPI change of current year (e.g., UR 1988 and CPI 1989).

reflected the substantial increase in inflationary expectations, which became self-fulfilling when they led to rapid price and wage increases as business and labor tried to make up for declines in real income to cushion their incomes against further price increases. In the mid-1980s, both unemployment and inflation declined from the previous high levels during the recessions of 1980 and 1981–82, as the fuller utilization of resources during this period raised productivity by spreading fixed overhead costs over greater quantities of output. The higher productivity also was an incentive to business to hold down the rate of price increases even though the economy was expanding. Inflation also slowed in this period because of international developments: oil prices fell following the weakening of the Organization of Petroleum Exporting Countries cartel and the international value of the dollar increased in the first half of the 1980s, intensifying price competition from imported products. Unemployment and inflation fluctuated from the late 1980s to the early 1990s with no distinct upward or downward trends.

In the mid-1990s, unemployment and inflation again both declined. One explanation offered for this improved Phillips Curve tradeoff is the greater production efficiencies obtained from downsizing and innovations in the workplace that became prominent in the 1980s and continued into the 1990s. While there are anecdotal reports of such productivity improvements, however, the productivity

Figure 2.2e **Phillips Curve: 1990–96**

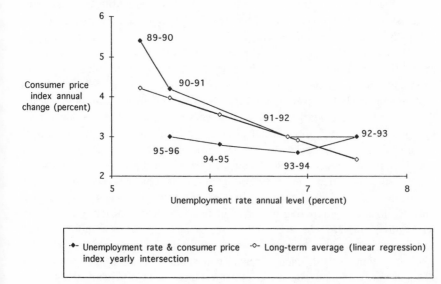

Note: Unemployment rate of previous year corresponds to CPI change of current year (e.g., UR 1995 and CPI 1996).

data show only small efficiency increases in the 1990s (Chapter 10). Another possible factor in the improved Phillips Curve tradeoff is the intensified global competition from abroad, although this would only be qualitative because there is currently no way to quantify it (Chapter 6).

Examples of other long-term factors affecting the Phillips Curve tradeoff are tariffs and other import restrictions (lowered by the North American Free Trade Agreement in the 1990s), farm subsidy price supports (replaced by farm income supports in the 1990s), minimum wages (increased in the 1990s), monopolistic pricing (more aggressive antitrust enforcement in the 1990s), deregulation of industry pricing (expanded in the 1990s), and social compacts between business and labor to hold down price and wage increases (not apparent in the 1990s). The tradeoff improves when these factors change in the direction of causing lower prices, and it rises when changes in these factors tend to raise prices. These changes in the threshold UR are referred to as improving or worsening the Phillips Curve tradeoff noted above. Overall, changes in the structural factors noted here for the 1990s suggest a modest improvement in the long-term Phillips Curve tradeoff by allowing a lower UR without increasing inflation, although this is a qualitative judgment because the effects of the structural changes are not quantifiable. If this improvement occurs, it will appear graphically in a shift of the Phillips Curve to the left.

The theoretical Phillips Curve tradeoff is most apparent in practice when inflation and unemployment are in relatively low ranges. During other periods, the experience often diverges from the theory. For example, low unemployment and high inflation may not be compatible over sustained periods as spending by households and businesses is moderated or lowered because the higher prices reduce the purchasing power of their incomes, leading to lower economic growth and higher unemployment. High unemployment and low inflation may lead to a prolonged period of stagnating economic growth. And the worst of both worlds, high unemployment and high inflation, lowers living conditions, inhibits business investment, and causes social discord until the abnormal expectations of spiraling inflation disappear. By contrast, low unemployment and low inflation may be compatible as a result of continuing workplace production efficiencies and global competition. They may also be bolstered if business and labor pursue a concerted anti-inflation policy by moderating price and wage increases and thus maintain the purchasing power of incomes, as Robert Kuttner notes.[6] But while this is attractive in an overall sense, because of wide variations in wage and price levels and movements in any recent period among various industries and occupations, it is difficult to obtain widespread agreement for uniform national patterns of moderate wage and price increases. In general, the graphic depictions of the changing tradeoffs between unemployment and inflation provided by the Phillips Curve are useful for exposing fault lines in the economy that may be remedied or worsened by economic events and policies affecting the tradeoff noted above.

The analyst should consider Phillips Curve analyses of inflation and unemployment most relevant during periods when both unemployment and inflation are relatively low. The assessment of the Phillips Curve should include qualitative judgments of the effect of long-term structural changes in the economy on the Phillips Curve tradeoff between unemployment and inflation.

Growth Cycles in Relation to Okun's Law and the Phillips Curve

Growth cycles provide an overview of fluctuations in economic activity in the context of steady long-term trends in economic growth (Chapter 1 details growth cycle concepts). In highlighting when current economic movements are above, below, or in line with the long-term growth of the economy, growth cycles are a unique tool for taking stock of the direction and momentum of the economy. Specifically, by integrating the fluctuating growth expansion and growth recession periods with steady long-term growth trends, growth cycles give a two-dimensional reading of the economy in contrast to the one-dimensional reading of business cycle fluctuations.

The leading and long-leading indexes of growth cycles suggest the future direction of the coincident index of growth cycles. Because the coincident index is the gauge for determining the expansion and recession phases of growth cycles, the leading indexes are harbingers of the future thrust of economic activity. When the two leading indexes move in the same direction, there is a greater likelihood that the coincident index will follow the same direction than when the leading indexes do not move in tandem.

Growth cycles are implicitly associated with Okun's Law and the Phillips Curve discussed in the previous sections on Economic Growth and Unemployment and on Unemployment versus Inflation. The longer a growth expansion period continues, the greater the tendency for economic growth to be sufficiently robust to drive down the unemployment rate to the minimum level without accelerating inflation (Okun's Law), and in turn the greater the tendency for the lower unemployment rate to approach the point where the tradeoff with inflation worsens (Phillips Curve). The opposite conditions obtain the longer a growth recession period continues—that is, the greater the tendency for slow or declining economic growth to result in rising unemployment and for the higher unemployment to lessen the chances of a worsening tradeoff with inflation. The integration of growth cycles with Okun's Law and the Phillips Curve gives a dynamic macro perspective to significant changes occurring in the overall economy.

The analyst should monitor the coincident index of the growth cycle to assess whether there is an approaching shift from a growth expansion to a growth recession, or vice versa. This should be supplemented by reference to the growth cycle leading indexes. The analyst should also evaluate the patterns of growth expansions and growth recessions in the context of Okun's Law and the Phillips Curve.

FISCAL, MONETARY, AND INCOMES POLICIES

The federal government and the Federal Reserve attempt on a continuing basis through fiscal and monetary policies, respectively, to moderate cyclical fluctuations and maintain steady long-term economic growth. Fiscal policy refers to the influence of federal government spending and taxation by the President and Congress. Monetary policy is the influence of the Federal Reserve on bank credit, interest rates, and the money supply. The federal government also occasionally uses incomes policies to curb inflation through voluntary guidelines or mandatory controls on prices and wages.

Although there is considerable sophistication in analyzing the effects of fiscal, monetary, and incomes policies, the causes of and remedies for business cycles and economic growth are complex, and the application of these policies is in part quantitative but also includes considerable qualitative judgment. Economic policies explicitly or implicitly take many factors into account: purely economic considerations such as balancing sales, production, employment, investment, prices, and interest rates; and political and other influences such as wars, harvests, consumer and business optimism and pessimism, international tensions, cartels, and protectionism.

Perhaps the major achievement of these policy tools is that no recession since World War II has degenerated into a cataclysm such as the depression of the 1930s.[7] In addition, the 1961–69 period went nine years without a recession, the 1982–90 period approached eight years without a recession, and the 1991–97 period has gone six years without a recession at the time of this writing in the spring of 1997. By historical standards, these expansions are very long. The first two periods, however, were tarnished by large increases in military spending that bolstered production and employment (in the 1960s for the Vietnam War and in the 1980s for the Cold War). By contrast, the expansion in the 1990s has occurred after the Cold War ended and when military spending has actually declined. The first two periods had fueled the hope that fiscal and monetary policies can maintain steady growth without recession or inflation. But the hope was dashed by the recessions and inflation in the 1970s and early 1980s and the recession in the early 1990s. There is much less hope in the 1990s that it is possible to prevent future recessions through fiscal and monetary policies because the economy is far too complex and unpredictable for problems to be diagnosed sufficiently far in advance and for the fiscal and monetary remedies to be timely enough to elicit the necessary response in the private sector to turn a pending recession into a mere slowdown in economic growth.

Fiscal, monetary, and incomes policies impact the economy in different ways. Before proceeding with the substantive aspects of the policies, it is useful background to contrast the institutional differences among them that affect the way they are carried out.

Fiscal policy is conducted through federal spending and taxes, which are aimed at influencing the long-term growth and cyclical movements of the economy. But fiscal policy is developed in the broader context of the role of government in the life of the nation. In the free, democratic society of the United States, federal, state, and local governments provide the institutions and services for enhancing the well-being of the nation's inhabitants. What governments do is ultimately determined at the ballot box when citizens elect their representatives. In general, governments are responsible for activities that in whole or in part are best done collectively for the common good, such as defense, elections, police, courts, health, education, transportation, income maintenance, environment, and other foundations of life. Taxation aims to finance that spending consistent with concepts of ability-to-pay, work and investment incentives, and efficient tax collection. When spending exceeds tax collections, the deficit is financed by borrowing, which in turn leads to spending in later years for the interest payments on the loans used to finance the deficit.

Thus, fiscal policies are developed as a subtext to the federal government's budget priorities for particular programs and taxes. The federal government, in contrast to state and local governments, is most suited to conduct fiscal policies, as noted below. Also, there is a long lag before the spending and tax changes impact the economy because of a lengthy process in putting them into effect.

First, the negotiation process between Congress and the President usually takes over a year to resolve to complete each year's fiscal budget. Second, these legislated changes then go through additional steps to make them operational: on the spending side, federal agencies must obligate funds to be spent, sign contracts and make other provisions for the work to be done, and pay for the work done before the new spending enters the income stream; on the revenue side, the Internal Revenue Service must write regulations and design tax forms to conform to the new laws before the new taxes can be collected.

By contrast, monetary policies aim solely at influencing the economy's growth rate, and in this respect pay particular attention to the inflationary aspects of economic growth rates at different stages of the business cycle. They affect the economy through their influence on bank credit, interest rates, and the money supply. Monetary policies are modified throughout the year by the Federal Reserve and can be and often are put into immediate effect when policy changes are adopted.

Because incomes policies interfere with the marketplace in determining prices and wages, they are used only when an upward spiral in prices is so great that the traditional fiscal and monetary policies are considered inadequate for getting inflation under control. The corollary is that incomes policies are always treated as a temporary emergency measure that is ended when the inflation crisis is over. In implementing incomes policies, government agencies are set up to develop standards for allowable price and wage increases, with variations for particular industries. Efforts to obtain compliance with voluntary price and wage guidelines have incentives such as being a prerequisite for bidding on government contracts, while compliance with mandatory incomes policies requires a much larger enforcement bureaucracy that includes penalties for violating the price and wage controls.

Differences in implementing the three types of policies due to their institutional differences may be summarized as follows. First, fiscal policy is derived as an outgrowth of spending priorities for government programs and tax legislation, while the primary purpose of monetary and incomes policies is to influence the economy. Second, monetary policy is more flexible than fiscal policy because changes in Federal Reserve actions affecting bank credit and interest rates can be made quickly, while spending and tax changes require a lengthy political and operational process. Third, incomes policies are only temporary, while fiscal and monetary polices are ongoing on a continuing basis, and changes are easier to make in income policies than in fiscal policy but less flexible than in monetary policy.

Fiscal Policy

Fiscal policy is use of the overall federal government budget spending and taxation levels to foster economic growth without stimulating inflation or causing a recession. The limitation of fiscal policy to the federal government, as distinct from state and local governments, reflects the fact that there is no national control over the spending and taxing actions of state and local governments. Nevertheless, while there is no national direction to the fiscal actions of state and local governments, estimates of the results of these governments' fiscal actions are included here.

A budget surplus (receipts exceed spending) results in the government taking money out of the income stream of households and businesses, a budget deficit (spending exceeds receipts) puts money into the income stream, and a balanced budget (receipts equal spending) has no effect on the income stream. Thus, the first-order effects of the federal budget are a surplus restrains economic growth through the reduction in income and related spending, a deficit stimulates economic growth through the increase in income and related spending, and a balanced budget is neutral with regard to growth because total income and spending is unaffected.

This generalization is modified and may even be reversed by several secondary effects of the budget position. First, when viewing changes in the budget position on economic growth over time, the importance of the absolute levels is lessened by whether they are increasing or decreasing. Thus, if a budget surplus in period 1 becomes smaller in period 2, the budget is less restraining in period 2 because it takes a smaller amount of money out of the income stream; analogously, if a budget deficit in period 1 becomes smaller in period 2, the budget is less stimulative in period 2. Second, a budget deficit tends to cause higher interest rates than a budget surplus, since the government must borrow money to finance the deficit. And the higher interest rates restrain spending by other borrowers, in turn leading to a lower growth rate, in contrast to the first-order effect of a higher growth rate. Analogously, a budget surplus tends to lower interest rates as the government does not need to borrow funds for that part of the budget (it may still borrow funds for its existing debt that cumulated from previous deficits). And the lower interest rates stimulate spending by other borrowers, leading to a higher growth rate than the first-order effect. Third, contrary to general perceptions, a balanced budget actually stimulates spending in subsequent rounds of spending cumulating over time to the total amount of the first-order spending through what is known as the balanced-budget multiplier.

Government budgets affect the economy in two ways, one through cyclical expansions and recessions and one through economic growth. The effect of government budgets on expansions and recessions is referred to as "automatic stabilizers." The effect of budgets on economic growth is referred to as the "structural budget."

Automatic Stabilizers

Automatic stabilizers are built-in institutionalized aspects of government budgets that cause government spending and tax collections, without direct intervention

Figure 2.3a **Change in Government Budgets toward a Surplus (+) or Deficit (–) as a Percentage of the Gross Domestic Product, 1960s to 1990s: Expansions**

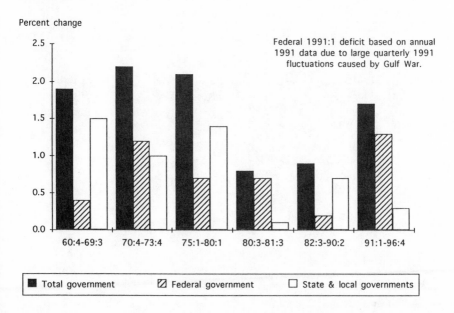

Note: Based on U.S. Bureau of Economic Analysis data in current dollars. Number after colon is quarter of year.

of new government programs, to move in the opposite direction or in less extreme patterns than trends in the overall economy. For example, the inherent nature of unemployment insurance is to put more money in the income stream in recessions than in expansions. Budget outlays for unemployment insurance rise in recessions and decline in expansions. The progressive income tax removes proportionately more income from households in expansions and less in recessions. Thus, these stabilizers automatically move consumer purchasing power in a countercyclical direction, lowering the growth of purchasing power during expansions and raising the growth of purchasing power during recessions. This is a two-step process, in which the economy initially impacts the budget, and then in a second-round feedback, the modified budget impacts the economy.

Figures 2.3a and 2.3b show this experience separately for the combined total of all governments, the federal government, and the aggregate of all state and local governments during the business cycles from the 1960s to the 1990s. In relating government budgets to the overall economy, the figures depict the change in the budget surplus or deficit for each expansion (from trough to peak) and for each recession (from peak to trough) in relation to the average gross

Figure 2.3b **Change in Government Budgets toward a Surplus (+) or Deficit (–) as a Percentage of the Gross Domestic Product, 1960s to 1990s: Recessions**

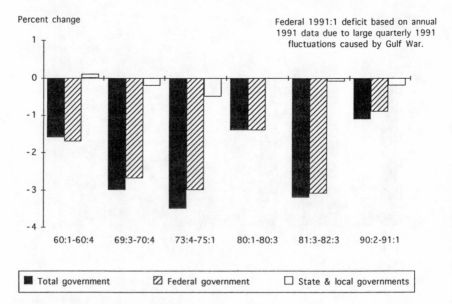

Note: Based on U.S. Bureau of Economic Analysis data in current dollars. Number after colon is quarter of year.

domestic product in the period. If the budget surplus increases or the deficit decreases, the change is positive; and if the deficit increases or the surplus decreases, the change is negative. *Thus, the analysis focuses on the direction of the change of the surplus or deficit during the expansion or recession, not on whether the budget is in surplus or deficit.*

Government budgets typically restrain income growth in expansions and boost incomes in recessions, which fits the concept of the stabilizing role. These patterns reflect the combined effects of economic growth, the tax laws, and inflation on tax receipts and spending.

During the six expansions from the 1960s to the 1990s, budgets for the combined total of all governments moved in a stabilizing (i.e., restraining) direction on all occasions, although they differed in magnitude. The restraint was 1 to 2 percent in the expansions from the 1960s to the 1990s. The restraining impact declined in the 1980s and increased in the 1990s due to substantial shifts in the federal budget deficit. In terms of the relative restraint between the federal and the state and local budgets, each was more restraining in three of the six expansions from the 1960s to the 1990s.

During the six recessions from the 1960s to the 1990s, budgets for the combined total of all governments were stabilizing (i.e., stimulating) on all occasions. The stimulating effect fluctuated typically in the 1 to 3 percent range, although it was at the low end of the range in two of the three recessions in the 1980s and 1990s. Overall, the federal budget was far more stimulating than state and local budgets in the recession periods.

The general stabilizing movements of both the federal and the state and local budgets result from different patterns of spending and receipts. At both levels of government, expenditures and revenues increase in both expansions and recessions. In recessions, however, federal revenues increase far more slowly than state and local revenues, and the federal increase occurs only because of the increase in revenues from Social Security taxes. Federal revenue, other than that from Social Security taxes, falls in recessions because of the considerable reliance on income taxes as a source of revenue, as high unemployment and low business profits cause tax collections to drop. This decrease in recessions is enlarged by the progressivity in the federal income tax, in which proportionately lower taxes are paid as income decreases (analogously, during expansions proportionately higher taxes are paid as income increases).

By contrast, a much greater share of state and local tax collections comes from sales and property taxes, which are not as cyclically sensitive as income taxes. For example, in 1995 personal and corporate income taxes accounted for 53 percent of federal receipts and only 17 percent of state and local receipts. In addition, because unemployment insurance benefit payments are part of the federal budget but are not included in state and local budgets, they raise federal but not state and local outlays in recessions. This heightens the stabilizing impact of the federal budget in recessions and accounts for much of the disparity between federal and state and local budgets in stimulating the economy during recessions noted above (unemployment insurance is a joint federal-state program, but unemployment taxes paid by employers are held in a federal trust fund and thus are counted as receipts in the federal budget).

Government budgets tend to have a stabilizing effect on the economy, restraining economic growth during expansions and stimulating it during recessions. But this stabilizing effect was much less consistent in the 1980s and 1990s than in previous periods. The analyst should monitor these patterns to determine if this smaller role of government budgets in moderating cyclical movements has continued or been reversed, and to what extent the budgets impact the economy. This should be done separately for the federal and the aggregate of all state and local governments.

Structural Budget

The structural budget of the federal government is the size of the budget surplus or deficit independent of whether the economy is in an expansion or recession. It is a hypothetical budget that focuses on whether the budget inherently stimulates or restrains overall economic activity through its effect initially on the income stream of households and businesses and subsequently on their spending and investments and the resultant economic growth. It is stimulative when it is in deficit because more money is added to than is removed from the income stream, it is restraining when it is surplus because more money is removed from than is added to the income stream, and it is neutral when the budget is in balance because the balance has a zero effect on the income stream.

The structural budget assumes the economy is operating at its highest potential without leading to a greater rate of inflation. This is the concept of the potential gross domestic product (GDP), which is linked to the nonaccelerating inflation rate of unemployment (NAIRU), discussed earlier under economic growth and unemployment as one aspect of Okun's Law. The structural budget abstracts from short-term cyclical shifts in budget surpluses and deficits to postulate the size of the surplus or deficit that would occur in a steadily growing economy in which there are no cyclical expansions or recessions. The effect of the budget on the income stream occurs as a first-order result of changes in the budget position, but secondary impacts related to shifts in the direction of the surplus or deficit, the effect of the budget on interest rates, and the effect of the balanced-budget multiplier modify and may modify or reverse the first-round impacts on economic growth, as noted above in the introduction to this Fiscal Policy section.

The concept of the structural budget is limited to the federal government. In the American federal system, it is impractical to use state and local budgets as a fiscal policy tool because (1) each state or local economy is heavily integrated with economies in the surrounding region as well as by the national economy, so that the high economic leakages of such deliberate actions between states and localities vitiate their intended effects; (2) institutional aspects vary considerably—there are different constitutional limitations on debt, legislatures meet at different times of the year, and fiscal years cover different twelve-month periods; and (3) it is not politically feasible to have a coordinated fiscal policy for even the five or ten largest states (abstracting from the other states and the over three thousand localities), as the complexity resulting from the independence of the large number of states and local jurisdictions is far greater than for the federal budget, which itself is quite complicated merely in negotiating between Congress and the President.

Economic theory about how best to balance robust economic growth with low inflation has evolved over the years. In the 1960s a "fully employed" economy (defined as 3 to 4 percent unemployment) was regarded as desirable, and "full employment surplus" budgets were developed and used as a fiscal policy tool. Because the budget surplus generated from such high employment was found to be a "fiscal drag" on economic growth, it was a basic rationale for the tax cuts of the early 1960s. During the 1970s, the model was modified as the "high employment" budget, which raised the nonaccelerating inflation rate of unemployment (NAIRU) to 6 to 7 percent. In the 1980s the model was further changed to the "cyclically adjusted budget," which specified the budget position based on the economic growth trend at 6 percent unemployment.[8] The cyclically adjusted budget differed from previous models because it abstracted from a normative unemployment rate based on the NAIRU concept, although the 6 percent unemployment rate used in calculating economic growth was viewed by some as the NAIRU rate during the period. In 1997, the "structural budget" as prepared by the Congressional Budget Office (CBO) is based on the taxes and spending for unemployment and other income maintenance programs in current laws associated with a potential GDP that assumes a NAIRU of 5.8 percent.[9]

Some analysts believe the CBO NAIRU rate of 5.8 percent is too high for the 1990s and that the economy could have a higher potential GDP and a lower unemployment rate without igniting inflation. They cite the experience that unemployment declined continuously from 7.5 percent in 1992 to 5.4 percent in 1996, and fell further in the spring of 1997 to under 5 percent. And concomitantly, inflation lessened to under 3 percent, rather than accelerating.

But the CBO believes that the containment of inflation along with the declining unemployment in the 1990s reflects special factors unrelated to economic growth and the nation's productive capacity. Examples of the special factors are the slowdown in medical costs, lower computer prices, and technical changes to the consumer price index that lowered the CPI inflation rate slightly.

The range of NAIRU estimates in the mid-1990s is 5.2 to 6.3 percent, with most between 5.5 and 6.3 percent.[10] But other analysts have challenged the policy implications of using certain NAIRU estimates. For example, George Akerlof, William Dickens, and George Perry find that a steady inflation rate of 3 percent annually would allow for an unemployment rate of 5.2 percent, while actions taken to reduce the inflation rate of 3 percent to zero would raise the unemployment rate by 2.6 percentage points.[11] An innovative feature of this study is that it incorporates the "real world" tendency for workers to resist reductions in wage rates, while recognizing that wage cuts do in fact occur. Resistance to wage cuts results in a permanent shock to production costs, which is inflationary at the relatively low rates of inflation considered in the study. Unemployment would remain steady if the Federal Reserve succeeds in its attempts to accommodate the higher inflation through expanding the amount of bank credit available and thus keeping interest rates from rising. Or unemployment would rise if the Federal Reserve decides not to accommodate the higher inflation and succeeds in restraining bank credit and raising interest rates. In fact, the authors conclude that because of such wage rigidity, there is no unique NAIRU with higher sustained unemployment rates and very low sustained inflation rates. Federal Reserve economic policies are discussed in the next section on Monetary Policy and in Chapter 12.

From another vantage point and even more fundamentally, Robert Eisner questions the use of the NAIRU as an economic policy tool at all.[12] He cites contradictions in its theoretical underpinnings and the uncertainty that unemployment below the NAIRU drives up inflation. Use of the NAIRU concept is discussed further under Monetary Policy below.

The effect of the structural budget on the economy is driven in the first instance by whether the budget is in a surplus, deficit, or balanced position. As with the above automatic stabilizers, however, the greater policy interest is in the change in the budget from one period to the next. Thus, the budget exerts a greater stimulus to economic growth when the surplus is reduced or the deficit is increased, and analogously it has a greater restraining effect on economic growth when the surplus becomes higher or the deficit becomes lower.

The structural budget is a hypothetical concept that depends on the assumed noninflationary rate of unemployment (NAIRU). Before using a particular estimate of the structural budget, the analyst should review the NAIRU underlying its preparation to see if it adequately reflects the relationship between unemployment and inflation. Based on this review, the analyst should make the appropriate adjustments to the budget estimates consistent with the NAIRU deemed to be most relevant.

Monetary Policy

Monetary policies are associated with actions of the Federal Reserve System (FRS) that affect the reserves of commercial banks that are available for extending credit to households and businesses, and in turn the effect of such changes in the availability of credit on interest rates. Chapter 12 gives a more comprehensive explanation of the institutional framework of the FRS and its conduct of monetary policies. It suffices here to note that FRS monetary policies are determined by the Federal Open Market Committee (FOMC). The FOMC has twelve members; the seven governors of the Federal Reserve Board in Washington, D.C., are permanent members, four presidents of eleven of the twelve regional Federal Reserve Banks on a rotating basis, and the president of the Federal Reserve Bank of New York is a permanent member. All twelve FOMC members vote on what should happen to interest rates; their decisions are carried out through open market operations.

The FOMC meets eight times a year on a regular basis, and on other occasions as needed. The FOMC submits two reports to Congress every year under the Full Employment and Balanced Growth Act of 1978, one in February and one in July. The reports include the FOMC's assessment of the economy and its targets for money supply growth for the current calendar year. Reserve requirements and the discount rate are other tools of monetary policy; while important, changes in reserve requirements and the discount rate over the long run are not as significant as open market operations. The seven governors of the Federal Reserve Board have direct authority, independent of the FOMC, over reserve requirements. The discount rate is set by each Federal Reserve Bank, subject to Board approval. Day-to-day operations of monetary policy are linked to the federal funds interest rate described below.

Monetary policies impact both economic growth and inflation. When the FOMC acts to increase the amount of bank credit available for loans, it does so by increasing bank reserves through a general buying of federal government securities in its open market operations. This raises the price of the securities or lessens the decline in their price. This leads banks and other investors to sell at least part of their holdings of federal securities, either to realize a profit or lessen their losses on the original purchase price of the securities. By selling their securities, banks increase their reserves. The increase in reserves causes interest rates to decline or rise more slowly because banks make money by lending money, and when they have an increased amount of money to lend, they have a greater incentive to lower the price of money to increase the amount of loans they make, since they do not make money when their funds are idle. At the same time, when interest rates are lower, households and businesses have a greater incentive to borrow funds to finance purchases of housing, cars, vacations, machinery, inventories, and so on, all of which stimulate production and economic growth. Analogously, the reverse process occurs when the FOMC acts to decrease or slow down the growth of bank credit available by reducing bank reserves through selling federal government securities. The decrease in reserves causes interest rates to rise or decline more slowly, and households and businesses have less of an incentive to borrow money, which lowers production and economic growth.

The most sensitive indicator of changes in monetary policies is the federal funds interest rate, which is the interest rate that commercial banks charge on loans between banks.[13] The loans are usually for overnight, but they also include loans for a few days to over one year. The FOMC uses the federal funds rate as its main operational mechanism in influencing the amount of bank reserves available for credit. It does this by targeting the federal funds rate it desires based on its assessment of the need for stimulating or restraining economic growth. Large changes in federal funds rates indicate a change in FOMC policies, with higher rates pointing to a desired slowdown in economic growth and lower rates to a desired speedup in economic growth.

These general relationships between interest rates and economic growth and between interest rates and inflation have some qualifiers. *First,* during periods of high inflation, a greater availability of credit may lead to higher, rather than lower, interest rates. This reflects the expectation that the greater credit availability will stimulate borrowing and spending above the economy's capacity to produce and thus lead to growth rates that overheat the economy and cause accelerating inflation. Because lenders want to make a profit in the price levels that exist when their loans are paid back, interest rates include an "inflation premium," which is the expected increase in prices from the time the loan is made to the time it is paid back, and a higher expectation of inflation in turn raises interest rates. *Second,* FOMC policy changes on bank credit and interest rates affect the economy with long, imprecise, and differential lags on economic growth and inflation on the one hand, and inflation on the other. A rule of thumb is that changes in interest rates affect economic growth and employment one to two years after they occur, while they affect inflation about three years later. *Third,* nonmonetary factors, such as the federal budget deficit, foreign investment, the international value of the dollar, psychological moods of optimism and pessimism, and very high unemployment or inflation, complicate and may override monetary policies. The limited power of FOMC policies in the face of these nonmonetary factors is suggested by the expressions "pulling the string" and "pushing the string." Generally, the FOMC is considered to be more effective at slowing economic activity by raising interest rates (pulling the string) than at quickening economic activity by lowering interest rates (pushing the string).

In their overall thrust, the FOMC's actions and pronouncements emphasize the containment of inflation more than the lowering of unemployment. This reflects the view that price stability, defined variously as an inflation rate of zero to 2 percent inflation, does not distort economic decisions made by households and businesses. A zero inflation rate means that the overall price level for all goods and services, such as the consumer price index, does not change from one period to the next, although component items such as food and housing may rise or fall.

The idea is that the natural generative forces of American life are most likely to bring about the desirable goals of a growing number of jobs, high wages, and robust profits in an environment of price stability. The perception affects the conduct of monetary policy. Generally, members of the FOMC consider the economy to have a greater inflationary potential than some other analysts. Therefore, during cyclical expansions, the FOMC tends to restrain economic growth at higher unemployment levels, and with greater restraint, than some other analysts would suggest. Analogously, during cyclical recessions, the FOMC tends to stimulate economic growth at higher unemployment levels and with less stimulus than some other analysts.

Individual members of the FOMC have varying degrees of concern about inflation, however, including response to advance signs of a possible acceleration in inflation and of striving toward zero inflation. The starkest differences are between "hawks," who take a hard line in fighting a possible inflationary acceleration and in lowering inflation to zero, and "doves," who require more evidence of a possible inflationary acceleration and are more hesitant to strive toward zero inflation because of its possible consequences of higher unemployment.

Each member of the FOMC has individual views of the economy and votes accordingly on what monetary policy should be. For most members, their typical predilection in conducting monetary policy is an eclectic approach, in which a variety of economic indicators is assessed, and based on this review, votes are cast on whether monetary policies should be changed, and if so, in what direction. But this eclectic approach is not universal among FOMC members. There is another approach to monetary policy, called monetarism, that advocates following a steady growth rate in the money supply (checking deposits and currency in circulation) regardless of changes in economic conditions and its effect on interest rates. This is based on the premise that little is known about forecasting economic activity, and frequent changes in monetary policies cause undue uncertainty in the business community with the attendant volatility in interest rates and economic activity; by contrast, a steady and predictable growth in the money supply is conducive to a more certain economic environment, encouraging more business investment and a higher rate of long-term economic growth. A minority of FOMC members typically follows the monetarist approach. Opponents of monetarism contend that it is based on a simplistic view of the economy that would hamstring the FOMC in its job of fostering economic growth and employment and moderating inflation. Of course, at any particular point in time, the makeup of the FOMC membership determines whether the committee as a whole follows the eclectic or monetarist approach.

The FOMC as an entity does not use the NAIRU as an underlying tool in its deliberations (NAIRU is the nonaccelerating inflation rate of unemployment discussed previously in the sections on Okun's Law and Fiscal Policy: Structural Budget). But some FOMC members may use the NAIRU concept in their analyses, although they may have different estimates of the NAIRU level. If the economy is operating below its NAIRU potential and inflation is not accelerating, those members following the eclectic approach and using a NAIRU analysis would call for stimulating the economy through increasing the amount of credit that banks have to lend, which in turn tends to lower interest rates and stimulate economic growth. But if the economy is approaching or above its NAIRU potential and inflation is accelerating or is expected to accelerate, these same members would call for lessening the amount or slowing the growth of available bank credit to raise interest rates and slow economic growth. Still, in the dynamics of the FOMC meetings, individual predilections for eclecticism and monetarism, varying views on the actual level of the NAIRU and forecasts of economic growth and inflation, and hawk-dove attitudes on inflation are subject to modification in the discussions and persuasiveness of opposing arguments, with policy actions formulated to obtain unanimous or near-unanimous voting.

Because huge sums of money are involved in trading in bond markets when interest rates go up or down, there is a community of "Fed watchers" who try to anticipate what the FOMC will do in terms of monetary policy. In order to protect the economic effect of prospective monetary policy changes from being diminished, and to avoid unfair advantage to traders in the financial markets who get advance "leaks" of prospective changes in monetary policy, the FOMC closely guards its policy intentions until its policy statements are made public. For example, when a Reuters news service release reported that eight of twelve

Federal Reserve Bank presidents favored a tighter monetary policy shortly before the FOMC met in September 1996, the Federal Reserve instituted its own
investigation and also requested the Federal Bureau of Investigation to help trace
the source of the leak.[14] Such leaks could violate federal laws or Federal Reserve
confidentiality rules.

*In assessing the prospect for future movements in interest rates, the analyst
should consider the outlook for economic growth and inflation. In addition,
possible changes in Federal Reserve System monetary policies should be monitored for their effect on interest rates.*

Humphrey-Hawkins Act Unemployment and Inflation Goals:
Fiscal and Monetary Policies

The specifics of balancing unemployment and inflation have been and probably
always will be subject to debate. The debate reflects the predilections of those
who place a greater weight on lowering unemployment and those who stress the
greater importance of lowering inflation.

The Full Employment and Balance Growth Act of 1978, referred to as the
Humphrey-Hawkins Act (HH), established the first legislated numerical national
goals for unemployment and inflation. These were unemployment of 4 percent
and inflation (based on the consumer price index) of 3 percent by 1983, with a
further reduction of inflation to zero by 1988; however, the Act permits the
inflation goals to be relaxed if pursuing them would hinder achieving the unemployment goal. As noted previously, zero inflation means no change in overall
prices, although prices for particular goods and services may increase or decrease.

The HH goals were not met as of 1996. In 1983 unemployment was 9.6
percent and inflation was 3.2 percent, and in 1988 unemployment was 5.5 percent and inflation was 4.1 percent. But the Act's goals continue in effect, even
though the timetables have passed, unless and until the legislation is modified or
repealed, which has not occurred at the time of this writing in 1997. The Act's
goals were still not met by 1996, when unemployment was 5.3 percent and
inflation was 2.9 percent (guess), although unemployment was closer to the goal
of 4 percent than inflation was to the goal of zero.

As a matter of public policy, the question becomes, "What purpose do the HH
goals serve"? Such goals may be more important for their intangible effect on the
nation's outlook than on their tangible results. On the one hand, the goals represent a clearly defined objective for the nation, one that will bring significant
improvements and that encourages everyone to continue to strive to do better.
On the other hand, if the goals are unrealistic, they will not only be disregarded
but also may lead to cynicism that discourages efforts for improvement, and
thereby have a negative effect.

Developing meaningful goals requires balancing the tension between ideal aspirations and feasible achievements. In the author's opinion, the Humphrey-Hawkins goals are useful long-term guideposts for conducting fiscal and monetary policies.

Incomes Policies

From time to time, fiscal and monetary policies are supplemented with incomes policies, which are either voluntary price-wage guidelines or mandatory price-wage controls. Incomes policies diverge from the complete market determination of prices and wages, and they are instituted only when it is thought that fiscal and monetary policies are too blunt to have the desired effect in curbing inflationary behavior at the micro level by businesses and labor unions. They are resorted to as a temporary device to break the inflationary psychology engendered when prices and wages spiral upward with no end in sight, and when it is believed that a recession and high unemployment caused by restrictive fiscal and monetary policies are too high a price to pay for breaking the inflationary environment.

Mandatory price and wage controls were used in World War II, part of the Korean War (1950–51), and part of the Vietnam War (1971–73). Voluntary price-wage guidelines were used in 1962–65 and 1978–79. Economists debate their effectiveness. Some say they distort price, wage, and profit relationships among products, industries, and companies, and result in higher inflation after they are removed. Others say they hold inflation below what it would have been, without undue interference with market-determined prices and wages, as long as they are temporary. Because of their sporadic use, incomes policies are not analyzed in this book. But if they are used in the future, the analyst will have to take them into account in assessing economic movements.

BASIC ASPECTS OF ECONOMIC FORECASTING

The economic indicators discussed in this book are statistical measures of the past. As extrapolations from these historical indicators, macroeconomic forecasts may be viewed as another kind of economic indicator. Forecasts of economic growth, unemployment, inflation, interest rates, and other economic indicators are developed by government and private organizations. Some forecasts are proprietary and are not publicly available, although most are disseminated in summary form through the news media. Organizations that prepare such forecasts for public dissemination include Data Resources, Inc., Wharton Econometric Forecasting Associates, Blue Chip Economic Indicators, the Federal Reserve Bank of Philadelphia, university-affiliated research groups (such as those at Georgia State, Michigan, and the University of California at Los Angeles), the Congressional Budget Office, and the U.S. Council of Economic Advisers.

Because perceptions of the future have an important effect on spending, investment, and saving decisions, forecasts about the future of the economy provoke widespread interest. Households, businesses, and governments rely on these forecasts in making a variety of economic decisions. Thus, forecasts not only predict the economic future, they also may influence that future. For example, forecasts of future interest rates may affect a prospective homeowner's decision to buy, or a business owner's decision about whether to invest in new equipment or change the level of inventories. Economic forecasts also affect how the President and Congress budget and appropriate funds for federal programs and establish federal tax laws for stabilizing economic fluctuations; how the Federal Reserve conducts monetary policy; and how state and local governments determine whether and when to sell bonds for building schools, sewer treatment plants, or other capital facilities.

In controversies over public policies, economic forecasts spotlight the uncertainty of the future. Various forecasts provide divergent views of trends in the pace of economic growth and inflation, and these differences sharpen public debate on the likely outcome of private and public actions. Effective forecasts take into account the effect of current actions, such as current fiscal and monetary policies, on the future economy. Forecasts should help lead us to a better selection of goals and methods to improve economic well-being.

There are two kinds of economic forecasts: informal predictions based on personal experience and formal analyses derived from statistical research. Perceptions of householders and business owners about the overall economy and their own economic prospects constitute the informal type of economic forecast. Informal forecasts are likely to reflect knowledge gained from the news media as well as personal experience. Frequently, therefore, these forecasts implicitly incorporate elements of the formal macroeconomic forecasting, which is the subject of this chapter.

In economic as in political or weather forecasting, many scenarios are possible. The challenge in making any forecast is to recognize the range of these possibilities and determine which is most probable. Alternatively a forecast may seek to assess the likely effects of a given set of forecasting assumptions, often referred to as "What if" forecasting. For example, what would be the effect on the gross domestic product growth rate if the labor force remains stable over the forecast period? This section focuses on how such formal economic forecasts are developed and used in order to help the analyst make such forecasting judgments as well as to evaluate others' forecasts.

**Forecasting Methodology: Historical Analysis
and Future Assumptions**

Quite simply, a macroeconomic forecast uses past and current economic data to determine economic relationships and in turn uses these relationships to predict the future state of the economy. In interpreting the current data, a forecaster may utilize econometric models, analyses of past trends, or mechanical extrapolations of past trends. A forecast based on an econometric model uses sophisticated mathematical and statistical techniques in a system of equations to integrate the theoretical and empirical interrelationships among such economic variables as employment, inflation, interest rates, and the value of the dollar. The model builder exercises judgment in specifying which variables are included in the model and the mathematical form of the equations. The forecaster also exercises judgment in modifying the forecasts generated by the model. These adjustments reflect assessments of current economic trends and anticipated future developments that are too subtle to be incorporated in the structural equations of the model.

A forecast based on analyses of past trends extrapolates from the statistical experience of selected components of the economy to predict the likely future direction and pace of observed trends. Like economic modeling, these extrapolations incorporate the forecaster's judgment, the statistical relationships observed in past behavior of the components, and current data such as surveys of anticipated spending by households and businesses or prognostications of government budgets.

Mechanical forecasts extrapolate from the past trends of given variables to predict future developments. This forecasting technique is referred to as "autoregressive" because future rates of growth are projected only by patterns of the variable's past growth rates. For example, the future growth rate of the real gross domestic product (GDP) is determined solely by past growth rates of real GDP. Mathematical equations used in developing these autoregressive forecasts include the Box-Jenkins and autoregressive integrated moving average (ARIMA) methodologies. Autoregressive forecasts predict cyclical turning points as well as rates of growth. As in all forecasts, however, the identification of cyclical turning points is limited to short-term predictions (short-term forecasts are discussed in the next section). Autoregressive forecasts incorporate the forecaster's judgment primarily in specifying the mathematical structure of time lags in the forecasting equation, although the use of autoregressive methodology itself reflects the forecaster's judgment that an indicator's past behavior is the best predictor of its future movements. Contrary to the practice with econometric modeling, however, forecasters using autoregressive methodology typically accept the forecast yielded by the equation, rather than modify the forecast based on subjective judgments about more likely outcomes. There is no intrinsic reason for this tendency of autoregressive forecasters not to modify their forecasts, however.

Assumptions about fiscal and monetary policies, technology, and institutions are key to making a forecast. All forecasts—econometric models, analyses of trends, and mechanical extrapolations—explicitly or implicitly include such assumptions and try to capture the interactions among them. These economic, scientific, and political elements form the regime under which the economy operates. A sharp departure from past patterns can significantly affect historical relationships of income, spending, productivity, unemployment, inflation, business cycles, and economic growth. Forecasts that make different assumptions about the economic regime can vary substantially. For example, the significant reduction in the federal government budget deficit that occurred in the mid-1990s and a change in Federal Reserve monetary policies can alter the outlook for unemployment and inflation. Further examples abound: technological breakthroughs such as electric cars or superconductors, or more widespread adoption of existing technology, such as solar energy or robots, can create major new product markets; a shift in labor-management relations from wage givebacks to wage takebacks may affect the morale and consequently the productivity of workers; the large corporate debt resulting from junk bond financing of company takeovers may inhibit additional structures and equipment investment and make more companies vulnerable to bankruptcy during a recession; the tendency for transnational companies to conduct more research and development abroad may lower U.S. international competitiveness; an accelerated trend toward global warming may limit the production of certain items or change the method of producing them; and the reduction in post–Cold War federal government defense spending that occurred from the late 1980s to the mid-1990s may change to increases in the late 1990s, which could limit increases in social programs to address homelessness, crime, health, education, and the environment.

Short-term, Medium-term, and Long-term Forecasts

The distinctions among short-term, medium-term, and long-term forecasts are not precise. Moreover, terminology varies with the user. One extreme is seen in the preoccupation of some participants in financial markets with how the stock and bond markets are likely to respond to late-breaking news within the next few days; such a focus implicitly defines any period longer than a few days as long-term.

Generally, however, short-term forecasts refer to economic projections for periods of up to two years that typically chart movements on a quarterly or semiannual basis (less frequently, movements are charted monthly). Some short-term forecasts are prepared for as long as four years ahead, but they emphasize the first two years. Short-term forecasts center on the cyclical dimensions of the economy and highlight changes in the rates of economic growth, employment, and inflation, as well as identifying the cyclical turning points from expansion to recession to recovery. These forecasts typically assume a continuation of the economic, scientific, and political regime of the recent past, except for expected changes in fiscal and monetary policies. The short time frame under consideration limits the extent to which basic changes in economic arrangements, technology, and political factors may be expected to affect the mainstream of economic life.

Medium-term forecasts are associated with a three- to five-year horizon and chart changes on an annual basis. There is some overlap between medium-term forecasts and the latter part of short-term forecasts that extend four years into the future, although as noted above, quarterly or semiannual movements of short-term forecasts usually are not developed beyond the first two years. Medium-term forecasts incorporate more change in the economic, technical, and political regime than do short-term forecasts. The six-year plan of 1997 to reduce the federal government budget deficit to zero by 2002, although containing only the broad outlines of taxation and spending reductions that still have to be agreed to in specific legislation as of this writing in the spring of 1997, is an example of a medium-term forecast.

Long-term forecasts refer to projections extending more than five years. They typically predict the state of the economy year-by-year, although very long forecasts of twenty or more years may use averages of five- or ten-year periods. Over such long periods, fundamental changes can occur in the underlying regime of economic arrangements, technology, and political factors. Thus, long-term forecasts provide a framework for evaluating and planning for developments that require long lead times, such as the impact of demographic and industrial changes on education, job training, housing, transportation, and other public infrastructure. Like medium-term forecasts, long-term forecasts do not include cyclical turning points from expansion to recession to recovery because relationships of such short-term volatility are too complex to trace far into the future. Consequently, long-term forecasts do not predict recessions, although they do project varying rates of growth over the forecast period.

Forecasting Accuracy

Evaluating the accuracy of macroeconomic forecasts is an economic discipline in its own right. The recognized authority in this area is Stephen McNees, whose assessments of forecasts cover the 1950s to the 1990s. They include forecasts of the real gross national product, inflation, unemployment, and interest rates by the Council of Economic Advisers, Congressional Budget Office, Federal Reserve FOMC, and private forecasting organizations. Some highlights of the findings in his 1987, 1992, and 1995 studies are the following:[15]

- The least accurate forecasts occur at cyclical turning points of recessions and recoveries.
- Forecasts one year ahead by government and private forecasters were off the mark by plus or minus 1 to 1.3 percentage points for the real gross national product (GNP), plus or minus 0.6 to 0.9 percentage point for

inflation, and plus or minus 0.5 percentage point for the unemployment rate.

- Government and private forecasts are noticeably more accurate than forecasts based on simple extrapolations of growth rates for the previous year and for the average of the previous four years.
- Interest rates seem to be more difficult to forecast than the nonfinancial GNP, inflation, and unemployment indicators, based on comparisons with simple extrapolations of previous growth rates.

McNees also analyzed how a forecaster's judgment affects the accuracy of the forecast.[16] As noted above, forecasters invariably modify forecasts derived from the equations of econometric models. McNees studied the effect of these judgments on the accuracy of econometric forecasts by analyzing records kept by a sample of four forecasters who reported their forecasts before and after the judgmental changes were made. Their records suggested that the judgmental modifications typically improved the forecasts, with the greatest improvement observed in the first quarter. The accuracy of the adjustments lessened as the forecasts extended to eight quarters ahead, occasionally worsening the forecasts by going in the wrong direction or by making too large a change, but overall the judgmental modifications improved the forecasts.

In considering the effect of subjective judgments on forecasting error, it is important not to lose sight of the fact that all forecasts contain underlying judgments regardless of how rigorously quantitative they are. A forecaster makes subjective judgments when determining whether to develop an autoregressive or an econometric forecast, as well as during the development of the mathematical specifications of these autoregressive or econometric forecasts.

There are inherent methodological limitations in determining the complex interrelationships among the factors governing the economic future. In essence, a forecast is an extrapolation of past trends with allowances for expected continuities or discontinuities with the past. The complex nature of the economy, however, as well as the limits of statistical data, inhibit complete understanding of these trends. At an elementary level, many economic indicators that forecasters rely on are subject to substantial periodic revision, such as the GDP and the balance of trade. Any forecast is bound to be off if the indicators are revised after the forecast is made. Therefore, an analyst wishing to assess a forecast's accuracy must take into account the level of built-in "error" due to data revision. To do so requires data for the forecast period on the former, unrevised basis as well as on the revised basis, and such figures typically are not readily available. In this situation analysts typically attempt to approximate the unrevised data. One method of approximation is to determine the percentage difference between the unrevised and revised data for a period when both data sets were published and then to use this ratio to estimate unrevised figures for the forecast period.

Many other methodological problems complicate the art and science of forecasting, but the fundamental problem is the difficulty of quantifying accurately the relative importance and the significant interactions of the elements used in developing forecasts, such as the rate of economic growth, stage of the business cycle, income, consumption, investment, saving, productivity, inflation, interest rates, psychological moods of optimism and pessimism, and the value of the dollar for which statistical data exist, as well as such nonquantifiable factors as international political tensions. Forecasters use statistical analysis of trends in past years and their own judgment to estimate these relationships, but the estimates are necessarily rough. For one thing, they represent an average of the experience of past years; this experience may not capture the unique characteristics of the forecast period. Second, statistical relationships and judgments can only describe a plausible behavior in terms of what would be expected according to current economic theory and experience. They cannot fully explain how each factor actually interacts with the others in the economic system as a whole.

Given these inherent problems of forecasting, it is problematic that any single forecaster will consistently have the insight and luck to provide more accurate forecasts than those of all professional forecasters collectively. In fact, Victor Zarnowitz and Phillip Braun find that forecasting accuracy for the totality of several economic variables such as the gross national product, inflation, unemployment, and interest rates is generally increased by combining the predictions of a wide range of forecasters using diverse methodologies into an average "consensus" forecast giving equal weight to each forecast, in contrast to the majority of individual forecasts.[17] At the same time, McNees corroborates a previous Zarnowitz study that for a specific macroeconomic variable, roughly one-third of the forecasters predict more accurately than the consensus forecast for that variable.[18]

There are also varying aspects of gamesmanship in economic forecasting that lessen the credibility of individual as well as consensus forecasts. Two perspectives are cited here on this phenomenon. David Laster, Paul Bennett, and In Sun Geoum provide a rationale of why some forecasters deliberately prepare forecasts that diverge from what a perceived consensus forecast will be.[19] These forecasters put a greater emphasis on obtaining publicity for their firms by attempting to prepare the most accurate forecast in a given period. The presumption is that by making outlier forecasts, which tend to be unpopular in the profession, these forecasters can maximize their chances of being the most accurate in a given period. Independent forecasters, and to a lesser extent securities firms, are most likely to develop forecasts that diverge from the consensus. By contrast, industrial companies, banks, and to a lesser extent econometric modelers prepare forecasts that conform more closely to what the perceived consensus will be, a strategy that will tend to maximize long-term accuracy.

On the other hand, some forecasters may not want to be far off the mark if the consensus forecast turns out to be fairly accurate. Or to put it differently, they would rather be wrong as long as they are part of the pack. McNees notes that if consensus forecasts gain wide acceptance, some forecasters may modify their forecasts to be closer to what they think the consensus will be.[20] This behavior would reduce the independence of individual forecasts. It is unclear if it would lessen the accuracy of the consensus forecast.

The extent to which forecasts diverge from subsequent experience, however, provides lessons in the art and science of forecasting. When forecasting errors are large, they motivate analysts to discover what went wrong and why; that is, was the error due to a flaw in technical methodology or to intangible or new circumstances that were difficult to anticipate? Methodological flaws cover errors such as incorrectly specifying the relationships between unemployment and inflation or between the federal deficit and interest rates. Flaws in methodology can be corrected for the next round of forecasts, but little can be done to prevent forecast error due to the unpredictability of the future. Examples of unanticipated events include the intangible psychologically driven waves of foreign inflows and outflows of money caused by speculation, rather than observable changes in investment opportunities in the United States and abroad, or new events for which there is minimal previous experience, such as the political and economic upheavals in former communist countries. Thus, even in a world of perfect data, perfect quantification of the future would be highly unlikely.

Even a forecast that seems accurate may contain hidden errors. Forecasts sometimes quite accurately project overall economic growth, employment, and inflation, but incorporate significant offsetting errors in the components of the forecasting methodology. For example, offsetting errors may occur in specifying the relationships between unemployment and inflation, and the federal deficit and interest rates. Consequently, the forecast is right for the wrong reasons. While an accurate forecast may be comforting, if it results from poor methodology it may give a false sense of security regarding future forecasts. Unfortunately, an accurate forecast can hamper impartial evaluations of the methodology. The accurate results and the euphoria resulting from a successful forecast may make it difficult for the forecaster to suspect a problem with the methodology at the time.

Effect of Forecasts on Economic Behavior

There are contradictory ideas regarding how macroeconomic forecasts affect the behavior of households and businesses and thus affect the economy. Depending on how forecasts are translated into actions, they may function as a self-fulfilling prophecy or a self-correcting mechanism.

Forecasts become a self-fulfilling prophecy when households and businesses respond with actions that help the forecast come true. For example, a forecast of rising unemployment may cause households and businesses to cut back on spending because of insecurity about jobs and prospects for lower profits; thus, the forecast may bring on higher unemployment. A forecast of rising inflation may cause a spurt in current spending as consumers attempt to buy at current prices before expected price increases occur; this spurt in spending can itself bring on higher inflation. Indications of how the future is perceived are included in the stock price and consumer confidence components of the leading index of economic activity.

Forecasts function as a self-correcting mechanism when households and businesses take deliberate actions to help make the forecast inaccurate, which is a tenet of rational expectations theory. For example, a forecast of higher unemployment may cause businesses to lower prices and banks to lower interest rates in order to bolster the quantity of sales and loans, thereby stimulating spending and lowering unemployment. A forecast of higher prices may cause households to restrain spending because consumers fear their income will not keep up with inflation; at the same time, businesses and banks may respond by raising prices and interest rates to ensure they do not fall behind in the upward spiral, but the increases may be to such high levels that they restrain spending. Both of these actions would tend to lower inflation, although the latter one would have a delayed effect until after the initial increases in prices and interest rates dampen spending.

At any rate, assessing the self-fulfilling versus self-correcting functions of forecasts is impossible because currently there is no information on how forecasts affect household and business behavior. Intuitively, it seems that the functions coexist, but at the present time any estimates of their relative impact can only be conjectural. Moreover, Victor Zarnowitz and Phillip Braun dismiss self-fulfilling and self-correcting household, business, and government responses to economic forecasts as having no practical relevance.[21] They note that self-fulfilling and self-correcting actions assume the original forecast that engenders the responses is correct, but forecasts often are not correct. In addition, such public responses to economic forecasts assume widespread acceptance of a particular forecast among households, businesses, and governments, which they consider to be unrealistic.

REVIEW QUESTIONS

- Why is the nonaccelerating inflation rate of unemployment (NAIRU) used in developing Okun's Law?
- Using a formulation of Okun's Law that puts the break-even point for unemployment at an annual growth rate in the real gross domestic product (GDP) of 2 percent, the change in the unemployment rate of 0.5 percentage point for every one percentage point change in the real GDP above and below the break-even point, and a current unemployment rate of 5 percent, calculate the new unemployment rate for:

New unemployment rate
GDP growth of 4% _____

    GDP growth of 3% _____

    GDP growth of 2% _____

    GDP growth of 0% _____

    GDP growth of –1% _____

- The Phillips Curve tradeoff between unemployment and inflation breaks down in two economic environments: (a) when both unemployment and inflation are high, and (b) when both unemployment and inflation are declining. What causes the breakdown during these periods?
- Characterize the difference between automatic stabilizers and the structural budget of the federal government budget for their effects on the economy.
- Why is there sometimes great uncertainty about actions the Federal Reserve FOMC will take on monetary policy?
- What is your opinion of the usefulness of the NAIRU concept for fiscal and monetary policymaking? Explain.
- Which goal of the Full Employment and Balanced Growth Act of 1978 (Humphrey-Hawkins Act) is more likely to be realized, a 4 percent unemployment rate or a zero inflation rate? Explain.
- How does an econometric model differ from an autoregressive methodology as a forecasting technique?
- How do short-term, medium-term, and long-term forecasts differ from each other in content and purpose?
- What role does the forecaster's judgment play in macroeconomic forecasts?
- What are the virtues and defects of consensus forecasts?
- How can gamesmanship by economic forecasters affect the credibility of their forecasts?
- What are the necessary conditions for macroeconomic forecasts to affect the economy?

Extra Credit

- We see in the next chapter that the reported growth rate of the real GDP is subject to periodic long-term revisions. What does that say about Okun's Law?
- What developments in the next decade might push the Phillips Curve leftward? Rightward?

NOTES

    1. Arthur M. Okun, "Potential GNP: Its Measurement and Significance," *Proceedings of the Business and Economic Statistics Section,* American Statistical Association,

1962. Reprinted, with slight changes, in Arthur M. Okun, *The Political Economy of Prosperity,* (Norton, 1970), Appendix.

2. Geoffrey M.B. Tootell, "Restructuring, the NAIRU, and the Phillips Curve," *New England Economic Review,* Federal Reserve Bank of Boston, September/October 1994.

3. A.W. Phillips, "The Relation between Unemployment and the Rate of Change of Money Wage Rates in the United Kingdom, 1861–1957," *Economica,* November 1958.

4. Robert J. Gordon, *Macroeconomics,* 6th ed. (HarperCollins College Publishers, 1993), pp. 241–44.

5. The survey methodology for the unemployment rate changed in 1994 so that the 1990–92 and 1994–96 data are not strictly comparable. However, the effect of the methodology change on the unemployment rate has been estimated to have raised the rate by a few tenths of a percentage point. This would make the improvement in the tradeoff from the early to the mid-1990s even greater than indicated by the official data used here.

6. Robert Kuttner, *The Economic Illusion: False Choices between Prosperity and Social Justice* (Houghton Mifflin, 1984), p. 22 and ch. 4.

7. Besides fiscal and monetary policies, other factors preventing a depression include unemployment insurance and other income maintenance programs that provide a floor during recessions, bank deposit insurance, and active government intervention to stem a widespread financial collapse by failing banks.

8. Frank de Leeuw and Thomas M. Holloway, "Cyclical Adjustment of the Federal Budget and Federal Debt," *Survey of Current Business,* December 1983.

9. Congressional Budget Office, Congress of the United States, *The Economic and Budget Outlook: Fiscal Years 1998–2007,* January 1997, pp. 3–4.

10. Tootell, "Restructuring." See also Stuart E. Weiner, "Challenges to the Natural Rate Framework," *Economic Review,* Federal Reserve Bank of Kansas City, 2nd quarter, 1995, and George A. Akerlof, William T. Dickens, and George L. Perry, "The Macroeconomics of Low Inflation," *Brookings Papers on Economic Activity* 1 (1996).

11. Akerloff, Dickens, and Perry, "The Macroeconomics of Low Inflation." An alternative measure in the study indicates that inflation would rise to 5 percent before unemployment would decline from 5.8 to 5.2 percent, which only highlights the complexity of this issue.

12. Robert Eisner, *The Misunderstood Economy: What Counts and How to Count It* (Harvard Business School Press, 1996), ch. 8.

13. Federal Reserve Bank of Richmond, *Instruments of the Money Market,* 7th ed., 1993, ch. 2. This has a good discussion of federal funds.

14. John B. Berry and Pierre Thomas, "Fed Requests Probe to Find Source of Leak," *Washington Post,* September 23, 1996, p. A1.

15. Stephen K. McNees, "Forecasting Cyclical Turning Points: The Record in the Past Three Recessions," *New England Economic Review,* Federal Reserve Bank of Boston, March/April 1987. See also the following by McNees: "How Large are Economic Forecast Errors?" *New England Economic Review,* Federal Reserve Bank of Boston, July/August 1993; "An Assessment of the 'Official' Economic Forecasts," *New England Economic Review,* Federal Reserve Bank of Boston, July/August 1995.

16. Stephen K. McNees, "Man vs. Model? The Role of Judgment in Forecasting," *New England Economic Review,* Federal Reserve Bank of Boston, July/August 1990.

17. Victor Zarnowitz and Phillip Braun, "Twenty-two Years of the NBER–ASA Quarterly Economic Outlook Surveys: Aspects and Comparisons of Forecasting Performance," in *Business Cycles, Indicators, and Forecasting,* ed. by James H. Stock and Mark W. Watson (University of Chicago Press, 1993), pp. 67–68.

18. Stephen K. McNees, "The Uses and Abuses of 'Consensus' Forecasts," *Journal of*

Forecasting, 1992, pp. 703–10; and Victor Zarnowitz, "The Accuracy of Individual and Group Forecasts from Business Outlook Studies," *Journal of Forecasting,* 1984, pp. 11–26.

19. David Laster, Paul Bennett, and In Sun Geoum, "Rational Bias in Macroeconomic Forecasts," *Staff Reports,* No. 21, Federal Reserve Bank of New York, March 1997. The views expressed by the authors do not necessarily reflect those of the Federal Reserve Bank of New York or the Federal Reserve System.

20. McNees, "Uses and Abuses of 'Consensus' Forecasts."

21. Zarnowitz and Braun, "Twenty-Two Years of Quarterly Economic Outlook Surveys," pp. 14–15.

3
ECONOMIC GROWTH

The overall performance of the economy is reflected in its economic growth. The economic growth of a nation is the rate increase from one period to the next at which its workers and entrepreneurs produce goods and services. Growth of the American economy is generally positive, as it rises in many more years than it declines. While the thrust of the economy is clearly upward, these long-run positive growth rates vary over multiyear periods. Negative growth rates occur during shorter periods of business cycle recessions, typically within a twelve-month period, when the economy declines (growth rates and business cycles are discussed in Chapter 2).

Economic growth is important because it affects the material well-being and social harmony of the population, as well as U.S. influence in world affairs. Material well-being relates to basic aspects of life such as food, shelter, clothing, health, transportation, education, and the environment. Because a faster growth rate usually translates into greater employment and more generous income maintenance programs, the higher the growth rate, the greater the purchasing power of the incomes of the working and nonworking population. Higher real incomes tend to lessen social tensions through the improved living conditions they bring, although economic discontent is not the only cause of these tensions. Thus, greater material well-being may bring a greater emotional and spiritual happiness and social harmony, but it does not necessarily do so. In world affairs, while the United States has a unique prestige as the only superpower, its influence in obtaining international agreement for its economic, environmental, social, diplomatic and military policies is probably heightened when its own economy is perceived as being on a sound and robust footing.

In referring to economic growth, President John Kennedy said that a rising tide lifts all boats. The presumption is that persons on all steps of the income ladder benefit from a robust economy. But the presumption has been questioned for persons with low and modest incomes who have not shared in the greater prosperity and for persons who have lost their jobs because their skills are no longer marketable.

This chapter highlights the gross domestic product (GDP) as the primary measure of economic growth. Because the GDP construct is so large, its aggregate dimensions are covered in this chapter, but its major components on household, business, international, and investment-saving transactions are covered separately in Chapters 4 to 7, and government transactions are covered in Chapter 2.

In addition to the overall perspective on economic growth, the chapter includes an assessment of the components of economic growth associated with employment, capital, and productivity. These are major topics in their own right that are covered in more detail in Chapters 5, 8, and 10. The chapter also includes an analytic framework of the last year of cyclical expansions as a guide for assessing the likelihood of an impending recession.

GDP METHODOLOGY

The GDP is prepared quarterly by the Bureau of Economic Analysis in the U.S. Department of Commerce. It is published in BEA's monthly journal, the *Survey of Current Business.* The initial estimate for each quarter is published about one month after the quarter. This is followed by a series of revisions: they begin with revised estimates in the two subsequent months; the next revisions are published annually in the three succeeding years, usually in July; and lastly, the benchmark revision is prepared on a periodic five-year schedule. Every five-year benchmark revision results in its definitional, classification, and statistical changes being carried back to 1929, thus maintaining a consistent series of GDP data from 1929 forward.

The GDP summarizes in a single number the nation's total economic output valued in dollars. It is derived by organizing the various sectors of the economy—the household, business, government, and international sectors—into a system of spending and income accounts. These are referred to as the "national income and product accounts," "national economic accounts," or simply the "national accounts."

The summary GDP number consolidates spending and its counterpart income flows to represent the nation's output from two perspectives, the differing components of demand and supply. The *demand* concept (known as the "product side") refers to the end-use markets for goods and services produced in the United States. It appears in the national accounts as sales of these items to households, businesses, governments, and foreigners. The *supply* concept (known as the "income side") refers to the incomes and costs involved in producing these goods and services. It is shown in the accounts as workers' wages, business profits, interest payments, rental income, and depreciation allowances for business structures and equipment, and sales and property taxes.[1]

The product and income sides are economic counterparts that have strong interrelationships. At the simplest level, the incomes generated on the income side are the source of spending on the product side. Moreover, this is a continuing process as the spending for goods and services in turn generates income for their production, and so the process continues from income to spending to income, and so on. These interrelationships between income and spending are discussed in various chapters for the enrichment they give to the analysis.

Table 3.1 shows the product and income sides of the GDP in 1996 and their major components. The total value of goods and services produced in 1996 was $7.5 trillion. The figures indicate the dominance of consumer expenditures on the product side with 68 percent of the GDP, and employee compensation on the income side with 59 percent of the GDP. As discussed below under Analysis of Trends, however, these and the other components move at different rates over the business cycle.

Meaning of Production

The GDP is defined on a "value-added" basis. This means that as goods pass through the various stages of production—from raw materials to semifinished goods to final products—only the value that is added in each stage is counted for GDP purposes. If goods and services purchased from other businesses for use in production were included, their value would be endlessly recounted. The value-added method counts only the total resources used in producing the final item, as represented in the wage, profit, and other income-side components, and the final markets of the product side. This prevents double counting of items on the product side. The income-side methodology itself prevents double counting on the income side.

Another key point in defining production is that the GDP excludes capital gains and losses in the sale of securities, land, and used goods. These are considered valuation changes in the transfer of assets, and while they may have effects on future production, they do not change output at the time of the transfer. But brokerage charges associated with these transactions are in the GDP because the broker's service is current production.

The GDP measures production in terms of dollar costs, without making value judgments on the differential worth to society of the activities measured. Equal weight is given to purchases of goods and services for everyday living, investment for future production, and public services—food, housing, machinery, inventories, education, defense, and so on, are all valued strictly in dollar terms. Similarly, the labor and capital resources necessary to produce this output are measured strictly in dollar amounts as workers' wages and business profits. This objective measure of the nation's output may be contrasted to measures that could account for the nation's "welfare" or "well-being" by assigning a positive or negative value to activities based, not only on their marketplace value, but also on their intrinsic worth.

Table 3.1

Gross Domestic Product and Main Components: 1996

	Product Side	
	$ billions	percent
Gross Domestic Product	7,576.1	100.0
Personal Consumption Expenditures	5,151.4	68.0
Durable goods	632.1	8.3
Nondurable goods	1,545.1	20.4
Services	2,974.3	39.3
Gross Private Domestic Investment	1,117.0	14.7
Nonresidential[a]	791.1	10.4
Residential[b]	310.5	4.1
Inventory change	15.4	0.2
Net Exports	−98.7	−1.3
Exports	855.2	11.3
Imports	953.9	12.6
Government Consumption Expenditures and Gross Investment	1,406.4	18.6
Federal	523.1	6.9
State and local	883.3	11.7

	Income Side	
	$ billions	percent
Gross Domestic Product	7,576.1	100.0
Compensation of Employees	4,448.5	58.7
Wages and salaries	3,630.1	47.9
Supplements	818.4	10.8
Proprietors' income[c]	527.3	7.0
Farm	44.7	0.6
Nonfarm	482.6	6.4
Rental Income	115.0	1.5
Corporate Profits	670.2	8.8
Net Interest	403.3	5.3
Indirect Business Taxes[d]	617.9	8.2
Consumption of Fixed Capital[e]	845.5	11.2
Business Transfer Payments and Government Subsidy Payments Less Surplus of Government Enterprises	14.7	0.2
Rest of the World[f]	6.7	0.1
Statistical Discrepancy[g]	−75.1	−1.0

Source: Bureau of Economic Analysis, U.S. Department of Commerce, *Survey of Current Business,* March 1997.

[a]Business structures and equipment.

[b]New housing construction and improvements.

[c]Profits of unincorporated businesses.

[d]Mainly sales and property taxes.

[e]Mainly depreciable allowances.

[f]Payments less receipts (net) of profits of multinational companies generated outside the company's home country, net interest, and net wages paid to persons who work in foreign countries.

[g]Product-side total less income-side components shown above.

A GDP that accounted for welfare would measure the nonmaterial effects of activities by deducting from production for "bad" items and adding for "good" items over and above their value in the marketplace. Such a computation would assign greater value to industrial activity that protects the environment than to equally productive activity that harms the environment. Similarly, defense spending that deters war would be valued more highly than defense spending that results in destructive or war-provoking actions, although in practice such a distinction would be very difficult to make. A GDP that took welfare into account would also include the value of many "products" currently not valued in dollar terms, such as the increased leisure time resulting from a shorter work-week, the greater security resulting from improved police protection, and the market value of unpaid labor services of homemakers, parents, and volunteers. Such a GDP measure would also evaluate consumer goods such as autos, furniture, and appliances differently to incorporate the value of their services over the years of their useful life, as well as the actual dollar amount involved in producing the goods, which is included in the traditional GDP measure. In the 1970s, the Bureau of Economic Analysis began to develop estimates of such items that economists could use to modify the traditional GDP measures, but the project was discontinued for lack of funding.

Because the market value of unpaid labor services of homemakers is not included in the GDP, the long-term shift of women working as homemakers for no pay to working at paying jobs in the market economy has also raised the growth rate of the GDP, as David Korten points out.[2] The result is that increasing amounts of work previously done within the family for no money wages, such as housekeeping, food preparation, child care, and care of the elderly, are increasingly done and paid for in the marketplace, and are added to the GDP. Thus, with the passage of time, the GDP has increased simply because of the change in the societal way work is done at home. No estimates are available of the effect of this societal change on the economic growth rate, however.

At the same time, some nonmarket activities are included as "imputed" estimates in the GDP. The main ones are the rental value of owner-occupied housing, employer-paid health and life insurance premiums, and services provided by financial intermediaries without payment. Imputed items accounted for 13 percent of the GDP in 1996.

Real GDP and Inflation

Real GDP, which technically is "GDP in chained (1992) dollars," represents the quantity of goods and services produced abstracted from price increases or decreases. "Chained" dollars refers to the procedure of changing the proportions of the expenditures for various goods and services items every year in calculating indexes of price change (see Chapter 1 on Index Numbers). To correct for any bias in these calculations due to using the prices of the individual items in year 1 or year 2, the prices of both years are "chained" by multiplying them together and averaging them by a geometric mean.[3]

As of this writing, the real GDP incorporates 1992 as the base year for these calculations.[4] The base year is updated with every five-year benchmark, so that the next benchmark will have 1997 as the base year. Such price effects are included in the "GDP in current dollars," also known as nominal GDP.[5] The real GDP measures have little relevance in absolute terms, as they are difficult to relate to over time; for example, in 1998, it is difficult to think of spending in 1992 dollars. But real GDP data are the most important measures of the *rate of change in percentage terms* of the quantity of economic output from quarter to quarter and year to year. Thus, real GDP is the most comprehensive and widely accepted indicator of economic growth.

In its simplest form, GDP in current dollars is converted to real GDP by dividing the current-dollar data by the price change from one quarter to the next (or annually from one year to the next) for each of the detailed goods and services items in the GDP. The weights used in the GDP price measures are based on a "chain-type price index," which is the geometric mean of the expenditure patterns that are prepared on an annual basis noted above. For example, for changes from the third quarter of 1997 to the second quarter of 1998, the geometric mean is derived from the calendar-year expenditure patterns for 1997 and 1998 and are used as weights. This geometric weighting of expenditure patterns of two adjacent years is achieved on a historical basis only one and two years after the reference years because the annual data on expenditure patterns are first available in the year following the reference year (1997 data are first available in 1998 and 1998, data are first available in 1999). Thus, the contemporaneous GDP data that are prepared every quarter utilize a single year's expenditure patterns, which in themselves represent expenditure patterns of 1 to $1^{1}/_2$ years earlier (i.e., there is a continuous lag of 1 to $1^{1}/_2$ years in incorporating the latest expenditure patterns). For example, from the third quarter of 1997 to the second quarter of 1998, the expenditure patterns are based on the 1996 expenditure patterns, and then in the third quarter of 1998 they are based initially on 1997 expenditures.

The real GDP data also provide measures of price change. These indexes of inflation (rising prices) and deflation (falling prices) are based on the percentage distribution of the expenditure patterns of the component goods and service items used as weights to calculate price change from one period to the next. There are two variants of the GDP price measures. One is the chain-type price index discussed above. The other is the "implicit price deflator," which is derived by dividing current-dollar GDP by the chained-dollar GDP. The deflator reflects continuing shifts in tastes and spending patterns because it accounts for actual spending as new or substitute products replace old ones and as consumers choose between higher- and lower-priced products or between items with slow or rapid price increases. Thus, the expenditure weights continually change from one period to the next in this price measure.

These alternative price measures are very close in magnitude. In practice, the two measures of price change are often identical or differ by no more than 0.1 percentage point, except for the most recent quarter. Therefore, the two different estimates of GDP price change are not a problem for economic analysis.

In addition to the problem of weight structures, price indexes are beleaguered by the problem of accounting adequately for changes in the characteristics of the goods and services being priced. These indexes purport to measure price changes that result solely from a price increase or decrease, not one from changes in the quality or specifications of the item. For example, if a loaf of bread increases in price without a change in quality or size, that is a price increase for purposes of GDP measurement. But if the loaf increases in size as much as in price, there is no price change for GDP measurement. Or if the price of the bread is unchanged but the loaf is now larger or contains a nutritious new ingredient, a price decrease will be registered.

Price measurement issues are discussed more fully in Chapter 11 on Inflation. They are noted here to indicate that price measurement, and the price-derived GDP in chained dollars (real GDP), are imprecise concepts.

Government Budgets

Government consumption expenditures and gross investment covers current outlays for goods and services and depreciation charges on existing capital structures and equipment (consumption), and capital outlays for newly acquired structures and equipment (investment). They include purchases of goods and services from private industry, wages paid to government workers, and annual depreciation charges on structures and equipment over the lifetime of the assets.

The GDP measurement of government consumption and investment is less inclusive than that of expenditures in federal, state, and local official budgets. Thus, government consumption and investment excludes transfer payments to individuals for Social Security, unemployment benefits and other income maintenance programs, federal grants to state and local governments and state grants to local governments, interest on government debt, foreign economic aid, and government loans less repayments—all of which are included as spending in official government budgets. The spending generated by these transfer-type payments typically is reflected in the GDP in subsequent rounds, as the income received as transfers is used to buy goods and services in the same or later periods. For example, Social Security and other income maintenance payments, when spent, become consumer expenditures; state and local government spending of federal grants appears in state and local consumption and investment; foreign spending of economic aid on U.S. production appears in net exports; and interest payments on government debt and government loans and subsidies appear in the spending by the recipients of these funds in the domestic and foreign components of the GDP. Thus, while these transfer-type items are excluded from government consumption and investment in the GDP, they are accounted for subsequently in all GDP components, except to the extent they are used to reduce debt.

Nevertheless, the exclusion of these items from the GDP's accounting of the government sector limits one's view of the economic impact of government. For example, federal government consumption and investment expenditures in the GDP of $523 billion represented only 30 percent of all federal government outlays in 1996. One way to analyze more fully the economic impact of governments in the GDP framework is to use supplementary data in the national accounts on government statistical budgets that include transfer payments as well as consumption and investment, plus tax and other receipts collected by governments. These are similar to the official budgets, but are modified to make them more useful for estimating the effects of expenditures, receipts, and the budget surplus or deficit on economic activity.

Selected GDP Technical Topics

This section addresses several technical aspects of the GDP relevant to interpreting economic trends: alternative summary measures, seasonally adjusted annual rate, error range, the statistical discrepancy, net exports, and valuation adjustments.

Alternative Summary Measures

In addition to the GDP, other summary measures of the national accounts are available to better reflect special circumstances in the domestic or international economies. These measures are final sales of domestic product, gross domestic purchases, final sales to domestic purchasers, gross national product, and command-basis GDP. Another alternative GDP measure, GDP on the income side, is discussed in the Statistical Discrepancy section below.

Final sales of domestic product is the GDP excluding inventory change. In deriving final sales, an inventory increase is deducted from the GDP or an inventory decrease is added to the GDP. Inventory movements arise from differences between production and sales—inventories increase when production is larger than sales, and they decrease when sales are greater than production. Businesses augment or cut back on their stock of goods based on their perceptions of future sales and prices, or because of unexpected market developments such as substantially greater than anticipated rises or falls in sales, in which case the subsequent inventory depletion or accumulation is referred to as "unplanned." The unplanned changes may in turn generate deliberate actions to bring inventories into a desired balance with sales. Short-term inventory movements can be important signals that production may increase because inventories are low in relation to sales, or that production may decrease because inventories are relatively high.

It is also informative to assess the economy's performance independent of inventory movements by focusing on the strength of demand in all GDP markets as evidenced in final sales. For example, if sales are level or falling but production is adding to inventories, the overall GDP growth rate may not be sustainable. Or if sales are increasing and inventories are being depleted because of production bottlenecks, the GDP growth rate may fall below the longer-term sustainable level. The purpose of the final sales measure is to capture this underlying demand.

Gross domestic purchases is the GDP minus exports and plus imports. It focuses on the demand for goods and services in the United States, regardless of the country that produces the items. By excluding exports, it abstracts from foreign demand for American production, and by including imports, it includes American domestic demand that is not being met by American industry. Thus it focuses on purchases of goods and services in the United States.

Final sales to domestic purchasers are final sales minus exports and plus imports. It measures underlying demand in the U.S. domestic economy by excluding inventory movements from gross domestic purchases.

Gross national product is the GDP adjusted to include the effect of profits (dividends and retained earnings) and interest derived from foreign investments and of wages and salaries received from working in foreign countries. These are referred to as "factor income." The GNP is a residency concept, in contrast to the GDP, which is a geographic location concept of the fifty states and the District of Columbia. The GNP treats multinational corporations' profits according to the nationality of the company's ownership, and foreign workers' wages according to the nationality of the worker. In the GNP, profits and interest from foreign operations of U.S.-owned companies are included as business income, while profits from operations in the United States of foreign-owned companies are excluded from business income. Analogously, wages and salaries of U.S. residents working abroad are included in GNP, and wages and salaries of foreign residents working in the United States are excluded from GNP.

For some analyses of the American economy, the generation of incomes of U.S. companies and workers based on residency is most significant. Thus, foreign workers send some of their wage income to relatives in their home country, although they also spend money in the nation where they are working. And profits of a multinational company with affiliates in several countries accrue to the parent company in the home country and thus affect the company's business decisions on investment and operations worldwide, although the profits are in part generated from production and employment outside the home country. In sum, the GNP includes the profits of U.S.-owned companies earned from foreign operations and wages of U.S. residents employed abroad, and excludes profits of foreign-owned companies from their U.S. operations and wages of foreign workers employed in the United States. This reverses their treatment in the GDP.

Command-basis GNP represents the "command" by U.S. residents over goods and services produced. It responds to the problem that as prices for exported and imported items diverge and substantially change the terms of trade (the ratio of export prices to import prices), the conventional deflation of exports and imports by their respective price indexes distorts real GNP growth rates and thus gives U.S. residents a misleading higher or lower claim on U.S. production than actually exists. The problem results from the accounting need to subtract imports from exports and payments of factor income from receipts of factor income in the net foreign transaction component of the GNP. This is done to offset the inclusion of imports in the other product-side GNP components of consumer expenditures, business investment, and government consumption and investment. If imports were not subtracted from exports, GNP would be overstated because it would include foreign production, and the product and income sides of the GNP would not balance because income-side wages and profits do not exist for imports (this also applies to the GDP and is discussed more fully in the later section on Net Exports). The command-basis measure is prepared for the GNP rather than the GDP because the GNP national concept is considered more relevant to the command-basis idea than the GDP concept of incomes derived from economic activity within the fifty states and the District of Columbia.

The problem occurs when important internationally traded items such as petroleum have relatively large price changes. For example, for some years in the 1970s and in 1980, when the price of imported oil rose very sharply, chained-dollar imports were much lower than current-dollar imports. This in turn raised chained-dollar net exports (net exports are exports minus imports) and therefore real GNP. It suggested that Americans had a greater supply from which to "command" goods and services because of the higher import prices. This is an anomaly of the accounting need to deduct imports because higher import prices actually lower the availability of goods and services for consumption. Analogously, the oil price decline from 1981 to 1986 falsely suggests a lower command of goods and services over that period in the conventional GNP.

Command GNP handles such problems by changing the deflation of prices of net exports in real GNP. The conventional GNP method deflates exports and imports separately by export and import prices, and then subtracts chained-dollar imports from chained-dollar exports. Command GNP deflates net exports in a single step, using import prices as the only deflator (export prices as the single deflator would yield similar results). This device tends to moderate the anomalies produced by the accounting need to subtract imports in the net export component.

Seasonally Adjusted Annual Rate

The GDP is estimated quarterly, but the figure for each quarter is published as if the activity in the quarter were at an annual rate. Specifically, the annual rate shows how much the economy would grow over a year if it continued growing for the next three quarters at the same rate as it grew in the latest quarter. This facilitates comparison of the economy's current volume with past and projected annual levels. Two measures are involved in this concept: the first is the GDP absolute level for the quarter at an annual rate, and the second is the percentage change in this level from the preceding quarter at an annual rate.

The GDP level is the sum of the seasonally adjusted data for the three months of the quarter, multiplied by four to raise it to an annual level. For example, for the first quarter of the year, the seasonally adjusted data for January, February, and March are summed, and the total is multiplied by four. The resulting number is the quarterly GDP at a seasonally adjusted annual rate. Because the quarter includes activity for three months, the GDP in a particular month of a quarter can decline (or rise) even if it rises (or declines) for the quarter as a whole.

To derive an annual percentage rate of change in the current-quarter GDP from the preceding quarter, the relative change for the present quarter is compounded to represent an annual rate. The procedure is to raise the rate of growth or decline in the current quarter to the fourth power, subtract 1.0, and multiply by 100, as follows:

$$\left(\frac{\text{Seasonally adjusted annual GDP (current quarter)}}{\text{Seasonally adjusted annual GDP (previous quarter)}} \right)^4 -1.0 \times 100$$

Percentage changes from quarter to quarter or year to year are published for major GDP aggregates except inventory change and net exports, because these components of the GDP can be either positive or negative, and a percentage change is not relevant between two periods that do not have the same sign, or for two periods that both have negative signs. To avoid confusion, the BEA reports only measures of economic activity that can be calculated on a regular basis. Thus, percentage changes for exports and imports are published separately.

Error Range

The contemporaneous GDP estimates published in each of the three months after each quarter are provisional, as is evident from the size of the revisions made as more complete and accurate information becomes available. Experience with these revisions has shown that, in nine cases out of ten, their likely effect on seasonally adjusted annual growth rates for quarterly real GDP is in the ranges indicated in Table 3.2. Thus, when real GDP for the second quarter of 1996 was first reported to have increased at an annual rate of 4.2 percent, the chances were nine out of ten that the final figure would fall somewhere between 1.2 and 7.2 percent. There is also a tendency for revisions, which incorporate new and additional data, to raise growth rates or lower the rate of decline. This is reflected in Table 3.2, in which the range above the early estimate is usually larger than the range below it.

Table 3.2

Probable Revisions to Quarterly Real GDP Annual Growth Rates
(percentage points)

Publication schedule of initial and revised GDP data for the same quarter	Average without regard to sign (plus or minus)	Range
Advance to final	0.6	−1.1 to 1.6
Preliminary to final	0.4	−0.5 to 0.7
Advance to latest	1.4	−3.0 to 3.0
Preliminary to latest	1.3	−2.3 to 2.9
Final to latest	1.5	−2.5 to 2.9

Source: Bureau of Economic Analysis, U.S. Department of Commerce, News Release, "National Income and Products Accounts," August 1, 1996.

Note: Based on nine of ten revisions from the 1996 GDP benchmark revision for 1981 to 1992.

Advance: One month after the quarter

Preliminary: Two months after the quarter

Final: Three months after the quarter

Latest: Most recent annual and five-year benchmark revisions

The table shows two sets of revision ranges. One set focuses on the revisions that occur on a contemporaneous basis. These are revisions made between the advance and preliminary GDP published one and two months after the quarter, and the final GDP published three months after the quarter, which are close in time to the quarter in question. The other set focuses on subsequent revisions of these three early estimates based on the annual revision prepared every July and on the still later five-year benchmark GDP revisions, both of which are far more distant from the quarter in question.

Both sets of revisions are sizable, but as would be expected, those associated with the annual and five-year benchmark revisions are greater than those between the GDP published one to three months after the quarter. However, policymakers responsible for setting fiscal and monetary policies to influence the economy clearly cannot apply such high revision ranges in their analyses of the current rate of economic growth. Further, to be timely, economic policymakers must respond to trends based on contemporaneous GDP figures before the annual and five-year benchmark revisions become available. For current policy analysis, then, a more workable measure of revision range is the average without regard to sign, also shown in Table 3.2. These data, which combine the revision ranges into a single number and thus moderate the extremes appearing in the actual ranges, indicate notably lower error ranges of approximately plus or minus 0.6 percentage point between the one-month and three-month estimates, and plus or minus 1.3 to 1.5 percentage points between the three contemporaneous estimates and the annual and five-year benchmark revisions.

In contrast to the high error ranges associated with the revisions, the average without regard to sign provides at least a workable error range.[6] In actuality, however, whether one uses the revision ranges or the average without regard to sign, the error range for revisions to the GDP is still high, which underscores the need to observe the trend for at least two consecutive quarters before using it as a basis for changing economic policies. But even current trends of three consecutive quarters can be misleading for economic policy analysis, as occurred in 1989–90 (see Chapter 1 under Revisions). In general, one should also wait for the final estimate three months after the quarter before concluding that the numbers reflect the actual circumstances of the quarter. The overall lesson is that no single GDP figure should be interpreted to indicate a new trend or validate an existing one, but instead should be viewed in the context of trends for previous quarters to determine whether a change is occurring.

Statistical Discrepancy

Conceptually, the grand totals of the product and income sides of the GDP represent the equivalent output of goods and services, although arrived at from different perspectives. In practice, limitations in the underlying data mean that the totals are rarely equal. The data are obtained from a variety of surveys, tax records, and other sources that have varying comparability with the GDP concepts. They also have varying degrees of accuracy because the survey samples are not necessarily representative and the respondents may provide erroneous information.

The difference between the output totals on the product and income sides is the net effect of these inconsistencies and inaccuracies and is referred to as the "statistical discrepancy." The discrepancy is not systematic from quarter to quarter, as different data problems continually occur. By convention, the discrepancy is calculated as the product side minus the income side, and this number appears on the income side of the accounts. In most cases the overstatement and understatement among the individual data items are probably offsetting, which results in the statistical discrepancy's being smaller than if the gross deficiencies were added without regard to their over- or understatement.

From the user's perspective, the discrepancy allows alternative GDP growth rates to be calculated from the product- and income-side information. These upper and lower bounds recognize that, due to data shortcomings, neither the product nor income side is inherently more accurate and that "reality" is more a range than a precise number.

For analytical purposes, the user should be aware that a noticeable change in the discrepancy could affect the growth rate. For example, in an $8 trillion GDP, assume a change in the statistical discrepancy from –$10 billion in the first quarter to $40 billion in the second quarter of the year. If the GDP on the product side grows at a rate of 2 percent in the second quarter, the alternative growth rate on the income side (adjusted for the statistical discrepancy) for the second quarter is 1.4 percent. Based on Okun's Law, discussed in Chapter 2, the product side growth rate of 2 percent maintains a stable unemployment rate, while a growth rate of 1.4 percent raises the unemployment rate by about 0.3 percentage point. Such a range suggests a weaker economy than that shown only by the product side estimate in this illustration.

Net Exports

Net exports of goods and services is the GDP component that represents U.S. transactions with other countries. It is derived by subtracting imports from exports. The net concept is necessary to keep the product and income sides of the GDP in balance, due to the special situation of imports.

Because imports are produced abroad, their production does not generate wages and profits in the United States, and thus no income-side payments are associated with their production. Imported items do appear on the product side, however, as households, businesses, and governments buy the imported goods and services. If nothing is done to offset purchases in the consumption, investment, and government components on the product side, that side would be higher than the income side, and it would appear that imports are produced in the United States. Therefore, imports are deducted from exports in the net export because imports are not produced in the United States.

The deduction of imports, however, causes the net export component to appear as a deceptively small share of the GDP. In 1996, for example, net exports were −$99 billion ($855 billion of exports minus $954 billion of imports), or −1.3 percent of the GDP. This relatively small net number masks the much higher actual economic impact of exports and imports separately, as exports were 11.3 percent and imports were 12.6 percent of the GDP in 1996.

While net exports give an overall view of the differential effect of exports and imports and of money flows between the United States and other countries (and can be important for foreign-exchange values and U.S. monetary policies), exports and imports taken separately are more relevant for assessing the impact of international trade on American production and prices. Exports and imports affect and are affected differentially by employment and inflation in the United States, American competitiveness in international markets, the value of the dollar, and the pace of the American and world economies.

Valuation Adjustments for Inventories and Depreciation

Special adjustments are made for the effect of price movements on inventories and on depreciation allowances for equipment and structures as conventionally reported by companies. These adjustments are particularly important during periods of high inflation and when depreciation allowances in the tax laws differ substantially from the use of capital facilities in business practice.

In both cases, the purpose of the adjustments is to reflect the replacement cost of inventories and capital facilities based on prices when they are used up, as distinct from prices at the time the inventories and capital facilities were acquired (their historical cost). Doing so eliminates the effect of valuation gains and losses on inventories due to price increases and decreases of goods since they were acquired. And for capital facilities, the adjustment provides a truer picture of the actual costs of replacing outmoded or inefficient plants and equipment as compared with the depreciation deductions allowed in income tax laws.

The *inventory valuation adjustment* (IVA) appears in the change in business inventories on the product side and in business profits on the income side of the GDP. During periods of rising inventory prices, the IVA is negative to offset valuation profits when goods are sold; when prices are falling, the IVA is positive to offset the valuation losses. Since prices generally are rising, the IVA is typically negative, although the amounts vary considerably depending on the inflation rate. For example, the IVA moved from $5 billion in 1991 to −$30 billion in 1995 and to −$8 billion in 1996. These trends reflected changes in the inflation rate of various commodities in the producer price indexes for crude materials, intermediate materials, and finished goods.

The data cited here refer to the IVA on the product side. The product- and income-side estimates of the IVA differ because they represent different accounting systems. The levels are of the same general magnitude and the year-to-year movements are almost always the same. Because inventories are continually replenished and sold at current prices, the IVA provides a more realistic assessment of actual inventory buildups and depletions and of business profits.

The *capital consumption adjustment* (CCAdj) affects the income side of the GDP, and appears as an offsetting item, with different signs, to business profits and capital consumption allowances (mainly depreciation). Thus, the CCAdj does not affect total GDP, but it does affect the distribution between profits and depreciation. Because profits are an important element driving future investment in capital facilities, large shifts in the CCAdj can affect business investment in structures and equipment.

The CCAdj reflects the fact that the actual usage of capital facilities by business (known as economic depreciation) differs from the depreciation based on tax-law provisions (known as tax depreciation). While tax depreciation is based on statutorily defined schedules, economic depreciation is a closer approximation of actual depreciation in industry practice both in terms of the expected lifetime of the asset and the rate at which it is depreciated over the years. Estimates of economic depreciation are based on actual service lives for various types of equipment and structures as indicated by industry surveys conducted in the 1970s by the U.S. Department of the Treasury, by information collected from regulatory agencies, and from studies of prices on used equipment and structures in resale markets.

The CCAdj is affected by the tax laws and inflation. When the tax laws allow accelerated depreciation schedules, which permit businesses to recoup the original cost of capital facilities faster than businesses actually use them up, the CCAdj appears as a positive item in business profits and a negative item in capital consumption allowances. When prices of capital goods are rising and thus raising the cost of new capital facilities, the CCAdj is deducted from profits and added to capital consumption allowances. The opposite occurs when the tax laws require slower depreciation rates than those at which business tends to use up capital facilities or when capital goods prices are falling. The CCAdj tends to be smaller when the tax laws have few investment incentives or disincentives in their own right, and larger when tax-generated investment incentives and disincentives are great. Thus, the smaller the CCAdj is, the closer the depreciation assumptions of the tax laws are to economic reality.

The CCAdj for unincorporated farm businesses and rental income of persons reflects changes in the capital goods inflation rate, but does not include differentials between tax-law depreciation and actual business practice in the "using up" of capital facilities. The absence of this distinction occurs because (1) there are limited reliable data to prepare such estimates for unincorporated farm businesses and rental property income, and (2) rental income is composed mainly of "rent" for owner-occupied dwellings that is imputed as if it were a cash payment to a landlord, but for which no depreciation is taken on the individual income tax return.

ANALYSIS OF TRENDS

This part of the chapter covers the main patterns shown by American business cycles from the 1945–48 expansion to the expansion beginning in 1991 (which was in progress in the spring of 1997, when the manuscript was completed) and highlights the major factors driving these trends. The period represents a major change from the depression of the 1930s and World War II both in the nature of the economy and the tools available for moderating business cycles. In addition to the patterns of economic growth as represented by the gross domestic product (GDP), this part addresses the following topics: (1) the last year of cyclical expansions; (2) alternative macro measures of the GDP; and (3) sources of growth of the GDP.

There have been ten expansions and nine recessions in the half century since World War II, as measured from the expansion of 1945–48 to the expansion that began in the spring of 1991, which was in progress in the spring of 1997 when the manuscript was completed. There was a recession from February to October

Table 3.3

Duration of Expansions and Recessions Related to the Real Gross Domestic Product

Expansions		Recessions	
	Duration (quarters)		Duration (quarters)
1945:4T–48:4P[a]	12	1948:4P–49:4T	4
1949:4T–53:3P	15	1953:3P–54:2T	3
1954:2T–57:3P	13	1957:3P–58:2T	3
1958:2T–60:1P	7	1960:1P–60:4T	3
1960:4T–69:3P	35	1969:3P–70:4T	5
1970:4T–73:4P	12	1973:4P–75:1T	5
1975:1T–80:1P	20	1980:1P–80:3T	2
1980:3T–81:3P	4	1981:3P–82:3T	4
1982:3T–90:2P	31	1990:2P–91:1T	3
1991:1T[b]			

Source: Monthly cyclical turning points established by the National Bureau of Economic Research were adapted by the author to quarterly GDP measures. See text.

Notes: Number after colon is quarter of year.

P = peak. High point of expansion before economy turns down into recession.

T = trough. Low point of recession before economy turns up into recovery.

[a]Quarterly real GDP data are not available before 1947. Use of 1945:4 as the start of the 1945–48 expansion follows the designation by the National Bureau of Economic Research of November 1945 as the beginning of the expansion.

[b]The expansion that began in 1991 was in progress in the spring of 1997 when the manuscript was completed.

1945, but because it was so closely linked to the war and the demobilization, it is not included in this analysis. The subsequent expansion from 1945 to 1948 was affected by the backlog of housing and consumer durables that were produced at very low levels in the depression of the 1930s due to the low incomes then, and the minimal output of these items during World War II as the concentration was on military production. This backlog, coupled with the higher incomes derived from wartime production in the place of production for the civilian economy, resulted in large amounts of household savings at the end of the war. Thus, the war had an important, although indirect, effect. The 1948–49 recession was the first postwar cyclical movement that was sufficiently removed from the war not to have been affected by the war's aftermath.

Table 3.3 shows the beginning and ending quarters of expansions and recessions for the business cycles since the end of World War II. The turning point used here to mark the peak of expansions and the trough of recessions is the change in direction of the real gross domestic product (GDP). It is based on the cyclical turning points established by the National Bureau of Economic Research

(NBER) discussed in Chapter 1. Because the NBER cyclical turning points are on a monthly basis, and the GDP is prepared on a calendar-quarterly basis, there is an ambiguity in dovetailing the monthly and quarterly turning points. Thus, one month in the quarter can be the peak of the expansion and the next month in the same quarter can be the beginning of the recession (the same situation occurs when the trough month of the recession and the following first month of the recovery are in the same quarter). To avoid this ambiguity, the convention adopted here is to use the first quarter closest to the NBER monthly turning point in which the real GDP changed directions. For expansions, this is the first quarter that the real GDP turned upward from the previous recession, and for recessions it is the first quarter the real GDP turned down from the previous expansion. The result for the duration of the expansion and recession periods is that the quarters in equivalent months in Table 3.3 mostly are the same or differ by no more than one month from the NBER monthly durations. The exceptions in expansions are that the NBER measures are three months shorter for 1958–60 and two more months for 1975–80, and in recessions the NBER measures are four months longer for 1969–70 and four months shorter in 1981–82.

The postwar period expansions averaged 4 years in peacetime and $4^1/_2$ years including wartime cycles, and recessions averaged 1 year in both cases, as noted in Chapter 1. The duration of individual cycles varies widely around these averages, however. The expansion of the 1960s lasted 9 years, the expansion of the 1980s lasted 8 years, and the expansion of the 1990s has been in progress for 6 years as of this writing in the spring of 1997, while there were very short expansions of 2 years and 1 year in the 1950s and 1980s, respectively.

Real GDP Movements

This section covers the movements of the real GDP aggregates and its main components, long-term trends, cyclical expansions and recessions, alternative GDP aggregate measures, and the sources of GDP growth since World War II. To put the period in a longer context, the discussion first briefly contrasts trends in economic growth during the twentieth century before and after World War II.

Trends Before and After World War II

Table 3.4 shows long-term trends in real GDP during the twentieth century.[7] The first part of the century, from 1901 to 1929, included the period before and after World War I culminating with the high point of 1929 before the depression of the 1930s. The subsequent periods from the 1930s to the 1990s had considerably varied economic conditions. The 1929–39 period was dominated by the Great Depression of the 1930s. The 1939–48 years comprised World War II and the transition after the war to a peacetime economy. Incomes were bolstered consid-

Table 3.4

Annual Growth of Real GDP

	Percent
1901–29	3.0
1929–39	0.9
1939–48	6.2
1948–59	3.6
1959–69	4.4
1969–79	3.2
1979–89	2.7
1989–96	1.9

Sources: 1901–29: Michael P. Niemira and Phillip A. Klein, *Forecasting Financial and Economic Cycles* (Wiley, 1994), Appendix A. The data represent the GNP, not the GDP. This definitional difference is insignificant for long-term trends generally and specifically because such definitional differences are overwhelmed by the large statistical errors in the early estimates. See text. 1929–96: Bureau of Economic Analysis, U.S. Department of Commerce.

Note: The author calculated the compounded annual rates.

erably by the employment growth associated with the high wartime production, but because there was little construction of housing and production of consumer durables, households had large amounts of savings after the war. Thus, the peacetime transition during 1945–48 reflected large increases in the demand for new housing and consumer durables stemming from backlogs created by (1) the low output and low incomes of the Great Depression, and (2) the curtailment of output for the civilian economy during the war years. These backlogs, together with the much greater household incomes and savings available after the war, coalesced for the greatly increased spending on housing and consumer durables after the war. The decades from the 1950s to the 1990s each had substantially different rates of economic growth, peaking in the 1960s and decelerating from the 1970s to the 1990s. They were also preoccupied internationally with the Cold War until the 1990s.

Long-term trends in real GDP that span several business cycles show distinct shifts in the annual growth rate. Generally, 1901–29, 1939–48, the 1950s, and the 1960s showed the highest growth rates, and the 1930s, 1970s, 1980s, and 1990s had the lowest growth rates. The highest growth rate for the entire period occurred during 1939–48, but that was a great exaggeration because it started from the low base at the end of the 1930s and was boosted by World War II and the immediate postwar period. The continuous decline in growth rates during the last three decades of the twentieth century was accompanied by periods of long and short expansions, as noted previously. The slower growth rates have increased the chances that children fall below the material living conditions of their parents, which is contrary to the history of the United States and a major challenge to correct in the twenty-first century.

A theoretical case could be made that fewer or possibly more uniform cyclical fluctuations result in faster economic growth, or vice versa. Looking more closely at the second half of the twentieth century, however, the evidence on the growth-cyclical relationship during 1948–96 is inconclusive. While the highest growth rate occurred during the expansion of the 1960s, which is the longest since World War II, the growth rate of the 1980s, which included the second longest postwar expansion as of this writing, was below that of the 1950s.

Such long-term comparisons are inherently tentative because the increasing accuracy of GDP measures over time limits the statistical comparability, particularly between the first and second halves of the century (see Chapter 1 under Changing Characteristics of Business Cycles Since the Nineteenth Century). Also, there is little documentation of the statistical methodology used in developing the estimates from 1901 to 1928. They were prepared by private researchers outside of the U.S. Bureau of Economic Analysis.

Overall Cyclical Movements

This analysis of real GDP and its main components highlights their movements over the ten expansion and nine recession periods since World War II. The measures cover the entire period of each expansion and recession, as well as the period leading up to the high point of the expansion before the economy turned down into a recession. Specifically, the data for each expansion represent the total movement from the low point of the previous recession (trough) to one year before the high point of the expansion (peak) is reached. The expansion from 1991 to 1997, ongoing at the time of this writing, is also included. The data for each recession represent the total movement from the high point of the previous expansion (peak) to the low point of the recession (trough).

Figures 3.1a and 3.1b depict these movements for expansions and recessions, respectively. *During expansions,* consumer expenditures for goods and services have movements very similar to those in GDP. This consistency between consumer expenditures and the GDP during expansions is not apparent during recessions (see below).[8] Private investment for nonresidential structures and equipment, housing, and inventory accumulation and depletion have much larger increases than the GDP and in general are the most volatile cyclical component of the GDP. Consumer expenditures and private investment are covered in Chapters 4 and 5.

Outlays for consumption and investment by the aggregate of federal, state, and local governments increase less than GDP, and in 1970–73 even showed a decrease. But this pattern is misleading because of the definition of government in the GDP. The government component of the GDP covers consumption and investment, but excludes transfer payments for Social Security, unemployment

Figure 3.1a **Gross Domestic Product and Main Components, 1960s to 1990s: Expansions**

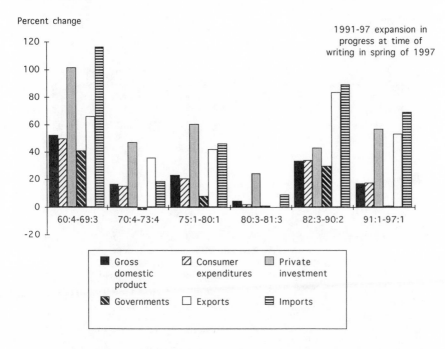

Note: Based on U.S. Bureau of Economic Analysis data in chained (1992) dollars. Number after colon is quarter of year.

benefits and various other income maintenance programs, federal government grants to state and local governments, interest on government debt, foreign aid, and government loans minus repayments, as noted in Methodology section under Government Budgets. Thus, the government component of the GDP considerably understates the impact of government outlays on the economy. The government role in the economy is covered in Chapter 2 under Fiscal Policy.

Exports and imports of goods and services typically rise much faster than the GDP during expansions. The faster rise of exports is a stimulus to the GDP, but the faster rise of imports lowers the GDP because imports are deducted from all other expenditures (see the Methodology section under Net Exports). The international dimensions of the U.S. economy are covered in Chapter 6.

During recessions, consumer expenditures decline less than the GDP and in some cases even rise. This has important cushioning effects in moderating the economic decline. Government consumption and investment also tend to decline less and even rise, which cushions the overall GDP decline. But this understates

Figure 3.1b **Gross Domestic Product and Main Components, 1960s to 1990s: Recessions**

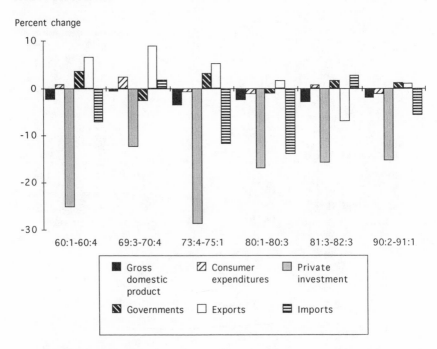

Note: Based on Bureau of Economic Analysis data in chained (1992) dollars. Number after colon is quarter of year.

the cushioning effect of actual government outlays, because the GDP definition of governments excludes unemployment benefits, which increase sharply during recessions (see above). Private investment declines much more than the GDP, and accounts for the bulk of the fall in the GDP. Exports tend to rise and imports tend to decline more than the GDP in recession periods, both of which moderate the GDP decline.

The contrasting movements of consumer expenditures and private investment during expansions and recessions reflect their intrinsically different characteristics. Consumer expenditures include a large component of necessities such as food, housing, and transportation, which are not drastically changed when incomes increase or decline in expansions and recessions, while the share of cyclically volatile consumer durable goods is much smaller (discussed further in Chapter 4). By contrast, private investment includes a larger amount of discretionary items for nonresidential structures and equipment and housing that are more readily deferred when incomes decline in recessions but which are significantly enlarged when incomes increase in expansions.

Last Year of Expansions

What clues do periods of cyclical expansion give of impending recessions? The last year of expansions before the economy reverses direction into recession is of interest because of insights it gives on the conditions that may lead to recession. Figures 3.2a (GDP product side) and 3.2b (GDP income side) focus on this period. To put the critical last year of the expansion in perspective, the figures include the GDP annual compound growth rate of the entire expansion beginning with the recovery from the previous recession up to but excluding the last year of the expansion; GDP 1 represents this period. GDP 2 and the other components represent the last year of the expansion. The figures cover all business cycles from the 1940s to the 1990s, except for the 1980:3 to 1981:3 expansion, because it only lasted one year. The 1991:1 to 1996:4 expansion was in progress at the time of this writing in the spring of 1997. It is included here to provide an example of how to analyze a contemporaneous situation, since the last year of an expansion is known only after the subsequent recession begins.

The figures in this section are complex and need to be studied together with the text.

GDP Product Side

Figure 3.2a on the product side indicates that the last year of the expansion shows a noticeably slower overall growth rate than in the preceding years of the expansion (GDP 1 vs. GDP 2). It suggests that a marked slowdown in the growth rate over a period of four quarters, compared to a more modest decline, raises the risk that the economy will slide into a recession. This was not evident in 1996:1–1997:1, which was part of the expansion in progress at the time of this writing, suggesting that a recession was not imminent at that time (discussed further below).

The difference between GDP 2 and final sales is inventory change. Because final sales exclude the volatile buildup and depletion of materials, semifinished goods, and finished goods inventories held by manufacturers, wholesalers, and retailers, they provide a closer approximation of underlying demand for goods and services than the GDP. On balance, GDP 2 and final sales differed only slightly in the last year of expansions. Consequently, inventory increases and decreases, whether deliberately made by businesses or which occur because of unanticipated changes in sales, appear as a marginal factor leading to recessions. While inventory movements are volatile from quarter-to-quarter, the volatility tends to wash out over a one-year period. Inventory movements mainly serve as a mechanism to adjust production to actual and anticipated changes in product sales. This is characterized by a buildup of inventories during expansions, and a depletion of inventories during recessions.

Consumer expenditures in the last year of expansions rose much more slowly

Figure 3.2a **GDP Product-Side Growth Rates in Last Year of Cyclical Expansions: 1960s to 1990s**

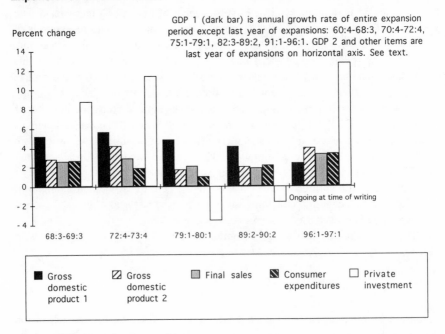

Percent change

GDP 1 (dark bar) is annual growth rate of entire expansion period except last year of expansions: 60:4-68:3, 70:4-72:4, 75:1-79:1, 82:3-89:2, 91:1-96:1. GDP 2 and other items are last year of expansions on horizontal axis. See text.

Ongoing at time of writing

68:3-69:3   72:4-73:4   79:1-80:1   89:2-90:2   96:1-97:1

■ Gross domestic product 1   ▨ Gross domestic product 2   ▨ Final sales   ◢ Consumer expenditures   ☐ Private investment

Note: Based on U.S. Bureau of Economic Analysis data in chained (1992) dollars. Number after colon is quarter of year.

than the GDP in 1972–73 and in 1979–80. Because consumer outlays account typically for two-thirds of the GDP (Table 3.1 indicates 68 percent in 1996), such differential movements are weighty in presaging recessions.

Private investment for nonresidential structures and equipment, housing, and inventory change is the most cyclically volatile component of the GDP. It also shows sharply different movements in the last year of various expansions. In 1968–69 and 1972–73, private investment increased far more than the GDP, while in 1979–80 and 1989–90, private investment declined. This decline in the last year of the expansions also is at variance with the persistently much larger increases in private investment than GDP for entire expansion periods, as noted above in Figure 3.1a. Because of the much larger increases of investment than other GDP components during expansions, a noticeable decline in the rate of growth or, even more so, an actual decline in investment suggests a higher risk of a subsequent recession.

Based on the product-side GDP, the expansion in progress during 1991–97 showed no sign of weakening in the 1996–97 period, at the time of this writing in the spring of 1997. Thus, from 1996:1 to 1997:1, the overall GDP growth rate

Figure 3.2b **GDP Income-Side Growth Rates in Last Year of Cyclical Expansions: 1960s to 1990s**

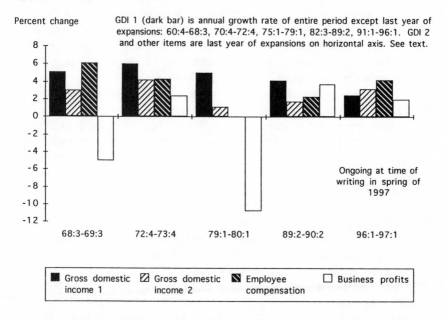

Percent change   GDI 1 (dark bar) is annual growth rate of entire period except last year of expansions: 60:4-68:3, 70:4-72:4, 75:1-79:1, 82:3-89:2, 91:1-96:1. GDI 2 and other items are last year of expansions on horizontal axis. See text.

Ongoing at time of writing in spring of 1997

Horizontal axis: 68:3-69:3   72:4-73:4   79:1-80:1   89:2-90:2   96:1-97:1

Legend:
■ Gross domestic income 1   ▨ Gross domestic income 2   ◩ Employee compensation   ☐ Business profits

Note: Based on U.S. Bureau of Economic Analysis data in chained (1992) dollars. Number after colon is quarter of year.

was noticeably higher than the average of the previous years. Private investment growth continued to be the major stimulus to growth, and consumer expenditures growth was similar to the GDP rate. This pattern shows no sign of an imminent recession.

GDP Income Side

The GDP on the income side excludes the statistical discrepancy, as discussed in the Methodology section. Figure 3.2b shows that the GDP on the income side, referred to as gross domestic income, has a noticeable decelerating growth rate in the last year of an expansion. This is similar to that of GDP on the product side in Figure 3.2a. Just as in the product-side figure, gross domestic income 1 (GDI 1) represents the entire expansion period except the last year of the expansion, and GDI 2 represents the last year of the expansion.

The primary income components for cyclical analysis are employee compensation and business profits. Employee compensation is the dominant income-side component, accounting typically for three-fifths of the GDI (Table 3.1 shows 59 percent in 1996). Employee compensation is composed of wages and salaries,

Social Security payments by the employer, and employer contributions for fringe benefits such as health insurance and pensions. To compute real, as distinct from current, dollars, the author deflated employee compensation in current dollars to 1992 dollars by the price index for consumer expenditures. Business profits are the sum of corporate profits and unincorporated profits (proprietors' income). The author deflated business profits in current dollars to 1992 dollars by the price index for business output in the national accounts.

Employee compensation rose at least as much as gross domestic income in the last year of expansions, with an exceptionally large increase in 1968–69. The exception to this pattern was 1979–80, when employee compensation showed no change over the four quarters. Thus, employee compensation typically, but not always, rose at least as much as gross domestic income in the last year of expansions. Because of this and its dominant share of gross domestic income, employee compensation generally, although not uniformly, limits large declines in GDI in the last year of expansions. While employee compensation is a major source of income for consumer expenditures on the product side, the two do not move in tandem in the last year of expansions. Consumer spending shows less strength than employee compensation in the last year of expansions. This reflects the role of savings, income less spending.

Business profits, the residual of sales less expenses, are the most cyclically volatile component of GDI. They declined sharply in 1968–69 and 1979–80, and rose noticeably less than GDI in 1972–73. The exception to this pattern of weakening profits in the last year of expansion was 1989–90, when profits rose noticeably more than GDI. Thus, business profits are typically, but not always, a harbinger of an impending recession. Business profits are a major source of income for private investment in the GDP product side. While these counterparts are both cyclically volatile, they typically do not move in tandem in the last year of expansions.

Based on the income-side GDI, the ongoing expansion of the 1991–97 period was generally strong when this was written in the spring of 1997. The GDI rose more from 1996:1 to 1997:1 than in the previous years of the expansion, and employee compensation increased more than the GDP in 1996–97. The exception was business profits, which rose noticeably less than the GDI in 1996–97. This is less robust than the GDP product-side movements noted above, but it still does not suggest an impending recession.

The last year of a cyclical expansion is of course known only with the benefit of hindsight after the recession begins. But the measures noted in this discussion provide the analyst with a technique for monitoring the strength of the expansion on a contemporaneous basis to assess whether the current period has signs of a fading expansion and thus of an impending recession. When a slowdown in the GDP growth rate over a recent four quarter period occurs, the movements of key components should be reviewed more closely. On the GDP product side, the main components to monitor are consumer expenditures and private investment.

On the GDP income side, the main components to monitor are employee com-pensation and business profits. The analyst should supplement this approach for detecting signs of an impending recession, which is done through the perspective of the GDP, with other economic indicators such as employment (Chapter 8), unemployment (Chapter 9), and the leading indicator system (Chapter 13).

Alternative GDP Measures of Economic Growth

The GDP numbers are subject to various sources of imprecision because they are prepared from a wide range of underlying data that do not necessarily match the GDP definitions and that reflect varying degrees of accuracy (see Methodology under Statistical Discrepancy and Error Range). The inherent statistical error in the GDP due to these limitations in the source data is not known. Differences between the GDP on the product and income sides are compounded because the two measures are prepared from many different data sources, which in itself introduces an unknown amount of inconsistency between them. Theoretically, if both measures were prepared from the same data sources, they would show the same GDP. Even here, it may not be so because the component data items such as sales and payrolls obtained from the same survey may be reported by a different number of survey respondents and with varying accuracy.

The result is that the GDP estimates on the product and income sides vary continually. The difference is called the "statistical discrepancy," which conven-tionally is calculated as the product-side estimate minus the income-side esti-mate. The GDP on the income side is referred to as the gross domestic income (GDI). The GDP and the GDI are considered to be equally accurate. They result in two different measures of economic growth, both of which are equally valid. Differences in the growth rates from one period to the next tend to be magnified when, in period 1 the product side is higher than the income side, and in period 2 the income side is higher than the product side. Generally the differential growth rates are larger on a quarterly than on an annual and multiyear basis, which probably results from offsetting inconsistencies and errors over time.

In addition, alternative definitional variations are prepared as slight modifica-tions to the GDP for analytical purposes, as noted in the Methodology section. These include final sales of domestic product, gross domestic purchases, final sales to domestic purchasers, gross national product, and command-basis gross national product.

Figure 3.3 illustrates the varying growth rates on a quarterly basis from 1993 to 1996 of three alternative measures: GDP, GDI, and final sales of domestic product. Final sales is included because of analytical interest in short-term inven-tory movements; final sales is the GDP minus inventory change. The growth rates among the three measures are occasionally quite close, as in 1993:4 and 1995:1. Between the definitionally consistent GDP and GDI, the variations range from under and over 0.5 percentage point, with exceptions of over one

Figure 3.3 **Alternative Gross Domestic Product Measures: Quarterly 1993:1 to 1997:1**

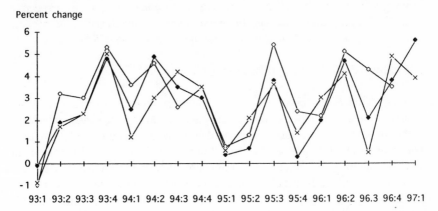

Percent change

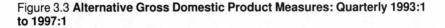

| -•- Gross domestic product | -◦- Gross domestic income (GDP minus statistical discrepancy) | -×- Final sales of domestic product (GDP minus inventory change) |

Note: Based on U.S. Bureau of Economics Analysis data. Number after colon is quarter of year.

percentage point occurring in 1993:2 and 1995:3. The growth rates of GDP or GDI are not typically higher in one measure than the other. The largest differences are between final sales on the one hand and GDP and GDI on the other, which would be expected because final sales differs definitionally from the others.

In assessing the quarterly movements of economic growth, the analyst should observe the alternative GDP and GDI measures to determine if statistical factors are causing them to show somewhat different movements. Because one measure is intrinsically no more accurate than the other, no single number represents reality. One way to resolve the difference is to treat each quarterly growth rate as being in a range between the upper and lower bounds. It is also useful to compare final sales with the GDP to determine if underlying demand represented by final sales is stronger or weaker than the GDP, which includes inventory change.

Components of Economic Growth

The nation's output of goods and services is produced by three basic elements: (1) labor input of workers, (2) services of capital physical facilities, and (3) productivity (i.e., efficiency). Thus, the GDP represents the quantity of the labor and capital resources used in production and their productivity, plus the productivity with which these resources are organized in the workplace. The latter productivity measure is referred to as multifactor productivity, as discussed below. Productivity is discussed more fully in Chapter 10.

Estimates of the three components of production in this section are based on the multifactor productivity measures prepared by the Bureau of Labor Statistics in the U.S. Department of Labor.[9] Productivity is discussed more extensively in Chapter 11.

Mathematically, the three growth components sum to business GDP in all periods as follows:

% change in output (GDP)   = % change in labor inputs × labor's share of costs
+ % change in capital inputs × capital's share of costs
+ % change in multifactor productivity

The GDP measure used in these estimates represents the private business sector only. It excludes the output, which is primarily the employee compensation of government employees and of paid employees of households, operating expenses of nonprofit institutions, and the rental value of owner-occupied housing. This modification of the traditional GDP is made because output is not measured independently of inputs, especially labor inputs, as is needed for productivity measurement. Implicit within some of these sectors is the assumption that output per hour, or labor productivity, does not change over time. Incorporating an obviously inaccurate assumption within the data would result in a biased measure of productivity.

The labor input measure represents the hours at work of employees, self-employed proprietors, and unpaid family workers. These are weighted to account for shifts to workers with more education and experience, or to relative increases in the compensation of these workers, which leads to greater measured labor input. The weights differ because the hours of workers with more schooling or experience are weighted more heavily to reflect differences in capabilities between workers. Thus, the weights differentiate among different groups of workers as separate and distinct inputs in the production process.

The capital services measure represents the stocks of physical assets used in production—business equipment, structures, inventories, and land. These are weighted by the income derived from their use in production. The income associated with these capital facilities in turn is based on a market rental value when the enterprise rents the items, or by an implicit rental value when the facilities are owned by the enterprise. Financial assets and owner-occupied housing are excluded because they do not directly involve the production of goods and services, although they have important indirect effects.

Multifactor productivity is a combination of many known and unknown ele-

Figure 3.4a **Components of Economic Growth, 1948–94: Annual Rates in Each Period**

Percent

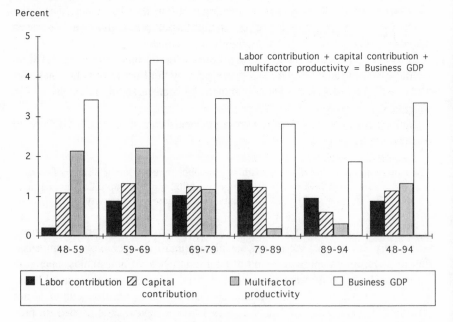

Note: Based on U.S. Bureau of Labor Statistics data.

ments that contribute to the efficiency of the economy. They include such items as managerial know-how, technology, quality of materials, utilization of productive capacity of firms, energy usage, transportation and distribution systems, and the interaction of these and all other factors. Changes in efficiencies associated with multifactor productivity often involve fundamental changes in efficiency that take relatively long to filter through the broad spectrum of industries in the economy.

Figures 3.4a and 3.4b show the labor and capital contributions together with multifactor productivity, which sum to business GDP, from 1948 to 1994.[10] Figure 3.4a depicts the annual growth rates of the labor, capital, and multifactor productivity components of growth by decade, and for the entire forty-six-year time span. Figure 3.4b converts these growth rates to their percentage contribution to business GDP for the same periods. There are two major patterns in the movements. First, as noted previously in this chapter, economic growth represented by the GDP declined continually in the 1970s to the 1990s, after peaking in the 1960s. Second, multifactor productivity declined relative to labor and capital in the 1980s and 1990s, although there was a small increase in the multifactor component in the 1990s.

Economic growth comes from labor, capital, and multifactor productivity with

Figure 3.4b **Components of Economic Growth, 1948–94: Percent Contribution**

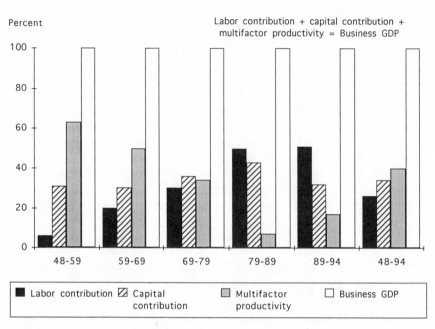

Note: Based on U.S. Bureau of Labor Statistics data. Calculated from measures in Figure 3.4a.

no distinctions among them. But in the long run, improvements in living conditions stem to an important extent from improvements in multifactor productivity. Assuming that the employment of persons and capital facilities increases at fairly steady rates in a growing economy, the key to increasing the size of the economic pie produced is productivity improvements. American perceptions, and for some the reality, of stagnating or even lower living conditions for the working population appeared around the late 1970s. These are typically associated with children having lower incomes than their parents, adjusted for inflation. While the problem of stagnating or declining living conditions has many causes, the slowdown in productivity improvement seems to be one of them.

In monitoring growth patterns of the GDP, the analyst should include the contributions to economic growth of the labor and capital inputs and of multifactor productivity. Generally, economic growth will be sustained if the rate of increase in labor and capital inputs is maintained, and accelerated improvements in living conditions have a greater probability of occurring with an accelerating rate of increase in multifactor productivity.

REVIEW QUESTIONS

- The GDP on the "product side" and the "income side" is the same in total, except for statistical problems. The components of the two measures differ substantively, however. What is the nature of the difference?
- What type of additional information would be needed to develop supplementary GDP measures that reflect a concept of well-being, in contrast to the existing concept of production?
- GDP data are provided in absolute current dollars, absolute dollars adjusted for inflation (real GDP), and rates of change of both.
  a. Why is the main interest in rates of change of real GDP?
  b. Give examples of analytical uses of the absolute GDP data in both current and inflation-adjusted dollars.
- Government consumption and investment in the GDP exclude transfer payments such as Social Security and unemployment benefits, even though they are part of government budgets and affect the economy.
  a. Why are transfer payments excluded?
  b. How is this limited measure of government dealt with in economic analysis?
- Why is it deceptive to look only at "net exports" (exports minus imports) in the GDP without considering the export and import components separately?
- Why are valuation adjustments for inventories and depreciation allowances more important during highly inflationary periods than when prices rise slowly?
- How do movements in economic growth differ between the periods before and after World War II? What are the statistical problems with these comparisons?
- What is an important component of the continuing slowdown in economic growth from the peak rate of the 1960s to the 1990s?
- During cyclical expansion and recession periods, why are consumer expenditures less volatile than private investment?
- What factors would you consider in assessing when an ongoing period has signs of the last year of a cyclical expansion?
- There are several alternative GDP measures: gross domestic income, final sales of domestic product, gross domestic purchases, final sales to domestic purchasers, gross national product, and command-basis GNP.
  a. How does gross domestic income differ from the alternative measures?
  b. How are the alternative measures used in economic analysis?

- Why are labor and capital contributions to economic growth associated with working harder, and multifactor productivity associated with working smarter?

Extra Credit

- For what reasons is real GDP a less-than-perfect measure of the output of the U.S. economy?
- Why do exports and imports of goods and services typically rise much faster than the GDP during expansions?
- What factors would cause multifactor productivity to decline relative to labor and capital contributions to economic growth in the 1980s and 1990s?

NOTES

1. Use of demand and supply terminology refers to the distinction between the components of the GDP on the product and income sides. In total, both sides measure "production." The difference between the two is in the demand and supply nature of the components.

2. David C. Korten, *When Corporations Rule the World* (Kumarian Press, and Berrett-Koehler, 1995), pp. 44–46.

3. Steven J. Landefeld and Robert P. Parker, "Preview of the Comprehensive Revision of the National Income and Product Accounts: BEA's New Featured Measures of Output and Prices," *Survey of Current Business,* July 1995.

4. Bureau of Economic Analysis, U.S. Department of Commerce, "Improved Estimates of the National Income and Product Accounts for 1959–95: Results of the Comprehensive Revision," *Survey of Current Business,* January/February 1996.

5. "Nominal" and "real" are the terms commonly used to denote the distinction in GDP measures with and without inflation. Some may object to these words as misleading; there is nothing nominal about the GDP in current dollars because this is the only actual GDP, and there is nothing real about GDP in chained dollars adjusted for inflation because in the everyday world, items are bought and sold in today's price, not in the unchanged prices of a particular year.

6. The average revision relative to the latest revised estimate of the percentage point change is much smaller than those in Table 3.2. While this measure is comforting over the long run, it does not negate the chances of sizable revisions in a particular period. See Allan H. Young, "Reliability and Accuracy of the Quarterly Estimates of GDP," *Survey of Current Business,* October 1993, Table 2, p. 34.

7. Because the growth rates are calculated from similar phases of the business cycle in which the final years of the comparison—1909, 1929, 1948, 1959, 1969, 1979, 1989, and 1996—are years of economic expansion, they provide a consistent representation of long-term trends; calculating the rates from terminal periods that include both expansion and recession years would distort the averages (see Chapter 1 under Calculating and Presenting Growth Rates).

8. Thus, although consumer expenditures are the dominant component of the GDP,

accounting for 68 percent of the GDP in 1996 (Table 3.1), the other components clearly influence the overall growth rate. Even during expansions, the similar movements of consumer expenditures and the GDP reflect the tendency for the differential movements of the other smaller components to be offsetting.

9. Bureau of Labor Statistics, U.S. Department of Labor, "Multifactor Productivity Trends, 1994," *News Release,* January 17, 1996.

10. These productivity data reflect the new index number chain-weighted methodology of the GDP adopted in the 1996 GDP benchmark revision, but they do not include the data revisions in the benchmark (Footnote 4). Totally revised data consistent with the GDP benchmark were not available at the time of this writing. Nevertheless, it is unlikely that the fully revised data would change the overall patterns discussed here.

4
HOUSEHOLD INCOME AND EXPENDITURE

The primary reason people work is to provide for the material well-being of themselves and their families. And once minimum living needs are satisfied, the ultimate purpose of economic activity becomes to raise material living conditions to as high a level as possible. Material well-being is represented by the incomes of households and the spending of their incomes to obtain goods and services for everyday living, such as food, clothing, housing, health, education, transportation, business and personal services, and entertainment.

Household income and expenditure are driving forces of the economy. They affect and are affected by employment and wages (Chapter 8), and impact investment in structures and equipment, which in turn are determinants of productivity (Chapters 5 and 10). By contrast, in a Garden of Eden environment in which all material needs are abundantly available without one's having to work for them, we would not speak about "the economy," or the accompanying topics of employment, inflation, investment, saving, and productivity.

Households buy goods and services using income obtained in the current period and from income obtained in previous periods that was not spent but accumulated as wealth assets. Purchases of goods and services are also financed from borrowing that is paid off in later periods. This continuing circular flow from income to expenditure to income to expenditure is the focal point of assessing the current status and future outlook of the household sector of the economy.

The household income and expenditure measures are prepared monthly by the Bureau of Economic Analysis in the U.S. Department of the Commerce.

METHODOLOGY

This section highlights the content and measurement used in preparing the economic indicators of household income and expenditure. It also includes household saving, borrowing, and debt, which are importantly linked to income and expenditure.

Table 4.1

Personal Income: 1996

	Billions of dollars	Percentage distribution
Total	6,449.5	100.0
Income from production	*4,593.6*	*71.2*
Wages and salaries	3,630.1	56.3
Fringe benefits	436.2	6.8
Self-employment	527.3	8.2
Income from investments	*1,083.8*	*16.8*
Rent	115.0	1.8
Dividends	230.6	3.6
Interest	738.2	11.4
Income from government transfers	*1,079.7*	*16.7*
Social Security	539.1	8.4
Unemployment insurance	22.1	0.3
Veterans benefits	21.9	0.3
Government employees' retirement	142.3	2.2
Aid to Families with Dependent Children	20.0	0.3
Other (Medicare, Medicaid, food stamps, other)	334.3	5.2
Less: Personal contributions for Social Security	*(307.5)*	*(4.8)*

Source: U.S. Bureau of Economic Analysis.
Note: Details do not equal totals due to rounding.

Personal income (PI) is the main source of consumer purchasing power used to buy goods and services. It primarily represents the income received by households, and comprises income derived from current production, investments, and transfer payments. Income from production covers money wages and salaries, fringe benefits, and profits from self-employment. Income from investments covers rent, interest, and dividends. Income from transfer payments covers Social Security, unemployment insurance, food stamps, Medicare, Medicaid, and other income maintenance programs. Social Security taxes paid by employees and employers are excluded from personal income. In addition to households, PI includes operating expenses of nonprofit organizations, plus the investment income of life insurance companies, noninsured pension funds, private nonprofit organizations, and trust funds. In 1995, income of households accounted for 95 percent of personal income.

Table 4.1 shows that in 1996, income from production accounted for 71.2 percent of personal income, income from investments for 16.8 percent, and income from government transfers for 16.7 percent. The total of these items, minus the 4.8 percent of employee contributions for Social Security, sums to 100 percent.

Disposable personal income (DPI) is a modification of personal income that reflects the fact that taxes are an important element affecting spending. DPI is personal income after the payment of income, estate, and gift taxes, and miscellaneous fines and penalty taxes (as noted, Social Security taxes paid by the employer and employee are excluded from personal income). It thus represents the actual purchasing power available to consumers from current income. Personal taxes accounted for 13.4 percent of personal income in 1996. Theoretically, DPI is more cyclically stable than PI because of the progressive income tax, a main attribute of the federal government income tax law. Under the progressive income tax, a higher proportion of income is paid as taxes as income of the recipient increases; and conversely, as recipient income declines, a lower proportion is paid in taxes. This progressivity should result in proportionately less of an increase in DPI than in PI during expansions, and in proportionately less of a decrease in DPI than in PI during recessions. The effect during expansions is to restrain income and spending growth, thus moderating economic growth and inflation. The effect during recessions is to shore up income and spending, thus moderating the declines in output and employment.

Consumer purchasing power refers to consumers' capability to finance spending. It encompasses personal income noted above, consumer installment loans, household savings in bank deposits, financial assets (money market accounts, stocks, bonds, etc.), and less liquid assets such as real estate. All of these sources may be used to finance consumer spending and repay consumer debt by liquidating savings and other assets, or by using these assets as collateral for further loans. The end result of using these financing sources for spending affects both spending and saving. We will see how this plays out in the following discussion of consumer expenditures and personal saving.

Consumer expenditures for goods and services account for approximately two-thirds of the gross domestic product (the GDP is discussed in Chapter 3). In addition to goods and service items bought for money in a market transaction, consumer expenditures include an imputed value for certain nonmarket items that are acquired for no payment. The largest nonmarket imputed items are the rental value of owner-occupied housing and certain services provided without charge by financial intermediaries. The imputed rental value was 8.8 percent and imputed financial services were 2.5 percent of consumer expenditures in 1994.

Personal saving is what is left of disposable personal income after all personal outlays.[1] Personal outlays consist mainly of consumer spending for goods and services (96.9 percent in 1996), but also include interest on loans paid by households to business, excluding home mortgage interest (2.8 percent), and net personal payments by U.S. households to foreigners (0.3 percent). The personal saving rate measures saving as a percentage of disposable personal income. The inclusion of operating expenses of nonprofit institutions in equal amounts in personal income and consumer expenditures lowers personal saving, amounting to 0.3 percentage point in 1996 (the personal saving rate was 4.9 percent in 1996). National saving, as distinct from personal saving, is covered in Chapter 7.

Personal outlays are financed by personal income plus other sources of consumer purchasing power (i.e., installment credit, existing savings, and loans obtained on real estate and other financial assets). Therefore, personal saving is affected by the use of credit, existing savings, and sale of existing assets as well as by current personal income. The total value of items bought on credit is included as spending when the purchase is made; in later periods, repayments of the principal of the loan are included as saving. In addition, while personal outlays exclude household purchases of homes and investments such as stocks, bonds, money market instruments, and real estate, personal saving includes the equity in these housing and investment transactions if they are financed from current income (the change in equity is discussed below).[2] But these items are not included in saving to the extent that they are financed by selling homes or other assets to other households or by interpersonal gifts (e.g., from parents to children). In general, personal saving is affected by transactions between households on the one hand, and businesses, governments, and foreigners on the other, but personal saving is not affected by transactions between households.

The net effect on saving of the use of loans and existing assets to finance consumer expenditures has the following attributes. Saving is reduced when a loan is used for spending, and saving is increased when the loan is paid off. Saving is reduced when consumers finance spending from existing savings or by selling real estate and financial assets to businesses, governments, or foreigners. And saving is increased when households build up equity in housing and in real estate and financial investments such as stocks and bonds as they pay off mortgage and other loans associated with the assets (changes in equity do not reflect price appreciation or depreciation of homes or investments). Saving is not affected by gifts between households, such as when parents give a house to their children; or by sales of homes, cars, and other assets between households, except for payments to intermediaries such as brokers' commissions and used-car-dealer markups.

ANALYSIS OF TRENDS

Consumer decisions to spend are affected by two broad considerations. One is the macroeconomic environment of production, employment, and inflation discussed in Chapters 2 and 3. The other is the individual consumer's purchasing power as reflected in household income, saving, borrowing, and debt.

Employment and price trends weigh heavily in the timing and types of consumer spending. Households in which the primary worker or workers are currently employed with little likelihood of being unemployed are among the best candidates to spend in the near future, both for necessities and deferrable items.

By contrast, households in which workers are employed but expect to be unemployed, or in which they are unemployed with low expectations of finding a job, are likely to curtail spending sharply for deferrable items, such as a new car, clothing, or recreation, while maintaining or somewhat reducing outlays for necessities. These households are far more constrained, both by a currently limited income and by the need to save for future spending, than are households with more secure job situations.

Consumer spending decisions are also affected by current and anticipated inflation. Ideally, consumers time their purchases to buy at the lowest price. For deferrable items, if prices are rising rapidly and inflation is expected to continue at a high rate, consumers are likely to feel it is better to buy immediately. If prices are rising now but are expected to decline within a certain period, consumers may defer some purchases. In addition to affecting timing, prices can also affect the overall amount of spending, depending on relative prices between necessities and deferrable items. For example, a sharp rise in gasoline prices may curtail spending for other items. Or if deferrable items (say, television sets) drop sharply in price, spending for these items may increase.

Two private organizations conduct surveys to track the combined effects of these employment and inflation factors on consumer attitudes toward spending: the University of Michigan's Survey Research Center publishes an "index of consumer sentiment," and The Conference Board publishes a "consumer confidence index." These indexes have been advance indicators of the turning points of business cycles, turning down before a general recessions sets in and turning up before a general recovery begins. As in the case of all such indexes giving advance signals, however, they should be viewed as giving general notions of future trends, rather than specific forecasts, since their timing varies from cycle to cycle and they sometimes give false signals (see Chapter 13 on the leading indicator system).

The two consumer attitude indexes supplement the outlook for the overall economy for their effects on consumers' spending decisions. In using the indexes for specific situations, however, the analyst should examine how well they performed in predicting consumer spending in the most recent six to twelve months.

Volatility of Consumer Durable Goods Spending

Consumer spending for all goods and services shows similar movements to the gross domestic product during cyclical expansions, and less volatility than the GDP during cyclical recessions, as noted in Chapter 3. The cyclical patterns of consumer expenditures and the GDP during expansions are similar because the differential movements of the other GDP components tend to offset each other. But during recessions, consumer expenditures cushion the effects of declining output from other sectors of the economy. While consumer expenditures account

Figure 4.1a **Business Cycle Movements of GDP and Consumer Expenditures, 1960s to 1990s: Expansions**

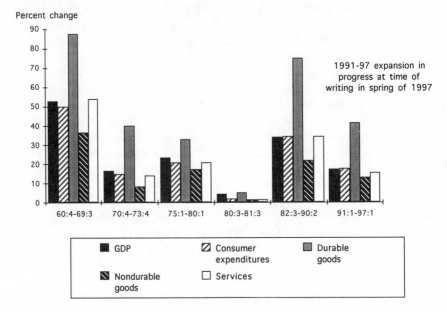

Percent change

1991-97 expansion in progress at time of writing in spring of 1997

60:4-69:3   70:4-73:4   75:1-80:1   80:3-81:3   82:3-90:2   91:1-97:1

■ GDP   ▨ Consumer   ■ Durable
                   expenditures   goods

◪ Nondurable   □ Services
   goods

Note: Based on U.S. Bureau of Economic Analysis data in chained (1992) dollars. Number after colon is quarter of year.

for the bulk of the GDP (68 percent in 1996), the other components do influence the GDP movements (Chapter 3).

However, there are large cyclical differences among the three broad categories of consumer expenditures—durable goods, nondurable goods, and services. Durable goods are items intended to last three or more years, such as cars, furniture, and household appliances. Nondurable goods, such as food, clothing, and gasoline, last less than three years. Services are noncommodity items such as housing rent (including both tenant rentals and nonmarket imputed rent for owner-occupied housing), utilities, public transportation, private education, medical care, and recreation.

Durable goods account for the smallest share of consumer outlays, ranging from 12 to 14 percent of the total. But because of the longer life of these items, it is easier for households to defer purchasing them when economic conditions such as wage earnings, unemployment, or inflation are adverse. Thus, while spending for durable goods is much smaller than that for nondurables and services, durable goods outlays are far more volatile over the business cycle.

Figures 4.1a and 4.1b indicate this volatility in both the expansion and reces-

Figure 4.1b **Business Cycle Movements of GDP and Consumer Expenditures, 1960s to 1990s: Recessions**

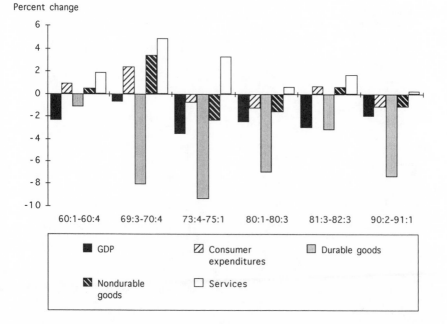

Note: Based on U.S. Bureau of Economic Analysis data in chained (1992) dollars. Number after colon is quarter of year.

sion phases of the business cycle in the six expansion and recessions from the 1960s to the 1990s. Durable goods spending increased more rapidly than did spending for nondurables and services in all six expansions. Durables typically increased two to three times faster than nondurables and services. During recessions, durable goods spending declined in all six downturns; nondurable goods purchases declined in three of the six recessions; and purchases of services increased in all recessions, although the services increase in the 1990–91 recession was only 0.2 percent, much smaller than in past recessions. In recessions when both durable and nondurable goods spending declined (1973–75, 1980, and 1990–91), the durable goods decline was much steeper.

Figure 4.2 shows the tendency for total consumer spending to be consistently more cyclically stable than the rest of the GDP. This results from the fact that services and nondurable goods spending is more stable than durable goods spending. Also, services spending is more stable than nondurable goods spending, and there has been a long-term shift from nondurables to the more stable services. From 1959 to 1996, nondurable goods dropped from 47 to 30 percent of

Figure 4.2 **Durable Goods, Nondurable Goods, and Services Shares of Total Consumer Expenditures: 1959–96**

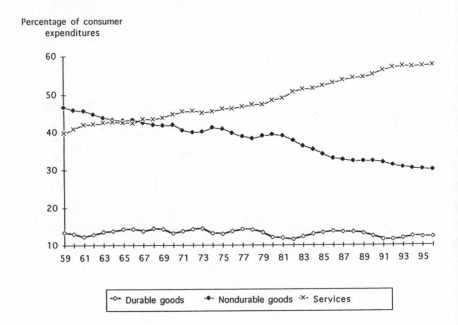

Note: Based on U.S. Bureau of Economic Analysis data in current dollars. The three components sum to 100 percent.

all consumer spending, while services increased from 40 to 58 percent. By contrast, durable goods spending fluctuated within 12 to 14 percent of consumer spending over the 1959–96 period.

The cyclicality of durables goods spending has been dampened by the greater stability of nondurable goods and services spending, in terms of total consumer spending. But this may not continue in the future if the service industries become more cyclically sensitive to changing growth patterns in the overall economy. A harbinger of this may be the anemic growth in services during the 1990–91 recession. If this occurs, consumer expenditures will have a less stabilizing impact on the economy. The analyst should monitor these components to determine if a change is occurring between the volatile and more stable components of consumer spending.

Personal Income

Figures 4.3a and 4.3b show the cyclical movements of real GDP, real personal income (PI), and real disposable personal income (DPI) during the six expan-

Figure 4.3a **Business Cycle Movements of GDP, Personal Income, and Disposable Personal Income, 1960s to 1990s: Expansions**

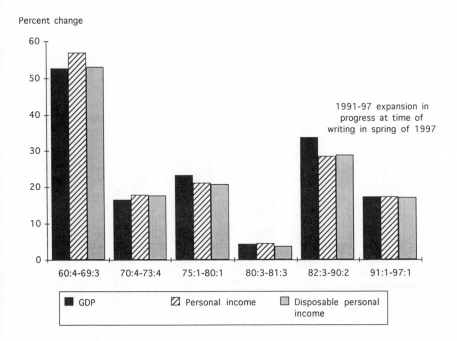

Note: Based on U.S. Bureau of Economic Analysis data in chained (1992) dollars. Number after colon is quarter of year.

sions and six recessions from the 1960s to the 1990s.[3] There is very little difference between the three indicators during expansions (Figure 4.3a). Thus, the effect of definitional distinctions among the indicators in terms of income from unemployment benefits (excluded from GDP and included in PI and DPI), and of personal income taxes (included in GDP and PI and excluded from DPI), was minimal and not always as expected during expansions. Personal income rose more than the GDP in three of the six expansions, which is contrary to the effect of lower unemployment benefits in PI during expansions. But DPI increased less than PI in five of the six expansions, which is consistent with the increasing income taxes paid during expansions.

By contrast, clear differences among the three indicators were apparent in recessions (Figure 4.3b). The GDP declined noticeably more than PI, and PI actually increased in the recessions of 1960 and 1969–70. This is consistent with the expectation stemming from the higher unemployment insurance benefits in PI during recessions and the treatment of corporate profits. For example, in the 1990–91 recession, unemployment benefits rose from an annual rate of $17

Figure 4.3b **Business Cycle Movements of GDP, Personal Income, and Disposable Personal Income, 1960s to 1990s: Recessions**

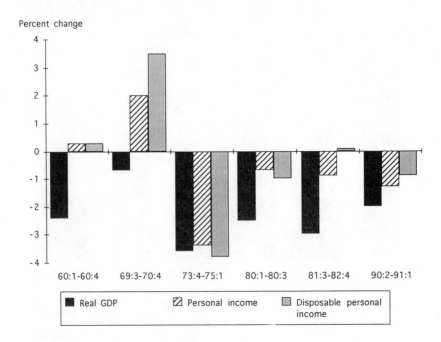

Note: Based on U.S. Bureau of Economic Analysis data in chained (1992) dollars. Number after colon is quarter of year.

billion in the second quarter of 1990 to $25 billion in the first quarter of 1991, or from 0.35 percent of personal income to 0.5 percent of personal income, respectively.[4]

Also, the highly cyclical undistributed corporate profits are included in the GDP and excluded from PI. But corporate dividend payments are part of PI and are more cyclically stable than the undistributed profits that are retained in the business and are in the GDP. Thus, unemployment insurance and corporate dividends in PI, and undistributed corporate profits in the GDP, were main factors softening the decline of 2 percent in GDP to a decline of 1.3 percent in PI in the 1990–91 recession.

In the distinction between PI and DPI, the expected pattern is for DPI to decline less or increase more than PI during recessions, due to the slowdown in income taxes paid during recessions. But the expected pattern occurred in only three of the six recessions—1969–70, 1981–82, and 1990–91.

Overall, the main characterization of the GDP, PI, and DPI measures during business cycles is the increase in unemployment benefits in PI and DPI

Figure 4.4 **Personal Saving Rate: 1959–96**

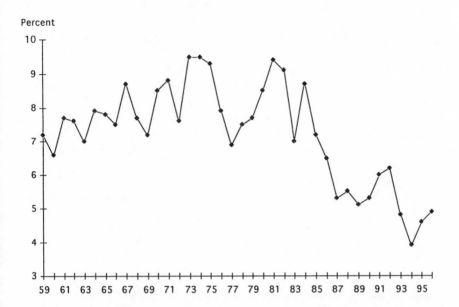

Note: Based on U.S. Bureau of Economic Analysis data. Personal saving as a percentage of disposable personal income.

and the decline in undistributed profits in the GDP during recessions. Differences among the three indicators during expansions are negligible.

The analyst should monitor the movements of the GDP, PI, and DPI to determine if they are following their expected patterns of cyclical stability. A break with expected patterns lessens economywide cyclical stability. The differential movements among the three indictors are of analytical interest mainly during recessions.

Personal Saving

Personal saving is of interest for its effect on decisions by households of how much to spend in the current period and on spending plans for the future. Personal saving is what is left of disposable income after all personal outlays are made, as noted in the Methodology section. The saving rate measures saving as a percentage of disposable personal income.

Figure 4.4 shows the saving rate during 1959–96. It is volatile from year to year, and has varied considerably from the decades of the 1960s to the 1990s. Generally, the saving rate was in the 7 to 8 percent range in the 1960s, the 8 to 9 percent range in the 1970s and early 1980s, and the 4 to 5 percent range in the late 1980s and the 1990s. These variations in the saving rate result from substantially different spending rates for the same income level. For example, in 1996, the saving rate was 4.9 percent and real consumer expenditures increased by 2.5 percent. Assuming the same levels of income and inflation, if the saving rate had been 6 percent, real consumer spending would have increased by only 1.3 percent in 1996, resulting in much slower economic growth for the year.[5]

Figure 4.4 shows no discernible difference in saving rates between expansion and recession periods.

In projecting saving rates to anticipate consumer spending, the analyst should prepare saving rates that appear appropriate for that phase of the business cycle. These projections require considerable judgment regarding consumer behavior, including the use of consumer installment credit and existing assets to finance spending, because over the years consumer behavior has not displayed the repetitive patterns that are essential for developing quantitative relationships.

Household Credit and Debt

Consumer credit loans augment consumer purchasing power and thus increase consumer expenditures. When an item is purchased on credit, the entire cost of the item is counted as a consumer expenditure at the time of the purchase, and as the loan is paid off, the repayments are counted as personal saving, as noted in the Methodology section. The other side of consumer credit is that it is a debt, which is a depressant on future spending because of the need to pay off the debt.

Consumer Credit

Consumer credit data provided by the Federal Reserve Board encompass loans to households by banks, credit companies, and retail stores. The loans cover automobiles, credit cards, and other items such as mobile homes, home improvements, education, vacations, vans, pickup trucks, and recreational vehicles. They include loans with an option to repay in two or more monthly payments, plus those scheduled to be repaid in a lump sum, including single-payment loans, charge accounts, and service credit. Secured and unsecured loans are included, except those with secured real estate. Securitized consumer loans—loans made by finance companies, banks, and retailers that are sold as securities—are included. The data exclude home mortgages, but because of classification problems in the reporting from lending organizations, in practice the data probably include consumer loans backed by housing equity as well as consumer loans used for business purposes. The extent of this is unknown, though a 1990 Federal Reserve Board study considered them to be relatively small at that time.[6] Automobile leasing is also excluded from the consumer credit data.

Figure 4.5 shows the relationship of the annual percentage change between

Figure 4.5 **Consumer Credit versus Consumer Expenditures, Annual Percentage Change: 1960–96**

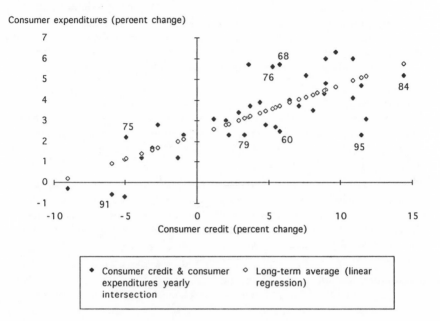

Note: Based on Federal Reserve Board and U.S. Bureau of Economic Analysis data in chained (1992) dollars.

consumer credit outstanding and consumer expenditures. Both the credit and expenditure data are adjusted for inflation in 1992 dollars based on the consumer expenditures' chain price index in the gross domestic product. Over the 1960–96 period, there is a general direct relationship between the two, as reflected in the long-term average line that slopes upward to the right. This means that on average, when consumer credit increases, so do consumer expenditures, and similarly consumer credit and consumer expenditures decrease in tandem. There also is a wide year-to-year variation in the relationship, however, as indicated by the dispersion of the individual years (black diamonds) around the long-term line (white diamonds). Thus, although consumer credit is important in financing consumer spending, other factors such as household income, prices, and consumer confidence often significantly lessen the influence of consumer credit.

Consumer Debt

While consumer credit is a source of financing for consumer expenditures, it also creates a debt burden that at times inhibits household spending. An overall measure of the debt burden is the ratio of consumer installment credit to personal income. As the ratio increases, there probably is a level when households retrench in spending because of an unwillingness to take on additional debt, or because lenders, noting the higher debt burdens and associated increase in loan delinquencies, become stricter in extending credit to consumers. But it is difficult to infer from historical experience what that level is.

There is a complex interaction among household incomes, debt burden, and delinquencies, as Jonathan McCarthy notes.[7] Households change their spending patterns more in line with changes in their incomes and income prospects than with their debt burden. This is reflected in the tendency for consumer spending to change direction before directional changes in household financial liabilities. At the same time, banks use their knowledge of customers' income prospects to decide on the creditworthiness of their customers. Thus, the confluence of more stringent credit rationing by banks and higher delinquency rates may have a common linkage in lower income prospects of bank customers.

Bankruptcy trends are another signal of debt burden problems, as reported by the American Bankruptcy Institute. Owing to a societal lessening of the stigma of bankruptcy and legislative reductions in the consequences of bankruptcy, there may be a greater willingness of individuals to take on more debt than they can afford in the 1990s, as noted by Lawrence Lindsey.[8] Thus, rising bankruptcy rates may in part reflect a lessening reluctance to declare bankruptcy than a worsening of personal finances.

Two financial developments of the mid-1990s do not seem to have had a significant effect on consumer debt burden, according to the Federal Reserve Board's Survey of Consumer Finances for 1992 and 1995.[9] One is the increased use of credit cards as a convenience in place of cash or a check. Even though consumers are making greater use of credit cards, the increase is confined to people who merely use the cards for convenience and pay their balance each month. Therefore, the increased use of credit has not raised the debt/income ratio.

The other financial development of the mid-1990s is for households to use consumer credit to invest in the stock market. It may be that this borrowing is relatively small and so has not raised the debt/income ratio.

Consumer credit outstanding as a percentage of personal income rose strongly after World War II, although with short-term interruptions, from 7 percent in 1948 to 16 percent in the early 1960s. But Figure 4.6 shows that it then fluctuated within a band of 14 to 17 percent from the 1960s to the early 1990s, with another rise to 18.5 percent in 1996.[10] The long-term average line indicates the tendency for the consumer credit debt burden to rise slowly from 1959 to 1996. Also, cyclical conditions have a strong bearing on the year-to-year movements of the debt burden. This is apparent in the sharp declines in the debt burden in recession years, when higher unemployment and lower incomes and lower consumer confidence lead to net repayments of loans outstanding (repayments of existing loans exceed new loans), in contrast to expansion years, which

Figure 4.6 **Consumer Credit Outstanding as a Percentage of Personal Income: 1959–96**

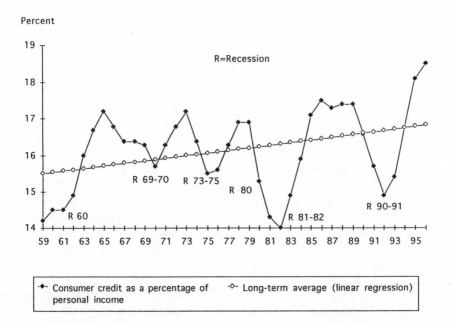

Note: Based on Federal Reserve Board and U.S. Bureau of Economic Analysis data in current dollars.

show net additions of loans outstanding (new loans exceed repayments of existing loans).

The analyst should include consumer credit and debt as a supplement to personal income, saving, and spending patterns for durable goods, nondurables, and services in assessing the strength of the household sector of the economy. In particular, household credit and debt should be monitored for any tendency to overheat the economy during cyclical expansions or snowball a decline during cyclical recessions.

REVIEW QUESTIONS

- Household spending is important in moderating the extremes of cyclical expansions and recessions.
    a. What factors are responsible for this?
    b. Give an example of what could change this in the future.
- Both unemployment benefits and the progressive income tax give greater stability to disposable personal income over business cycles.

a. Explain.

b. How can the indexing of inflation in the tax laws affect this in highly inflationary periods?

- Why is the saving rate problematic in short-term forecasts of consumer spending?
- Why does the relationship between consumer credit and consumer spending vary in different stages of the business cycle?
- Give examples of how consumer debt can adversely affect economic growth.

Extra Credit

- Services have grown from 40 percent of consumer expenditures in 1959 to 58 percent in 1996. What factors are responsible for this growth?
- The consumer debt/income ratio turns down after the onset of a cyclical recession and turns up after the onset of a cyclical recovery. Why does this ratio lag the turning points of the business cycle?

NOTES

1. An alternative measure of personal saving, developed by the Federal Reserve Board as part of the flow of funds accounts, is based on the change in net assets of households—that is, assets less liabilities. The assets are ownership of bank deposits, securities, pension reserves, owner-occupied homes, consumer durables, and unincorporated business structures, equipment, and inventories. The liabilities are debt and borrowing by households and unincorporated businesses. These measures are always higher than those derived from disposable personal income less personal outlays discussed in the text. The differential mainly reflects the definitional difference in the treatment of consumer durables (the flow of funds accounts includes, and the personal income measure excludes, consumer durables as saving), and the different databases used in preparing both measures.

The two measures cannot be reconciled statistically because the various sources of the differences cannot be quantified. For the type of economic analysis discussed in this book, either measure is acceptable so long as the same one is used over time, although most references to personal saving are to the income less outlays measure. The following article includes a good summary of the differences between the two saving measures: Lynn Elaine Browne with Joshua Gleason, "The Saving Mystery, or Where Did the Money Go?" *New England Economic Review,* Federal Reserve Bank of Boston, September/October 1996.

2. Residential construction is defined as investment in the gross domestic product (Chapters 3 and 5).

3. The U.S. Bureau of Economic Analysis adjusts disposable personal income for inflation by the implicit price deflator for personal consumption expenditures, but does not adjust personal income for inflation. Therefore, the author adjusted personal income for inflation by the implicit price deflator for consumer expenditures. The implicit price deflator is discussed in Chapter 3 under Methodology: Real GDP and Inflation.

4. Although the 1990–91 recession ended in the first quarter of 1991, according to

the National Bureau of Economic Research (see Chapter 3 under Analysis of Trends), unemployment insurance benefits continued to rise for five quarters after the recession was declared to have ended, peaking at $40 billion and accounting for 0.8 percent of personal income in the second quarter of 1992 (it was 0.5 percent of personal income at the bottom of the recession in the first quarter of 1991). This reflected the sluggish rise in employment in the recovery following the recession, as employment first began rising in 1993. Unemployment insurance benefits then declined to annual levels of $22 billion in 1995 and 1996. Employment and unemployment are covered in Chapters 8 and 9.

5. The decision to spend or the decision to save is a chicken-and-egg question of which comes first. Both are probably involved in household actions.

6. Glenn B. Canner, Charles A. Luckett, and Thomas A. Durkin, "Mortgage Financing," *Federal Reserve Bulletin*, August 1990.

7. Jonathan McCarthy, "Debt, Delinquencies, and Consumer Spending," *Current Issues in Economics and Finance,* Federal Reserve Bank of New York, February 1997.

8. Lawrence B. Lindsey, "Statement Before the Committee on Banking and Financial Services of the U.S. House of Representatives," *Federal Reserve Bulletin,* November 1996, pp. 1000–1007.

9. Ibid.

10. Use of disposable personal income instead of personal income in the denominator of the consumer debt burden measure raises the proportion by about 2 to 3 percentage points, but the movements over time are similar in both measures.

5
BUSINESS PROFITS, NONRESIDENTIAL INVESTMENT, AND HOUSING

This chapter has two parts: (1) the relationship between business profits and nonresidential investment in structures and equipment, and (2) the short-term and long-terms factors affecting new housing investment.

The data on profits, investment, and housing are components of the gross domestic product (Chapter 3). They are prepared quarterly by the Bureau of Economic Analysis in the U.S. Department of Commerce. Other data sources used in analyzing investment and housing are noted in the chapter.

BUSINESS PROFITS AND NONRESIDENTIAL INVESTMENT

Business investment in nonresidential structures and equipment provides the industrial capacity to produce goods and services for household, business, government, and export markets. These capital investments raise economic growth and productivity (Chapters 3 and 10). They cover all privately owned buildings (e.g., factories, offices, stores), nonbuilding structures (e.g., roads, power plants, telephone lines, oil and gas well drilling), machinery, vehicles, computers, furniture, and other equipment lasting two or more years. The structures and equipment are used for first-time investments in new businesses and to expand, replace, and modernize existing capital facilities in for-profit, not-for-profit, farm, and nonfarm activities. The dollar value of the purchased structures and equipment depreciates over the life span of each item and thus becomes an annual cost of production, which appears as depreciation allowances on business income tax returns and in the income side of the gross domestic product (Chapter 3).

The share of nonresidential investment in the gross domestic product (GDP) typically ranged from 9 to 11 percent from the 1950s to the 1990s, with structures accounting for 3 to 4 percent and equipment for 6 to 7 percent. The overall proportion generally rose from 9 percent in the 1950s to a peak of 13 percent in

Figure 5.1a **Business Cycle Movements of GDP, Business Profits, and Nonresidential Investment, 1960s to 1990s: Expansions**

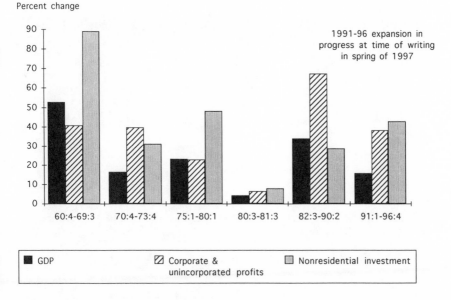

Percent change

1991-96 expansion in progress at time of writing in spring of 1997

■ GDP   ☑ Corporate & unincorporated profits   ☐ Nonresidential investment

Note: Based on U.S. Bureau of Economic Analysis data in chained (1992) dollars. Number after colon is quarter of year.

1981, then gradually declined to 9 percent in the early 1990s, and subsequently turned up, reaching 10.4 percent in 1996. The equipment component rose faster than the GDP and the structures component rose slower than the GDP over the period, resulting in the equipment share of the GDP rising and the structures share of the GDP declining. In 1996, equipment accounted for 7.6 percent and structures for 2.8 percent of the GDP. The dominance of equipment reflects the more rapid replacement of deteriorating and outmoded equipment than structures, and the increasingly efficient use of space within buildings.

Figures 5.1a and 5.1b show the cyclical movements of inflation-adjusted GDP and nonresidential investment from the 1960s to the 1990s. The figures indicate that structures and equipment spending is noticeably more volatile than the overall economy, increasing more than the GDP in five of the six expansions, and declining more than the GDP in five of the six recessions.[1] The sharp cyclical patterns arise because such investment is often deferrable, and it is difficult to anticipate the demand for goods and services produced with these capital facilities. Investment is deferrable because businesses can often make do with existing facilities, although doing so may result in profits below

Figure 5.1b **Business Cycle Movements of GDP, Business Profits, and Nonresidential Investment, 1960s to 1990s: Recessions**

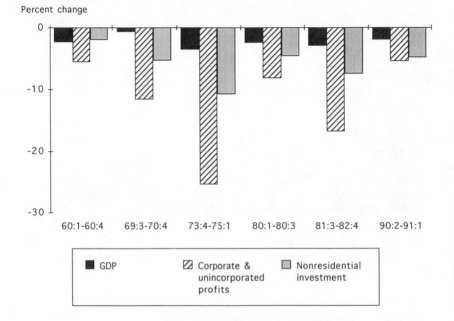

Percent change

Note: Based on U.S. Bureau of Economic Analysis data in chained (1992) dollars. Number after colon is quarter of year.

their potential: such facilities are less efficient than more modern technology would allow and are unable to meet sudden surges in demand. The difficulty of anticipating demand results in waves of optimism and pessimism, which in turn lead to substantial additions of capital facilities during expansions, only to be followed by overcapacity in recessions and accompanying deep cutbacks in investment outlays. The Dun & Bradstreet Corporation publishes quarterly measures of business optimism based on surveys of executives' expectations for sales and profits.

The Role of Profits

Because the basic purpose of business is to make a profit, anticipated profits are the engine that drives investments in nonresidential capital facilities. Anticipated profits are affected by perceptions of whether trends in past profits will continue at similar rates or if the future movements will turn decidedly higher or lower.

Profits are sales of goods and services less the costs of producing the goods and services, and as a residual reflect the movements of both sales and costs.

Sales are the outcome of the demand and price for a firm's product. Costs represent the firm's purchases of materials and services, wages paid to its workers, and other expenses. If profits are rising and markets are expanding, business tends to be optimistic that markets for its products will grow; it is thus encouraged to invest in new facilities to supply those markets. In contrast, during periods of declining profits and shrinking markets, there is little urgency to expand productive capacity, and a greater share of capital investments is used for replacing and modernizing existing facilities in order to lower production costs.

Profits provide financing for structures and equipment investments in two ways. First, as internally generated funds from company operations, profits provide money to buy the capital facilities. Second, a business's profits are a key factor in lenders' and investors' decisions to provide external funds through bank loans, debt instruments (e.g., bonds), and equity capital (e.g., stock).

There was a long-term decline in profits as a percentage of the GDP from 24 percent in the late 1940s and early 1950s to 11 percent in the early 1980s. The number then generally rose, reaching a high of 15.8 percent in 1996. The long-term relative decline in profits is difficult to explain, other than to state that business as a whole did not pass along costs into higher prices sufficiently to maintain profit margins, apparently because demand for its goods and services was not considered strong enough to sustain the higher prices. Other explanations, such as that profits in the earlier years were too high or that business feared government antitrust actions or price controls if prices were increased to maintain the earlier profit margins, are difficult to substantiate.

Figures 5.1a and 5.1b also show the cyclical pattern of business profits. The profits measure, which includes the total of both corporate and unincorporated business profits, is adjusted for inflation by the implicit price deflator for the business sector component of the GDP. During expansions, business profits showed no consistent pattern of rising faster or slower than the GDP and nonresidential investment, but during recessions business profits typically declined far more than both the GDP and nonresidential investment. This reflects the fact of profits being a residual of sales less costs. During expansions, sales and costs move in relatively similar patterns; but during recessions, sales declined much more than costs, because many costs are "fixed" limiting a firm's flexibility to reduce them if the enterprise stays in business.

Figures 5.2a and 5.2b show the cyclical movements of inflation-adjusted business profits and the investment components of structures and equipment from the 1960s to the 1990s. During expansions, equipment investments typically increase much faster than those for structures. The small increase in structures investment in the 1991–97 expansion reflects the continued decline in structures investments from the 1990–91 recession well into the subsequent recovery, with the upturn first occurring in the second quarter of 1994. During recessions, equipment de-

Figure 5.2a **Business Cycle Movements of Business Profits and Nonresidential Investment, 1960s to 1990s: Expansions**

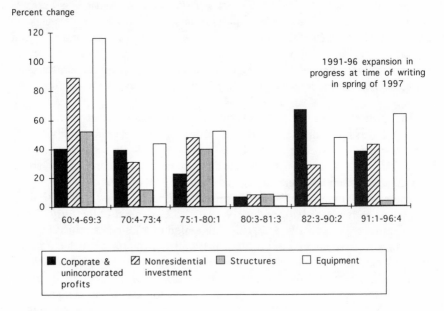

Note: Based on U.S. Bureau of Economic Analysis data in chained (1992) dollars. Number after colon is quarter of year.

clined more than structures in four of the six recessions (structures increased in the 1960 recession).

GDP, Profits, and Nonresidential Investment

The growth of the economy represented by the gross domestic product (GDP) and private enterprise incentives represented by business profits are underlying macroeconomic factors affecting investments in structures and equipment. Figures 5.3a and 5.3b show the long-term relationships from 1959 to 1996 between (1) the GDP and nonresidential investment, and (2) business profits and nonresidential investment. The black diamonds are the actual plotting points of the individual years at which the GDP on the horizontal axis intersects nonresidential investment on the vertical axis (Figure 5.3a), and at which business profits on the horizontal axis intersects nonresidential investment on the vertical axis (Figure 5.3b). The white diamonds represent the long-term average relationship in both figures.

Both figures indicate a direct relationship with the long-term trend line sloping upward to the right. This indicates that the GDP (Figure 5.3a) and business

Figure 5.2b **Business Cycle Movements of Business Profits and Nonresidential Investment, 1960s to 1990s: Recessions**

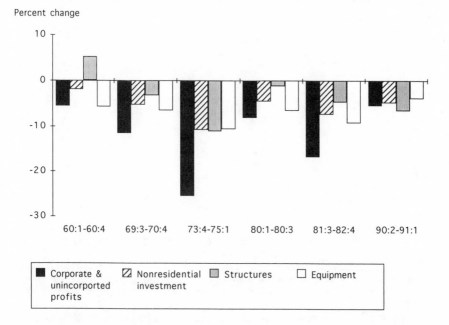

Note: Based on U.S. Bureau of Economics Analysis data in chained (1992) dollars. Number after colon is quarter of year.

profits (Figure 5.3b) typically move in the same direction as nonresidential investment. Generally there is a closer relationship between the GDP and nonresidential investment than between business profits and nonresidential investment. This is apparent in the dispersion of the individual years around the long-term line, where the black diamonds are closer to the white diamonds in Figure 5.3a than they are in Figure 5.3b. It suggests that the growth of production governs year-to-year nonresidential investments more closely than do the more volatile yearly movements of business profits.

Capacity Utilization and Nonresidential Investment

As a supplement to the GDP and business profits, capacity utilization rates (CURs) in the manufacturing, mining, and electric and gas utilities industries provide an additional perspective on the factors driving nonresidential investment. The CURs indicate the proportion of capacity in structures and equipment facilities used in production. For example, if a factory with the capacity to produce 1,000 cans of paint a month actually produces 800 cans a month, its

Figure 5.3a **GDP versus Nonresidential Investment: 1959–96**

Structures & equipment investment (billions of 1992 dollars)

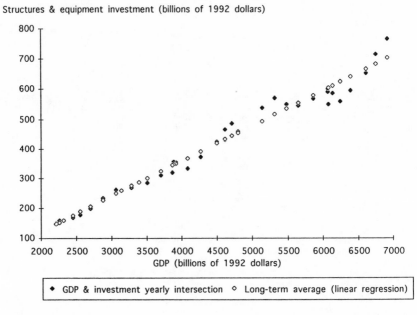

GDP (billions of 1992 dollars)

| ◆ GDP & investment yearly intersection | ○ Long-term average (linear regression) |

Note: Based on U.S. Bureau of Economic Analysis data in chained (1992) dollars.

utilization rate is 80 percent. Mathematically, the CUR is the ratio of production in the numerator and capacity in the denominator. The measure of unused capacity is obtained by subtracting the utilization rate from 100 percent. In practice, preparation of the capacity measures in the various industries is often very indirect and represents only a broad order of magnitude. The CUR measures are prepared monthly by the Federal Reserve Board.[2]

Theoretically, the direction and level of CURs indicate the demand for nonresidential investment and the degree of inflationary pressure in the economy. Rising CURs tend to reduce unit costs of production for a time, as the existing stock of structures and equipment produces a greater volume of goods. The cost advantage of the larger volume (increasing returns to scale) continues until the utilization rate reaches a level at which further increases in production raise unit costs because of machinery breakdowns, increasing use of outmoded and less reliable equipment, hiring of less productive workers as unemployment falls, and laxness by managements in holding down costs.[3]

The specific point at which the turnaround occurs on costs, and consequently on structures and equipment investment and on inflation, varies among industries and is hard to quantify precisely. The observed turnaround zone is based on movements of the data—it does not mean that company decisions to invest or

Figure 5.3b **Business Profits versus Nonresidential Investment: 1959–96**

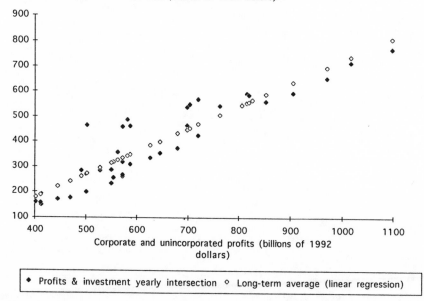

Structures & equipment investment (billions of 1992 dollars)

Corporate and unincorporated profits (billions of 1992 dollars)

◆ Profits & investment yearly intersection ○ Long-term average (linear regression)

Note: Based on U.S. Bureau of Economic Analysis data in chained (1992) dollars.

change prices are linked to a particular CUR zone. The rising production costs at the higher utilization rates spur companies to reduce costs by increasing capacity through new investment in structures and equipment. By contrast, relatively low and falling CURs reduce business incentives to expand capacity, and replacements of run-down and outmoded capacity account for greater shares of nonresidential investment during such periods. Analogously, increasing production costs foster higher prices, and decreasing costs foster stable or declining prices.

CURs are provided only for the manufacturing, mining, and utilities industries. Although these industries cover a limited part of the overall economy, they are capital intensive and so have a significant impact on capital investment. For example, they accounted for 21 percent of the GDP and 40 percent of nonresidential investment in 1994.

Figure 5.4 shows the relationship between the CUR for the total of all manufacturing, mining, and utilities industries and the annual change in inflation-adjusted nonresidential investment. The long-term average line slopes upward to the right, indicating a direct relationship between the CUR and investment in which both indicators typically move in the same direction, which would be theoretically expected. The individual years are also quite widely dispersed

Figure 5.4 **Capacity Utilization versus Nonresidential Investment: 1967–96**

Structures & equipment investment annual change (percent)

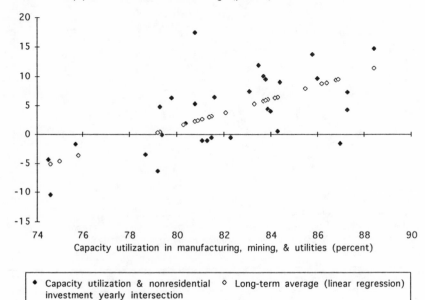

Capacity utilization in manufacturing, mining, & utilities (percent)

| ◆ Capacity utilization & nonresidential investment yearly intersection | ◇ Long-term average (linear regression) |

Note: Based on Federal Reserve Board and U.S. Bureau of Economic Analysis data in chained (1992) dollars.

around the long-term line, however, which means that the relationship varies widely from year to year.

Another factor complicating the relationship between the CUR and investment is the CUR's tendency to function as a threshold in this relationship, or what is sometimes referred to as a "flashpoint." That is, above a particular CUR level, businesses are assumed to increase structures and equipment expenditures substantially to expand capacity in order to meet the increased demand for their products, while below the threshold businesses are assumed to retrench capital spending and concentrate on modernizing by replacing inefficient and outmoded facilities rather than on expanding capacity. The CUR threshold for all manufacturing industries is sometimes thought to be in the 83–85 percent zone. Statistical analyses of such thresholds are at best very weak, however.

New Orders for Nondefense Capital Equipment

The most concrete short-term advance indicator of nonresidential investments is the commitment of company funds to begin work on an investment project. Such information is included in the Census Bureau survey data on new orders received by manufacturers of nondefense capital goods. These monthly data are used by The Conference Board in preparing the system of leading indicators (Chapter 13).

The reader should keep in mind a few basic differences between the data on equipment orders on the one hand, and nonresidential investments on the other. First, the equipment orders data exclude construction work on structures. Second, the orders data are for part or all of an investment project, but they do not specify when the spending for the project will occur. This is particularly pertinent for large-scale projects with lead times of more than one year. Third, the orders data do not give precise coverage of equipment purchases by American business because they exclude U.S. imports of capital equipment, while they include U.S. exports of capital equipment that are not part of investment in the United States.

The analyst should follow several steps in monitoring the strength and outlook for nonresidential investment. The first is to focus on the movements of the GDP and business profits. Generally, the linkage between the GDP and investment is closer to that between profits and investment; however, there is more confidence in the analysis if both the GDP and profits show similar movements. The next step is to compare the level and movements of capacity utilization with the pattern of investment. While the capacity utilization relationship is weaker than the GDP and profits analyses, it is a check on those approaches. On the most current basis, the data on manufacturers' orders for capital goods are an early indicator of concrete company actions taken on equipment investment.

HOUSING

The housing component of private investment covers the value of new construction of privately owned single-family (including townhouse) and multifamily permanent-site housing units, mobile home housing units, nonhousekeeping dormitories, fraternity and sorority houses, and doctors' and nurses' homes, and improvements consisting of additions, alterations, and major replacements to existing residential structures. The residential investment category of the gross domestic product (GDP) also includes brokers' commissions on the sale of new and existing housing and the net purchase of existing residential structures between the private and public sectors. After reviewing overall trends based on all residential investment, this section focuses on the new housing unit component—single-family homes, townhouses, apartments, and mobile homes.

Table 5.1 shows that the component shares of residential investment are dominated by new housing units, accounting for 62 percent of the total in 1996. They are followed by improvements (26 percent) and brokers' real estate commissions (13 percent). On a rounded basis, these represent the entire 100 percent.

Table 5.1

Residential Investment: 1996

	Billions of dollars	Percent
Total	303.0	100.0
New housing units	189.2	62.4
Single-family	155.2	51.2
Multifamily	20.6	6.8
Mobile homes	13.5	4.5
Improvements	75.4	24.9
Brokers' commissions	39.4	13.0
Other (nonhousekeeping)	0.1	0.03
Net purchases of used structures		
between the private and public sectors	(1.1)	−0.4

Source: U.S. Bureau of Economic Analysis.
Note: Details do not equal totals due to rounding.

Residential investment has not grown as fast as the overall economy from the 1960s to the 1990s. Residential investment as a percentage of the GDP rose from 4.6 percent in the 1960s to 5 percent in the 1970s, and then declined to 4.4 percent in the 1980s and 4 percent in the mid-1990s. This mainly reflects the slowdown in population and household growth from the 1960s to the 1990s (future demographic trends are covered under Long-term Factors below). In addition, it reflects the durability of housing, because if housing is properly maintained, it has an exceptionally long life. Also, most of the substandard housing existing before World War II has been replaced.

Although the residential investment share of the GDP is small compared with other components, it has secondary and cyclical impacts that are not apparent from size alone. The secondary impacts result from the tendency for the purchase of a new home to generate additional spending on household appliances, furniture, and other consumer durables.[4] The cyclical impact has two aspects. In terms of timing, the number of housing starts, building permits issued by local governments for housing construction, and the value of residential investment in inflation-adjusted dollars are all classified as leading indicators of the overall economy—turning up in a recession before the recovery begins and turning down in an expansion before the recession begins (Chapter 13).[5] In a short-term perspective, this tends to stabilize the cyclical aspects of the economy. But Figures 5.5a and 5.5b indicate that residential construction increases the volatility of business cycles.

Figures 5.5a and 5.5b show the cyclical movements of residential investment and the GDP from the 1960s to the 1990s. Residential investment increased more than the GDP in four of the six expansions during this period. The exceptions

Figure 5.5a **Business Cycle Movements of GDP and Housing, 1960s to 1990s: Expansions**

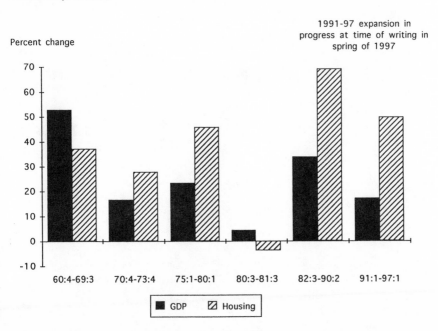

Note: Based on U.S. Bureau of Economics Analysis data in chained (1992) dollars. Number after colon is quarter of year.

were the 1960s expansion when residential investment rose less than the GDP, and the 1980–81 expansion when residential investment declined. Residential investment declined more than the GDP in five of the six recessions. The exception was the 1969–70 recession, when residential investment increased.

Figure 5.6 shows the movement of privately owned housing starts from 1959 to 1996. The annual average for the period is 1.5 million starts. The peak levels of over 2 million units occurred in the early and late 1970s, and the low levels of slightly above 1 million units occurred in the mid-1960s, mid-1970s, early 1980s, and early 1990s. The year-to-year movements are quite volatile. There is a slight decline in the long-term average line.

New Housing Demand

The market for new housing reflects both long-term and short-term factors. The long-term factors determine the number and cost of housing units needed over a period of about a decade, and the short-term factors affect the yearly movements that vary around the average annual levels implied by the long-term needs.

Figure 5.5b **Business Cycle Movements of GDP and Housing, 1960s to 1990s: Recessions**

Percent change

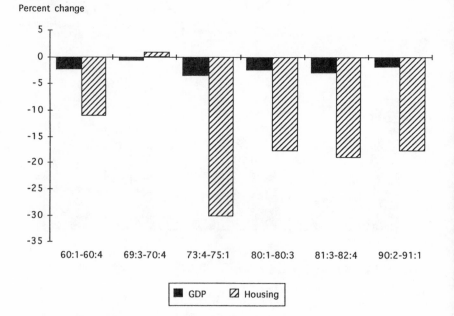

Note: Based on U.S. Bureau of Economic Analysis data in chained (1992) dollars. Number after colon is quarter of year.

Long-term Factors[6]

Over the long run, the market for new housing construction is driven mainly by demographic trends of population and households that include both national totals and geographic subnational migrations. Population trends are associated with birth and death rates, immigration and emigration between the United States and other countries, and regional migration between localities within the United States. Household formation reflects the tendency for individuals to set up separate living quarters (a household includes a family, a single person living alone, or unrelated persons sharing a house or apartment). The number of households is determined by marriage and divorce rates, adult children moving out of their parents' homes or moving back with their parents, and unrelated individuals sharing a house or apartment. Based on these demographic factors, the number of households is expected to increase by 1.2 million annually from the late 1990s to 2010.

Secondary long-term factors for new housing include the replacement of existing housing removed from the housing inventory. The lost housing results

Figure 5.6 **Private Housing Starts: 1959–96**

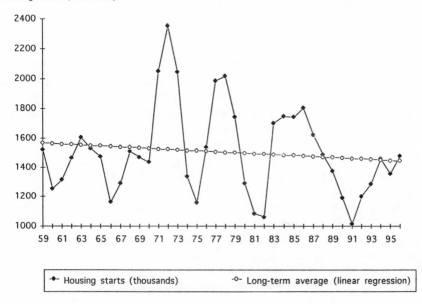

Housing starts (thousands)

```
-•- Housing starts (thousands)          -○- Long-term average (linear regression)
```

Note: Based on U.S. Bureau of the Census data.

from destruction due to natural disasters such as fires, floods, hurricanes, and earthquakes, deliberate demolition of substandard housing, and the net effects of conversions between residential and nonresidential use and between single-family and multifamily housing. The secondary new housing demand also includes the market for second homes. The net effect of the housing stock removals and the second home market is projected at 300,000 housing units annually from the late 1990s to 2010.

The combination of 1.2 million new households plus the 300,000 housing units associated with replacements of the lost housing stock and the demand for second homes leads to an annual average market for 1.5 million new housing units from the late 1990s to 2010. Because the household projections represent national totals, however, they do not include the effect of new housing demand due to geographic migration within the United States. Allowing for an additional 200,000 housing units to accommodate households that move from one community to another, when some communities gain more households than they lose to other communities, the total annual level of new housing units needed from the late 1990s to 2010 is 1.7 million.[7]

In addition to the above factors, which focus on the number of housing units, the size and amenities of the housing units determine their costs and the residential investment dollar expenditures. These are affected by the demand for single-family housing and townhouses in contrast to apartment dwellings and mobile homes, as single-family and townhouse structures have more costly construction costs than apartment housing and mobile homes for each housing unit. Generally, the demand for single family housing and townhouses is greatest for households in the 35–54-year-old age groups, while that for apartment housing is largest in the 34-and-under year-old age group. Projected household trends between the late 1990s and 2010 indicate little change in the age distribution between households in the under 34-year-old and the 35–54-year-old groups, which suggest little change in the distribution between single-family and apartment housing during the fifteen-year period.

The size and amenities of permanent-site housing units and mobile homes, such as the number of rooms, bathrooms, and comfort features, are largely determined by affordability, which is reflected in household income levels and its distribution. Unlike future household trends, which are importantly determined by the known births in previous years, future household incomes and the distribution of household incomes are more difficult to project because they are driven by problematic factors of economic growth and the distribution of incomes in the various low-, middle-, and high-income categories.

Short-term Factors

While housing demand from year to year reflects the long-term factors noted above, it also fluctuates in the short term. These movements reflect the effects of business cycle expansions and recessions on employment, interest rates, and inflation. In expansions, as employment and incomes rise, more households have sufficient income to qualify for mortgage loans to buy housing or to rent costlier new apartments, both of which stimulate residential investment. This increase in purchasing power is partially offset during expansions by higher inflation and mortgage interest rates and the resultant higher cost of housing, but the net effect is increased housing demand and residential investment, except for the last phase of an expansion when housing demand turns down, as noted previously. The opposite occurs in recessions, when falling employment lessens the demand for housing, although this decline during recessions is tempered by reduced inflation and interest rates, the accompanying slower rise or the decline in housing costs, and the earlier upturn in housing construction than in the recovery of the overall economy, as noted previously.

Figure 5.7 shows the relationship of mortgage interest rates and housing starts from 1963 to 1996. The interest rate data reflect the annual average rate charged on mortgages for new single-family homes (interest rates for new multifamily housing have similar movements). Each black diamond shows the average mortgage interest rate (horizontally) and the number of housing starts (vertically) for a particular year during the period. The long-term average of white diamonds

Figure 5.7 **Mortgage Interest Rates versus Private Housing Starts: 1963–96**

Private housing starts (thousands)

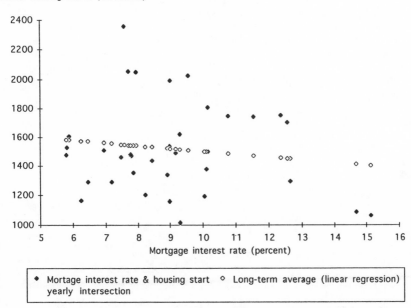

Mortgage interest rate (percent)

| ◆ | Mortage interest rate & housing start | ○ | Long-term average (linear regression) |
| | yearly intersection | | |

Note: Based on Federal Housing Finance Board and U.S. Bureau of the Census data.

slopes downward to the right, indicating an inverse relationship in which interest rates and housing starts typically move in opposite directions, which would be expected theoretically. Nevertheless, the individual years vary widely around the long-term line, with relatively large differences in the year-to-year movements.

Figure 5.8 shows the relationship between unemployment and housing starts from 1959 to 1996. As with interest rates, there is an inverse relationship between unemployment and housing starts, which also is intuitively expected. Similarly, there is a wide dispersion of the individual years around the long-term line, indicating a large variation in the yearly movements. Analogous calculations comparing employment and employment growth with housing starts resulted in even weaker relationships.

The absence of strong statistical relationships between interest rates and unemployment on the one hand and housing starts on the other does not diminish their importance in household decisions on whether and when to buy a house or apartment. The short-term housing market is obviously far more complex than would be revealed in simple comparisons of single economic indicators with housing starts.

This points up the difficulty of using national relationships for forecasting

Figure 5.8 **Unemployment Rate versus Housing Starts: 1959–96**

Private housing starts (thousands)

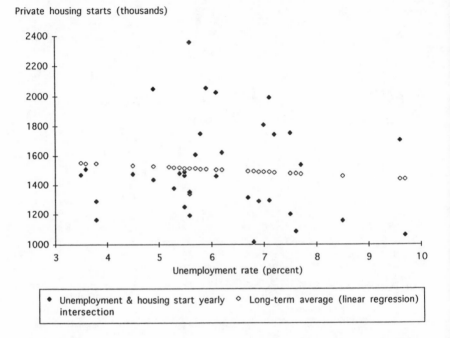

Note: Based on U.S. Bureau of Labor Statistics and U.S. Bureau of the Census data.

housing demand. It suggests that because of large variations in the demographics and incomes among local housing markets, short-term forecasts of housing demand are more relevant for metropolitan areas than for the nation as a whole.

In anticipating the future demand for housing, the analyst should consider both long-term factors such as demographic trends and short-term cyclical movements in the economy. Unless substantial changes are expected in household formation or in private or government programs to replace substandard housing, the long-term demand is shaped largely by existing demographic trends. By contrast, short-term cyclical forecasts of housing demand are subject to much greater uncertainty because of the complexity of the interactions among the factors affecting the short-term movements.

REVIEW QUESTIONS

- What makes investments in nonresidential structures and equipment have extreme cyclical movements?
- Distinguish the differing roles of the GDP and business profits in influencing nonresidential investment.

- Why is capacity utilization a useful indicator of nonresidential investment if it covers only 21 percent of the overall economy?
- How do manufacturers' orders for capital equipment differ in nature from the GDP, profits, and capacity utilization as indicators of nonresidential investment?
- Residential investment accounts for only 4 percent of the GDP, but it gets a lot of analytic attention. Why?
- Why is the distinction made between short-term and long-term factors affecting housing forecasts?
- Although demographic trends are not typically a critical factor affecting short-term housing forecasts, give an example of when demographic movements can have a noticeable impact on such forecasts.

Extra Credit

- Why is the relationship between manufacturing capacity utilization and unit manufacturing costs not a simple one?
- Explain why homebuilding activity turns down before the end of a cyclical expansion and turns up before an overall recovery begins.

NOTES

1. The decline in recessions is more than shown here because nonresidential investment typically declines after a recession has ended and turns up into a cyclical recovery. Thus, nonresidential investment is a lagging indicator in recessions in the system of leading indicators (Chapter 13).

2. See Chapter 11 under Inflation and Capacity Utilization for a description of the CUR methodology.

3. In prosperous times, managers probably have less pressure to seek more efficient operations than they do in periods of slow growth or recessions, when businesses tend to be more aggressive in cutting costs. These practices over the business cycle are difficult to quantify, but they are intuitively plausible and also appear anecdotally in the press. They are related in the economic literature to the idea of "X-efficiency," which typically associates differences in competitive pressures in monopolistic and more competitive industries. X-efficiency may have less of an impact in the era of global competition and business downsizing of the 1990s compared with previous periods, but there is no such indication at the time of this writing in the spring of 1997. Harvey Leibenstein, "Allocative Efficiency vs. 'X-Efficiency,' " *American Economic Review,* June 1996.

F.M. Schereer, *Industrial Market Structure and Economic Performance,* 2d ed. (Rand McNally, 1980), pp. 464–66.

4. Technically, residential investment in the GDP is represented by the construction of housing. The reference in the text to purchases of housing is used because it is associated with the new homeowner, who has a tendency to buy appliances, furniture, and other items.

5. A housing start is designated in the month when the excavation work begins for the foundation of the building. Each single-family house, townhouse, and apartment in a multifamily building is counted as one housing start. But because of differences in the

size, amenities, and structural aspects of the various types of housing, the amount of construction work done is measured in the dollar value of housing construction.

6. Two good discussions of long-term housing factors were published in the mid-1990s. The long-term outlook in this section is based on the data and projections presented in these studies and on the author's analysis of the data. See Joint Center of Housing Studies of Harvard University, *The State of the Nation's Housing* (National Association of Home Builders of the United States, 1996); and *Home Builders Forecast*, December 1995.

7. This geographic movement includes several housing market adjustments in the areas that have a net decline in households. For example, some housing left behind is converted to office and retail use. There may simply be higher housing vacancy rates. And some houses may be sold at distressed prices.

6
THE UNITED STATES IN
THE WORLD ECONOMY

The term "continuing internationalization of the U.S. economy" refers to the growing interdependence of the U.S. economy with those of other nations in three major ways. One is the exports of goods and services produced in the United States and sold abroad, and the imports of goods and services produced in other countries and bought by U.S. residents. The second is the output and employment generated by foreign investments of U.S.-owned companies abroad and by foreign-owned companies in the United States. The third is financial investments in stocks and bonds by U.S. residents in foreign securities and by foreign residents in U.S. securities.

Foreign trade and foreign investments bring increasing competition and efficiencies into the U.S. economy, although they also bring dislocations of workers and firms. The increasing internationalization also increases the sensitivity of the U.S. economy to foreign economic and political developments.

This chapter first summarizes the methodological characteristics of the data on international transactions in the balance-of-payments measures and their relationship to the international data in the gross domestic product. It then highlights the factors affecting exports and imports of goods, services, and income on foreign investments, and their relationship to international investments.

METHODOLOGY

The data on international economic transactions comprise exports and imports of goods and services, income on foreign investments, and the international flows of money that pay for the foreign trade in goods and services and for the foreign investments in the United States and abroad. The statistical measures are prepared quarterly by the Bureau of Economic Analysis in the U.S. Department of Commerce. The international transactions data are often referred to as the balance of payments.

Table 6.1

U.S. International Transactions: 1996 (billions of dollars)

	Goods	Services	Investment income	Goods, services, and investment income
Exports	611.5	223.9	196.9	1,032.5
Imports	799.3	150.4	205.3	1,155.1
Balance (exports minus imports)	−187.8	73.5	−8.4	−122.6

Source: U.S. Bureau of Economic Analysis.
Note: Details do not equal totals due to rounding.

Foreign trade in goods covers agricultural, mineral, and manufactured items produced in the United States and sold abroad (exports), and such items produced in other countries and bought in the United States (imports). Foreign trade in services covers travel, transportation, royalties and license fees, insurance, telecommunications, and business services sold abroad by U.S. companies, and such services that foreign parties sell to the United States. It also covers U.S. military sales contracts, direct defense expenditures, and miscellaneous U.S. government services.

Foreign investment refers to purchases by U.S.-owned companies and U.S. residents of assets in other countries, and by foreign residents of assets in the United States. There are two broad categories of foreign investments. Foreign *direct* investment is defined as ownership or control, direct or indirect, by residents of one country of 10 percent or more of the voting securities of a corporation in another country, or the equivalent interest in an unincorporated enterprise. Foreign *portfolio* investment is the ownership or control of less than 10 percent of a company's voting securities, plus foreign party holdings of company and government bonds. Income on foreign investments covers the profits from direct investment, dividends on stocks, and interest. Income receipts represent returns to U.S. residents on U.S. investments abroad (exports), and income payments are returns to foreign residents on their investments in the United States (imports).

Table 6.1 shows the U.S. international transactions for goods, services, and investment income for 1996. Goods account for the major share, 59 percent of exports and 69 percent of imports. Service exports are larger than investment income receipts, while investment income payments are larger than service imports. The balance on goods, services, and income is −$123 billion, which reflects the excess of goods imports that is only partially reduced by the excess of services exports; there is a relatively small excess of investment income payments.

Table 6.2

Statistical Discrepancy: 1990–96 (billions of dollars)

1990	46.5
1991	−26.8
1992	−23.1
1993	43.6
1994	13.7
1995	31.5
1996	−53.1

Source: U.S. Bureau of Economic Analysis.

Conceptually, the sum of foreign trade in goods and services, income on foreign investments, and unilateral transfers abroad such as personal remittances that foreign workers send home and government-to-government grants on the one hand, must equal the capital flows between nations that are used to finance these transactions on the other. In practice, however, these opposite sides of the coin do not equal each other due to statistical limitations in the data. The difference is referred to as the statistical discrepancy. A positive statistical discrepancy means that net capital inflows of money into the United States exceed those indicated by the data on trade, investment income, and unilateral transfers, while a negative statistical discrepancy indicates that net capital outflows of money from the United States exceed that indicated by the trade, investment, and unilateral transactions. The statistical discrepancy reflects omissions in all categories, but the major problem is generally considered to be in the capital rather than the trade transactions. The statistical discrepancy is a net figure of the sum of the individual categories, some of which overstate and some of which understate the true values. Thus, some of the errors are offsetting, which means that the statistical discrepancy is smaller than would appear if all the errors both above and below the true values were aggregated, that is, if they were summed without regard to sign. But such a number cannot be calculated because the true values are not known.

Table 6.2 shows the statistical discrepancy from 1990 to 1996. It ranged from $46 billion in 1990 to −$53 billion in 1996. The largest year-to-year movements were in 1990–91 and 1995–96, with noticeable but smaller movements in other years. Large yearly movements in the discrepancy reflect a fair amount of inconsistency in the data underlying the measures from year to year.

Exports and imports of goods and services also enter into the calculation of the gross domestic product (GDP). As discussed in Chapter 3, exports and imports are counted in the GDP as a net number, exports minus imports. The net figure is a relatively small number, ranging from about +1 to −2 percent of the GDP yearly from the 1960s to the 1990s, with the sign depending on whether exports are larger or smaller than imports. This net share of the GDP shifted from a surplus of exports averaging 0.3 percent of the GDP in the 1960s to a surplus of imports averaging 1 percent of the GDP in the 1990s. The net number is a bookkeeping technique to avoid double counting in the GDP because the GDP includes imports in the consumption, investment, and government categories. The net number grossly understates the importance of foreign trade in the economy. As indicated below, exports account for over 10 percent of the GDP and imports for over 11 percent of the GDP in the 1990s. But the net number is relevant for assessing America's competitive position in the world economy, the foreign exchange value of the dollar, and possibly the extent of protectionist sentiment. These factors, in turn, influence the volumes of exports and imports.

The international transactions data on goods and services are modified slightly for inclusion in the GDP. The differences in descending order of importance are the geographic coverage of U.S. territories and Puerto Rico, imputed interest for certain financial services provided without payment, and the treatment of gold. Other international transactions in the balance of payments cover capital movements for foreign investments, bank and nonbank financial transactions, and government official reserve assets. While these capital movements are not part of the GDP, they reflect economic activity that affects the foreign exchange value of the dollar, which in turn influences exports and imports of goods and services, and thereby the GDP.

Also, within the national income and product accounts, there is a difference in the treatment of exports and imports between the GDP and the gross national product (GNP), as noted in Chapter 3. The GDP does not measure international investment income of profits, dividends, and interest, or wage income of foreign workers when these factor incomes flow into or out of the United States. By contrast, the GNP includes these investment and wage flows. For example, the GNP treats profits from the operations of multinational firms abroad when the firm abroad is owned or controlled by U.S. parties as a receipt of factor income, and it treats profits of multinational firms operating in the United States when the firm is owned or controlled by foreign parties as a payment of factor income. In this regard, the GNP is consistent with the balance on goods, services, and income.

DEMAND FOR EXPORTS AND IMPORTS

The volumes of exports and imports are determined by three general economic factors: economic growth at home (for imports) and abroad (for exports), relative domestic prices for competing U.S. and foreign goods and services, and the foreign exchange value of the U.S. dollar. The ways in which these factors work are summarized below. In addition, exports and imports are affected by the quality of U.S. and foreign goods and services and other nonprice factors, including tariffs, quotas, and nontariff barriers such as domestic-content laws requiring that imported goods contain minimum amounts of domestically produced items.

Directional Impact of Factors Affecting Exports and Imports of Goods and Services

Demand factor	Exports	Imports
Economic growth abroad	Higher growth, higher U.S. exports	_____
Economic activity in U.S.	_____	Higher growth, higher imports
U.S. prices relative to foreign prices for the same item	Higher U.S. prices, lower exports	Higher U.S. prices, higher imports
Value of the U.S. dollar	Higher dollar, lower exports	Higher dollar, higher imports

The foreign trade of the United States became increasingly important in the overall economy from the 1960s to the 1990s. As a proportion of the gross domestic product (GDP), exports of goods and services averaged 10.5 percent and imports averaged 11.5 percent during 1990–96, compared with 4.9 percent for exports and 4.6 percent for imports in the 1960s. In 1996, the volume of both exports and imports was larger than consumer spending for durable goods, nonresidential investment, or housing investment, and the volume of imports was slightly larger than state and local government budget expenditures.

The relationship of exports and imports to American business cycles is more tenuous than those of the other GDP components because of factors outside the United States that affect foreign trade. For example, economic activity and price movements in the United States are not always paralleled in other countries, and the value of the dollar is affected by factors only partially influenced by American actions, such as interest rate differentials between the United States and other countries or political stability abroad.

Figures 6.1a and 6.1b show exports and imports of goods and services in relation to the GDP over the business cycles from the 1960s to the 1990s. Exports increased more than the GDP in five of the six expansions during the period. The exception was the 1980–81 expansion, when exports declined very slightly (the figure shows no change, not the actual decline). Imports increased more than the GDP in all six expansions. In the recessions, exports increased in five of the six cases. Imports decreased in four of the six recessions, and by much more than the decline in the GDP. The tendency of imports to follow

Figure 6.1a **Gross Domestic Product, Exports, and Imports, 1960s to 1990s: Expansions**

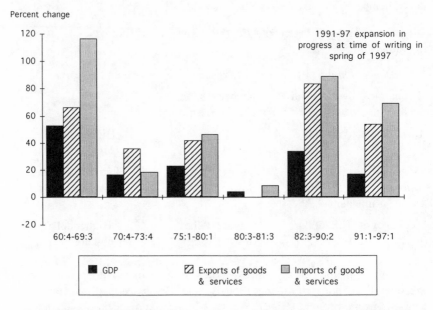

Note: Based on U.S. Bureau of Economic Analysis data in chained (1992) dollars. Number after colon is quarter of year.

business cycle movements more closely than exports reflects the fact that the income reduction resulting from a recession cuts U.S. demand for foreign-made items, but not the foreign demand for U.S. exports. Foreign demand for U.S. exports is affected by business cycles abroad, which may not coincide with U.S. cycles.

Relative Importance of Demand Factors

This section first discusses the relative importance of the general demand factors summarized above—economic growth in the United States and abroad, relative prices in the United States and abroad, and the value of the U.S. dollar. The section also discusses the relationships of the globalization of production and the terms of trade to exports and imports.

Economic Growth and Relative Prices

In assessing the importance of the three general factors driving exports and imports—economic activity at home and abroad, relative prices in the United

Figure 6.1b **Gross Domestic Product, Exports, and Imports, 1960s to 1990s: Recessions**

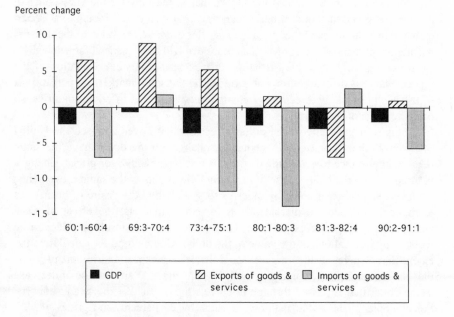

Note: Based on U.S. Bureau of Economic Analysis data in chained (1992) dollars. Number after colon is quarter of year.

States and foreign countries, and the value of the U.S. dollar, one must note that the relationships among these factors are not simple. For example, while exports are directly related to economic activity abroad, they also indirectly reflect economic activity at home: when business is booming in the United States, American companies may be less aggressive in marketing exports, while in recessions they may be more aggressive. Similarly, prices and exchange rates interact with each other, as an anticipated high rate of inflation in a country may reduce the value of its currency.

With these caveats as background, several studies in the 1980s indicated that economic growth at home and abroad (measured, for example, by the GDP) has a larger effect on exports and imports than do prices, although the differential lessens in later years.[1] For example, in the first year, a 1 percent change in GDP growth has two to four times the effect on exports and imports as does a 1 percent change in inflation. As of this writing in the spring of 1997, no similar studies have appeared since then, although there seems to be a consensus that the relationships have not changed significantly in the 1990s. This is a topic where new analyses are desirable.

Value of the U.S. Dollar

The foreign exchange value of the U.S. dollar is the price of the U.S. dollar in relation to the currency unit of other countries. That is, it is the amount of a foreign currency that can be purchased with a dollar. For example, the value of the dollar is the number of Japanese yen or Mexican pesos that will be exchanged for a dollar.

In one respect, the value of the dollar represents the stock valuation of the United States as a corporation that is traded on the stock market. As perceptions of the health of the U.S. economy change relative to that of other countries, so does the value of the dollar.

Changes in the value of the dollar affect relative prices between the United States and other countries. Conceptually, changes in the dollar have the same relative importance to economic activity as was noted above for prices. Changes in prices and in the value of the dollar do not always show the same movements, however. Prices are affected by other factors, including the desire of businesses to maintain or increase market shares in export markets, the effect of price changes on profit margins, and the willingness of sellers to allow prices to be dictated by fluctuations in the value of the dollar. One method for calculating the extent that changes in the value of the dollar affect export and import prices is the "passthrough rate," which estimates the percentage of an increase or decrease in the dollar that is passed through to change the prices of exports and imports. For example, if the dollar declines in value by 20 percent, and prices of U.S. exports (in foreign currency terms) decline by 15 percent, the passthrough is 75 percent (15 divided by 20). Using this same decline of 20 percent in the value of the dollar for U.S. imports, if the dollar price of U.S. imports rises by 10 percent, the passthrough is 50 percent (10 divided by 20).

Passthrough experience previously could be calculated from information provided in the U.S. import and export price indexes prepared by the U.S. Bureau of Labor Statistics. Unfortunately, these data are no longer available, due to budget cutbacks in statistical programs.

According to one widely cited theory, over the long run the value of the dollar is established according to the concept of purchasing power parity (PPP). This theory starts with a hypothesized period in which the American and other economies are considered to be in balance, with the existing unemployment, inflation, and foreign trade balances consistent with a sustainable steady rate of economic growth. The prices of goods and services in the United States and other countries, which are reflected in the value of the dollar in relation to currencies of those countries during this "equilibrium" period, are used as the base from which to calculate future price changes. As subsequent price movements in the U.S. and in foreign countries diverge (for example, U.S. prices rise faster than prices in England), the value of the dollar would fall proportionately to the relative rise of American prices in order to maintain the PPP of the base period between the dollar and the pound.

Despite the appeal of the theory, it is difficult to argue that foreign currency values typically move in accord with the PPP concept because (1) it is difficult to determine the base period when economies were in balance; and (2) the base period may become obsolete due to productivity changes, investment opportunities, resource supplies (such as discoveries of oil), interest rates, and political stability. Hence, the PPP concept is difficult to apply to economic events, particularly during periods when international economic relationships change substantially.

PPP is measured by the real exchange rate of the dollar. The real exchange rate is the nominal rate, which is the familiar one used in actual transactions, adjusted for price levels in the United States and other nations. Thus, the real exchange rate represents the value of the dollar in terms of the inflation-adjusted costs of U.S. exports and imports. Trade-weighted nominal and real measures of the value of the dollar are computed by combining the dollar exchange rates for several nations into a single figure by using the export and import trade volumes of the United States and the other nations as weights. The theoretical PPP concept works perfectly if the real value of the dollar is constant over time.[2] The real value of the dollar varies considerably over time, however, as noted below. Thus, the PPP is of little value in determining if the dollar is "overvalued" and likely to depreciate, or if it is "undervalued" and likely to appreciate.

Figure 6.2 shows Federal Reserve Board measures of the trade-weighted nominal and real value of the dollar from 1973 to 1996. Both have fluctuated widely and in similar patterns—declining from 1976 to 1980, rising sharply in the early 1980s and declining sharply in the late 1980s, and then with noticeably smaller fluctuations in the 1990s. Thus, the real exchange rate has not been constant, as posited by the PPP theory. The relatively close correspondence between the nominal and real exchange rates means that price inflation in the United States and other nations tends to be similar. The Morgan Guaranty Trust Company of New York and the Federal Reserve Bank of Dallas prepare measures of the nominal and real value of the dollar that include different countries' currencies and weight the export and import trade volumes differently. However, these measures also show a real exchange rate that fluctuates considerably and in patterns similar to those of the nominal rates.

Globalization of Production

"Globalization of production" refers to a long-term manufacturing trend in which some companies whose basic ownership and operations are in one country establish production plants in foreign countries. Examples are when a U.S. automaker (for example, General Motors) produces cars in Brazil and when a Japanese automaker (for example, Toyota) produces cars in the United States. American cars produced in Brazil are not a U.S. export, and Japanese cars produced in the United States are not a U.S. import. But the components and parts for these cars

Figure 6.2 **Value of the Dollar, 1973–96**

March 1973=100

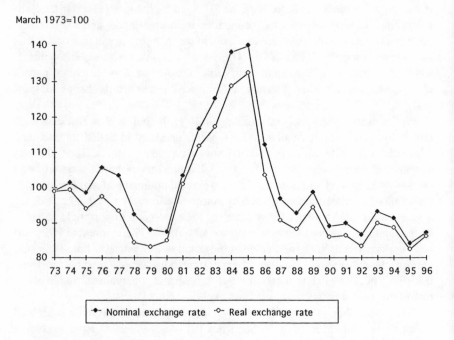

-•- Nominal exchange rate   -○- Real exchange rate

Note: Based on Federal Reserve Board data. Real = nominal adjusted for consumer price index changes in United States and abroad.

that are produced in the company's home country are exports and imports—the parts and components produced in the United States and incorporated in the cars made in Brazil are a U.S. export, and the parts and components produced in Japan and incorporated in the cars made in the United States are a U.S. import. Also, the profits attributable to these companies' foreign operations are incorporated in the income components of the balance of payments and the GNP, with profits of U.S. companies in Brazil being a U.S. receipt of factor income, and profits of Japanese companies in the United States being a U.S. payment of factor income.

The globalization of production is relatively small in terms of the overall output of the U.S. economy. Foreign companies operating in the U.S. averaged 6 percent of the U.S. gross domestic business product during 1990–94, rising from under 3 percent in the late 1970s and 5 percent in the late 1980s.[3] Employment in these foreign companies followed a pattern similar to that of the gross product. For example, as a proportion of private employment in the United States, foreign companies averaged 5 percent during 1990–94, compared with 4.5 percent in 1988 and 1989. Not reflected in these measures, however, is that most of the top jobs in a foreign-owned company are held by foreign nationals, rather than by U.S. citizens.

Most of the value of the output of the foreign companies operating in the United States is produced in the United States (referred to as "local content"), although the importation of foreign-made parts and components is not negligible. For example, of the total amount of purchase materials and services used in production, these companies purchased 80 percent from U.S. companies and imported 20 percent from abroad in 1991.[4]

For U.S. companies operating abroad in host countries that represent about 90 percent of U.S. company output abroad, the U.S. company output was 3 percent of the GDP of those countries in 1994. This 3 percent share of GDP is not strictly comparable to the 6 percent share of gross domestic business product (GDBP) noted above for foreign companies operating in the United States due to differences between GDP and GDBP and other statistical aspects of the two measures.[5] The 3 percent share of foreign-country GDP accounted for by U.S. companies operating abroad probably would be about 0.5 to 1 percentage point higher if it were fully consistent with the 6 percent share for foreign companies operating in the United States, but the actual difference is not known.[6]

The U.S. content of materials used by U.S. companies abroad was 9 percent, and the foreign content of materials used by those companies was 91 percent of the value of their production (sales and inventory change) in 1991.

Terms of Trade

The relative movements of export and import prices are tracked by the terms of trade, which is defined as the ratio of the price of exports (numerator) to the price of imports (denominator). When the terms of trade are rising (export prices rising more or falling less than import prices), export receipts are proportionately greater than import payments for the same quantity of exports and imports, which tends to cause a greater trade surplus or a lower trade deficit. And when the terms of trade are declining (export prices falling or rising less than import prices), the price relationships foster a higher trade deficit or a lower trade surplus.

The terms of trade are only a first approximation of the effect of price movements on the dollar value of exports and imports because they do not include the effects of price movements on quantities sold. For example, when a country's terms of trade are rising, it could receive more imports for a given level of exports, which could lead to a greater volume of imports than exports. In addition, measures of the terms of trade before 1984 are suspect for very long-term analysis because price information until then was based on "unit value indexes." Unit value indexes are affected by shifts in purchases of different quality merchandise in the same category and thus do not reflect price movements for the same product; for example, a shift in imports from lower-priced to higher-priced

Figure 6.3 **Terms of Trade for Exports and Imports of Goods and Services: 1959–96**

Ratio (1992=100)

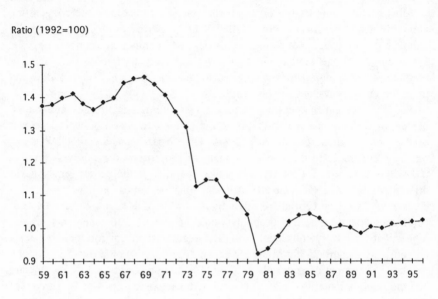

Note: Based on U.S. Bureau of Economic Analysis data. Export price index divided by import price index.

cars raises the import unit value index, even though the price of both models is unchanged. Beginning with 1984, however, the U.S. Bureau of Labor Statistics provides import and export price indexes that distinguish all goods, and a limited number of services, of different quality, which greatly enhance the validity of foreign trade price movements.

Figure 6.3 shows the terms of trade from 1959 to 1996 for exports and imports of goods and services based on the price indexes used in adjusting export and import values for inflation. The terms of trade declined from the 1.4 range in the 1960s to 0.9 in 1980, and after rebounding to slightly above 1 in the mid-1980s, fluctuated around 1 from 1987 to 1996. At the 1.0 level, the terms of trade are neutral, as the price level of all U.S. exports is the same as the price level of all U.S. imports. The essentially neutral movement in the terms of trade from the mid-1980s to the mid-1990s suggests that it is highly unlikely that prices of the types of goods and services that the U.S. exports in relation to the different composition of the goods and services that it imports significantly affect its balance of payments. Also, the movements from the mid-1980s to the mid-1990s are more reliable than the movements in previous periods because of the introduction of the new foreign trade price measures noted above.

Figure 6.4 **Balance on Goods, Services, and Investment Income, Surplus (+) and Deficit (–): 1963–96**

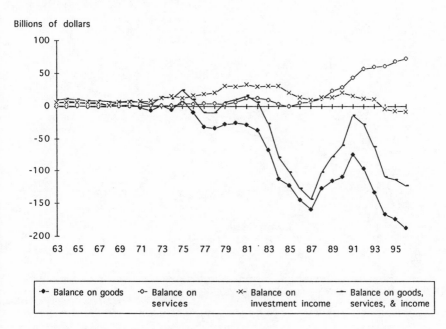

Billions of dollars

	Balance on goods	Balance on services	Balance on investment income	Balance on goods, services, & income

Note: Based on U.S. Bureau of Economic Analysis data.

Balance of Payments and External Debt

Figure 6.4 shows the balance of payments for the total of all international transactions and the main components goods, services, and investment income from 1963 to 1996. The dominant item is the balance on goods, as the movements of goods and the total of all transactions are similar. Goods began having a decided negative balance in the mid-1970s, reaching a low of $160 billion in 1987, and after rebounding to a smaller negative balance of $74 billion in 1991, goods declined again to a further low of $190 billion in 1996. The total of all international transactions had a continuing negative balance from the early 1980s to the 1990s. By contrast, the balances on services and investment income were generally positive, although with quite different movements. Thus, from 1985 to 1996, the services balance became increasingly positive, while the investment income balance declined from being positive to a negative position. The net effect from the 1970s to the 1990s of the varying movements of the components on the movement of the total of all international transactions was that while the total mirrored the movements of the goods component, the more positive balances of services and investment income resulted in (1) the total having a positive balance

Figure 6.5 **U.S. International Investment Position Using Current Cost Valuation: 1982–95**

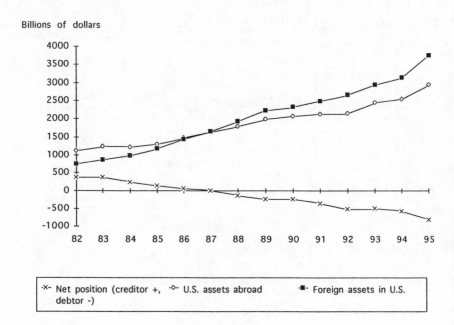

Billions of dollars

-×- Net position (creditor +, debtor -)   -◇- U.S. assets abroad   -■- Foreign assets in U.S.

Note: Based on U.S. Bureau of Economic Analysis data.

and goods having a negative balance, or (2) the total having a smaller negative balance than goods.

Figure 6.5 shows the U.S. international investment position from 1982 to 1996. As a result of the balance-of-payments deficits of the 1980s, foreigners have greater claims on the United States than the United States has on assets abroad for the first time since before World War I. The United States declined to its net debtor status of $11 billion in 1987, and this debt mushroomed to $814 billion by 1995. The increased net debt reflects the greater increases in foreign-owned assets in the United States compared with the increases in U.S.-owned assets abroad.

Figure 6.6 compares an alternative method of measuring the investment position with that in Figure 6.5. Estimates of the investment position in Figure 6.5 are based on the valuation of investment in current costs. Specifically, the direct investment tangible assets of structures, equipment, and land are valued in the prices of replacing them in the current period. The alternative measure is the market value. Market value of the direct investment position is based on indexes of stock market prices of companies, and thus also includes the market value of intangible assets such as patents, trademarks, management, and name recognition

Figure 6.6 **U.S. Net International Investment Position Using Alternative Valuation Methods: 1982–95**

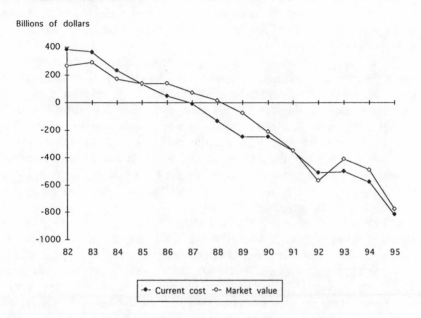

Note: Based on U.S. Bureau of Economic Analysis data.

(intangible assets are not included in the current-cost method). The current-cost and market value measures generally track each other, although one is not consistently higher than the other. Generally, the current-cost measure fluctuates less than the market value measure, which reflects the year-to-year volatility in stock market prices that are used in the market value calculations.

Typically, the deterioration in the U.S. balance of payments and the international investment position in the 1980s and 1990s is attributed to four main developments. First, during the 1980s, the U.S. economy as measured by the GDP grew faster than most other industrialized nations, which raised U.S. imports relative to exports. Only Japan's economy grew faster, but this growth did not lead to significantly higher imports from the United States due to nontariff barriers associated with government procurement, wholesale and retail trade distribution, and technical product standards that discriminate against foreign products in Japan. Second, during the first half of the 1980s the value of the dollar increased sharply due to high interest rates in the United States, resulting from heavy government borrowing to finance the large federal government budget deficits. These higher interest rates attracted foreign funds that in turn drove up the value of the dollar and made U.S. products more expensive in world markets; consequently, U.S. exports increased less than imports. Third, the influx of foreign funds attracted by these higher interest rates also caused greater income payments to foreigners on their investments in the United States. Fourth, Asian industrializing nations with wage rates much lower than those in the United States were increasingly competitive in the 1980s and made significant inroads in American markets.

The standard prescription for reversing the deterioration has been to undo the four developments of the 1980s that are blamed for causing the decline—that is, the United States should substantially reduce its federal government budget deficit, industrialized nations should promote faster growth in their economies through stimulative fiscal and monetary policies, Japan should reduce its non-tariff barriers, and the Asian industrializing nations should pay higher wages to their workers to reduce the differential with wages in industrialized countries. In fact, such changes occurred in varying degrees in two of the four categories in the 1990s—a lower U.S. federal government budget deficit, and a reduction in Japan's nontariff barriers.

Growth rates in other industrialized nations have not accelerated, however, although the governments and central banks of Germany and Japan have at times tried to stimulate their economies. Given the dominant impact of economic activity at home and abroad on U.S. exports and imports noted previously under Relative Importance of Demand Factors, this appears as a key link in any prospect for reducing the U.S. current account deficit and turning it into annual surpluses. The balance of payments must show continuing and large annual surpluses in order to reduce the net debtor position during the first decade of the twenty-first century. With respect to wage rates in the Asian and Latin American industrializing countries, they are so much lower than those in the United States that fundamental breakthroughs in the presence and clout of labor unions in those countries are necessary to lower the wage differentials to any meaningful extent. But such an influence of labor unions in those countries shows no sign of occurring in the late 1990s.

A basic problem with the prescribed changes is that they ignore the fact that the new economic environment of large U.S. balance-of-payments deficits has a life of its own. An economy is not like a driver in a car who, having taken a wrong turn, can simply turn around and drive back to the right road. The loss of markets by American companies in the United States and abroad has altered the economic landscape. Moreover, in hindsight the trend toward increasingly competitive foreign markets is of long duration. Although the decline in U.S. competitiveness accelerated rapidly during the 1980s, the decline actually appears to have begun in the early 1970s when the trade deficit in goods first emerged.

Thus, although the changes mentioned above would no doubt be conducive to a U.S. resurgence, they will not make the foreign competition go away. New foreign companies on the scene will continue to compete by moderating price increases and developing new and improved products to maintain and increase their share of world markets. To make a comeback, American companies must compete in terms of price, quality, and product specifications. Reviving the role of the United States in the world economy will require long-run commitments by American businesses to regain the prestige of U.S.-made products, including investing in new production facilities in the United States regardless of fluctuations in the value of the dollar.

What is the problem with chronic balance-of-payments deficits and growing debt to other nations? Imports and foreign investments in the United States are not intrinsically bad. In fact, they improve living conditions by competing with American industry through lower prices and higher quality products. But there is a problem when deficits and debt are large. Because current account deficits signify a loss of production and employment in the United States, large deficits suggest that better living conditions due to higher quality and lower prices from increased foreign competition will be outweighed by the loss of wage and profit income due to the lower economic activity in the United States, even though the U.S. unemployment rate in early 1997 of 5 percent was at its lowest level since 1973. While there are no quantitative measures of when deficits are "large," a problem is evident when American-made products for some items are difficult to find or when American products are, or are perceived to be, inferior. That has been the case in the 1980s and the 1990s.

It has also been the experience of industrialized countries, such as the United States, that they are vulnerable to losing their market positions in some products to industrializing countries. This reflects the ability of industrializing countries to duplicate some products with modern equipment and low wages that sell at lower prices. Thus, the pressure is continuously on industrialized countries to develop new and better products to maintain their overall positions in domestic and world markets.

The large and growing debt owed to foreigners adversely affects U.S. well-being in three ways. First, it leads to a net outflow of U.S. interest and profits payments to other nations on their investments in the United States. This outflow reduces domestic business income available for investment in U.S. industry, ultimately lowering living conditions in the United States. Second, a large foreign debt lessens U.S. control over its economic affairs because the need to manage the debt burden constrains Federal Reserve actions in guiding the domestic economy. The Federal Reserve typically makes decisions to tighten credit and raise interest rates, or loosen credit and lower interest rates, in response to the state of the domestic economy. However, credit and interest rates also have complex relationships to the value of the dollar. Thus, when foreign debt is large, Federal Reserve Board decisions become complicated by concerns about how foreign investors will react to proposed actions. Third, the debt lowers respect for the United States abroad and ultimately will lead to a loss of leadership in world political affairs, as noted by Benjamin Friedman.[7] While the U.S. economy in general has become sounder than it was in 1988 when this view was expressed, such as the lower unemployment rate and the lower federal government budget deficit in the mid-1990s, the current account deficit signifies a fault line in the U.S. competitive position in world markets.

The analyst should focus on three broad issues affecting the United States in the world economy:

1. For periods up to one year, greater weight should be given to changes in economic growth than to relative prices at home and abroad for their effect on the volume of export and import trade, given similar percentage changes in economic activity and prices. Over longer periods, although economic activity is still more important, relative prices merit greater attention. But if there is a large change in relative prices, such as one resulting from a sizable depreciation in the value of the dollar, the price effect could be larger than changes in economic activity.

2. Changes in the size of the annual federal government budget deficit and in the ownership of the federal debt by foreigners should be monitored to determine the influence of foreign investors on the value of the dollar. When foreigners buy greater amounts of federal bonds and other debt securities, the effect is to raise the value of the dollar, and when they buy lesser amounts or are a net seller of government securities, the effect is to lower value of the dollar. In addition, foreigners may change the volume of their investments in the United States independently of changes in federal government finances, and such investment changes should be assessed for their impact on the value of the dollar.

3. The actions of U.S. industry in competing for world markets in terms of product quality, prices, and product preferences should be monitored from anecdotal reports in newspapers and the trade press for clues about the likelihood of future changes in the balance of payments.

REVIEW QUESTIONS

- Why are exports more related to economic growth abroad while imports are more related to economic growth in the United States?
- How are product prices in world markets affected by changes in the value of the U.S. dollar?
- What short-term and long-term factors would tend to improve the competitive position of the United States in the world economy?
- Why are the globalization of production and the terms of trade long-term rather than short-term factors?
- Why would a reversal of the problems generally assumed to have caused the deterioration of the U.S. balance of payments and the United States increasingly to be a debtor nation in the 1980s and 1990s not necessarily result in a surplus in the U.S. balance of payments in the twenty-first century?
- What are the problems with continued large deficits in the U.S. balance of payments and the associated growing foreign debt?

Extra Credit

- Comment on the following statement: "What is amazing about the foreign-trade component of the GDP is how, both over the course of the business cycle and over the long run, the changes in both exports and imports tend to mirror the changes in GDP." (The statement, of course, is totally wrong.)
- Why does the United States have a trade deficit in goods and a trade surplus in services?

NOTES

1. Morris Goldstein and Mohsin S. Khan, "Income and Price Effects in Foreign Trade," in *Handbook of International Economics,* vol. 2, ed. R.W. Jones and P.B. Kenen (Elsevier, 1985).

2. Jane Marrinan, "Exchange Rate Determination: Sorting Out Theory and Evidence," *New England Economic Review,* Federal Reserve Bank of Boston, November/December, 1989, p. 44.

Cletus C. Coughlin and Kees Koedijk, "What Do We Know About the Long-Run Real Exchange Rate?" *Review,* The Federal Reserve Bank of St. Louis, January/February 1990, p. 37.

3. Mahnaz Fahim-Nader and William J. Zeile, "Foreign Direct Investment in the United States: New Investment in 1995 and Affiliate Operations in 1994," *Survey of Current Business,* July 1996.

4. William J. Zeile, "Merchandise Trade of U.S. Affiliates of Foreign Companies," *Survey of Current Business,* October 1993, p. 63.

5. Raymond J. Mataloni Jr. and Mahnaz Fahim-Nader, "Operations of U.S. Multinational Companies: Preliminary Results from the 1994 Benchmark Survey," *Survey of Current Business,* December 1996, pp. 18–19.

6. GDBP is GDP less the output of households, nonprofit institutions, and federal, state, and local general government. GDBP typically is 14 to 15 percent less than GDP. It should also be noted that these overall estimates of U.S. companies operating abroad and of foreign companies of several nations operating in the United States themselves are not comparable. One estimate measures the output of one country's companies, those of the United States operating in many countries abroad, while the other measures the companies of many foreign nations operating in one country, the United States. Bilateral comparisons of the foreign operations of U.S. companies in one country with the companies of one foreign country operating in the United States, such as between the United States and England, would be more comparable.

7. Benjamin M. Friedman, *Day of Reckoning: The Consequences of American Economic Policy under Reagan and After* (Random House, 1988), p. 13.

World power and influence have historically accrued to creditor nations. It is not coincidental that America emerged as a world power simultaneously with our transition as a debtor nation dependent on foreign capital for our initial industrialization, to a creditor supplying investment capital to the rest of the world. But we are now a debtor again, and our future role in world affairs is questionable. People simply do not regard their workers, their tenants, and their debtors in the same light as their employers, their landlords, and their creditors. Over time the respect and even deference that America earned as a world banker will gradually shift to the new creditor countries that are able to supply resources where we cannot. And America's influence over nations and events will ebb.

Most Americans continue to think of themselves as creditors. We readily offer unsolicited advice to other debtor countries, as if they had fallen into a trap that we had successfully avoided. Meanwhile, the Japanese and Germans appear still to think of themselves as debtors. As a result, world leadership arrangements do not yet reflect our changed circumstances or theirs. But self-perceptions on both sides will soon catch up with the new reality, in which our financial problems circumscribe our scope for maneuver in world affairs while other countries' financial strength does the opposite. Just how large a departure that reality represents from recent history will depend in part on whether, and how, we change our economic policy.

7
INVESTMENT AND SAVING

Higher rates of investment and saving are typically viewed as leading to better living conditions in the United States and greater prestige for the United States around the world. Investment and saving as a percentage of the gross national product (GNP) declined from the early 1980s to the early 1990s and then rebounded during 1994–96.[1] Many economists advocate that the nation continue the upward trend for investment (vs. consumption) that began in the mid-1990s. This view assumes that economic policies that succeed in raising the saving rate will lead to more private and government investment in structures and equipment, which in turn will boost productivity growth and improve U.S. competitiveness in world markets in the twenty-first century. The end result would be better living conditions in the United States and more prestige abroad.

Investment and saving are by definition equivalent. This reflects the stylized definitions that equate the saving and investment components in the GDP accounting system, as well as the common-sense notion that investment cannot occur without saving. The link between saving and investment is not as simple as often portrayed, however, and in fact is an elusive concept that makes it difficult to understand the overall relationship. Investment and saving decisions are made by different actors and for different reasons. Also, only certain transactions are defined as investments in the investment-saving equivalence discussed here. For example, purchases of existing assets such as company buyouts and mergers, new issues of company stocks, and loans in credit markets are not defined as investments in the context of this chapter, although if they were included, there may have been no decline in the relative shares of investment and saving during the 1980s and early 1990s.

This chapter analyzes four aspects of investment and saving: (1) accounting equivalence of investment and saving; (2) theory and dynamics of the investment-saving relationship; (3) trends in investment and saving from 1960s to the 1990s; (4) implications of the investment and saving movements. The investment-saving framework also interrelates several topics discussed far more fully in Chapters 2 through 6.

ACCOUNTING EQUIVALENCE OF
INVESTMENT AND SAVING

The conventional method of equating national investment to saving is through the national income and product accounts. Summary measures of the national accounts are represented by the GDP. Investment and saving cover private, government, domestic, and international economic transactions of the U.S. economy. The equivalence of investment and saving is based on the following syllogism:

> Gross domestic production = Gross domestic income
> Production = Consumption* + Investment
> Income = Consumption* + Saving
> Therefore: Investment = Saving

---

*Consumption has a broad definition in this instance.
Thus, C = consumer spending + government consumption + exports.
This definition implicitly includes imports, since imported finished
goods as well as imported materials used in production are
represented in the consumer, government, and export figures.

By centering on investment spending and saving flows out of current production, however, this syllogism obscures the relationship's true nature. To understand better how investment equals saving, it is useful to think of their functional roles as assets for increasing future production and income. Thus, the sum totals of investment and saving are equivalent because they are counterparts of a balance sheet. Investment represents the acquisition of assets to generate future income, and saving represents the forgoing of current consumption to provide the financial resources to purchase the assets.

Because investment and saving have specific meanings in this context that are far more limited than those in general usage, the terms are defined here to help clarify the concept. Even with these definitions, however, it will be obvious as the discussion proceeds that the above syllogism is deceptively simple and that the relationship between investment and saving is especially complex and difficult to get an overall grasp of for economic analysis.

Saving Components

National saving is the accumulation of certain assets by households, businesses, and governments through the excess of income over expenditures.

Personal saving is the part of disposable personal income that is not spent on goods, services, interest payments on loans, or net personal transfers to foreigners. It includes changes in the equity ownership of securities and real estate, but not changes in the valuation of the investments due to capital gains and losses. Profits of unincorporated businesses are included in personal saving, as these profits are part of personal income (Chapter 4). This measure of personal saving is calculated as a residual of disposable personal income minus personal outlays, based on the national accounts. An alternative estimate of personal saving represents the change from one period to the next in household assets minus household liabilities, based on the flow of funds accounts prepared by the Federal Reserve Board.[2] Generally, the national accounts saving rate has less volatile yearly movements than the flow of funds saving rate, although both have similar movements over long-term periods. The two saving rates differ in level because the flow of funds measure includes purchases of consumer durable goods as saving, while the national accounts measure includes consumer durable purchases as spending. Therefore, the flow of funds saving rate is always higher. Indeed, the treatment of all consumer durables as spending in the national accounts is problematic, as noted by Lynn Browne and Joshua Gleason.[3] For example, labor-saving household appliances have been a stimulus to more women working in outside employment, and cars have given workers more job mobility, both of which are characteristic of investment rather than of saving.

Business saving is undistributed corporate profits (retained earnings after the payment of corporate income taxes and the distribution of dividends to stockholders). Business saving also includes depreciation charges of both corporations and unincorporated business. By including depreciation allowances, business saving represents the broad measure of business cash flow. Profits of unincorporated businesses are included in personal saving, as noted above.

Government saving represents depreciation allowances on government-owned structures and equipment, plus the surplus or deficit of government budgets. Government budget surpluses or deficits are calculated as the difference between government revenues and government consumption expenditures. Government revenues are obtained from tax receipts, user fees, interest receipts, and other sources of income. Government consumption expenditures cover outlays for goods and services except structures and equipment, transfer payments for Social Security and other income maintenance programs, federal grants to state governments and state grants to local governments, interest payments on government debt, and depreciation allowances for existing government structures and equipment. Statistical estimates of government budget surpluses and deficits in the national accounts differ from surpluses and deficits in official legislated budgets of the federal, state, and local governments.[4] Saving occurs when there is a budget surplus (i.e., when government revenues exceed expenditures), and dissaving occurs when there is a budget deficit (i.e., when expenditures exceed revenues). A government budget deficit reduces national saving because it is financed from the private saving of households, businesses, and foreigners. Specifically, government deficits absorb some private saving when households and businesses purchase government bonds and other debt securities, which reduces the private saving available for financing private investment.

Investment Components

National investment covers gross private domestic investment, gross government investment, and net foreign investment.

Gross private domestic investment covers capital outlays for nonresidential structures and equipment and housing before depreciation of existing facilities is deducted (Chapter 5), and the change in business inventories. But there are several anomalies with these definitions in the national accounts as they relate to the ownership and leasing of cars, household appliances in newly constructed housing, and outlays for education and business research and development, which makes the notion of investment a problematic concept, as Robert Eisner points out.[5] The data represent investments in the United States by both U.S.-owned business and foreign-owned business. They exclude financial investments in stocks and bonds (although, as noted above, a household equity ownership of stocks and bonds is defined as personal saving), purchases of existing nonresidential structures and equipment facilities and housing except for the sales commissions associated with the purchases (such purchases transfer national assets but do not increase them), and business spending for research, development, education, and training (returns on such outlays are difficult to estimate).

Gross government investment covers expenditures for government-owned structures and equipment by the federal, state, and local governments. They include such outlays for civilian and defense needs.

Net foreign investment mainly represents the difference of exports of goods, services, and income received from U.S. investments abroad, less imports of goods, services, and income payments on foreign investments in the United States. It also includes net unilateral transfer payments of households, businesses, and governments between the United States and other countries. When net foreign investment is positive, U.S. residents acquire more foreign assets than foreigners acquire U.S. assets. When it is negative, foreigners acquire more U.S. assets than U.S. residents acquire foreign assets, which results in net foreign disinvestment. Foreign disinvestment reduces national investment because it reduces U.S. net ownership of assets.

Overall Dimensions

Table 7.1 summarizes the main components of saving and investment in 1996. Gross saving of $1,275.9 billion represents private saving of $1,161 billion and government saving of $115 billion. Gross investment of $1,200.8 billion represents private investment of $1,117 billion, government investment of $233.3 billion, and net foreign disinvestment of $149.5 billion. The difference

Table 7.1

Gross Saving and Investment: 1996

	Billions of dollars
Gross Saving	*1,275.9*
Gross private saving[a]	*1,161.0*
Personal saving	271.6
Undistributed corporate profits	192.9
Business depreciation allowances	696.5
Gross government saving[b]	*115.0*
Federal	−54.6
Depreciation allowances	72.5
Current surplus or deficit (−)	−127.1
State and local	169.6
Depreciation allowances	76.6
Current surplus or deficit (−)	93.0
Gross Investment	*1,200.8*
Gross private domestic investment	*1,117.0*
Nonresidential structures	214.3
Producers' durable equipment	576.8
Residential	310.5
Inventory change	15.4
Gross government investment	*233.3*
Federal	58.2
Structures	13.1
Equipment	45.2
State and local	155.3
Structures	125.6
Equipment	29.7
Net foreign investment	*−149.5*
Exports less imports of goods and services	−98.7
U.S. receipts less payments of profits and interest on foreign investments	−8.9
Transfer payments by persons, business, and governments	−41.9
Statistical Discrepancy	*−75.1*

Source: U.S. Bureau of Economic Analysis.

Note: Details do not equal totals due to rounding.

[a]Includes wage accruals less disbursements. These mainly are timing differences of year-end bonus payments between when they are included as wages in national income (accrual), which is used here as overall saving, in contrast to wages in personal income and saving (disbursement). In 1996, the difference between wage accruals and disbursements was zero.

[b]See note 4 at end of the chapter for the distinction between government budget surpluses and deficits in the national income and product accounts used here, in contrast to those in official government budgets.

between gross saving ($1,275.9 billion) and gross investment ($1,200.8 billion) is the statistical discrepancy ($75.1 billion).

The statistical discrepancy is defined as the difference between the product and income sides of the gross domestic product (GDP), which results from inaccuracies and inconsistencies in the various data sources, as noted in Chapter 3 (the statistical discrepancy is the same for both the GDP and the GNP). The saving and investment measure includes the entire statistical discrepancy because the measure encompasses those elements among the product and income sides of the household, business, government, and foreign sectors of the GDP for which the underlying data are derived from unrelated data sources, and thus contain the sum total of the statistical inaccuracies and inconsistencies. The statistical discrepancy in Table 7.1 is calculated as gross investment less gross saving. Thus, the discrepancy is positive when investment exceeds saving and negative when saving exceeds investment.

THEORY AND DYNAMICS OF THE INVESTMENT-SAVING RELATIONSHIP

In economic theory, a distinction is made between actual and planned investment and saving. The equivalence discussed above refers to actual investment and saving, that is, after the fact. Planned investment and planned saving are not necessarily equal because investors and savers are mostly different parties with differing motivations. Thus, before the actual transactions occur, investors may plan to acquire assets that cost more than savers plan to accumulate, or vice versa.

Not all households, businesses, and governments invest the same portion of their savings. Some invest the total amount of their savings, while others invest only a portion. The accumulation of savings by some households and businesses is used by others to finance their investments. The investment-saving equivalence occurs after a myriad of intermediate transactions by lenders, borrowers, and savers in the financial system. In turn, these transactions both influence and are influenced by the continuous fluctuations in interest rates that occur in the marketplace.

What are these intermediate transactions? Banks create deposits when they extend loans to households and businesses; households and businesses purchase commercial paper and bonds that provide direct loans to businesses; companies raise new equity capital by selling new corporate stock to households and businesses; and federal, state, and local governments borrow funds by issuing debt instruments such as bonds. Businesses invest part of the borrowed and equity funds in nonresidential structures and equipment, housing, and inventories, and part of these funds are used for purposes such as wage payments to their employees, to pay off previous debt, and to increase cash balances. Households use their borrowed funds for purchases of goods and services, to pay off previous debt, and to increase their cash balances. Governments use part of their borrowed funds for investment in structures and equipment, and part for purchases of goods and services, wage payments to their employees, to pay off previous debt, and to increase cash balances. Even this highly simplified summary indicates the complexity of the dynamic nature of the investment-saving relationship.

To understand how new saving generated from production in a quarter, year, or other period is equivalent to investment in the same period, recall the identity equations in the earlier section on the accounting equivalence of investment and saving, which reflects actual, as distinguished from planned, saving and investment. Current production not consumed by households, government, and exports must be absorbed by business investment because investment is the only other outlet for the production. The buildup or depletion of inventories is the accounting balance wheel that makes investment always equal to saving. For example, suppose investment for nonresidential structures and equipment and housing is strong and exports exceed imports, but domestic production does not keep pace with this investment growth. The result will be that investments use up more goods than are produced, which will reduce the inventory level in the previous period by the equivalent amount. In contrast, suppose investment for nonresidential structures and equipment and housing is weak and imports exceed exports, but domestic production is not scaled back to the slower pace of these investments. Then the investments will use up fewer goods than are produced and thus raise inventories by the equivalent amount. In this process, inventory movements on the "product side" of the GDP also have a myriad of counterpart movements on the "income side" of the GDP, as personal, business, and government incomes directly reflect changes in production.

Trends from the 1960s to the 1990s

Figures 7.1a, 7.1b, and 7.1c show gross saving as a percentage of the gross national product (GNP) in the aggregate and separately for the volatile and stable components from 1959 to 1996. Figure 7.1a highlights the long-term decline in the saving share of the GNP, though there are several periods from the 1960s to the 1990s when the saving share rose. For example, the general decline in the share from 20.7 percent in 1981 to 14.2 percent 1993 was followed by a rebound to 16.9 percent by 1996.

Figure 7.1b shows the saving components that have the most volatile year-to-year movements—personal saving, the federal government budget surplus or deficit, and undistributed corporate profits. Personal saving was 5 to 6 percent of the GNP from the 1960s to the early 1980s, declined to 3 percent by the early 1990s, and rose to 3.6 percent by 1996. The federal budget had a surplus for most of the 1960s within 1 percent of the GNP, deficits within 1 to 5 percent in the 1970s, deficits within 2 to 5 percent in the 1980s, and a decline in the deficit from 4.5 percent in 1992 to 1.7 percent in 1996. Undistributed corporate profits

Figure 7.1a **Gross Saving as a Percentage of the Gross National Product: 1959–96**

Percent of GNP

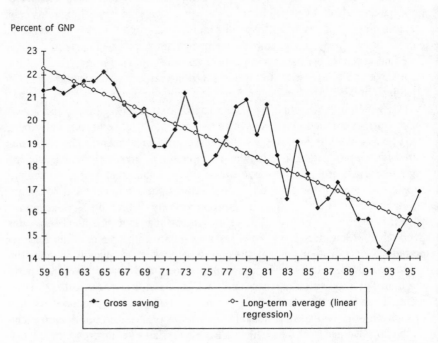

Note: Based on U.S. Bureau of Economic Analysis data.

were typically 2 to 3 percent of the GNP, the main exceptions being 4 percent in the mid-1960s and 1 percent in the early 1980s.

Figure 7.1c shows the saving components with the most stable year-to-year movements—business depreciation allowances, government depreciation allowances, and the state and local governments budget surplus. Business depreciation allowances rose from 8 percent of the GNP in the 1960s and early 1970s to 11 percent in the early 1980s, and gradually declined to 9.2 percent by 1996. Government depreciation allowances declined from 2.7 percent of the GNP in the early 1960s to 2 percent in the 1990s. The budget surplus of all state and local governments was 2 percent of the GNP from the 1960s to the mid-1980s and then declined to 1.2 percent by 1996.

Figure 7.2a shows gross investment and the main components of investment as a percentage of the GNP from 1960 to 1996. Gross investment is the mirror image of gross saving in Figure 7.1, except that investment includes the statistical discrepancy noted previously.

Figure 7.2b shows the investment components of private nonresidential structures and equipment, private residential structures, government structures and

Figure 7.1b **Volatile Components of Gross Saving as a Percentage of the Gross National Product: 1959–96**

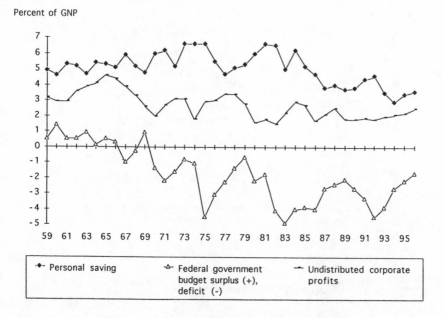

Percent of GNP

*— Personal saving   -△- Federal government budget surplus (+), deficit (-)   —⌃— Undistributed corporate profits

Note: Based on U.S. Bureau of Economic Analysis data.

equipment, and net foreign investment and disinvestment. Private nonresidential investment rose from 9 percent of the GNP in the early 1960s to 12–13 percent in the early 1980s, declined to 9 percent in the early 1990s, and rose to 10.5 percent by 1996. Residential investment was typically 4 to 5 percent of the GNP from the 1960s to the 1990s. Government investment declined from 5.5 percent of the GNP in the early 1960s to 3 percent in the 1990s. Net foreign investment was less than 1 percent of the GNP for most of the 1960s and 1970s, declined to a disinvestment of 3 percent in the mid-1980s, and was a disinvestment of 1 to 2 percent from the late 1980s to the 1990s. With respect to the year-to-year volatility, nonresidential, residential, and net foreign investment were the most volatile components, and government investment was the least volatile.

Implications of the Investment and Saving Movements

The dominant factor causing the decline in saving relative to the GNP from 1981 to 1993 and the subsequent increase in the investment-saving shares during 1994–96 were the marked changes in the federal government's budget deficit over the fifteen-year period. Thus, the generally rising federal government bud-

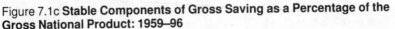

Figure 7.1c **Stable Components of Gross Saving as a Percentage of the Gross National Product: 1959–96**

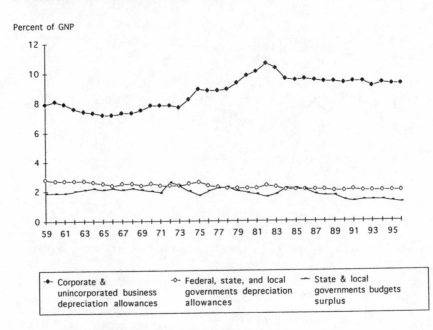

Percent of GNP

-◆- Corporate & unincorporated business depreciation allowances	-○- Federal, state, and local governments depreciation allowances	— State & local governments budgets surplus

Note: Based on U.S. Bureau of Economic Analysis data.

get deficits from the early 1980s to the early 1990s were followed by declining budget deficits in the mid-1990s. These deficits were major depressants on saving over the period, although their effect lessened in the mid-1990s. A secondary component causing the savings decline was the fall in personal saving.[6] The main components causing the decline in investment relative to the GNP from the early 1980s to the early 1990s and the subsequent rebound in the mid-1990s were private nonresidential structures and equipment and net foreign disinvestment.

As of this writing in the spring of 1997, the major improvements in the U.S. economy in the mid-1990s have been the increasing job growth and lower unemployment accompanied by tolerable inflation (see Chapter 11 for this definition of inflation). Economic growth and productivity increases have not accelerated. Private investment in structures and equipment increased, as it typically does during cyclical expansions. The international economic deterioration continued, as the deficit in the U.S. balance of payments and the U.S. net debtor position showed further increases.

The economy is far too complex to attribute the improved employment and modest inflation of the mid-1990s to the relative rise in investment and saving, which itself primarily reflects the decline in the federal government budget defi-

Figure 7.2a **Gross Investment as a Percentage of the Gross National Product: 1959–96**

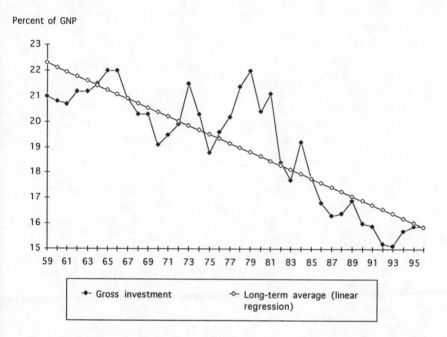

Percent of GNP

Note: Based on U.S. Bureau of Economic Analysis data.

cit. The major benefit from the lower federal deficit probably is the lessening pressure on interest rates, which in turn encourages greater borrowing and re-lated spending by households, businesses, and governments, while keeping busi-ness financial costs and thus inflation down through the subdued interest rates. This is preferable to the method of containing inflation by raising interest rates in order to reduce spending, which in turn leads to lower economic growth and lower employment (Chapter 12 covers interest rates).

Additionally, there is a question about whether a lower level of relative con-sumption actually raises investment and saving, due to the income effects of the lower consumption, as Robert Eisner notes.[7] Thus, if the lower consumption results in lower incomes of workers and businesses, both investment and saving will decline because of the lower incomes. In this dynamic setting, incomes are the balance wheel between saving and investment, in contrast to the static invest-ment-saving accounting identity noted previously in which inventory change is the balance wheel. With respect to the federal government budget deficit, the lower incomes can arise from a lower federal government budget deficit either through deliberately legislated lower federal spending or deliberately legislated higher federal taxes, independent of the business cycle effect on both spending

Figure 7.2b **Components of Gross Investment as a Percentage of the Gross National Product: 1959–96**

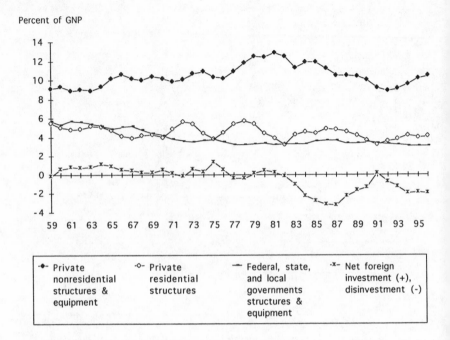

Note: Based on U.S. Bureau of Economic Analysis data.

and revenues (see Chapter 2). Also, while lower federal deficits bring lower interest rates, the lower incomes brought by the reduced deficits may reduce spending more than the lower interest rates increase spending.

The supposition of many economists that the U.S. economy would benefit from lower consumption and higher investment and saving was noted at the beginning of the chapter. But it is difficult to specify what a desirable proportion of GNP investment and saving would be. This reflects the fact that the investment-saving structure is an elusive concept in the aggregate due to two problematic characteristics. First, the household, business, government, and international sectors reflect such different functions that it is difficult to think of them as combining into aggregate measures of investment and saving. Second, there are fundamental problems with how some components of saving and investment are defined. In these cases, the definitions are unrealistic in terms of how the economy functions, as noted in the earlier sections on the saving and investment components.

In assessing the effect of the investment-saving relationship, the analyst should include both the short-term and long-term effects. The short term is dominated by the cyclical expansion and recession effects of the economy on private investment in structures and equipment, the federal government budget deficit, and the international exports and imports of goods and services. The long-term factors are changes in the legislated federal government budget expenditures and taxes, the investment behavior of U.S. businesses, the skills of U.S. workers, and the competitive position of U.S. businesses in world markets. These filter to the various industries slowly as their effects take long to be widely felt and acted on, in contrast to the quicker response to short-term cyclical movements.

REVIEW QUESTIONS

- How do planned investment and saving differ from actual investment and saving for economic analysis?
- Why are inventories and incomes the balance wheels of investment and saving? How do they differ in their economic effects?
- What were the main factors contributing to the relative decline in investment and saving from the early 1980s to the early 1990s? What caused the investment-saving rebound in the mid-1990s?
- What is the difficulty in grasping the significance of the investment and saving aggregates?
- How would you differentiate short-term from long-term factors in assessing future movements in investment and saving?

Extra Credit

- If General Motors issues new shares of corporate stock and uses the proceeds of the sales to buy new assembly-line machinery, should the purchase of the new shares count as investment? Explain.

NOTES

1. Due to technical factors related to the international component of the investment-saving measure, investment and saving are calculated as a percentage of the gross national product (GNP), rather than of the gross domestic product (GDP). The GNP, rather than the GDP, is used because the investment-saving account includes foreign investment income receipts minus foreign investment income payments, which are included in the GNP but not in the GDP. In practice, there is little difference between the GDP and GNP in long-term analyses, which is the focus of the investment-saving relationship. Because the GDP is the featured measure of economic growth by the U.S. Bureau of Economic Analysis, which prepares the national income and product accounts, the GDP is highlighted in the book. Chapter 3 covers the national accounts.

2. Lynn Elaine Browne with Joshua Gleason, "The Saving Mystery, or Where Did the Money Go?" *New England Economic Review*, Federal Reserve Bank of Boston, September/October 1996. This article includes a good summary of the differences in the two saving measures.

3. Ibid., p. 26.

4. Federal government investment expenditures for structures and equipment totaled $64 billion, and federal government consumption outlays of depreciation allowances on existing structures and equipment were $69.8 billion in 1996. The statistical budget estimates in the national income and product accounts used in this analysis exclude the investment expenditures and include the consumption depreciation allowances. By contrast, the official federal government budget of the U.S. Office of Management and Budget includes the investment expenditures but excludes the consumption depreciation expenditures. On this basis alone, the national accounts federal budget deficit was $5.8 billion (69.8 − 64.0) higher than the official government budget deficit. Other differences of item content and timing between the official and the national accounts statistical federal budgets cause additional differences in the surplus and deficit estimates between the statistical and official federal government budgets. Differences of item content include the treatment of government loans, purchases and sales of land, government contributions to federal employee retirement funds, and budgets of U.S. territories outside the United States and the Commonwealth of Puerto Rico. Differences of timing include variations in the accrual, cash, and delivery methods of recording when revenues are received and when expenditures are made.

For state and local government budgets, the official budgets typically exclude investment expenditures, particularly those for structures financed through long-term bonds, in contrast to the official federal budget, which includes these expenditures. The state and local governments official budgets typically exclude depreciation allowance expenditures on existing structures and equipment from their surplus and deficit calculations, similar to that in the official federal government budget. In 1996, investment expenditures by the aggregate of all state and local governments were $138.9 billion for structures and $30.5 billion for equipment, and consumption expenditures for depreciation allowances were $57 billion. Assuming that structures expenditures are not included and equipment expenditures are included in the official budgets of all state and local governments, the adjustments for the equipment expenditures and depreciation allowances in the national accounts statistical budget increase expenditures by a net amount of $26.5 (57.0 − 30.5) and thus would lower the surplus in the official budgets by that amount, although there is no compilation of the official budgets for the aggregate of all state and local governments. The surplus in the state and local national accounts statistical budget was $93 billion in 1996.

5. Robert Eisner, *The Misunderstood Economy: What Counts and How to Count It* (Harvard Business School Press, 1994), pp. 51–54. For example, if a household leases a new car from an automobile dealer, the value of the new car is defined as investment, but if the household buys the new car, it is defined as consumption. Analogously, if a newly constructed house includes a built-in range, refrigerator, dishwasher, or other appliance provided by the builder as part of the purchase price of the house, the appliances are defined as investment, but if the homeowner purchases the same appliances separately, they are defined as consumption. And some expenditures made in the present that defer current income with the intent that they will lead to a future income have all the earmarks of investment, such as outlays for education and research and development, but education outlays are classified as consumption and research and development outlays are defined as a current business expense.

6. Browne and Gleason, "The Saving Mystery." See also Jagadeesh Gokhale, Laurence J. Kotlikoff, and John Sabelhaus, "Understanding the Postwar Decline in U.S. Saving: A Cohort Analysis," *Brookings Papers on Economic Activity* 1 (1996). These two studies conclude that the savings decline from the early 1980s to the early 1990s mainly reflects the increased medical expenditures financed by the greater Medicare and Medic-

aid government transfers to households. This includes both the greater consumer medical expenditures and the consequent lower personal saving rate, plus the greater federal government budget deficits arising from the increased government programs. While the rising medical expenditures financed by the government transfer programs contributed to the savings decline, they were undertaken in the context of large reductions in the tax base and large increases in defense spending that were not offset by spending reductions in other government programs. Thus, the concentration on medical programs as the cause of the savings decline does not square with the federal budget realities of the period.

7. Eisner, *The Misunderstood Economy,* pp. 38–40.

8
EMPLOYMENT AND WAGES

Employment and wages are basic to the incomes of workers and the labor costs of employers. It is important to take both aspects into account in assessing the overall economy.

From the workers' perspective, their employment and the wages they receive is the primary source of income for themselves and their families. Thus, employment and wages are the key determinants of the economic well-being of the vast majority of the population. Income derived from work also gives people the intangible, but vitally important, feeling of self-esteem and dignity. And the hope of a higher material well-being through stable and higher-paying jobs enhances a work ethic of responsibility and pride in the work product, in contrast to a feeling of alienation that comes from hopelessness.

From the employers' perspective, workers are essential in producing the goods and services of their enterprises. Labor costs of wages and fringe benefits plus all other production expenses must be covered by the prices of goods and services sold for the enterprises to make a profit and stay in business. Consequently, employers have a direct interest in having workers who are productive at wage levels that allow the firms to compete in the marketplace.

This chapter discusses three main topics: employment, worker earnings, and employer costs. The data series are prepared monthly and quarterly by the Bureau of Labor Statistics in the U.S. Department of Labor.

EMPLOYMENT

This discussion centers on persons working in jobs located in the fifty states and the District of Columbia. They cover jobs held by U.S. citizens and noncitizens working in both civilian and defense activities. Persons who are members of the armed forces of the United States are not included in the employment measures.

Methodology

Two alternative surveys provide data on trends in employment: (1) a survey of establishments where the employees work, and (2) a survey of households where the employees live.[1] They generally have parallel movements over time, but because they use different definitions and data collection methods, they sometimes have different monthly and even cyclical patterns. Therefore, it is important to know which figures are used in particular analyses. The employment surveys are prepared monthly.

There are two basic distinctions between the two surveys. The establishment survey provides a count of jobs, which includes all jobs of multiple jobholders, with the emphasis on the industry and geographic location of the business establishments. By contrast, the household survey counts employed persons, who are counted only once even if they have more than one job, with the emphasis on the demographic and socioeconomic characteristics of the workers.

Establishment Survey

Employment data based on the establishment survey are collected from private businesses, the federal government, and state and local governments. The data are derived from a sample of employers for the pay period that includes the twelfth day of the month (the establishment survey is also referred to as the payroll survey). Samples of the establishments (places of work) are surveyed for private businesses and state and local governments by statistical agencies within state departments of labor under a federal/state cooperative agreement with the BLS. The data are collected primarily through touch-tone data entry by the employer. Alternative collection modes are electronic data interchange, voice recognition technology, computer-assisted telephone interview, and mail. Data covering all federal government civilian employees, including the Department of Defense, are provided by the U.S. Office of Personnel Management (armed forces military personnel and employees of the Central Intelligence Agency and the National Security Agency are excluded).

Data are obtained on the number of all workers employed, including those from the lowest pay scales to company executives, and part-time and full-time workers. The survey is a count of jobs and thus includes all jobs, including those workers with more than one job, as long as each job is on an employer's payroll. The survey excludes the self-employed, farm workers, domestic workers, and unpaid family workers.

The monthly sample of nearly 400,000 employer establishments covered about 41 percent of all nonagricultural employment in 1996. The monthly figures go through two sets of revisions. They are initially published as "preliminary" in each of the first two months after the survey is taken, and in the third month are "final" based on the most complete returns from the employer sample.

Table 8.1

Percentage Difference between the Benchmark and Final Monthly Estimate of Employment for the Establishment Survey

	(+: benchmark more than monthly survey −: benchmark less than monthly survey)
1990	−0.2
1991	−0.6
1992	−0.1
1993	+0.2
1994	+0.7
1995	+0.5
1996	Less than +0.05

Source: U.S. Bureau of Labor Statistics.

The chances are that in two of three cases, the monthly level of employment will be revised by plus or minus 65,000 workers between the preliminary number and the revision two months later.

The initial monthly estimates are subsequently revised annually to conform to benchmark numbers for the month of March, which are based on data from the universe of all employers reporting their unemployment insurance tax payments to the state government employment offices. The new March levels are then used to revise the previous eleven months, which were based on data obtained from the sample of employers, and extrapolations are carried forward to the most current month as well. The unemployment insurance reports covered 97.5 percent of all nonagricultural employment in 1995; these are supplemented by other reports for industries exempt from unemployment laws, such as those available from Social Security records.

Table 8.1 shows that over 1990–96, the benchmark revisions for all employees ranged from −0.6 percent to 0.7 percent. Despite the relatively small revisions in annual benchmarks, there remain some long-standing concerns regarding the sampling procedures for the employer survey. One issue is how up-to-date the sample of participating firms is. Because new firms starting in business are added to the universe frame only once each quarter, the monthly survey data first reflect these firms' employment several months after the firms have been in operation. The understatement of employment due to the delayed inclusion of new firms in the sample is compensated by a statistical adjustment for the new firms' additional employment. This is based on benchmark revisions of the past three years and differential growth rates between the two most recent quarters and the past several years. The result of this procedure is that, in addition to the late introduction of new firms, it adjusts for other sources of error, including the late identification of firms that have gone out of business and a variety of other differences between the benchmark and monthly estimates.

A second issue is the sample of firms used in the survey. Because the current sample is not a probability sample, the representativeness of the sample in terms of the distribution of small-, medium-, and large-size firms is uncertain, and therefore a sampling error cannot be calculated for it. While formal sampling error estimates do not exist for the establishment survey, the annual benchmark provides a comprehensive annual measure of overall survey error, containing both sampling and nonsampling components. Thus, the existing range of past benchmark revisions is analogous to a range of sampling error (i.e., a confidence interval) and suggests that a true probability sample would not result in significantly different annual levels, although it could result in noticeably different monthly movements during the year. The Bureau of Labor Statistics is conducting a research program in the late 1990s to have the establishment survey based on a probability sample. If this research demonstrates that a probability sample is feasible, a probability sample could be implemented over several years if adequate funding becomes available.

Household Survey

Employment data based on the survey of households are derived from a sample survey of residences in which the worker or workers live. In the household survey, employed persons include those individuals sixteen years and older who worked at least one hour as paid employees, the self-employed, and workers in a family business who worked at least fifteen hours a week, in nonfarm and farm activities. Thus, the employed population consists of wage earners and those who work for profit, the latter being the self-employed and unpaid workers in family businesses who are assumed to share in the profits. All persons are counted equally if they are paid for an hour or more per week. If a person has two or more jobs, the job with the most hours worked in the week is the only one counted. And the hours worked for all jobs are assigned to that job. Since 1994, data on the number of multiple jobholders have been collected each month in the household survey for analytical use.

The household survey employment data are obtained from a monthly survey of a sample of about 50,000 households, called the Current Population Survey (CPS), which the Census Bureau conducts for the Bureau of Labor Statistics. The sample is representative of the distribution of households in small and large metropolitan areas and in rural areas. It undergoes a major revision every ten years to be consistent with the most recent decennial population census. As of this writing, the sample is based on the 1990 census of population beginning in 1994. The sample is also updated annually on a limited basis to reflect current changes in residential locations due to new construction based on housing start data prepared by the Census Bureau. The chances are that in two of three cases, the sampling error for employment is plus or minus 312,000 workers for the monthly level and 235,000 workers for the month-to-month change.

In order to reduce the reporting burden on any group of households, the sample is divided into eight subsamples (panels) that are rotated over a sixteen-month period. Each subsample is surveyed for four consecutive months, is then dropped from the survey for eight months, and is subsequently resurveyed for the following four months. At the end of the sixteen months, the subsample is eliminated from the sample and replaced with a new panel of households. The result of this procedure is that every month 25 percent of households in the sample is either new to the survey or is returning to it after an eight-month hiatus. Correspondingly, 25 percent of the sample households drops out of the survey every month.

The survey refers to the individual's employment status during the calendar week that includes the twelfth day of the month. The survey is conducted mainly by telephone interviews, supplemented by personal visits as necessary. The CPS data are also used to estimate the unemployment rate (Chapter 9).

In two cases out of three, the monthly level of employment is within a range of plus or minus 293,000 persons, and the monthly change in employment is within a range of plus or minus 216,000 persons. By way of perspective, civilian employment in the household survey in December 1996 totaled 128 million and the monthly change from November was 211,000.

Overall Comparisons of the Two Surveys

The establishment survey counts all paying jobs of nonagricultural employees on employer payrolls in U.S. enterprises and governments. It includes all jobs held by each worker (not just the primary one, as in the household survey), workers under sixteen years old, residents of Canada and Mexico who commute to the United States for work, and institutionalized persons on payroll jobs. All of these are excluded from the household survey. By contrast, the establishment survey excludes the self-employed; residents of the United States who commute to jobs in Canada and Mexico; private household, agricultural, and unpaid family workers; workers in international organizations such as the United Nations and foreign embassies; and workers on the job rolls but temporarily not receiving pay, such as those on strike or on unpaid vacations or sick leave. All of these are in the household survey, with the exception of persons living on the premises of foreign embassies. In addition, there are substantial differences in the sampling and data collection aspects in the surveys.

The net effect of these differences in coverage is that the household survey shows more employment than the employer survey. In 1996, average employment in the household survey was 126.7 million, compared with 119.6 in the establishment survey. Reconciliations of both measures, when they are put on as similar a definitional basis as the available data will allow, reduce the difference substantially. For example, the reconciliation in 1996 resulted in the establishment survey having about 2 million more in employment than the household survey.

Statistically, both surveys have strengths and weaknesses. The information source for the establishment survey is better because the data are obtained from employer payroll records, which are used for tax returns, rather than from answers by household members, which are not documented. Two weaknesses of the establishment survey are related to the survey sample and the statistical estimating procedures. One is that it is not based on a probability survey, and although research is under way to convert it to a probability sample, such a new sample design will require adequate funding in future years to implement it, as noted previously. A second is that statistical adjustments are necessary to compensate for the lateness of new firms getting into the survey sample, which may in turn cause a problem with the monthly data, as noted below under Monthly Movements.

The household survey is better in terms of general sample survey methodology as it has a probability sample, in contrast to the nonprobability sample of the establishment survey. A primary weakness of the household survey is its reliance on a household member to provide the data. While the respondent is an adult member of the household, there is no documentation of the member's responses to the survey questions, and different members of the household may respond to the survey from month-to-month differently. Errors associated with the survey respondent's answers to questions are referred to as nonsampling errors. Examples of such nonsampling errors are the inability to obtain information on all persons in the sample, differences in the interpretation of the questions by different respondents in the same household from month to month, inability or unwillingness of respondents to provide correct information, and inability to recall information.

Both surveys have seasonal adjustment problems during the summer months from June to September associated with school vacations. These may be mitigated in future years with increases in year-round schooling, but they introduce an uncertainty in the monthly employment movements during the summer. The seasonal problem with the establishment survey is that secretaries, janitors, cafeteria workers, and other support staff are carried on the payrolls as year-round (twelve-months) employees in some school systems, but as school-year (less than twelve months) employees in other school systems. The seasonal problem with the household survey involves the timing of when students end school in May and June and enter the labor market, and when students leave the labor market in August and September and go back to school. The difficulty is that the household survey respondent does not always know when the student members of the household change their schooling and work status.

The two surveys also differ in terms of data revisions. The establishment survey data are revised in a routinized program from the initial monthly estimates to the annual benchmarks. By contrast, the initial monthly estimates of the household survey typically are not revised.

Over the years, the establishment survey has been considered to better mea-

Table 8.2

Employment Growth, Establishment versus Household Surveys: 1948–96
(annual percentage growth)

	Establishment survey	Household survey
1948–59	5.7	8.9
1959–69	2.8	1.9
1969–79	2.5	2.4
1978–89	1.9	1.7
1989–96	1.5	1.1
1948–96	2.1	1.6

Source: U.S. Bureau of Labor Statistics.

sure the monthly change in total employment. The author believes that neither survey is superior, however, and that the movements of employment are usually best represented as being within the upper and lower bounds of both surveys. This is discussed further below.

Analysis of Trends

The long-term movements of the two surveys are similar, although not identical. Table 8.2 shows both surveys' movements in nonagricultural employment at compound annual rates for the 1950s to the 1990s. The decade increases were highest for the 1950s, the second highest increases were in the 1960s and 1970s, and the increases declined further in the 1980s and 1990s.[2] Over the forty-eight years from 1948 to 1996, employment based on the establishment survey increased at an annual rate of 2.1 percent, higher than the growth of 1.6 percent in the household survey. The establishment survey had higher growth rates in all decades except the 1950s.

Monthly Movements

Figures 8.1a, 8.1b, and 8.1c show monthly employment trends of both surveys from 1991 to 1996. The establishment survey data show a steadier pattern in one direction in all cases except one month in 1996, in contrast to the household survey, which had several month-to-month interruptions in direction.

These monthly differences are perplexing because it is not known whether the labor market actually has the employer survey's relatively smooth monthly movements or the household survey's monthly volatility (the data in both surveys are seasonally adjusted). At the same time, the varying short-term movements of the two surveys may simply reflect the difference in coverage and statistical procedures noted in the previous section on Methodology.

Figure 8.1a **Monthly Employment from Establishment and Household
Surveys: 1991–92**

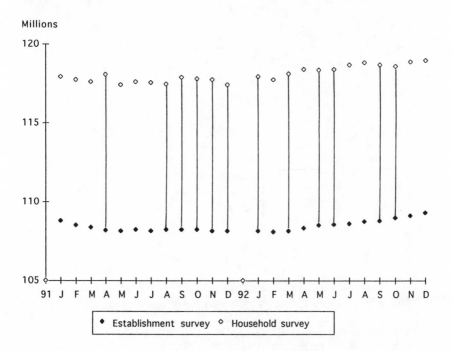

Note: Vertical lines indicate months when the two surveys moved in opposite directions.

It is difficult to say which survey better depicts the actual economy. The author's view is that the actual economy moves with some fits and starts, rather than smoothly in the same direction from one month to the next. But both surveys have limitations in this regard. It is possible that the generally smoother movements of the establishment survey result from the statistical adjustments used to compensate for the delay in the introduction of new firms starting in business in the establishment sample. It is also possible that the monthly volatility of the household survey is exaggerated because, in some households, different household members respond to the survey from month to month.

While these monthly differences raise uncertainty about the employment movements, they also have a positive effect, as they point up the lack of perfection in any statistical survey. To deal with this, the analyst should compare the employment patterns of both surveys. If they are similar, they may be considered to confirm the movements. If they differ significantly, definitional and statistical differences between the surveys should be examined to see if there is a reasonable explanation. If there is no plausible explanation, the movement for that short period may be treated as within the lower and upper bounds of both surveys.

Figure 8.1b **Monthly Employment from Establishment and Household Surveys: 1993–94**

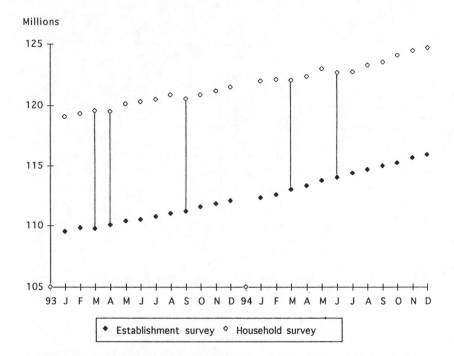

Millions

Note: Vertical lines indicate months when the two surveys moved in opposite directions.

Cyclical Movements

Figures 8.2a and 8.2b show the changes in both employment surveys and in the gross domestic product (GDP) adjusted for inflation during the expansions and recessions from the 1960s to the 1990s (the cyclical turning points are the same as those used in Chapter 3 for the GDP). The establishment survey showed more extreme cyclical movements, increasing more in expansions and decreasing more in recessions than the household survey (employment in the household survey actually increased in the 1960 and the 1969–70 recessions). The differentials were much smaller from the 1970s to the 1990s than in the previous decades, however.

Employment as measured in both surveys is typically less cyclical than the GDP, rising less in expansions and falling less in recessions. The GDP is more cyclical because in addition to employment, it takes into account weekly hours worked and productivity, both of which are highly cyclical. Weekly hours are discussed later in this chapter, and productivity is covered in Chapter 10.

Figure 8.1c **Monthly Employment from Establishment and Household Surveys: 1995–96**

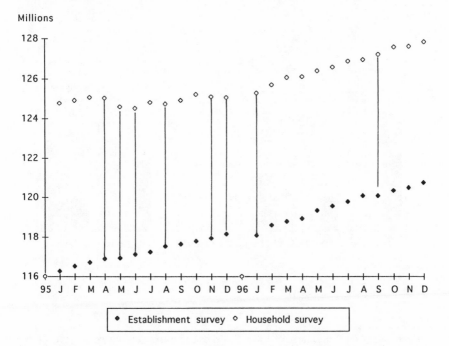

Note: Vertical lines indicate months when the two surveys moved in opposite directions.

John Stinson suggests reasons for the varying cyclical patterns based on qualitative assessments of the likely effect of the differences between the two surveys.[3] In recessions, two situations lead to employment decreases in the employer survey and no decrease in the household survey. These are cases in which a dual job-holder loses one job, and cases in which a person loses a job with a large employer who is a respondent in the employer survey and switches to a marginal employer who is not in the employer survey (perhaps even switching to the underground economy). In expansions, the reverse situation occurs for persons who had been with marginal employers not in the employer survey and switch as demand increases to larger employers that are in the employer survey; this appears as an employment increase in the employer survey but as no change in the household survey. Another supposition on the greater cyclical volatility of the employer survey is considered more speculative: it is possible that because the persons typically undercounted in household surveys, such as minority males, are those with the greatest cyclical changes in employment, the undercount may reduce that survey's employment fluctuations. In analyzing the effect of undercoverage in the household survey, Alexander Korns found it tended to dampen cyclical fluctuations.[4]

Figure 8.2a **Business Cycle Movements of Employment and the Gross Domestic Product, 1960s to 1990s: Expansions**

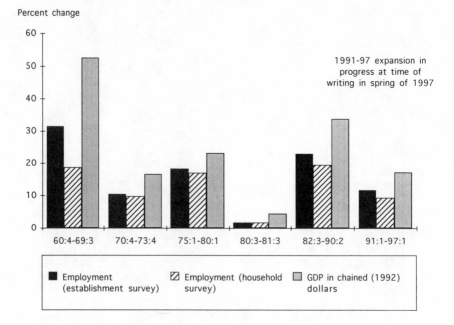

Note: Based on U.S. Bureau of Labor Statistics and Bureau of Economic Analysis data. Number after colon is quarter of year.

There also are cyclical fluctuations in self-employment, which is included in the household and excluded from the establishment survey. Self-employment as a share of total employment in nonagricultural industries has remained stable at 7 percent from 1967 to 1996. Previously, it declined from 12 percent in 1948 to 7 percent in 1967. A small part of the decline resulted from a refinement in the household survey methodology in 1967 that excluded persons from being classified as self-employed even if they were a primary owner of a corporation, as John Bregger points out.[5] The decline in self-employment in agriculture was even greater, largely reflecting the reduction in small farming. Self-employment increases in expansions along with other employment, but in recessions it tends to decline less sharply and to start increasing sooner than wage and salary employment, as Eugene Becker notes.[6] These countercyclical movements in recessions may result from two factors: (a) persons who are self-employed as a second job, and thus are counted only in their primary job in the household survey, are counted as self-employed when they lose their employee job, and (b) some workers who have lost their jobs and are not able to find another one try self-employment and thus are still counted in the household survey.

Figure 8.2b **Business Cycle Movements of Employment and the Gross Domestic Product, 1960s to 1990s: Recessions**

Percent change

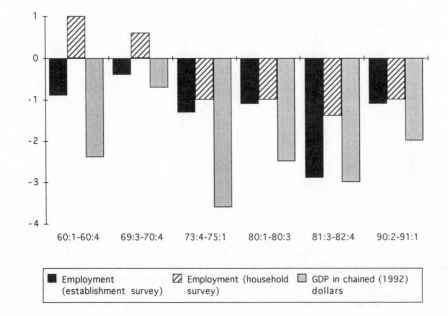

| Employment (establishment survey) | Employment (household survey) | GDP in chained (1992) dollars |

Note: Based on U.S. Bureau of Labor Statistics and Bureau of Economic Analysis data. Number after colon is quarter of year.

Employment-Population Ratio versus the Labor Force Participation Rate

Two measures of the linkage of the working-age population to job markets are the employment-population ratio (EPR) and the labor force participation rate (LFPR). They represent seemingly slightly different aspects of job markets, with the difference being that the EPR is limited to employment, while the LFPR includes unemployment as well as employment. The EPR is the proportion of the population of working age that has jobs, and the LFPR is the proportion of the population that is working or is seeking a job. Both measures are based on data from the household survey.

Mathematically, they are calculated as follows:

$$EPR = \frac{Employment}{Noninstitutional\ population^{**}} \quad LFPR = \frac{Employment + unemployment^*}{Noninstitutional\ population^{**}}$$

*The labor force is defined as the sum of employment and unemployment
**Persons 16 years and older who are not in hospitals, nursing homes, jails, etc.

Figure 8.3 **Employment-Population Ratio versus the Labor Force Participation Rate: 1947–96**

Employment and labor force as a percentage of the noninstitutional population

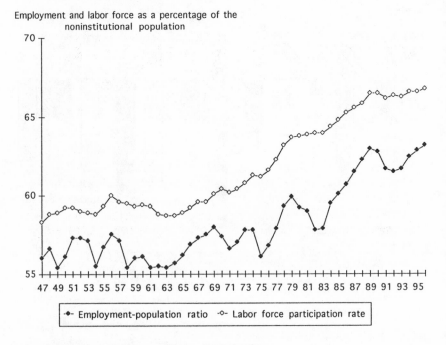

◆- Employment-population ratio ◦- Labor force participation rate

Note: Based on U.S. Bureau of Labor Statistics data.

Because the EPR excludes unemployment, it is not affected by people moving between unemployment and outside the labor force. By contrast, the LFPR includes these movements into and out of unemployment. Persons are counted as unemployed if they are actively looking for work in the official measure of unemployment (Chapter 9 covers unemployment). Since the noninstitutional population is the denominator in both measures, and it increases steadily over time, the movements of both the EPR and the LFPR are dominated by changes in the numerator.

Figure 8.3 shows the movements of the EPR and the LFPR from 1947 to 1996. Both have a generally rising trend from the 1960s to the 1990s, but the EPR has far more volatile year-to-year movements than the LFPR. The sharp changes in employment in the EPR were offset by the opposite movements of unemployment that are included in the LFPR, causing the less volatile movements in the LFPR.

Because the EPR better portrays the tendency of the working-age population to have jobs than the LFPR, the analyst should focus on the EPR in assessing the momentum of employment growth of the noninstitutional population.

WAGE EARNINGS

Wage-earning data represent wage income from the perspective of the worker. This contrasts with data on wage costs, which reflect the perspective of the employer (wage costs are covered below). Earnings of the average worker reflect the hours on the job and the hourly pay rate, or the salary rate, for the worker's pay period. Hours worked, hourly pay rates, and salary rates are averages for all private nonfarm industries and most occupations and therefore change when jobs shift between industries or occupations that have longer or shorter workweeks or higher or lower pay rates, such as between manufacturing and services or between clerks and pharmacists.

The hours and earnings data are obtained from the establishment survey of the U.S. Bureau of Labor Statistics discussed in the previous section on employment. They are averages for the total of full-time and part-time workers and of overtime hours that are paid a premium over the straight-time rate in private nonagricultural industries. Technically, they reflect "hours paid for," which includes hours of paid vacations and sick leave, as well as actual working time on the job.

The data on hours and earnings are limited to "production workers" in the goods-producing industries and "nonsupervisory workers" in the service-producing industries, which in all industries exclude executives and managers.[7] In manufacturing, construction, and mining, workers engaged in professional, technical, office, and sales activities are excluded as well. Thus, the data for workers in the goods-producing industries represent "line" workers as distinct from administrative and support employees. By contrast, the data on employment in the previous section cover workers at all levels, including officers of corporations, executives, and managers.

Worker Hours, Worker Earnings, and Household Income

Weekly Hours

Weekly hours represent the average length of the workweek and are an early indicator of changes in labor utilization. Typically, employers change existing employees' hours before hiring new employees when sales strengthen during a recession, and before laying off workers when sales weaken during an expansion. Because recent sales trends may be reversed in a short period, it is simpler for employers to adjust work schedules first. Hiring new employees involves administrative costs and training time, which may not be justified by future business activity. Laying off workers in temporary downturns may result in losing efficient labor to other employers just as demand picks up. Retaining workers during slack periods that are expected to be of short duration is one way to avoid this possibility. Other factors encourage employers not to lay off workers immediately before there is a more definitive indication of sales trends. They recognize the importance of the job to the worker and, on a personal level, some may be reluctant to lay anyone off. Employers also seek to avoid higher unemployment insurance premiums, which can result from increasing layoffs because the premiums are based on the unemployment experience of the firm's employees.

The number for average weekly hours in manufacturing industries is so sensitive to changes in demand that it is a component of the composite index of leading indicators (see Chapter 13). It includes overtime and usually ranges from 39 to 41 hours. For short periods, typically of one to three months, it has fallen below 39 hours in some recessions, and less frequently has risen above 41 hours in expansions. In the mid-1990s, it averaged 42 hours in 1994, 41.6 hours in both 1995 and 1996, and at the end of 1996 reached 42 hours.

On average, it takes at least three months for the weekly hours data on manufacturing to establish a cyclical upward or downward trend. A one- or two-month upward or downward movement is affected by too many factors to be considered a statistically reliable trend. Even within the longer expansion and recession periods, however, the weekly hours series is quite erratic.

Because of the volatility of the weekly hours data, the analyst should consider current trends in weekly hours only as a broad clue to developments in labor markets.

Weekly Earnings vs. Disposable Personal Income

Two alternative measures of employees' incomes provide evidence on trends in the material well-being of workers. One is the data on average weekly earnings per worker adjusted for inflation, which is derived from the establishment survey discussed in this chapter. The other is disposable personal income per capita adjusted for inflation, which is associated with Household Income and Expenditure, covered in Chapter 4.

Weekly earnings of workers represent the money wages for straight-time and overtime pay, employer-paid vacations, and employer-paid sick leave, before employee deductions for income and Social Security taxes, group insurance, private unemployment insurance, bonds, union dues, or any other deductions. They exclude bonuses that are not earned and paid regularly each pay period, tips, in-kind payments such as the value of free rent or meals, and employer-paid noncash fringe benefits such as health insurance and retirement plans. The data are referred to as "gross weekly earnings" because they are before the payment of income and Social Security taxes.

Disposable personal income (DPI) per capita is a far more comprehensive measure than weekly earnings per worker (DPI is prepared by the U.S. Bureau of Economic Analysis). Personal income includes the combined job earnings of all workers in the household, such as the combined earnings of both spouses, plus

Figure 8.4 **Average Weekly Earnings per Worker and Disposable Personal Income per Capita Adjusted for Inflation: 1959–96**

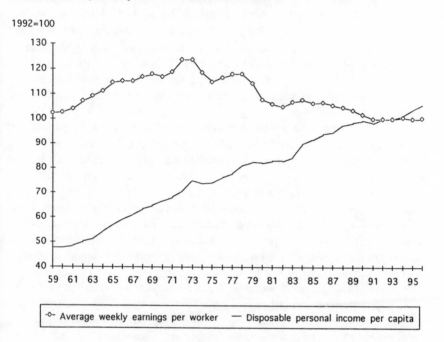

1992=100

-○- Average weekly earnings per worker   — Disposable personal income per capita

Note: Based on U.S. Bureau of Labor Statistics and U.S. Bureau of Economic Analysis data.

income received by all household members from self-employment, interest, dividends, rent, unemployment insurance, Social Security, and other income maintenance programs. Since DPI measures personal income after the payment of income, estate, and gift taxes (Social Security taxes paid by the employee and employer are excluded from personal income), DPI represents the purchasing power of the household incomes. DPI per capita is the income per person including all adults and children.

Figure 8.4 shows the trend of weekly earnings per worker and DPI per capita adjusted for inflation from 1959 to 1996 on an index of 1992 = 100. Real weekly earnings rose during the 1960s and peaked in the early 1970s, but subsequently declined through the 1990s to below the 1959 level. There were only short-term interruptions in the declining trend. By contrast, DPI per capita rose continuously over the 1959–96 period to twice the 1959 level in the mid-1990s, with only a few interruptions in the rising trend. Thus, the two measures give starkly contrasting patterns of the overall change in the material well-being of the nation's households.

Which one better represents the material well-being of the population? From the vantage point of the wage income derived from working, the average worker has fallen behind. This reflects both the relative decline in the higher-paying jobs from industry restructuring and the slowdown in wage increases for the same job. But from the vantage point of total income from all sources, the average person has experienced ever-better conditions. This stems mainly from the increasing proportion of families in which both spouses have paying jobs and the rising receipt of income maintenance payments from Social Security, Medicare, Medicaid, and food stamps.

Because both measures are for an "average" worker or person, they mask vast differences among individual households, some being above and others being below the average. Nevertheless, the contrasting averages point up fault lines in the economic lives of the people. Many adults of this generation have not reached the income levels and living conditions of their parents, even with both spouses working, contrary to the historical tendency for children to have better living conditions. This strongly suggests that higher job earnings are essential for economic conditions to improve for each new generation. Neither working spouses nor more generous income maintenance programs are enough to produce this result without better paying jobs.

Because of the critical importance of job earnings to the material well-being of the population, the analyst should assess the factors that most heavily affect pay scales, such as shifts between higher- and lower-paying industrial jobs and the bargaining position of workers and employers. These items typically change gradually over time, although there may be some instances when more dramatic changes occur.

WAGE COSTS VERSUS WAGE EARNINGS

Viewed from the perspective of the employer, money wages and salaries and fringe benefits are a cost of production that affect the prices of the goods and services produced and the profits of the enterprise. The most appropriate measure of compensation costs is the quarterly employment cost index (ECI) prepared by the U.S. Bureau of Labor Statistics.

The ECI covers money wages and salaries and noncash fringe benefits such as employer-provided health and retirement plans in all private nonfarm industries and state and local governments for workers at all levels of responsibility. The ECI maintains a stable composition of industries and occupations, so it is not affected by shifts in production between high- and low-wage industries or between high- and low-wage occupations within industries. The composition is changed every ten years. As of this writing, it is based on the industry and occupational distributions in the 1990 census of population. By contrast, the average weekly earnings data discussed in the previous section are affected by the shifting composition of industries and occupations. Also, the weekly earnings

Figure 8.5a **Employment Cost Index versus the Consumer Price Index: 1980–96**

Percent change, December to December

Note: Based on U.S. Bureau of Labor Statistics data.

data exclude nonwage cash payments and noncash fringe benefits.

Figure 8.5a shows annual changes from 1980 to 1996 in the consumer price index (CPI), and in the ECI for private nonfarm industries separately for compensation (wages, salaries, and fringe benefits) and for wages and salaries. Following the decline in the ECI increases from 9 to 10 percent in the early 1980s to 3 percent in the mid-1980s, the increases rose to 5 percent in the late 1980s and then declined to 3 percent in the mid-1990s. The compensation and the wage and salary measures differed by less than one percentage point, with one exception. Compensation had larger increases than wages and salaries except in the mid-1980s and 1995 and 1996. The 1995–96 reversal of the pattern reflected the slowdown in noncash fringe benefit health insurance premiums paid by employers in those two years.

The CPI in this perspective indicates the price movements of the goods and services sold by the nation's enterprises (the CPI is discussed more fully in Chapter 11). The difference between the CPI and the ECI is the movement in the rate of profit, abstracting from changes in the quantity of goods and services sold. When the CPI rises more than the ECI, then profit margins would be rising,

Figure 8.5b **Employment Cost Index Minus Productivity Growth versus the Consumer Price Index: 1980–96**

Percent change, December to December

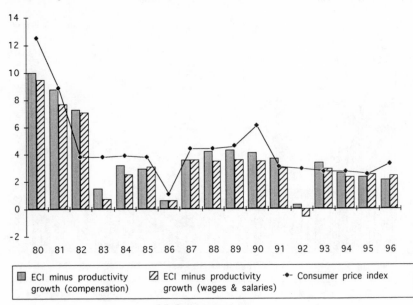

Note: Based on U.S. Bureau of Labor Statistics data.

and when the CPI rises less than ECI, profit margins would be declining. Figure 8.5a indicates that the CPI rose less than the ECI in most years, which suggests that profit margins generally declined over the 1980–96 period. Figure 8.5a does not adjust for productivity, however, which is a key part of the production process.

Figure 8.5b adjusts Figure 8.5a for productivity change (productivity is discussed more fully in Chapter 10). Specifically, Figure 8.5b is the ECI minus productivity change. Productivity is the efficiency of the use of materials, services, labor, equipment, and other resources used in producing goods and services. The ECI less productivity gives a more realistic picture of actual changing labor costs in the production process than the ECI without the adjustment because productivity is an essential ingredient of production.

The result of the productivity adjustment included in Figure 8.5b indicates that the CPI increased more than the ECI in most years. This suggest that profit margins generally increased over the 1980–96 period, contrary to the above pattern of declining profit margins in Figure 8.5a without the productivity adjustment.

Figure 8.6 shows annual changes in average weekly earnings for private nonfarm industries adjusted for inflation from 1959 to 1996. Weekly earnings

Figure 8.6 **Average Weekly Earnings per Worker Adjusted for Inflation: 1959–96**

1982 dollars

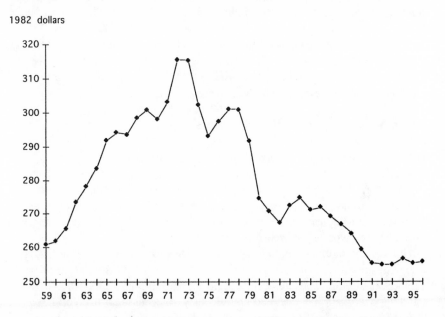

Note: Based on U.S. Bureau of Labor Statistics data for private nonfarm industries.

represent wages from the viewpoint of workers. They reflect the effects of the changing distributions of high- and low-wage industries and occupations, as noted in the previous section. And adjusted for inflation, the earnings data indicate whether the purchasing power of worker earnings increased or decreased. When weekly earnings increase more than the CPI, the purchasing power of the inflation-adjusted worker earnings increases, and when weekly earnings increase less than the CPI, worker purchasing power declines. Figure 8.6 indicates that the inflation-adjusted weekly earnings generally rose from 1959 to 1972, declined from 1972 to 1993 to below the level in the early 1960s, and rose very little during 1994–96. Overall, worker purchasing power in the 1990s is at its lowest level over the entire thirty-seven-year period.

Wage Setting: Interrelationship of Wage Costs and Earnings

Wage rates are determined by many factors, such as relative shortages or surpluses of workers with various skills in local labor markets, feelings of security by workers about their jobs, union membership, and the use of temporary workers and independent contractors.

There is also a general framework within which employers and workers agree on a wage that pertains to the above discussion—profits to the employer and purchasing power to the worker. Figures 8.5b and 8.6 contrast the perspective of profits and purchasing power between employers and workers—Figure 8.5b on the ECI from the viewpoint of employers, and Figure 8.6 on weekly earnings from the viewpoint of workers. The CPI appears as a counterpart in both figures, in one as the selling price of items produced by employers, and in the other as the buying price of items bought by worker consumers.

Union, Nonunion, and Contingent Workers

The bargaining position of workers and employers is also affected by the relative proportions of union workers, nonunion workers, and the employment of temporary workers and independent contractors, who are referred to as "contingent workers." Money wages, fringe benefits, job security, and occupational health and safety are highest for union members and lowest for contingent workers, with nonunion workers between the two.

Union negotiating strength is directly related to the proportion of workers who are unionized, with worker bargaining power being stronger with large numbers than with small numbers. Union membership as a proportion of wage and salary workers has declined continuously since the end of World War II, from 35.5 percent in 1945, to 23 percent in 1980, to 16 percent in 1990, to 14.5 percent in 1996.[8] There are also wide variations by industry. In 1996, for example, unionized workers accounted for 1.9 percent of farm workers, 10.2 percent of private nonfarm workers, and 37.7 percent of federal, state, and local government workers.[9] In the late 1990s, unions began drives to unionize more business establishments and thus reverse the long-term decline in the numbers and economic impact of unions.

Although unions represent a relatively small share of all American workers, unions influence wage incomes and working conditions of nonunionized workers as well. Because unions are the dominant bargaining agent in several industries, their compensation patterns are often a guideline for compensation of nonunion workers in the same industry or company. For example, some nonunion companies have a policy of raising wages when wages in their union counterpart companies are increased, and thus maintain the same differential between union and nonunion wages. The aim is to reduce the incentive of nonunion workers to join a union.

At the lowest pole of the bargaining position, increasing use of contingent workers raises the bargaining position of employers in relation to both union and nonunion workers. Estimates of contingent workers range from 2.2 percent to 4.9 percent of all employed workers in 1995, depending on the definition of contingent workers.[10] The lower estimate refers to workers who expect their current job to last for an additional year or less, and who had worked at their jobs for one year or less. It also excludes self-employed workers and independent contractors. The higher estimate includes all wage and salary workers who expect their current jobs to terminate at some time in the future, regardless of how long they have been on the job (this relaxes the one-year limitation of the low estimate). It also includes self-employed workers, temporary workers, independent contractors, and contract company workers who do not expect their current assignment to last for more than one year, which includes the less than one year they have already been on that assignment. In a survey conducted by the Upjohn Institute, Susan Houseman notes that employers say their main reasons for hiring contingent workers are fluctuations in workload, absences of regular workers, and to a lesser extent screening candidates for regular jobs, with lower wages, health insurance, and other fringe benefits paid to contingent workers being less important.[11]

The analyst should monitor trends affecting both sides of the bargaining table: efforts by unions to make up for previous losses in the purchasing power of worker wages, to raise worker wages above the inflation rate, and to provide more job security, in contrast to efforts of employers in holding down wage costs. These are affected by how each side perceives the relationship between compensation and job security. If a strong linkage between compensation and job security is assumed, compensation tends to increase less than if job security is not an overriding issue. The tensions among union, nonunion, and contingent workers should be included in the assessment of the bargaining power relationship.

REVIEW QUESTIONS

- What are the strengths and weaknesses of the establishment and household surveys of employment?
- Are differences in the movements of the two measures of employment more significant for periods within one year or for longer periods? Explain.
- Why is the employment-population ratio a more significant measure of employment movements than the labor force participation rate?
- Employers tend to change the weekly hours of workers in response to changes in company sales before hiring or laying off workers. What statistical property does this give the weekly hours data?
- What caused the sharply differing movements between the average weekly earnings and the disposable personal income per capita data from the 1970s to the 1990s?
- How does the economic significance of the employment cost index differ from that of the average weekly earnings data?
- Explain the differing roles of the consumer price index when it is compared with the employment cost index and the average weekly earnings data.

- How are union wage levels related to the employment and wages of nonunion and contingent workers?

Extra Credit

- What effects may the underground economy have on the accuracy of the household and establishment employment surveys?
- Suppose the next decennial census in the year 2000 shows that the government has been understating the U.S. population. What would this imply for the relative accuracy of the household and establishment employment measures?

NOTES

1. Bureau of Labor Statistics, U.S. Department of Labor, *Handbook of Methods,* April 1997, chs. 1 and 2; and Bureau of Labor Statistics, U.S. Department of Labor, *Employment and Earnings,* every month, Explanatory Notes and Estimates of Error. These sources provide detailed descriptions of both the household and establishment survey methodologies.

2. The 1950s are calculated from 1948–59, instead of 1949–59 or 1950–59, because 1949 was a recession year and 1950 was a recovery year, while 1948 and 1959 were both expansion peak years before the onset of a recession. The treatment here is consistent with the beginning and ending years for the other decades, 1959–69, 1969–79, 1979–89, 1989–96 (1996 was an ongoing expansion at the time of this writing). To use 1949–59 or 1950–59 for the 1950s would distort the calculation. This issue is covered in Chapter 1 under Calculating and Presenting Growth Rates, Beginning and Ending Dates.

3. John F. Stinson Jr., "Comparison of Nonagricultural Employment Estimates from Two Surveys," *Employment and Earnings,* March 1983.

4. Alexander Korns, "Cyclical Fluctuations in the Difference Between the Payroll and Household Measures of Employment," *Survey of Current Business,* May 1979.

5. John E. Bregger, "Measuring self-employment in the United States," *Monthly Labor Review,* January/February 1996. For example, self-employment as a share of total employment in nonagricultural industries declined from 8.7 percent in 1966 to 7.3 percent in 1967. Most of this large one-year decline probably stemmed from a new question added to the household survey in 1967 that asked survey respondents who identified themselves as self-employed if their businesses were incorporated. Since 1967, if the business is incorporated, even the primary owner is classified as a wage and salary employee, because legally, the owner is an employee of the corporation.

6. Eugene H. Becker, "Self-employed workers: an update to 1983," *Monthly Labor Review,* July 1984.

7. In manufacturing, mining, and construction, for employees up through the level of working supervisors, "production" designates workers who engage directly in the work. The analogous designation in other industries—transportation, utilities, trade, finance, and other services—is "nonsupervisory" workers.

8. For 1945, these percentages are limited to organizations officially designated as unions, but by the 1970s they include employee associations of professional groups that subsequently began to act as unions, such as the National Education Association and the

Fraternal Orders of Police. See Larry T. Adams, "Changing employment patterns of organized workers," *Monthly Labor Review,* February 1985.

9. Bureau of Labor Statistics, U.S. Department of Labor, "Union Members in 1996," *Employment and Earnings,* January 1997, Table 42.

10. Anne E. Polivka, "Contingent and alternative work arrangements, defined," *Monthly Labor Review,* October 1996.

11. Susan N. Houseman, "New Institute Survey on Flexible Staffing Arrangements," *Employment Research* (W. E. Upjohn Institute for Employment Research. Spring 1997).

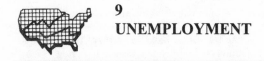

9
UNEMPLOYMENT

The topics of unemployment in this chapter and of employment in Chapter 8 center on what they indicate about economic growth and material living conditions. They also affect the economy in intangible ways, such as their influence on personal satisfaction and social stability. Though these factors are not strictly "economic," they can affect economic developments. For example, voters experiencing high unemployment are more likely to vote for politicians who offer new economic theories and the promise of job creation. While such cause-and-effect relationships are difficult to quantify, the analyst should bear them in mind when considering the economic policy implications of unemployment and employment data.

UNEMPLOYMENT RATE

The unemployment rate (UR) is prepared monthly by the Bureau of Labor Statistics in the U.S. Department of Labor based on data obtained from a survey of a sample of households.[1] The UR is defined as the proportion of the nation's noninstitutional population sixteen years and older that is out of work, actively looking for a job, and available for work. It is a relative measure of the degree of slack in job markets. At the most simplistic level, a relatively high UR indicates that production probably can be increased without generating inflation because the available labor supply will tend to moderate wage rate increases and in some cases reduce wage rates. Conversely, in periods of low unemployment, high economic growth is more likely to raise wages—the tighter labor supply pushes up wages as more experienced and more productive workers are bid away from firm to firm on all steps of the skill ladder, which increases job openings for the less experienced and less productive workers. Of course, the overall UR may mask significant differences among local markets, occupations, industries, and demographic groups.

Contrary to this model, it does not always happen that high unemployment is associated with low inflation, and that low unemployment is associated with high inflation. In fact, the opposite occurred in the early 1980s and the mid-1990s. In the early 1980s, unemployment and inflation were both high, while in the mid-1990s, unemployment and inflation were both low. The nature of such differences is discussed in Chapter 5 under Capacity Utilization and Nonresidential Investment.

Methodology

There are several measures of unemployment. The basic difference among the various measures is the definition of the unemployed. The framework for all the measures is noninstitutionalized persons living in the United States who are sixteen years or older and who are not members of the U.S. armed forces. They exclude persons confined to institutions such as nursing homes or jails. By excluding the armed forces, the measures represent the civilian labor force.

Mathematically, the unemployment rate (UR) is calculated as follows:

$$UR = \frac{\text{Unemployed persons}}{\text{Employed + unemployed persons (labor force)}} \times 100$$

The official and most widely accepted UR defines the labor force as consisting of all persons at least sixteen years old who have a job or are actively seeking and available to work. The employment component includes all persons who did any work at all (at least one hour), as paid employees, persons working in their own business (self-employment), persons working at nonpaid jobs in a family business for at least fifteen hours a week, as well as those temporarily absent from their job or business due to vacations, illness, or other reasons. Thus, the employed population consists of full-time and part-time wage earners and of those who work for profit, the latter being the self-employed and unpaid workers in family businesses who are assumed to share in the profits. Persons who have more than one job are counted only once, in their primary job, which is the one from which they derive the most income. Supplementary data are provided on multiple jobholders, those who have more than one job, for analytical use (Chapter 9 covers employment).

Unemployed persons are those who had no employment during the survey reference week, were available to work except for temporary illness, and had actively looked for employment some time during the four-week period ending with the survey reference week. The survey reference week is the week (Sunday to Saturday) that includes the twelfth day of the month. The survey is conducted during the following week. Examples of an active job search are having a job interview; contacting an employer for a job interview; contacting an employment agency, friends, or relatives; sending out résumés; answering a job advertisement; placing an advertisement in a newspaper; or checking a union or professional register. By contrast, looking at job advertisements or attending job-training programs or courses is defined as a passive search for work, and does not meet the criterion of being unemployed.

Persons aged sixteen years and over who are not employed or unemployed are classified as "not in the labor force." "Discouraged workers" are persons sixteen and older who want a job and have looked for work in the last twelve months, but are not currently looking for a job because they believe jobs are unavailable in their area or in their line of work, or because they believe they would not qualify for existing job openings. Typically, discouraged workers range from 0.3 to 0.6 percent of the labor force, tending toward the lower number in expansions and the higher in recessions.

The information used in deriving the UR is obtained from a monthly survey of a sample of about 50,000 households, called the Current Population Survey (CPS). Responses are actually obtained from about 47,000 households each month. For the remaining 3,000 households, no responses are obtained due to absence, impassable roads, refusals, or for other reasons. The U.S. Bureau of the Census conducts the survey for the U.S. Bureau of Labor Statistics.

In order to avoid placing too heavy a burden on the households selected for the sample, one-fourth of the households in the sample is changed each month. Each household is interviewed for four months, dropped from the rotation for the next eight months, and then is again interviewed for the subsequent four months; participation in the survey ends after this sixteen-month period. As indicated by the survey questions summarized below, persons are not directly asked whether they are unemployed. Instead, they are asked a series of questions to determine if they are working (employed) or actively seeking employment (unemployment). Unemployment is determined from the respondent answers to all the questions; this ensures that the same unemployment definitions are used for all survey participants. Other groups of questions are asked to determine employment and labor force status, full-time and part-time work, earnings, multiple jobholders, discouraged workers, industry and occupation, and other labor market indicators.

A personal interview is conducted for nearly all households that are in the CPS sample survey the first and fifth month. For most of the remaining months in the sample, telephone interviewing is used. If an adult member of the household who answered the questions in one month is unavailable at the time of the interview in a subsequent month, another adult member of the household (such as a spouse) who is familiar with the individual's employment status may answer the questions by proxy.

The following CPS questions are asked of respondents who reported they had no job or business from which they were absent or on layoff:

Determination of Unemployment

- Have you been doing anything to find work during the last four weeks?
- What are all of the things you have done to find work during the last four

weeks? Follow-up questions to obtain specific job search actions. You said you have been trying to find work. How did you go about looking? Can you tell me more about what you did to search for work?

- Last week, could you have started a job if one had been offered? Follow-up if the answer is no. Why is that?

Characteristics of Unemployment

- Before you started looking for work, what were you doing: working, going to school, or something else?
  Follow-up if the answer is "Working."
  Did you lose or quit that job, or was it a temporary job that ended?
  When did you last work at that job or business? Month and year.
- As of the end of last week, how long have you been looking for work?
  Weeks, if possible. Otherwise, months or years.
- Have you been looking for full-time work of thirty-five hours or more per week?

Sampling Error

Estimates derived from a sample of only 50,000 households may not be fully representative of the demographic and economic characteristics of America's 99.6 million households as of 1995. The chances are that in two of three cases, the sampling error in the monthly movement of the UR is plus or minus 0.1 percentage point. For example, if the UR is 5 percent, it most likely is in the range of 4.9 to 5.1 percent. Because of this sampling error, a single month-to-month change of plus or minus 0.1 percentage point is not statistically significant, but a change of plus or minus 0.2 percentage point is statistically significant. By the same token, cumulated changes in the UR in the same upward and downward direction of 0.1 percentage point a month for two or more months in a row are statistically significant. If the reliability range is raised to nineteen of twenty cases, the sampling error for the monthly movement rises to 0.2 percentage point, and the above example is increased accordingly. Thus, a UR of 5 percent would have an error range of 4.8 to 5.2 percent, and a monthly movement would have to be at least plus or minus 0.3 percentage point to be statistically significant.

Alternative Measures of Labor Underutilization

Table 9.1 provides six alternative measures of labor underutilization that are referred to as U-1 to U-6 for 1996.[2] The numbers are based on the household survey labor force data and reflect different ways of counting unemployment. Alternative monthly estimates U-1 to U-3 are seasonally adjusted, but the

Table 9.1

Alternative Measures of Labor Underutilization: 1996

	Percent
U-1. Persons unemployed 15 weeks or longer, as a percentage of the civilian labor force	1.7
U-2. Job losers and persons who completed temporary jobs, as a percentage of the civilian labor force	2.5
U-3. Total unemployed, as a percentage of the civilian labor force (official unemployment rate)	*5.4*
U-4. U-3 plus discouraged workers, as a percentage of the civilian labor force plus discouraged workers	5.7
U-5. U-4 plus all other marginally attached workers, as a percentage of the civilian labor force plus all marginally attached workers	6.5
U-6. U-5 plus total employed part-time because full-time jobs are not available	9.7

Source: U.S. Bureau of Labor Statistics.

monthly estimates for U-4 to U-6 are not. The seasonal differentials are small, however, and do not affect the patterns described here.

The narrowest alternative measure (U-1) is limited to persons who are unemployed for fifteen weeks or longer. The broadest alternative (U-6) comprises the official designation of unemployed persons described above under Methodology, plus "discouraged" workers who do not look for work because they think there are no jobs for them, plus other "marginally attached" workers who are currently neither working nor looking for work, but indicate that they want and are available for a job and have looked for work sometime in the past twelve months, plus persons working part-time who would work full-time if such jobs were available.[3] The range between these extremes is considerable—1.7 to 9.7 percent, with the official definition of unemployment (U-3) at 5.4 percent.

The official UR, U-3, is the most widely accepted measure. It is the most neutral in terms of value judgments related to labor force definitions. It includes all unemployed workers and gives equal weight to each unemployed person, regardless of age, duration of unemployment, reason for not working at the previous job, and full-time or part-time labor force status. Other URs are provided, such as those by age, gender, color, Hispanic origin, and family relationship, which highlight differences among various population groups in obtaining work. In addition, there is a measure of unemployment based on unemployment insurance benefit payments, which is based on different data and is not comparable to the six labor force alternative measures, as discussed later.

Although their movements over time are similar, the different unemployment definitions indicate a varying absolute range of slackness in the economy. They therefore tend to be cited selectively by persons characterizing the extent of unemployment, depending on social or political perspectives. For example, those who wish to emphasize the economy's success in generating employment highlight the U-1 end of the spectrum with the lowest URs (political conservatives), and those who wish to emphasize the economy's failure to provide jobs highlight the U-6 end with the highest URs (political liberals). This does not necessarily reflect the tendency of the political party in power, which whether liberal or conservative, would seek to show it is providing more jobs.

The analyst should monitor the alternative measures of labor underutilization for changes in differential rates among the various labor force classifications. Significant changes in the differentials could suggest subsequent impacts on persons entering and leaving the labor force, the official unemployment rate, and wages.

ANALYSIS OF TRENDS

Demographic Changes Affecting the Labor Force and Unemployment

Long-term demographic movements over decades and for shorter cyclical movements have different characteristics in labor force and UR analysis. Demographic movements reflect both population growth and labor force participation rates. Cyclical movements are linked more closely to economic growth (Chapter 3) and employment (Chapter 8).

Long-term Population and Labor Force Movements

Population changes resulting from long-term birthrate cycles have the most pronounced impact on the labor force over five- and ten-year periods, mainly because of the lag in the effect of birthrates in previous decades until the children reach working-age in later decades. Changing immigration, emigration, and death rates are less important factors affecting the working-age population. For example, the low birthrates of the depression in the 1930s led to a low annual increase (compounded) of the working-age population in the 1950s of 1 percent. But the baby boom of the late 1940s and the 1950s resulted in faster average annual increases in the working-age population of 1.5 percent in the 1960s and 2.1 percent in the 1970s. The subsequent drop in birthrates during the 1960s and 1970s lowered the annual working-age population increases in the 1980s to 1.2 percent and in the 1990s (1990–96) to 1.1 percent.

The labor force is the sum of employed and unemployed persons, as noted previously in the Methodology section. The labor force participation rate (LFPR) represents the number of persons in the labor force as a proportion of the population sixteen years and older.

Table 9.2 shows the LFPR from the 1950s to 1996 separately for males and females 16 years and older, and for teenagers 16–19 years old. Changes in the

Table 9.2

Labor Force Participation Rates: 1950–96

	Total[a]	Males[a]	Females[a]	Teenagers[b]
1950	59.2	86.4	33.9	51.8
1960	59.4	83.3	37.7	47.5
1970	60.4	79.7	43.3	49.9
1980	63.8	77.4	51.5	56.7
1990	66.5	76.4	57.5	53.7
1996	66.8	74.9	59.3	52.3

Source: U.S. Bureau of Labor Statistics.
Note: Represents the labor force as a percentage of the noninstitutionalized population separately for males, females, and teenagers.
[a] 16 years and older.
[b] 16–19 years old.

LFPR over the long run reflect changes in life-style and perceptions of the availability of jobs. The combined participation rate for males and females increased from 59 percent in 1950 to 67 percent in 1996. This overall increase is the net effect of the increasing proportion of women pursuing a career that more than offset the declining proportion of men in the labor force, who had shorter working careers by retiring earlier. The rate for females rose from 34 percent in 1950 to 59 percent in 1996, while that for males declined from 86 to 75 percent over the same period. The direction of the patterns was consistent from the 1950s to the 1990s, although with males having the largest decreases in the 1950s and 1960s, and females having the largest increases in the 1960s, 1970s, and 1980s. The total LFPR changed very little in both the 1950s and the 1990s.

The LFPR for teenagers fluctuated from the 1950s to the 1990s, as teenagers showed changing proclivities to enter the labor market while in high school and after. The teenage rate declined in the 1950s, increased in the 1960s and 1970s, and decreased in the 1980s and 1990s. Generally, one-half of all teenagers have been in the labor force since the end of World War II.

Figure 9.1 shows the distribution of adult men, adult women, and teenagers as a percentage of the total labor force from 1950 to 1996. Adult men and women are defined as those twenty years and older. The three components sum to 100 percent. (This differs from the LFPRs in Table 9.2, which are calculated separately for each of the three groups.) The proportion of women in the labor force rose continuously from 27 percent in 1950 to 43 percent in 1996, and the proportion of men declined continuously from 66 percent in 1950 to 51 percent in 1996. By contrast, the proportion of teenagers fluctuated over the period, rising from 7 percent in 1950 and 1960 to 9 percent in 1970 and 1980, and declining to 6

Figure 9.1 **Men, Women, and Teenagers as a Percentage of the Labor Force: 1950–96**

Percent

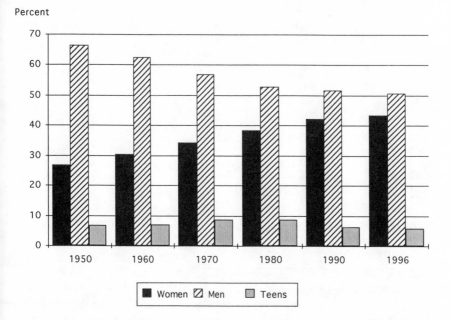

Note: Based on U.S. Bureau of Labor Statistics data. Men and women 20 years and older; teens 16–19 years.

percent in 1990 and 1996 (the decline actually continued during the 1990s, from 6.2 percent in 1990 to 5.8 percent in 1996).

Effect of Changing Demographics on Unemployment

Unemployment would not be affected by changing distributions of men, women, and teenagers in the labor force if the three groups had similar URs. Table 9.3 shows the URs for men and women 20 years and older, and for teenagers 16–19 years old, from 1950 to 1996. These indicate that the URs for men were 0.5 to 1.5 percentage points lower than those for women until the 1980s, but that the differential disappeared and in some years reversed itself in the 1980s and 1990s. By contrast, teenage URs were two to three times higher than adult rates during the five decades. Thus, the total UR is affected by the differential URs for men and women until the 1980s, and for teenagers over the entire period.

The result is that the increasing proportion of women and the decreasing proportion of men in the labor force increased the total UR from 1950 to 1980, but not from 1980 to 1996. While the labor force gender trends of the 1980s and

Table 9.3

Unemployment Rates: 1950–96

	Total	Men[a]	Women[a]	Teenagers[b]
1950	5.3	4.7	5.1	12.2
1960	5.5	4.7	5.1	14.7
1970	4.9	3.5	4.8	15.3
1975	8.5	6.8	8.0	19.9
1980	7.1	5.9	6.4	17.8
1982	9.7	8.8	8.3	23.2
1984	7.5	6.6	6.8	18.9
1986	7.0	6.1	6.2	18.3
1988	5.5	4.8	4.9	15.3
1990	5.6	5.0	4.9	15.5
1992	7.5	7.1	6.3	20.1
1994	6.1	5.4	5.4	17.6
1996	5.4	4.6	4.8	16.7

Source: U.S. Bureau of Labor Statistics.
[a]20 years and older.
[b]16–19 years old.

1990s continued those of the previous decades, they did not affect the total UR in the 1980s and 1990s because the URs for men and women were similar in the later decades. The changing proportions of teenagers did affect the overall UR, however, raising it from the 1950s to the 1970s, and lowering it in the 1980s and 1990s.

Paul Flaim estimated that if the labor force composition had remained the same between 1959 and 1979, the civilian UR would have been 1.4 percentage points lower than it was in 1979 (4.4 percent compared with the actual 5.8 percent).[4] The study found that most of the rise in unemployment due to demographic factors over the period resulted from the increased number of teenagers in the population rather than from the increasing labor force participation rates of women, because of the much higher teenage URs than those for men and women. In addition, the decline in the teenage share of the work force in the 1980s accounted for approximately 0.5 percentage point of the 0.6 percentage point decline in the UR from 1979 to 1989—that is, approximately 80 percent of the decade decline in the UR.[5] The study also projected that the lower birthrates of baby-boom parents will contribute to a further UR decline in the 1990s by 0.3 percentage point because of the continued decline in the proportion of teens in the labor force.

The analyst should assess long-run shifts in the demographic composition of the labor force and in LFPRs to determine when changes in direction are likely to affect the UR. This includes the maturing of children into the teens and of the teens into the twenties, and shifts in the LFPR for adults and teenagers.

Relation of Persons Receiving Unemployment Insurance
Benefits to the Labor Force Measure of Unemployment

A different measure of unemployment based on persons collecting unemployment insurance benefit payments is provided weekly by the Employment and
Training Administration in the U.S. Department of Labor. Its main use for macroeconomic analysis is that the data on persons filing initial claims for benefit
payments when they first become unemployed are a component of the composite
index of leading indicators (Chapter 13). In addition, because the data on all
persons receiving unemployment insurance benefits (not just those who are initially unemployed) are available weekly, and because the monthly movements
(the average of the four weeks) tend to be similar or in the same direction,
although not identical to those for the household UR, they are suggestive of the
forthcoming monthly household UR.

The unemployment insurance data coverage is limited to persons filing claims
for unemployment insurance benefits and consequently is a much less comprehensive unemployment measure than those based on the labor force household survey discussed above. In 1996, for example, on average 2.65 million
unemployed workers were receiving benefits under state and federal unemployment insurance programs, compared with 7.24 million workers counted as unemployed in the labor force survey. Thus, insured unemployment represented only
37 percent of all unemployment. Overall, in 1996 the insured UR was 2.3 percent (persons receiving unemployment insurance benefits as a percentage of all
persons covered under unemployment insurance programs), compared with the
labor force UR of 5.4 percent. The reason is that insured unemployment excludes
such groups as young persons looking for their first job after graduation, former
workers who are reentering the labor force, those who have exhausted their
unemployment benefits, and those who are otherwise ineligible for unemployment benefits. By contrast, all persons in these groups who meet the labor force
criteria of actively seeking work are included in the labor force measure of
unemployment.

The generosity of the unemployment insurance benefit payments varies both
in the dollar amounts and the eligibility criteria among the various state governments. In general, only workers who meet the following requirements can receive unemployment insurance payments:

- Applied for benefit payments
- Lost their job, with exceptions in some states for those who quit their jobs
  with good cause
- Previously worked long enough to be eligible for benefit payments (e.g.,
  six months)
- Have not exhausted the period during which they may collect the payments (typically, twenty-six weeks)

The tightened administration of unemployment insurance benefits by state governments during the 1980s and 1990s also probably contributed to the declining URs in those periods. The more restricted interpretation of the eligibility criterion for receiving unemployment benefits probably led some unemployed workers to take a less satisfactory job than they would have held out for had they received unemployment benefits. Estimates of the impact of the administration of unemployment insurance on job search and job acceptance, however, and consequently on insured unemployment and labor force unemployment, are not available.

In assessing future effects of the administration of unemployment insurance programs on unemployment, the analyst should monitor the tendency of the various state governments to become more generous or more stringent in the interpretation of who is eligible to receive unemployment benefits. Increasing generosity would tend to raise the UR, while greater stringency would tend to lower the UR.

Impact of Cyclical Movements on the Labor Force and Unemployment

During cyclical expansions and recessions, changes in the LFPR of persons entering and leaving the labor market are dominated by short-term economic conditions. Typically, more people enter the labor force in expansions than in recessions, as the prospects of finding a job are higher in expansions than in recessions. Yet even in recessions there tends to be a general upward thrust in participation because of the underlying upward trend.

Monthly and quarterly movements of the LFPR are key items affecting the cyclical UR because they indicate how individuals perceive their immediate chances of finding work. Intuitively, one would expect that more persons would enter the labor force during expansions than during recessions because they would be more hopeful of getting a job when the economy is growing. This is borne out in the actual movements of discouraged workers during expansions and recessions. The effect has also been observed in studies related particularly to periods of recession and high unemployment. The issue during periods of high unemployment is if one member of a family loses a job—whether this causes another family member to seek work to supplement the family's income (the added-worker effect), or if the declining job market discourages some people from seeking work (the discouraged-worker effect). The studies have indicated that the discouraged-worker effect is greater than the added-worker effect, as noted by Robert Pindyck and David Rubinfeld.[6] One reason the additional-worker effect is not stronger is that the large increases that have occurred in the female labor force participation rate (discussed previously) have reduced the pool of "additional workers."

The movement of discouraged workers in and out of the labor force also affects the UR, as Edward Steinberg notes.[7] During expansions, a greater opti-

Figure 9.2 **Civilian Unemployment Rate: 1967–97**

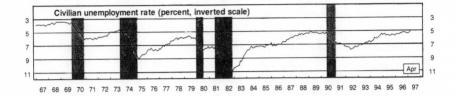

Note: Based on U.S. Bureau of Labor Statistics and National Bureau of Economic Research data. Vertical bars are recession periods.

mism about job prospects dampens the decline in the UR, if the previously discouraged workers who enter the labor force find jobs at a lower rate than that for the labor force as a whole. Conversely, during recessions, when declining employment causes large numbers to withdraw from the labor market because of the pessimistic outlook for jobs, the rise in discouraged workers dampens the increase in the UR. Thus, the effects of job prospects on the perceptions of discouraged workers tend to understate the improvements in the economy during expansions, and understate the deterioration of the economy during recessions.

In some months these movements in and out of the labor force lead to UR changes that are contrary to changes in employment. In such cases, large numbers of persons leaving the labor force lower the UR, while large numbers of persons entering the labor force raise the UR. This usually occurs for marginal UR movements that are not statistically significant, which give a different picture of the economy than the employment movements. For example, in January, July, and November 1996 and January 1997, the UR increased by 0.1 percentage point (not statistically significant), while employment increased.

Over the post–World War II business cycles, the UR moved as expected—declining in expansions and rising in recessions. The only exception was the expansion from 1945 to 1948; the exceptionally low UR of 1.9 percent in 1945 was not sustained in the subsequent demobilization of war production and the reduction of the resident armed forces (from 11.4 million in 1945 to 1.5 million in 1948). Thus, the UR averaged 3.9 percent in 1946 and 1947 and 3.8 percent in 1948. In retrospect, these were the lowest "peacetime" URs in the postwar period, as noted below. The relatively low URs in 1946–48 resulted from the strong civilian economy, and from the return of many veterans to full-time schooling, which removed them from the labor force. In terms of timing at cyclical turning points, the UR is a leading indicator at the peak of expansions and a lagging indicator at the trough of recessions (Chapter 13).

Figure 9.2 shows the UR at the peaks of expansions and troughs of recessions from 1967 to 1996 (the vertical scale is inverted from its usual position).[8] Three long-term features of the UR movements are noteworthy. First, unemployment levels worsened during the 1970s and early 1980s, drifting upward so that typically the low point at the peak of each expansion was higher than it was at the peak of the previous expansion. But this pattern was reversed at the peak of the 1982–90 expansion, as the UR was below the peaks of the two previous expansions. These developments are related to the changing demographic composition of the labor force discussed previously. Second, the UR has not been below 3 percent other than in 1952–53 during the Korean War, and it was below 4 percent for a sustained period only in 1966–69 during the Vietnam War. Third, the decline in the UR below 5 percent in 1997 brought the UR to its lowest level since 1973.

The analyst should evaluate fluctuating movements in and out of the labor force for their effect on the UR. The labor force movements of discouraged workers lessen the UR declines in expansions and lessen the UR increases in recessions.

Unemployment Goals

Economic analysis has a major policy interest in determining the lowest UR level that can be sustained over long periods without causing inflation. Over the years this concept has been referred to variously as "full," "maximum," or "high" employment, "natural" unemployment, and the "nonaccelerating inflation rate of unemployment." Regardless of the terminology, the intent is to establish a UR toward which the nation should strive.

The goal of achieving a minimum level of unemployment, corresponding to a notion of "full employment," without causing inflation has changed. In the 1960s it was believed the lowest feasible UR was 3 to 4 percent. In the 1970s this number rose to 5 to 7 percent. The Full Employment and Balanced Growth Act of 1978 specified unemployment goals of 4 percent (Chapter 2).

In estimating a minimum UR, it is assumed there will always be some unemployment, for two reasons. First, there is never a perfect match between persons in the labor force and the skills required by employers because of residual outmoded skills from declining industries; lack of training; geographic immobility of workers; or age, race, gender, and other discrimination in hiring; all of which are referred to as "structural unemployment." Second, there is an inherent time lag in finding jobs whether persons are newly entering the labor force or whether they have lost their jobs, which is referred to as "frictional unemployment." In practice, determining a minimum UR that would accommodate both structural and frictional unemployment, without causing additional price inflation, has been based on past relationships between unemployment and inflation, rather than on an analysis of what the micro labor markets in the economy would generate. This approach is referred to as the nonaccelerating inflation rate of unemployment, or NAIRU (Chapter 2). Although a micro analysis is theoretically more appealing than the NAIRU approach, it would require an assessment of the myriad transactions of buyers and sellers in product, labor, and financial markets that could be translated into the overall macro economy. This is a monumental task, and the methodology of economics is not yet capable of doing it.

The analyst should monitor reports in the press that suggest changes in structural and frictional unemployment that could lead to changes in minimum UR levels.

Note on Job Vacancy Data

One approach for assessing the magnitude of unemployment is to compare it with available job vacancies. To make such a comparison meaningfully, the distribution of job skills among the unemployed would have to be matched with those required in available jobs. Only with appropriate data on both of these factors would it be plausible to make unemployment-vacancy comparisons at the macro level. If there were a reasonable match, it could be assumed that part of the unemployment could be absorbed.

No such information is available that would permit absolute comparisons with unemployment levels, however. The U.S. Bureau of Labor Statistics has conducted actual and experimental vacancy surveys of employers in the past, but all have been discontinued because they were considered too expensive.

The Conference Board provides data on employer hiring plans from help-wanted newspaper advertisements. They are collected from one newspaper in each of fifty-one local labor markets. This sample is raised to an estimated national total by the national employment proportions accounted for by the sample labor markets. The data are provided monthly as an index of the percent change in the number of jobs advertised. The index is a leading indicator at business expansion peaks and a lagging indicator at business recession troughs (Chapter 13).

The help-wanted data broadly estimate the relative change in job vacancies. But they are not comprehensive or representative enough to be converted to absolute levels for comparisons with the actual number of unemployed persons because many jobs are not advertised in newspapers. The help-wanted measure also does not distinguish job vacancies by occupational skills, which could be matched with counterpart data on the skills of the unemployed. This is necessary to obtain specific data on occupational job shortages and surpluses. Thus, while some job vacancy data are available from the help-wanted advertising measure, data limitations prevent their use for assessing the overall magnitude of unemployment.

REVIEW QUESTIONS

- The household survey of the labor force does not ask the direct question of the respondent, "Are you unemployed?" What are the strengths and weaknesses of this survey technique?

- In some months, the unemployment rate declines when employment declines. Why?
- Characterize how the official unemployment rate differs from other unemployment measures that include special groupings of unemployed workers.
- Why is the official unemployment rate higher than the one based on unemployment insurance data?
- How did the demographic changes in the labor force affect unemployment rates in the 1980s and 1990s?
- What aspects of the labor force would have to change to have zero unemployment?
- How could the availability of job vacancy data be used to lower the unemployment rate in the short run and in the long run?

Extra Credit

- Chapter 2 of the 1977 *Economic Report of the President* analyzes the relationship between inflation and the "demographically adjusted unemployment rate." What do you think the "demographically adjusted UR" is, and why would analysts focus on it, rather than on the traditional UR, to explain changes in inflation?
- Table 9.3 shows that the UR for women typically exceeded the UR for men before 1980, but since then the two rates are very similar. What explains the closing of the male-female UR gap?
- How would policies designed to combat structural unemployment differ from those designed to combat unemployment related to recession?

NOTES

1. Bureau of Labor Statistics, U.S. Department of Labor, *BLS Handbook of Methods,* April 1997, ch. 1. Bureau of Labor Statistics, U.S. Department of Labor, *Employment and Earnings,* Explanatory Notes and Estimates of Error, every month. These sources provide detailed descriptions of the unemployment statistics methodology.

2. John E. Bregger and Steven E. Haugen, "BLS introduces new range of alternative unemployment measures," *Monthly Labor Review,* October 1995.

3. Marginally attached workers other than attached workers are not currently looking for work because of such problems as child care or transportation.

4. Paul O. Flaim, "Population changes, the baby boom, and the unemployment rate," *Monthly Labor Review,* August 1990.

5. The decline in the UR from 1979 to 1989 as reported at the time of this writing is 0.5 percentage point. This probably reflects a revision in the data from the time the study was made, which reported a decline of 0.6 percentage point. On its face, the revised data suggest that all of the decline was accounted for by the decline in the teenage labor force, rather than all but 0.1 percentage point cited in the study. It is likely that if the study

were conducted with the revised data, however, there would still be a small part of the decline not accounted for by teenagers.

6. Robert S. Pindyck and Daniel L. Rubinfeld, *Microeconomics,* 3d ed. (Prentice-Hall, 1995), p. 7.

7. Edward Steinberg, "The Cycle of Discouraged Workers," *The Margin,* September/October 1990, p. 39.

8. The vertical scale in Figure 9.2 shows the lowest number at the top and the highest number at the bottom, which is contrary to the typical order. The typical treatment shows a rising graph when the numbers are rising, in line with the general perception that more is better. But in the case of unemployment, less is better. So the scale is inverted to show that less unemployment is better.

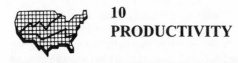

10
PRODUCTIVITY

Increasing the output of goods and services is a key factor in improving the material well-being of the population and maintaining a secure defense. There are two ways to increase the volume of goods and services available for private and public use: increase the amount of labor and capital equipment used as inputs in production, or increase the efficiency of these factors in producing the output. The latter defines the economy's productivity and is a primary factor determining the growth of the nation's total output (the contribution of productivity to economic growth is covered in Chapter 3). Productivity is increased through improvements in technology and equipment; education and skills of the workforce; executive direction; managerial know-how; public-sector spending that substitutes for private spending infrastructure such as for roads, airports, and sewers; and many other factors.

Productivity refers to the efficiency of producing goods and services. In the context of a firm or a worker, increasing productivity is an important element in generating greater profits and wages. In the context of the nation, rising productivity is fundamental to improvements in living conditions. Sustained productivity increases over time are the basic means by which the economy generates overall improved living conditions for each generation. Higher productivity is required for children to have a higher level of material well-being than their parents, and concomitantly for the nation to have the resources to protect itself against foreign enemies.

At the same time, new technology can temporarily lower productivity. Productivity may be reduced in the initial transition period when lack of familiarity with new equipment causes workers to take longer to do a job than they took with the older technology, or when breakdowns and bugs occur in the new equipment and have to be corrected. Problems associated with the introduction of new computer systems and advanced telephone systems are recent examples of this phenomenon. Additionally, because new technology causes some workers to be unemployed or to work at lower-paying jobs, not everyone shares equally in productivity improvements.

Productivity is not an unmixed blessing. Rising productivity can cause employment dislocation because the introduction of new technology changes or eliminates some jobs. Displaced workers with outmoded skills may not be able to find new jobs or may find only lower-paid work. At the economywide level, rising productivity does not necessarily lead to higher unemployment or lower wages because other workers find better-paying jobs in new fields. Thus, the greater incomes and lower prices attributable to rising productivity cause overall spending and employment to increase. But this does not alleviate the hurt of those workers who cannot obtain new jobs, or only jobs at much below the wages of their previous jobs that were eliminated. It points up the need for cushioning the effect of lost jobs through job retraining and other assistance to displaced workers.

Productivity measures are prepared by the Bureau of Labor Statistics in the U.S. Department of Labor. There are two basic measures of productivity, labor productivity and multifactor productivity. Labor productivity data are provided quarterly and multifactor productivity data are provided annually. This chapter covers both measures for the business sector of the economy and for the total of all manufacturing industries. Thus, the chapter provides four productivity measures: labor productivity in the business sector, multifactor productivity in the business sector, labor productivity in manufacturing, and multifactor productivity in manufacturing.

METHODOLOGY

Productivity is the output of items produced in relation to the inputs required for the production of the items.[1] Mathematically, this is expressed as follows:

$$\text{Productivity} = \frac{\text{Output}}{\text{Input}}$$

Labor Productivity: Business Sector

The broadest measure of labor productivity is the output of goods and services per hour worked in the business sector of the economy. Mathematically, labor productivity in the business sector is expressed as follows:

$$\text{Labor productivity} = \frac{\text{Output}}{\text{Input}} = \frac{\text{Business GDP}^*}{\text{Labor hours}^{**}} = \begin{array}{l}\text{Real GDP per labor hour in} \\ \text{the business sector}\end{array}$$

*Gross domestic product, excluding households, not-for-profit organizations, rental value of owner-occupied housing, and general government, adjusted for inflation.
**Hours worked by paid employees, the self-employed, and unpaid family workers.

Output is represented by the gross domestic product (GDP) in the business sector, adjusted for inflation. Business GDP is smaller than the GDP, as described below. The GDP comprises the goods and services produced in the household, business, and government sectors of the economy (Chapter 3). The GDP is defined on a value-added basis that covers the labor costs, depreciation costs on equipment and structures, business profits, interest, and sales and property taxes in producing the nation's output. This excludes the purchases of intermediate goods and services from other industries. Otherwise, the intermediate items would result in continuous double-counting, with the production of the same goods and services being re-counted as they become components in successive stages of fabrication until they are incorporated in a final end-use item. For example, steel sheets are used in the manufacture of an automobile. A steel sheet originates with the extraction of iron ore, and the iron ore in turn goes through several stages of fabrication, including the use of other products, until it is finally transformed into a steel sheet.

Because of statistical problems in measuring the productivity of household, not-for-profit organization, and government workers, the output of these sectors in the GDP is defined as the inputs of wages and salaries paid to their workers. Since the outputs equal the inputs of these sectors, there is no measured change in their productivity. Therefore, the output measure used in estimating both labor and multifactor productivity excludes the output of households, not-for-profit organizations, rental value of owner-occupied housing, and general government, because to include them would bias the productivity measures downward.[2] The rental value of owner-occupied housing in the GDP is also excluded because there is no corresponding input for it. The resultant measure of output is the GDP in the business sector.

Input comprises the labor hours used in production. Labor hours are the product of the number of employees and their average weekly hours. Labor hours include paid employees, the self-employed, and unpaid family workers. The definition of hours represents hours at work, which is limited to time at the job site and includes paid time to travel between job sites, coffee breaks, and machine downtime. It excludes paid leave for vacations, sickness, or other reasons, which is associated with data on "hours paid" (Chapter 8). The data on hours for the self-employed and family workers are less clear. Given the nature of the compensation for these groups, measures of their labor input can be described as "hours worked" or "hours paid."[3]

Returning to the quotient in the mathematical expression above, which is labor productivity, we see that labor productivity is an aggregate of all the factors contributing to productivity change, except for the labor hour inputs that are included as inputs in the denominator of the expression. The elements of this aggregate are not quantified. They include the skills and effort of workers not captured by the schooling, experience, and compensation surrogates in the labor hour inputs; the quantity and technology of capital equipment and structures;

executive direction; managerial know-how; level of output; utilization of industrial capacity; consumption of energy; quality of materials; roads, airports, sewers, and other public-sector infrastructure; and the interaction of these and all other factors not specified.

Multifactor Productivity: Business Sector

Because the labor productivity measure contains the effect of capital inputs, it does not provide estimates of the contribution to productivity separately for capital inputs and the aggregate of all other factors. Capital inputs are equipment, structures, land, and business inventories.

The multifactor productivity measure of output is GDP in the business sector, excluding government enterprises, adjusted for inflation. This is the same as the output measure of labor productivity, except for the exclusion of government enterprises (see note 2).

Multifactor productivity refines the estimate of labor inputs included in the above measure of labor productivity and adds a separate component of capital inputs. The labor hours data in multifactor productivity reflect statistical adjustments that give greater weight to workers with more schooling, experience, and higher compensation adjusted for inflation, to reflect differences in the capabilities between workers.[4] The assumption is that as the workforce is composed of an increasing proportion of workers with a greater amount of schooling, experience, and compensation, the workforce itself becomes more productive. By including this changing composition of the workforce in the labor hours inputs in the denominator of the productivity formula, the resultant multifactor productivity labor input measure abstracts from the effects of both the changing number of hours worked and the changing composition of the workforce on the nation's output. These adjustments are a surrogate for estimating the changing efficiency of the workforce, as direct data on overall labor efficiency are not available.

The capital inputs in multifactor productivity represent the services that flow from the stocks of capital. They include the rental value services of capital facilities, adjusted for inflation, used in the production of goods and services—equipment, structures, inventories, and land. The capital inputs incorporate the quantity and the composition of equipment and structures facilities. The quantity of capital is based on the value of (1) existing equipment and structures resulting from the cumulated investments in previous years minus the depreciation and removal of the facilities, (2) business inventories used in production, and (3) land. Adjustments for the composition of equipment and structures facilities are made by giving more weight to short-lived than to long-lived equipment items, because short-lived assets provide more services per year than long-lived assets per dollar of asset. Other adjustments are implicit in the inflation-adjusted equipment and structures facilities, as the price indexes used to estimate the quantity, as distinct from the current-dollar value of these facilities, include some estimates for quality change (Chapter 11). These adjustments are a surrogate for estimating the changing efficiency of capital facilities, as direct data on the overall efficiency of equipment and structures are not available.

Mathematically, multifactor productivity in the private business sector is expressed as follows:

$$\text{Multifactor productivity} = \frac{\text{Private business GDP*}}{\text{Weighted aggregate (Labor hours**, Capital services***)}}$$

= Real GDP per combined unit of multifactor input in the private business sector

*Same as business GDP in labor productivity above, excluding government enterprises.
**Hours worked by paid employees, the self-employed, and unpaid family workers, modified for the schooling, experience, and inflation-adjusted compensation of different groups of workers.
***Rental value of equipment, structures, inventories, and land adjusted for inflation. Depreciated value of equipment and structures modified for short-lived and long-lived equipment items.

By including both labor hours and capital services as inputs in the denominator, multifactor productivity is an aggregate of all the factors contributing to productivity, except labor hours and capital facilities. The elements of this aggregate are not quantified. They include changes in the skills and effort of workers not captured by the labor hours inputs; technology of capital equipment not captured by the capital facilities inputs; executive direction; managerial know-how; level of output; utilization of industrial capacity; energy consumption; quality of materials; roads, airports, sewers, and other public-sector infrastructure; and the interaction of these and all other factors.

Labor and Multifactor Productivity: Manufacturing

Labor and multifactor productivity measures for the total of all manufacturing industries differ in scope and in definitions of output and input from those in the above sections on productivity in the business sector of the economy. First, manufacturing accounts for an important, but limited, share of the economy—18 percent of the GDP in 1994. Second, outputs in the manufacturing industries represent the dollar value of shipments of products from manufacturing establishments adjusted for inflation, which incorporate intermediate purchases of goods and services, and thus is much larger than the GDP value-added output measure used for the business sector. Third, in addition to the labor and capital inputs of business sector multifactor productivity, inputs of manufacturing multifactor productivity include purchases of intermediate goods, services, and energy outside of manufacturing. This provides for the substitution effects among the labor, capital, and intermediate inputs.[5]

Mathematically, labor and multifactor productivity in manufacturing are expressed as follows:

$$\text{Labor productivity} = \frac{\text{Output}}{\text{Input}} = \frac{\text{Products shipped from manufacturing establishments*}}{\text{Labor hours**}}$$

*Adjusted for inflation.
**Hours worked by paid employees, the self-employed, and unpaid family workers modified for the schooling, experience, and inflation-adjusted compensation of different groups of workers.

$$\text{Multifactor productivity} = \frac{\text{Products shipped from manufacturing establishments*}}{\text{Weighted aggregate (Labor hours*, Capital services**, purchased materials, services, energy***}}$$

*Same as labor productivity above.
**Rental value of equipment, structures, inventories, and land adjusted for inflation. Depreciated value of equipment and structures modified for short-lived and long-lived equipment items.
***Adjusted for inflation.

ANALYSIS OF TRENDS

Figure 10.1 shows the average annual movements of labor productivity and multifactor productivity for the GDP business sector for the decades from 1948 to 1994.[6] The productivity slowdowns in the 1970s and the 1980s, and the continuation of the very low increases in the 1990s, appear in both measures. Annual increases in labor productivity declined from 3.5 percent in the 1950s and 1960s to 1.2 percent in the 1980s and 1990s. Annual increases in multifactor productivity declined from over 2 percent in the 1950s and 1960s to under 0.5 percent in the 1980s and 1990s. Over the entire forty-six-year period, labor productivity increased 2.4 percent and multifactor productivity increased 1.3 percent annually. Labor productivity rose about 1 percentage point more than multifactor productivity in each of the decades because capital services grew faster than hours and the composition of workers shifted toward more educated, and after 1979, more experienced workers.

Figure 10.2 shows the average annual movements of labor and multifactor productivity for the total of all manufacturing industries for the decades from 1950 to 1993.[7] These are not comparable with the business sector trends in Figure 10.1 because of the different definitions of output and input between manufacturing and the business sector noted in the Methodology section. This is particularly so for labor productivity, because the difference in the output definition is not

Figure 10.1 **Productivity in the Business Sector: 1948–94**

Annual percent change

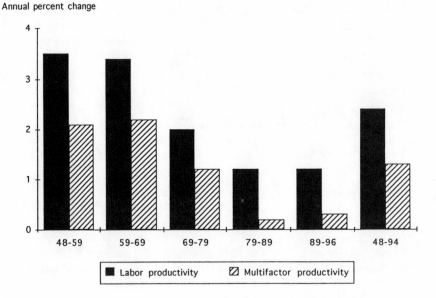

Note: Based on U.S. Bureau of Labor Statistics data.

compensated for by a comparable difference in the input definition. In the case of multifactor productivity, however, there is a rough correspondence between the manufacturing and business sector definitions, as the output data on shipments and the inclusion of intermediate purchases in the inputs of manufacturing reduce the definitional distinction from the GDP value-added definition of the business sector.

Labor productivity in manufacturing rose in the 1960s, continued at the same level in the 1970s, and declined slightly in the 1980s and 1990s. A distinguishing feature of these movements is that no decline occurred in the 1970s, contrary to the pattern in many productivity indicators. Multifactor productivity in manufacturing fluctuated noticeably from one decade to the next. A distinguishing feature is the sharp rise in productivity in the 1980s, which is not typical in other productivity indicators. Over the entire forty-three-year period, labor productivity increased at an annual rate of 2.5 percent and multifactor productivity increased 1.2 percent. Labor productivity rose about 1 percentage point more than multifactor productivity in the 1950s, 1960s, and 1980s, and 2.0 and 1.7 percentage points faster in the 1970s and 1990s. Manufacturing labor and multifactor productivity both declined during 1973–79 (not shown in Figure 10.2). Unlike the business sector, however, the slowdown in manufacturing was short-lived.

Figure 10.2 **Productivity in Manufacturing: 1950–93**

Annual percent change

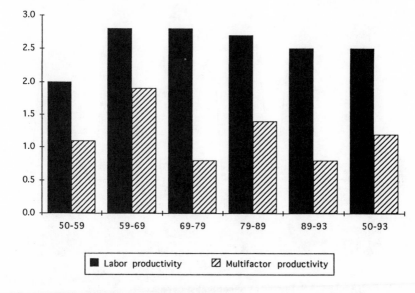

Note: Based on U.S. Bureau of Labor Statistics data.

Cyclical Movements

Figure 10.3 shows that the year-to-year movements of labor productivity in the business sector from 1960 to 1996 fluctuate considerably.[8] This is due to the sharper cyclical changes in the GDP output measure (numerator) than the changes in the labor hours input measure (denominator). Although not shown in the figure, the same phenomenon occurs in the quarterly movements.

The greater stability of the labor input measure than of the GDP output measure reflects the fact that because employers are uncertain if shifts in demand for their products are permanent or transitory, they resist hiring and laying off workers in response to initial changes in demand. Instead, they are more likely to partially adjust weekly hours of existing workers. Also, some workers whose skills are specific to the firm are too valuable to lay off every time demand slacks off, so employers tend to hoard some workers during recessions. The combination of these two patterns leads to labor input that is less cyclical than output, and therefore productivity appears to have a cyclical component. Further, capital, which is not part of the labor productivity measure, may also be more heavily utilized when demand increases, which may contribute to the cyclical productivity.

Lawrence Fulco points out that because of this practice of only partially

Figure 10.3 **Labor Productivity in the Business Sector: 1960–96**

Annual percent change

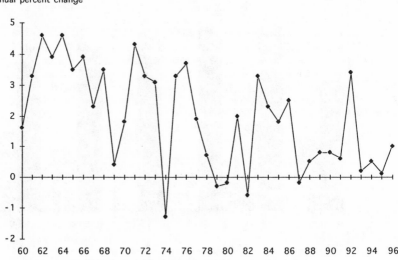

Note: Based on U.S. Bureau of Labor Statistics data.

changing labor input during periods of cyclical uncertainty, productivity rises more in expansions than in recessions, irrespective of changes in labor skills, capital equipment, and other basic factors affecting productivity.[9] And Matthew Shapiro finds that when changes in production and employment in manufacturing industries are accounted for by changes in capacity utilization rates and night shifts, there is no evidence of cyclical productivity.[10]

The underlying factors driving productivity cumulate slowly over time as they become more widely diffused throughout the economy, and thus do not have significant quarterly and annual changes. The long-term downward trend in Figure 10.3 is consistent with the general slowdown in productivity improvement in Figure 10.1.

Industrial Relationship of Productivity, Output, and Employment

Generally, it would be expected that if productivity increases more than output, employment declines, and if output increases more than productivity, employment rises. This pattern occurs in the following example of seven industries. Nevertheless, there are sure to be exceptions when employment change diverges from the expected direction due to special circumstances.

Figure 10.4 shows the movements of productivity and output in relation to

Figure 10.4 **Output and Employment in Seven Industries with Similar Productivity Growth: 1960–90**

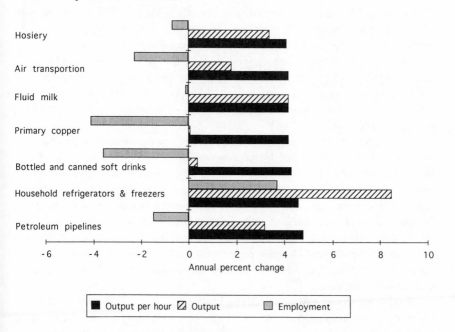

Note: Based on U.S. Bureau of Labor Statistics data.

employment change for seven industries with similar productivity growth of 4.1 to 4.8 percent annually from 1960 to 1990. Productivity growth noticeably exceeded output growth in five cases, and employment clearly declined in all five cases. Output growth noticeably exceeded the productivity growth in one case, and employment clearly increased. The productivity and output growth were the same in one case, and employment declined slightly. Typically, the larger the difference between output and productivity growth, the larger the change in employment.

These data do not support the concern that, at the industry level, advanced technology necessarily displaces workers and leads to lower employment in the aggregate. Thus, industry employment is closely related to the demand for each industry's products and productivity change.[11] But workers do lose their jobs because of the introduction of labor-saving machinery. Some of these displaced workers are not able to find new work, and others often can find new jobs only at lower wages, even while the industry they were in hires other workers. Job retraining and other assistance are used to alleviate the hardship faced by displaced workers. These programs have a limited success record, and more evaluation is needed to make them or other approaches more effective, as Yolanda Kodrzycki notes.[12]

Productivity Slowdown in the 1970s, 1980s, and 1990s

Higher worker incomes are the essential route for raising the living conditions of the broad spectrum of the population. And productivity increases are the best foundation for raising worker incomes over the long run, as greater productivity growth allows employers to pay higher wages while maintaining profit margins. The sharp drop in productivity growth in the 1970s and the continued low productivity increases in the 1980s and 1990s discussed previously are associated with the decline in worker weekly earnings adjusted for inflation during the same period (Chapter 8).

Various partial explanations have been offered for the substantial productivity slowdown in the 1970s. They include decreasing technological advances due to lower research and development spending, less investment in equipment and structures as higher energy prices caused business to use more labor relative to energy-using machinery, and more hours paid for than hours worked because of increases in paid vacations and sick leave. Actual measures of these and other possible reasons related to multifactor productivity by Jerome Mark and William Waldorf and by Edward Denison provide estimates that account for only about 20 percent of the decline, however, and the factors causing the slowdown are not well understood.[13]

Charles Morris and Michael Darby have suggested that the measured productivity growth slowdown in the 1970s is a statistical illusion associated with the price controls of the early 1970s.[14] Their analyses assume that the official price measures used to estimate the inflation-adjusted gross national product in 1973 understated price inflation and consequently overstated output and the productivity level in 1973. The idea is that without this distortion, there was a productivity slowdown from 1968 to 1973, but no further slowdown after 1973. Empirically substantiating the extent of the price measurement problem is difficult, however, and this view has not gained general acceptance over the official measure that shows productivity slowing down during most of the 1970s. It is also noteworthy that productivity slowdowns occurred in virtually all industrialized countries in the 1970s, most of which did not have price controls.

The continuation of low productivity increases in the 1980s and 1990s also is not understood. Some have speculated that efficiencies resulting from industry downsizing and computerization in the 1980s and 1990s should appear as greater productivity growth in the official data by the mid-1990s. They conclude that the effects of the downsizing and computerization are not observed as productivity improvements in the mid-1990s because there are deficiencies in the way productivity is measured. One such deficiency is the understatement of productivity in the service industries, because of the difficulty of measuring productivity in such fields as education, health, and legal services. Another data deficiency often cited is the overstatement of inflation in the consumer price index (CPI), which because the CPI is used to adjust output for inflation, causes output to be understated.

These assessments are questionable for several reasons:

- There had been a long-term shift from goods to services in the U.S. economy well before the 1970s, and this shift did not accelerate from the 1970s to the 1990s.
- The alleged overstatement of measured inflation in the CPI may be much smaller than claimed, and possibly more than offset by factors causing inflation to be understated (Chapter 11).
- Industry downsizing associated with discontinuing low-profit or unprofitable product lines is not in itself an increase in productivity.
- Downsizing associated with outsourcing activities previously done in-house to outside contractors tends to be an offset between manufacturing and service industries, with the outsourcing by manufacturers to service industry contractors raising measured manufacturing industry productivity and lowering measured service industry productivity.[15]
- The benchmark revision of the gross domestic product (GDP) in 1996 that incorporated a refined method for adjusting GDP for inflation showed only a small increase in the revised measure of economic growth from 3 to 3.2 percent annually over the 1959–94 period, and a decline in the revised measure of economic growth during the 1991–95 cyclical expansion from 3.1 to 2.5 percent annually.[16] These revisions did not change the overall picture of slow productivity growth from the 1970s to the 1990s.
- The returns to computer investments would probably have to increase substantially for the application of computers to significantly raise the rate of overall growth of the economy, as Daniel Sichel points out.[17] Also, if the adaptation of computers is viewed as a continuation of previous technological innovations in office automation and communications during the nineteenth and twentieth centuries, the use of computers is not likely to lead to large increases in productivity.

Comparison with Other Countries

Table 10.1 shows productivity based on the GDP per employed person for the United States and five other industrialized nations and industrializing Korea from 1976 to 1995, with the United States indexed as 100 in all years. The productivity level in the United States in 1995 was higher than in other industrialized countries, although the gap has been narrowing. In 1995, productivity in France and West Germany was 2 and 7 percent below the United States; productivity in Canada and Japan was 16 and 18 percent below the U.S.; productivity in the United Kingdom was 24 percent below the United

Table 10.1

International Productivity Levels: 1976–95 (GDP per employed person: U.S. = 100)

	1976	1980	1985	1990	1995
United States	100.0	100.0	100.0	100.0	100.0
France	80.4	87.3	89.3	96.5	97.7
West Germany	80.3	84.8	85.3	89.9	93.2
Canada	83.5	83.2	84.5	83.6	83.6
Japan	63.3	70.9	74.5	83.3	81.7
United Kingdom	64.2	66.7	70.3	72.4	75.5
Korea	22.0	25.1	31.6	40.5	49.1

Source: U.S. Bureau of Labor Statistics.

States; and productivity in Korea was 51 percent below the United States.

In an assessment of international productivity movements from the 1860s to the 1980s, William Baumol, Sue Anne Blackman, and Edward Wolff develop the idea that international productivity levels tend to converge in the long run.[18] This occurs because new technology is transferred relatively rapidly from the country in which it was developed to other nations. An imitating country often narrows the productivity gap created by the new technology in a process of "catch-up," and sometimes, because of a wider and more advanced exploitation of the new technology, even surpasses the originating country. Though the U.S. advantage in the level of productivity has narrowed, the authors of the study conclude that the growth in productivity in the United States remains sufficiently high so that the United States is not in danger of losing its overall advantage. The accuracy of this forecast will be one determinant of the U.S. competitive position in the world economy (Chapter 5).

The tendency for productivity to converge among nations requires that nations have the institutional and cultural traits that facilitate the adoption of new technologies. The receptivity to new technologies is an important factor affecting the rate of convergence of particular nations.

Productivity and international competitiveness are related, but they are not the same. Productivity directly affects living conditions through its relationship to wages, as noted previously. International competitiveness directly affects the ability of U.S. industry to sell its products at home and abroad. Demand for U.S. products increases at home and abroad as U.S. competitiveness increases. Generally, a greater demand for U.S. products fosters higher worker incomes as it leads to more jobs and higher wages. And rising productivity increases U.S. international competitiveness, as higher productivity helps make U.S. prices competitive with those of other countries.

Productivity and Inflation

Prices are determined by both the markets for goods and services (demand) and production costs (supply). This section focuses on the supply effects. Price inflation is discussed more fully in Chapter 11.

Productivity affects inflation through its effect on the costs of producing goods and services. If costs rise, business will be motivated to increase prices in order to maintain profits rates (profits as a percentage of sales). If costs remain the same or decline, they do not exert a pressure for higher prices to maintain profit rates. In fact, if costs decline, prices can decline and profits still be maintained.

A key item affecting production costs is the relation between employee compensation per hour and productivity, which is referred to as unit labor costs (ULC).[19] ULC also may be expressed as compensation per unit of output, because "labor hours" is the common term in compensation per hour and productivity that cancels out in the mathematical expression below. Mathematically, ULC are expressed as follows:

$$\text{Unit labor costs} = \frac{\text{Compensation per hour}}{\text{Productivity}} = \frac{\dfrac{\text{Compensation}^*}{\text{Labor hours}}}{\dfrac{\text{Output}}{\text{Labor hours}}} = \frac{\text{Compensation}}{\text{Output}}$$

*Wages and salaries plus fringe benefits

If compensation per hour increases more than productivity, ULC increase and there is an upward pressure on prices. If compensation per hour increases less than productivity, ULC decrease and there is downward pressure on prices.

Figure 10.5 shows the annual change in ULC and the GDP implicit price deflator for the business sector from 1960 to 1996. The figure indicates parallel movements in both indicators. The differential movements typically were within 1 to 2 percentage points in the 1980s and within 1 percentage point in the 1990s. Sometimes prices increased more than ULC, and other times ULC increased more than prices, but there is no pattern in these directional differences.

The analyst should include the following aspects of productivity in assessing their future effects on the economy:

- *It is essential to distinguish between short-term cyclical and long-term structural changes in productivity. Only structural changes have long-term substantive impacts on the efficiency of producing goods and services.*
- *By abstracting from the quantity and some attributes of the quality of labor and capital inputs, multifactor productivity focuses attention on an aggregate of other features of the economy that affect productivity. Be-*

Figure 10.5 **Unit Labor Costs and Prices in the Business Sector: 1980–96**

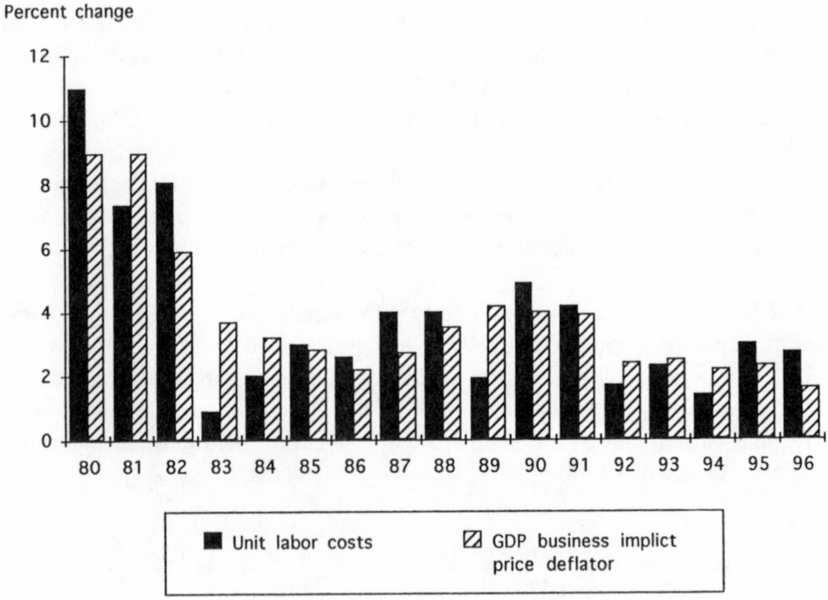

Percent change

Note: Based on U.S. Bureau of Labor Statistics and U.S. Bureau of Economic Analysis data.

cause the elements of this aggregate are not quantified, changes in their future impact on productivity are probably best monitored from anecdotal reports in the press.

- Changes in productivity levels between the United States and other countries are a broad indicator for assessing the future competitive position of the United States in the world economy.
- Unit labor costs are a broad indicator of inflationary price pressures stemming from production costs.

REVIEW QUESTIONS

- How does productivity affect living conditions?
- Why are cyclical changes in productivity a problematic indicator of fundamental changes in productivity?
- What analytic interest does multifactor productivity add to the traditional measure of labor productivity?
- Although the level of U.S. productivity is noticeably higher than productivity in Japan and Germany, those nations are major competitors of the

United States in the world economy. What factors other than productivity could account for this?

- Assuming that prices are determined solely by unit labor costs, calculate the effect of the changes in productivity and compensation on the inflation rate from the following:

Productivity	Compensation per hour	Inflation				
		2%	6%	9%	−1%	−6%
5%	4%	_____	_____	_____	_____	_____
2	4	_____	_____	_____	_____	_____
0	6	_____	_____	_____	_____	_____

Extra Credit

- Why does labor productivity grow faster than multifactor productivity?
- Figure 10.3 shows that labor productivity actually declined in 1974, 1980, and 1982. What development in the economy caused the decline? Explain.
- *The Misunderstood Economy* by Robert Eisner (p. 24) prompts this question: Suppose a person who has been keeping house full-time joins the labor force, gets a job in the business sector, and is less productive than the average worker. What happens to the official measure of labor productivity? How would your answer differ if housework were counted as part of the business sector?

NOTES

1. Bureau of Labor Statistics, U.S. Department of Labor, *BLS Handbook of Methods,* April 1997, ch. 10. This provides a detailed description of the productivity statistics methodology.

2. General government covers government functions that are financed from tax revenues. General government accounts for the preponderance of government functions. Government enterprises are government functions that cover a substantial part of their operating costs by selling goods and services to the public.

3. Mary Jablonski, Kent Kunze, and Phyllis Flohr Otto, "Hours at work: a new base for BLS productivity measures," *Monthly Labor Review,* February 1990.

4. Bureau of Labor Statistics, U.S. Department of Labor, *Labor Composition and U.S. Productivity Growth,* Bulletin 2426, October 1993.

5. Because manufacturing is one segment of the economy, the substitution effect between the labor and capital inputs on the one hand, and the intermediate inputs on the other, is important. By contrast, intermediates cancel out in the economywide business sector measure.

6. The measures are based on the gross domestic product (GDP) data before the 1996 GDP benchmark revision (Chapter 3), and thus end with 1994. The pre-benchmark data are used because the necessary detailed GDP data to estimate multifactor productivity were not available at the time of this writing in the spring of 1997. However, the differential movements between labor and multifactor productivity probably will not be significantly different when the revised GDP data are available because the productivity measures had already been based on a statistical procedure related to index numbers for estimating inflation-adjusted GDP very similar to that used in the 1996 GDP benchmark revision. The revised underlying data incorporated in the 1996 revision probably will have little effect on the GDP output data when they are incorporated in the productivity numbers.

The 1950s are calculated from 1948–59, instead of 1949–59, because 1949 was a recession year and 1959 was an expansion year, which would distort the calculation. The beginning and ending years for the other decades are expansion periods, 1959–69, 1969–79, 1979–89, and 1989–96. To maintain this consistency of using all terminal years as expansion periods, the entire five decades are calcualted as 1948–96. This issue is discussed more fully in Chapter 1 under Calculating and Presenting Growth Rates, Beginning and Ending Dates.

7. The data characteristics are the same as those in note 4 for the business sector, other than the terminal year dates. The manufacturing data begin with 1949 and end with 1993. Because 1949 was a recession year, the data series here start with 1950.

8. The data are based on the 1996 benchmark GDP revisions.

9. Lawrence J. Fulco, "Strong post-recession gain in productivity contributes to slow growth in labor costs," *Monthly Labor Review*, December 1994.

10. Matthew D. Shapiro, "Macroeconomic Implications of Variation in the Workweek of Capital," *Brookings Papers on Economic Activity* 2 (1996).

11. Jerome A. Mark, "Technological change and employment: some results from BLS research," *Monthly Labor Review*, April 1987.

12. Yolanda K. Kodrzycki, "Training Programs for Displaced Workers: What Do They Accomplish?" *New England Economic Review*, May/June 1997.

13. Jerome A. Mark, William H. Waldorf, et al., *Trends in Multifactor Productivity*, Bureau of Labor Statistics, U.S. Department of Labor, Bulletin 2178, September 1983, chs. III and IV. See also Edward F. Denison, *Trends in Economic Growth, 1929–82* (Brookings Institution, 1985).

14. Charles S. Morris, "The Productivity 'Slowdown': A Sectoral Analysis," *Economic Review*, Federal Reserve Bank of Kansas City, April 1984. See also Michael R. Darby, "The U.S. Productivity Slowdown: A Case of Statistical Myopia," *American Economic Review*, June 1984.

15. Sharon Kozicki, "The Productivity Slowdown: Diverging Trends in the Manufacturing and Service Sectors," *Economic Review*, Federal Reserve Bank of Kansas City, First quarter 1997.

16. Bureau of Economic Analysis, U.S. Department of Commerce, "Improved Estimates of the National Income and Product Accounts for 1959–95: Results of the Comprehensive Revision," *Survey of Current Business*, January/February 1996, Tables 17 and 20.

17. Daniel E. Sichel, *The Computer Revolution: An Economic Perspective* (Brookings Institution, 1997), ch. 5.

18. William J. Baumol, Sue Anne Blackman, and Edward N. Wolff, *Productivity and American Leadership: The Long View* (MIT Press, 1989), ch. 13.

19. Bureau of Labor Statistics, U.S. Department of Labor, *BLS Handbook of Methods*, April 1997, ch. 10.

11
INFLATION

Prices influence and reflect many aspects of the private and government sectors of the economy. They are both a driving force and a culmination of the various elements of demand and supply in the marketplace. Different geographic, industrial, financial, real estate, and labor markets vary considerably in their competitive and monopolistic features, and prices are the summation of the varying degrees of market imperfections. Prices are also affected by extramarket considerations, such as war or threat of war, the environment, and natural disasters (e.g., drought, floods, earthquakes).

Prices of goods and services vary considerably among individual items bought and sold in the marketplace. There is the intrinsic difference in the absolute price of one item in comparison to another at a point in time, such as the price of a car and of a college tuition. There are continuing differences in the movements of prices over time, such as price changes of a car and of college tuition from one year to the next. Some items rise in price more than others, some decline in price more than others, and some are unchanged from one period to the next. These differential price movements reflect actual or perceived shortages or surpluses among buyers and sellers and varying degrees of price competition for particular items. Changes in overall prices for the total of all goods and services are the net effect of the varying upward, downward, and stable movements of the vast number of items sold in markets around the United States.

Inflation is the general term given to a rise in overall prices for the total of all goods and services, and deflation represents a decline in overall prices. Zero inflation occurs when there is no change in overall prices. It results from offsetting price increases and decreases among the individual items. There are also varying degrees of inflation that have differential effects on the economy. In general, overall price movements affect the economic well-being of the population in the following way: people are better off if their incomes increase more than prices increase or if their incomes fall less than prices fall.

This chapter focuses on the movements of overall prices represented by the consumer price index (CPI), the producer price indexes (PPIs), and the gross domestic product (GDP) price indexes. The CPI and the PPIs are prepared monthly by the Bureau of Labor Statistics in the U.S. Department of Labor. The GDP price indexes are prepared quarterly by the Bureau of Economic Analysis in the U.S. Department of Commerce. Topics covered in the chapter are as follows:

- General characteristics of inflation
- Methodology and issues of price indexes
- Proposed methodological changes to the CPI
- Price movements of the major price indexes
- Transmission of price change by stage of processing
- Inflation and capacity utilization
- Domestic inflation and imports
- Misery index

Inflation is also discussed in the context of other chapters. These are inflation and unemployment (Chapter 2), inflation and unit labor costs (Chapter 10), and inflation and interest rates (Chapter 12).

GENERAL CHARACTERISTICS OF INFLATION

This section highlights two background aspects of inflation: contrasting rates of inflation, and price expectations and price structure.

Contrasting Rates of Inflation

There are varying inflationary gradations that both affect and are affected by the economy quite differently. Examples of these gradations are core inflation, accelerating inflation versus disinflation, creeping inflation versus hyperinflation, and tolerable inflation.

Core inflation is an objective measure of price change that excludes changes in energy and food prices. It is sometimes called the "underlying rate of inflation" because it abstracts from price fluctuations in food and energy that may have nothing to do with underlying price pressures in the economy. Food prices fluctuate in large part due to changes in the weather associated with rainfall and frosts, as well as with natural disasters of floods and hurricanes. These physical elements directly affect plantings and harvests of grains, fruits, and vegetables, which in turn affect cattle prices through feed-grain prices, with larger harvests tending to lower prices and smaller harvests tending to raise prices. Energy prices fluctuate as the discipline of member nations in maintaining cartel prices among the Organization of Petroleum Exporting Countries (OPEC) strengthens and weakens. When the nations tend to regulate their oil production in line with

OPEC guidelines, the effect is to bolster prices, and when they do not follow the production guidelines, the effect is to weaken prices. Daniel Yergin illuminates the political problems of maintaining discipline among the OPEC nations in adhering to agreed-on country output quotas.[1]

Accelerating inflation and disinflation represent objective opposite rates of inflation. Accelerating inflation occurs when the rate of inflation increases, say, from 2 percent in period one to 3 percent in period two. Disinflation occurs when the rate of inflation decreases, as from 3 percent in period one to 2 percent in period two. Two vivid periods of an accelerating inflation followed by a disinflation appeared over the span of the late 1960s to the mid-1980s.

The accelerating inflation that began in the late 1960s continued although with interruptions in the 1970s and ended in 1980 based on the CPI and in 1981 based on the GDP chain price index. The inflation acceleration in the late 1960s resulted from the combined effect of strong economic growth and the Vietnam War buildup, with limited and delayed tax increases that would restrain the inflationary pressures. In the 1970s, several factors converged to cause a general tendency toward a sharp acceleration in the inflation: energy prices increased substantially when OPEC became an effective cartel in 1973; the international value of the dollar (Chapter 6) declined following the shift to floating foreign exchange rates; unit labor costs rose because of a productivity slowdown (Chapter 10); and accelerating wage increases associated with a wage-price spiral fed by an inflationary psychology of expected continued higher inflation. The general inflation acceleration was temporarily interrupted by mandatory price controls in 1971–74 and by the 1973–75 recession.

The disinflation from 1980–81 to 1996 reflected a general turnaround in the above factors during the first half of the 1980s. The reversal was marked by a weakening in the discipline of OPEC as a cartel; higher interest rates fostered by the Federal Reserve, which influenced a rise in the value of the dollar and the onset of the 1981–82 recession (Chapter 12); and intensified weakening of the long-term declining membership of labor unions symbolized by the federal government's breaking of the air traffic controllers strike and their union (Chapter 8).

Creeping inflation and hyperinflation are qualitative terms for sharply differing rates of inflation. Creeping inflation is characterized by annual inflation rates of 1 to 2 percent such as those from the most of the 1950s through the first half of the 1960s. Hyperinflation reflects annual inflation rates in double digits, such as the 10 to 14 percent range from 1979 to 1981. The term hyperinflation is typically reserved for much greater price increases, such as 1,000 percent a year or more, that occur from time to time in other countries.[2] In using this term for much lower price increases in the United States, the author believes that the much lower political tolerance for inflation in the United States before strong anti-inflation fiscal, monetary, and price-wage measures are taken, makes the lower threshold for hyperinflation relevant to the United States.

Tolerable inflation is another qualitative term, which typically represents an annual inflation rate of 3 to 5 percent. It incorporates a value judgment that implies inflation should be lower because the rate erodes the incomes of large segments of the population whose wages, profits from self-employment, or interest and dividends from investments do not keep pace with inflation. At the same time, the rate is not thought to cause extreme speculative behavior among households and businesses, nor does it lead to spiraling increases in interest rates (Chapter 12 covers interest rates). Inflation fluctuated in this range from the early 1980s to the mid-1990s, with the 1992–96 period consistently being at the low end of 3 percent.

Price Expectations and Price Structure

Consumer prices as measured by the average annual change in the CPI have risen in all years from the 1940s to the 1990s, except for 1949 and 1955. By contrast, consumer prices declined in four years of the 1920s and six years of the 1930s. Thus, inflation seems to be built into the economy since the end of the Great Depression of the 1930s. One reason is that some prices and wages are set by multiyear contracts that call for scheduled increases over the life of the contract regardless of changing economic conditions. Another is that while some prices and wages actually decline during recessions or during periods of slow economic growth, the more typical experience during such periods is that the rate of increase only slows. Businesses and workers apparently believe that while price and wage declines would increase the quantity of goods and services sold and the number of workers employed, such increases would be insufficient to offset the resultant decline in company profits or of worker incomes.

Expectations of price change are an important intangible to monitor because they affect the behavior of businesses, labor, lenders, and borrowers in the determination of prices, wages, and interest rates. Expectations, at least temporarily, tend to be self-fulfilling forecasts. For example, when there is an expectation of high inflation, the various groups try to insulate themselves by raising price, wage, and interest rate demands in order to maintain the purchasing power of their future incomes. Similarly, an expectation of low inflation leads to smaller price, wage, and interest rate demands. Inflationary expectations helped fuel the large price increases in the 1970s, while lower inflationary expectations in the 1980s and 1990s helped moderate price increases in those decades.

A structural tendency toward measured inflation results from the continuing shift in the American economy from the consumption of commodities to the consumption of services. For example, the consumer price index for commodities increased at an annual rate of 3.5 percent, compared with an annual increase of 5.2 percent for services from 1950 to the 1996. This pattern of higher price increases for services occurred in all decades of the period. The higher rate of increase for services is partly due to the higher labor content in the production of services in contrast to commodities, which use proportionately more machinery in their production. Services do not benefit as much as commodities from cost-saving productivity improvements in machinery (Chapter 10 covers productivity). Another part of the difference reflects statistical difficulties in quantifying quality changes in services such as housing, transportation, medical care, education, and entertainment. If quality improvements are understated in services, the price increases would be overstated (discussed in the following two sections, Methodology and Issues of Price Indexes, and Proposed Methodological Changes to the CPI).

METHODOLOGY AND ISSUES OF
PRICE INDEXES

As an introduction to this section, the reader will find it useful to review the section in Chapter 1 on Index Numbers. That discussion highlights the conceptual attributes and implications of index numbers.

Price indexes represent the combination of a wide range of goods and services into a single number in order to obtain an overall measure of price change from one period to the next. Two aspects in the preparation of price indexes have a major influence on the measured price change. One is how the various goods and services items are combined into a single number. The other is accounting for improvements or deterioration in the quality of the items being priced over time.

Combining Individual Items into a Single Index

The various goods and services items are combined into a single index according to the relative importance of each item, which sum to 100 percent. The proportions for the various items are referred to as "weights." The weights are based on the dollar sales volume of each item in a base period. The weights are updated periodically to reflect the changing importance of the various items included in the index. In the CPI, for example, data on consumer purchases of specific goods and services items are obtained from surveys of households in geographic areas around the country conducted for the Bureau of Labor Statistics by the Census Bureau.[3] These spending patterns (i.e., weights) are updated about every ten years—the weights from 1987 to 1997 reflect the household spending patterns in 1982–84. Beginning in 1998, the CPI weights represent the spending patterns during 1993–95.

The weights for some indexes represent a few years and for other indexes a single year, depending on the availability of the underlying data used in constructing the index. The weights for the CPI reflect household spending patterns for a few years, as noted above. The weights for the PPIs, which are based on the five-year economic censuses, reflect commodity and industry output patterns for 1992, as of this writing in 1997. The weighting structure of the PPIs will next be updated to represent 1997 output patterns when the 1997 economic census data become available. The GDP chain price indexes represent weights that are updated every year based on the most recent expenditure patterns for the household, business, government, and international sectors of the economy (Chapter 3).

The CPI: General Attributes and Illustrative Index Calculation

Because of the prominence of the CPI as the key measure of inflation in the U.S. economy, this and several following sections focus on the basic methodological aspects of the structure and preparation of the CPI.

General Attributes

The CPI measures the relative change in prices as the percent movement between two periods. It does not measure the dollar amount of the costs. Thus, while CPIs are prepared for local areas as well as for the national level, comparisons of the CPIs between local areas only indicate the differential rates of inflation between the areas, but not the relative level of prices in the two areas. For example, the CPIs for the New York and the Cleveland metropolitan areas may indicate prices rising more in Cleveland than in New York, but in dollars it may cost more to live in New York.

The CPI incorporates the actual transaction price of the item. This includes sales taxes, premiums and discounts from list prices, and import duties. In practice, there probably are a minority of cases in which actual prices net of premiums and discounts from list prices are not obtained.

The CPI is sometimes referred to as the cost-of-living index, although it does not conform to a theoretical cost of living. A cost-of-living index allows for the substitution of perfect substitute products when the substitute product has a lower price, while the CPI does not permit this substitution, as Patrick Jackman points out.[4] Thus, a cost-of-living index measures price movements associated with the minimum expenditures necessary to maintain a constant standard of living. In contrast, the CPI measures price movements for purchasing only the same items between two periods, regardless of the availability of lower-priced substitutes. The CPI also does not include other attributes of a cost-of-living index, such as accounting for household preferences between work and leisure, how changes in income tax rates affect the household's after-tax income and thus the household's financial ability to buy the same goods and services as in the base period, and social problems of crime and pollution that cause households to move to other areas or buy protective items.

Table 11.1

Estimating the CPI for December 1996: Not Seasonally Adjusted
(1982–84 = 100)

	1 Base-period weights, Dec. 1986	2 Price change, Dec. 1986 to Dec. 1996 (ratio)	3 December 1990 proportions (Dec. 1986 = 100) 1 x 2
Food and beverages	17.758	1.412	25.076
Housing	42.791	1.381	59.101
Apparel and upkeep	6.309	1.212	7.647
Transportation	17.172	1.432	24.589
Medical care	5.749	1.833	10.538
Entertainment	4.385	1.424	6.245
Other	5.836	1.757	10.252
Total	100.000		143.449

Adjustment to 1982–84 = 100:
 CPI for Dec. 1986 (1982–84 = 100): 110.5
 CPI for Dec. 1996 (1986 = 100): 143.449—Column 3 total
 CPI for Dec. 1996 (1982–84 = 100): 158.511
 143.449 x 1.105
Note: 158.5 differs from actual 158.6 due to rounding.

December 1996 CPI	158.6
Less June 1996 CPI	156.7
equals: Index point change	1.9
Ratio of index point change (1.9/156.7)	0.012
Percentage change (0.012 x 100)	1.2

Illustrative Index Calculation

Table 11.1 shows the basic procedure for calculating a price index for a current period, using the monthly CPI as an example.[5] The weights of the major components are from the spending patterns introduced in 1987 using December 1986 as the base period. These are multiplied by the relative price change between December 1986 and December 1996 to obtain the proportions of each component in December 1996, and the proportions are summed to obtain the total CPI on a base of December 1986 = 100. To convert this level to the CPI base period of 1982–84 = 100, which is the actual base period used in the published CPI, the summed total is multiplied by the ratio of the CPI price change between 1982–84 and December 1986. The resultant index of 158.6 means that the CPI increased by 58.6 percent between 1982–84 and December 1996 (the difference from the calculated index of 158.5 is due to rounding).

In practice, the computations are made at a much greater level of detailed items within each major component. Food prices, for example, are calculated for a wide range of bakery, meat, dairy, produce items, beverages, and the like, and distinctions are made between food consumed in homes and restaurants. The percentage change in the CPI between any two periods is calculated as the relative movement in the CPI levels between the periods. To illustrate, from June to December 1996, the CPI increased by 1.2 percent, as indicated in the lower bank of Table 11.1.

Price Effect of Updated CPI Weights

The effect of updating the CPI weights to reflect more recent spending patterns can be analyzed by comparing the CPI based on new weights to hypothetical figures based on continued use of old weights. For example, from 1983 to 1990, the CPI, calculated using 1982–84 spending patterns, increased 31.8 percent. The CPI increase is 31.4 percent for the same period, however, when calculated using the old 1972–73 spending patterns (as modified in 1983 for the new method of measuring housing costs). This differential is approximate since the estimates are calculated at summary levels for the major components of food and beverages, housing, apparel, transportation, medical care, entertainment, and all other items, rather than for the hundreds of detailed items. Previous changes in weights based on new spending patterns also had a relatively small impact on the overall CPI. Thus, the ten-year periods in which the weights remain constant do not appear to cause exceptional discontinuities in the measure of price change. Despite these relatively small effects on measured price change due to changing weights, the U.S. Bureau of Labor Statistics publishes the CPI using the old weights for a period of six months after the new weights are introduced, which allows users of the CPI to assess the impact of the new weights during a transition period.

Accounting for Quality Change in Price Indexes:
Illustrative for the CPI

An essential concept of a price index is that its movements from one period to the next reflect only those price changes for goods and services items that occur independently of quality changes. This section uses the CPI as an example of quality adjustments that are made to the market price that the buyer pays for the item to convert the market price to the price of the item for the CPI.

The CPI measure of quality change includes adjustments to the market price for the improvement or deterioration in the performance of an item. By contrast, no adjustments to the market price associated with changes in an item's aesthetic attributes are made in the CPI. For example, if a loaf of bread is increased (decreased) in size or nutrients, the changes are defined as quality improvements (deterioration).[6] Similarly, if an automobile's specifications are changed to increase (decrease) its braking power, maneuverability, impact safety, pollution

Table 11.2

Relationship of Quality Change and Market Price in the CPI

Quality change	Market price	CPI price
Improvement	Increase by amount of improvement cost	No change
Improvement	Increase less than improvement cost	Decrease
Improvement	No change	Decrease
Improvement	Increase more than improvement cost	Increase
Deterioration	Decrease by amount of deterioration cost	No change
Deterioration	Decrease less than deterioration cost	Increase
Deterioration	No change	Increase
Deterioration	Decrease more than deterioration cost	Decrease
No change	Increase	Increase
No change	Decrease	Decrease
No change	No change	No change

controls, or comfort, such changes are quality improvements (deterioration). By contrast, a change in styling such as sculptured lines or chrome in an automobile may result in a market price change, but styling is not defined as a quality change. Quality adjustments are discussed further below. The implementation of quality changes in CPI is governed by the availability of data on the extent of the change. The CPI reflects the changes only if the dollar value of the quality change can be quantified.

Table 11.2 shows how changes in the quality and market price of the item translate into the price used in the CPI. In the monthly pricing of an item in the CPI, the price is compared to the item's specifications to determine if changes in specifications have occurred since the previous month. If there is a change in the specifications, and an estimate of the production cost of the specification changes is obtained, the table indicates how they combine with the market price in the CPI. The various combinations indicate that an increase or decrease in the market price in the store may be an increase, no change, or decrease in the CPI, and that no change in the store price may be a price increase, decrease, or no change in the CPI.

For virtually all goods and services items, the quality adjustments are based on cost estimates associated with the quality change for producing the item. The adjustments are based on the premise that a quality improvement most likely means more and/or better labor or materials are required to produce the item, while a quality deterioration assumes fewer or lower-grade resources are used in producing the item. The cost estimates are obtained from the manufacturer or service provider of the item. For example, if the impact safety of an automobile is improved by a better airbag or a better construction of the frame of the car, the increased production cost of the improvement is obtained from the automobile manufacturer.

While the above example is of quality improvements, the same procedure applies for quality deterioration, which is presumed to be associated with a decrease in production costs. If no credible estimate of the production cost of the quality improvement or deterioration is available, the quality change is not incorporated in calculating the CPI.

The exception to the above technique of adjusting for quality change based on production costs occurs for apparel. Price changes for apparel diverge considerably from the production cost model, in which a quality improvement usually entails higher production costs, and a quality deterioration usually means lower production costs. Changes in apparel fashion are so rapid from year to year and from season to season that production costs are not relevant for capturing them. Thus, when the new fashions are first introduced at the beginning of each winter, spring, summer, and fall season, their prices typically are higher than the previous year's prices. But this high price is often short-lived, as the prices decline noticeably toward the end of each season.

To compensate for this continuing phenomenon, price changes for apparel are based on a "hedonic" price index. A hedonic price index traces the effect of a group of characteristics of a product that influence the price of the item both through the utility of the item to the buyer and the cost of making the item to the producer.[7] Such characteristics in the case of women's apparel include daytime versus nighttime style, number of pieces (one or two), fiber content, brand label (local store or national), size range, type of lining, and type of store (full service or discount). Using a considerable amount of data on these characteristics and the prices associated with them over time, statistical regressions are developed that estimate the expected change in price associated with them when the new fashions are introduced each season. The difference of the actual market price in the store less the expected price from the hedonic regressions is the measure of price change used in the CPI. A positive difference is an increase in the CPI, a negative difference is decrease in the CPI, and no difference is no change in the CPI. The incorporation of the hedonic price index actually raised the annual inflation rate for apparel by 0.2 percentage point from June to December 1991.[8]

A hedonic price index is also relevant in the counterintuitive situation in which items having improvements in quality decline in price. Computers are an example of this, where quality improvements in capacity, speed, and portability have been accompanied by lower prices. Work is under way as of this writing in 1997 on developing a hedonic index for computers and appliances in the CPI.[9]

Sampling Error in the CPI

Because the monthly price data are collected from a sample of retail and other businesses selling to households, the CPI is subject to errors associated with sampling rather than surveying an entire group. During the 1991–95 period, the median standard error was plus or minus .07 percent.[10] Thus, if the CPI increases from one month to the next by 0.2 percent, in two of three cases the true price increase ranges from 0.193 to 0.207 percent.

Proposed Methodological Changes to the CPI

The CPI is the most widely accepted gauge of inflation. It is used in four broad areas: (1) macroeconomic analysis and policies affecting economic growth, employment, and inflation; (2) cost-escalation formulas used to compensate for inflation in Social Security and other income-maintenance programs, wage contracts, pensions, business contracts; (3) adjustments to the gross domestic product for inflation to derive measures of economic growth; and (4) the indexing of federal individual income taxes for inflation to limit the inflation-induced bracket creep.

The CPI does not measure inflation perfectly, however, because of two exceptionally difficult problems. These are the classic index number problem of how frequently to change the weighting structure of the index, and the adjustment of market price data for quality change (discussed in Chapter 1 and above in this chapter). The weighting structure in the CPI of the proportion of goods and services purchased by households is updated at approximately ten-year intervals. This results in a lag in incorporating the extent to which households change their purchases to substitute items that are cheaper or have more slowly rising prices, and to new products primarily after the price of the new product declines. Research by the U.S. Bureau of Labor Statistics (BLS) indicates that this lag raises the annual CPI inflation rate by 0.15 percentage point above what it would be if the weights were updated every year. While the overall structure of the CPI maintains constant weights over the ten-year intervals, in practice many models of particular products are phased out by manufacturers or retailers and replaced by new products in the stores. These new products are incorporated in the CPI during the ten-year interval between major updates in the weighting structure through the collection of price data from a sample of retail stores every month. One-fifth of the retail establishments in the sample is changed every year to reflect shifts in shopping preferences such as toward discount stores.

Adjustments for quality change are substantial. The best available estimates of the overall effect of quality adjustments is for a component of the CPI for commodities and services that accounts for approximately 70 percent of the CPI (shelter is the main exclusion). During 1995, the quality adjustments to the market price lowered the price increase from 3.9 percentage points before the quality adjustments to 2.2 percentage points after the adjustments were made, accounting for a downward adjustment of 1.7 percentage points in the price increase.[11] Thus, the net effect of the quality adjustments was a substantial amount of quality improvements, as the CPI price increase was only 56 percent of the market price increase.

Outside analyses of the methods used in preparing the CPI are important and are a stimulus to improving the CPI methodology. One such analysis is the widely publicized 1996 study, prepared for the U.S. Senate's Finance Committee, which estimated that the CPI overstates inflation by 1.1 percent annually.[12] The overstatement is composed of 0.4 percentage point for the weighting structure, 0.6 percentage point for the combined total of quality adjustments and the late introduction of new products, and 0.1 percentage point for the lagging recognition of purchases in discount retail stores in contrast to full-service stores.

The BLS has questioned the methodology on which some of the study's estimates are based.[13] Examples of the questioned items are unsubstantiated judgments of the value to consumers of the increased variety of food and beverage products and the increased availability of restaurants; overstatement of the increase in the size of an average apartment, and an incorrect assumption that rents rise in proportion to the increase in apartment size (rents generally increase less than proportionately to apartment size); the assumption that the entire increase in the average age of automobiles on the road reflects an increase in their durability, and the incorrect assumption that the CPI does not correct for changes in durability of automobiles; conjecture on the value of improvements on furniture and fabrics with respect to removing stains and lessening children's accidents for which there are no quantitative estimates; sole use of a Sears catalogue to estimate apparel prices, which ignores the many other apparel brands, and which prices the same apparel items without regard to changes in fashion.

The BLS also notes that the Advisory Commission report does not address the deterioration in the quality of some goods and services. If the quality deterioration is not adequately taken into account in adjusting the market price for such items, the CPI would *understate* inflation. In fact, the improved measure of quality in apparel products using the hedonic methodology raised the inflation rate, as noted above. Examples of quality deterioration include unsafe toys; difficulty of assembling toys; lower-grade materials that diminish the appearance of an item after a short time, such as pressed wood covered by formica in place of solid wood or metal in kitchen cabinets; reduced convenience and comfort of air travel; inability to reach live people on a telephone; lack of clerks in stores; computer manuals that are incomprehensible for operating computers; and overstatement by producers of goods and services of the dollar cost increase of quality improvements, or understatement by producers of the dollar cost decrease of quality deteriorations. There is also the possibility of a downward bias in the CPI inflation rate when old products are dropped from the index after being replaced by substitute products.

This is not to downplay the existing quality, weighting, and other problems with the CPI that the study identifies. The BLS agrees with the need to improve the quality adjustments for computers, consumer appliances, and medical care. These adjustments will require additional funding, and because they present difficult methodological issues, will take some time to implement. Also, various research is under way on alternative methods for the weighting structure and other technical problems in the CPI, some of which are consistent with the commission's recommendations. Examples of the continuing research on the CPI problems that have resulted in methodological improvements are the following: the bias in the formula for incorporating new products that replace older models into the index between major benchmarkings has been corrected; and quality adjustments have been substantially improved for apparel, housing, and durable goods.

There has also been a critique by Dean Baker of the Advisory Commission's overall conclusion that the CPI overstates inflation by 1.1 percent annually.[14] Thus, an annual 1.1 percent overstatement of inflation implies an implausibly large amount of poverty in the United States in past years. The argument is based on the following methodology. When income in current dollars is adjusted for inflation to obtain "real" income, if inflation has been lower than indicated by the CPI rate, then real incomes have risen more than the official measures of real income. Consequently, if incomes rose more than indicated by the official measures, then incomes in the past were lower than indicated by the official measures. This would result in a greater number of households with incomes below the poverty income threshold in the past than indicated in the official numbers, and therefore more households living in poverty in the past than has been thought to be the case.

For example, allowing for modest reductions in the inflation bias in the CPI due to the continuing improvements in the CPI from 1960 to 1994, Baker found that the inflation-adjusted income of the median family of four in 1960 was just 13 percent above the poverty level adopted in the early 1960s, which implies that the vast majority of all families were in poverty in 1960. But the official poverty standard adopted in the early 1960s, which has remained unchanged substantively through the 1990s (the income threshold is just adjusted for inflation over the years), was approximately only one-half of median family income.[15] This resulted in 18 percent of all families being classified in poverty in 1960, based on the official poverty count.[16] Simply stated, the inflation-adjusted income implied by the estimated 1.1 percent overstatement of inflation in the CPI means that most families were living in poverty in the early 1960s, which is unrealistic in terms of the perceptions of the times and is contrary to the official poverty statistics. And extending this pattern into the future, Baker finds that coming generations in the twenty-first century will have much higher incomes than their parents, which is contrary to the experience at the end of the twentieth century.

Conclusions

1. In the author's opinion, there is no compelling evidence of the extent to which the CPI overstates or understates inflation. Research on the problems in both directions should go forward. In fact, it may be that because of a long-held

notion that the CPI overstates inflation, a disproportionate part of the research has addressed problems that overstate inflation, such as the weighting structure and quantifying quality improvements. But, as noted above, there are problems of deteriorating quality for some goods and services, which if not adequately adjusted for, lead to an understatement of inflation. Thus, the CPI research should include specific attention to problems of quality deterioration. The research should also include the effect on the inflation rate of dropping old products from the index when they are replaced by substitutes.

2. Beyond the question of how accurately the CPI measures inflation, a more fundamental problem is that the Advisory Commission's study has been politicized, which if taken down a mischievous road, has a dangerous potential for the U.S. democracy. Thus, as a way of reducing the federal government budget deficit, some members of Congress of both major political parties have proposed using the Advisory Commission's estimate of the overstatement of inflation as a basis for lowering the cost-of-living adjustments on benefit payments of Social Security and other entitlement programs. If elected officials conclude that it is desirable to lower cost-of-living adjustments for Social Security and other entitlements, they should do so explicitly, such as by stating that the adjustment will be based on a certain percentage of the CPI inflation rate. No adjustments should be made to the CPI itself because of political pressure, however. The CPI should not be contaminated by notions of what inflation should be to fit political agendas. Such actions would mean that politicians determine what prices are. It would be a dangerous precedent for the CPI and all economic indicators, because if Congress or the President does not like a particular number, they can make one up and apply subtle and not-so-subtle pressure through agency budgets to mandate its use. That would be analogous to proposed changes in the judicial system, which would allow Congress to impeach judges whose opinions it disagrees with, or to overturn court decisions it disagrees with. What then becomes of the constitutional separation of powers of the legislative, executive, and judicial branches of government?

Lively debate on the methodology of the CPI and other economic indicators is healthy. But the integrity of the data should be inviolate and overseen by professionals. The data should not be tainted in any way by political or nongovernment interference, as discussed in Chapter 1 under Data Integrity. Tampering with economic statistics in order to support a particular point of view is characteristic of dictatorships, where "facts" are created at whim. It undermines the credibility of the government and the underpinning of a free democratic society. The foundation of a democracy is that information provided by the government, including economic statistics, is factual and trustworthy. People may differ in their interpretation of the data, but the data themselves should be uncompromised. It would be tragically wrong to politicize the CPI by imposing a political determination of the inflation rate.

Figure 11.1 **Consumer Price Index: 1950–96**

Annual percent change

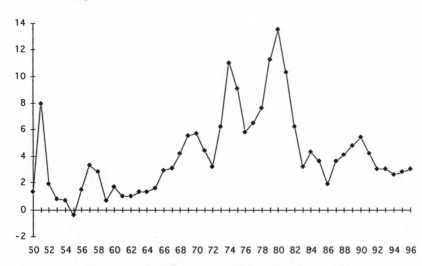

Note: Based on U.S. Bureau of Labor Statistics data.

PRICE MOVEMENTS OF THE MAJOR PRICE INDEXES

Figure 11.1 shows inflation rates in the CPI for 1950–96. The CPI increased at an average annual rate of 4.2 percent over the forty-six-year period. But it varied considerably over shorter periods. The extreme low was in 1955 (–0.4 percent), the only year in which overall prices declined. Prices had declined previously in 1949 (a recession year), six years in the 1930s, and four years in the 1920s. The extreme high was in 1980 (13.5 percent).

The varying price movements reflect the changing domestic and international events from 1950 to 1996, and reads like an economic and political history of the times.[17] The Korean War (1950–53) had an initial sharp rise in inflation, which declined substantially when mandatory price and wage controls were instituted. The 1954–65 period had an average annual inflation rate of 1.4 percent, with volatile price movements from 1954 to 1960 that included the end of the Korean War and three recessions, and slightly rising inflation from a low base during 1961–65 when economic growth was accelerating and voluntary price-wage guidelines were in effect. Inflation accelerated in the second half of the 1960s with the continued expansion in economic growth and the buildup of the Vietnam War.

The 1970–80 period had sharp gyrations in the inflation rate. It declined in 1971–72 due to new mandatory price and wage controls; rose sharply in 1973–

Table 11.3

Annual Inflation Rates for Four Price Indexes: 1948–96 (in percent)

	Consumer price index	Producer price index for finished goods	Gross domestic product chain price indexes	
			GDP	PCE[a]
1948–59	1.7	1.4	2.2	1.9
1959–69	2.3	1.4	2.3	2.1
1969–79	7.1	7.4	6.7	6.5
1979–89	5.5	3.9	5.0	5.3
1989–96	3.4	2.1	2.9	3.2
1948–96	4.0	3.0	3.8	3.8

Source: U.S. Bureau of Labor Statistics and U.S. Bureau of Economic Analysis.
[a]Personal consumption expenditures

74 from the oil price increases of the Arab oil boycott; declined in 1975–76 as oil prices rose less sharply and demand was weak in the aftermath of the 1973–75 recession (the end of the Vietnam War in 1975 had little effect, as defense expenditures had been steadily declining from its peak in 1968); and rose in 1977–80 due to the inflationary expectations of the price-wage spiral (which included a period of voluntary price-wage standards), and the oil price increases of the Iranian revolution.

The sharp disinflation during 1981–86 included a deep recession, accelerated weakness in the bargaining position of labor unions with the rising use of re-placement workers by companies and the federal government in the face of strikes, and weakness in oil prices stemming from energy conservation and the development of additional world sources of oil supplies that began in the 1970s. Inflation accelerated during 1987–90, during which economic growth was ini-tially strong but then slowed, and then turned down into the 1990–91 recession (the recession period also bracketed the Gulf War buildup and the war). Inflation was quite stable around 3 percent during 1992–96, as economic growth ranged from 2 to 3.5 percent.

Table 11.3 shows the annual inflation rates (compounded) for the CPI, pro-ducer price index for finished goods (PPI), and the gross domestic product (GDP) chain price indexes for the GDP and personal consumption expenditures (PCE) by decade from 1948 to 1996.[18] The inflation rate over the forty-eight-year period is 4 percent for the CPI, 3 percent for the PPI, and 3.8 percent for the GDP price indexes. Overall, during each of the decades, the CPI and the GDP price index inflation rates were within 0.5 percentage point of each other, and the differences between the CPI and the PPI ranged from 0.3 to 1.6 percentage points.

Table 11.4

CPI Movements at Cyclical Turning Points (three-month annual rates at expansion peak and recession trough)

Expansion peak		Recession trough	
November 1948	−4.3	October 1949	−0.6
July 1953	1.5	May 1954	−0.8
August 1957	4.1	April 1958	4.3
April 1960	2.3	February 1961	0.8
December 1969	6.3	November 1970	5.9
November 1973	8.2	March 1975	6.6
January 1980	15.8	July 1980	8.3
July 1981	11.7	November 1982	1.7

Source: John F. Early, Mary Lynn Schmidt, and Thomas J. Mosimann, "Inflation and the business cycle during the postwar period," *Monthly Labor Review,* November 1984, Table 1, p. 4.

The variations among the four indexes reflect differences in item content and weighting structures. The higher inflation rates of the CPI and the two GDP price indexes compared with the PPI largely reflect the inclusion of goods and services items in the CPI and GDP indexes, but only goods in the PPI. Services typically show more measured inflation than goods because they have a higher labor content and include items that are especially difficult to adjust for quality change, as noted previously under Price Expectations and Price Structure.

Because the weight structures of the CPI and PPI are changed every ten and five years respectively, while those of the GDP price indexes are changed every year, the GDP price indexes would tend to have lower price inflation due to their tendency to reflect more frequent substitution of items that have lower prices and smaller price increases. The item content is most similar between the CPI and the GDP consumer expenditure price index, and so these indexes would be expected to have the closest price movements on that basis, which did appear in the 1980s and 1990s. In the previous decades, however, the CPI and the total GDP price index had the closest price movements.

Cyclical Inflation Movements

Table 11.4 shows the pattern of CPI movements at the peak of expansions and trough of recessions in the eight complete business cycles from the end of World War II to the 1981–82 recession, each containing an expansion and recession (the analysis has not been updated to include the 1982–90 expansion and the 1990–91 recession). As would be expected, prices tend to rise faster in expansions and slower in subsequent recessions. There were, however, two exceptions:

in the 1949 recession, overall prices declined faster at the expansion peak than at the recession trough, and in the 1957–58 recession, prices increased faster at the recession trough than at the expansion peak. In both cases, food prices played a partial role. Because food prices are often driven by supply shortages or surpluses caused by weather conditions and harvests, they are not directly related to cyclical price fluctuations. Two additional factors in 1949 were the still-unsatisfied demand after World War II for automobiles and the rapidly growing market for television sets that propped up prices in 1949. While overall prices typically do not decline in recessions (slight declines occurred only in the first two of the nine postwar recessions), the slower rate of increase in recessions indicates they are responsive to declining sales volume. Prices for the broad groups of both commodities and services (not shown in the table) have the same pattern of faster increases in expansions.

The tendency in recessions for the rate of price increase to slow, rather than for prices to decline, reflects the business perception that price declines would not generate enough additional sales to raise profits. This reluctance to lower prices is referred to as the "stickiness" of prices.

TRANSMISSION OF PRICE CHANGE BY STAGE OF PROCESSING

An intuitively appealing idea in price analysis is that prices in each phase of production are passed along to the prices in subsequent stages of production. If these relationships can be developed empirically, it would significantly enhance the ability to forecast price movements of the overall economy, such as the producer price indexes (PPIs), the consumer price index (CPI), and the gross domestic product (GDP) price indexes.

The transmission of price movements from one phase of fabrication to the next starts with the very first phase, which reflects the fact that all goods originate in nature. The broad categories of products emanating from nature are water; crop, animal, and fish foods; cotton, linen, and wool fibers; lumber; sand and stone; metals; petroleum; and chemicals. They are initially produced in government (water reservoirs), agriculture, fishery, forestry, and mining industries. Following their initial production, they are refined in many processes in many different industries, and are incorporated in many different components and services, that ultimately become the completed goods and services used by households, businesses, and governments.

Ideally, if one product in each stage of fabrication is used only in that stage, it would be feasible to trace each product as it is transformed into another product. The problem is that the production process does not proceed in a straight line from natural materials to semi-finished goods to components to finished goods. A simplistic example of producing steel products of an automobile illustrates the process. The steel originates from the iron ore extracted from the ground. The iron ore is refined into steel, the steel is rolled into sheets, bars, or other shapes, and these are fabricated further to become part of the chassis, engine, and frame. But the iron ore was extracted from the ground using equipment, fuels, and services that themselves were produced from items much further along in the production process. This is multiplied many times over in many complex sequences for all of the natural materials and refined components of an automobile, which makes it impossible to develop a unidirectional sequence of the production process of the type noted above.

The PPIs have three broad categories of goods by stage of processing that provide the data for analyses and models of the transmission of inflation from one stage to the next: crude materials for further processing; intermediate materials, supplies, and components; and finished goods. The PPIs cover price movements of domestically produced goods only. They exclude services, construction, and imported goods, although imported items are indirectly included to the extent they are incorporated as components of the domestically produced items. Examples of the items in the three stages of processing are: crude materials for further processing (e.g., corn, soybeans, cattle, fluid milk, coal, crude petroleum, natural gas, raw cotton, sand and gravel, timber, metals); intermediate materials, supplies, and components (e.g., textiles, fabrics, commercial and industrial electric power and natural gas, refined petroleum, paper, chemicals, fertilizers, metal mill shapes, building materials, paper, glass, and metal containers, motors, generators, motor vehicle parts, photographic supplies, medical and surgical devices); and finished goods (fruits, vegetables, meat, dairy products, cooking oils, coffee, soft drinks, alcoholic beverages, apparel, furniture, appliances, newspapers, toys, automobiles, mobile homes, machinery, equipment, trucks, civilian aircraft, and ships).

Figure 11.2 shows the annual change in the three stage-of-processing PPIs from 1980 to 1996. It indicates that crude materials have the most volatile and finished goods the least volatile price movements, with intermediate materials between the two in volatility. One source of the volatility of crude materials prices is their sensitivity to supply shocks from natural disasters such as floods, droughts, frosts, hurricanes, and earthquakes, and from social and political events such as strikes and lockouts, shifting strong and weak discipline among members of cartels, revolutions, and wars. Also, many crude materials are traded in auction markets, where the effects of supply shocks can be quickly reflected in anticipating future inflation through futures prices, which may add to the volatility. By contrast, prices of intermediate materials and finished goods often are based on contracts for specified periods of time that limit the rapid price changes which are intrinsic to auction markets. More importantly, intermediate materials include many elements in their production beyond the use of crude materials, such as processed materials, components, supplies, services, and labor, that make them less susceptible to the supply shock vulnerability of crude materials alone. And finished goods are still further removed in their production costs from the initial supply shocks to crude materials.

Figure 11.2 **Producer Price Indexes by Stage of Processing: 1980–96**

Annual percent change

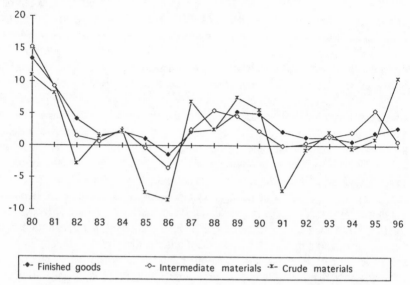

| -•- Finished goods | -◦- Intermediate materials | -×- Crude materials |

Note: Based on U.S. Bureau of Labor Statistics data.

Changes in demand also impact the transmission of inflation from one stage of processing to the next. These reflect such events as shifts between expansive and restrictive fiscal and monetary policies, or the introduction of new products at high prices and the subsequent maturation of the products at declining prices.

Figure 11.3 shows the annual price change in the PPI finished goods, CPI commodities, CPI commodities and services, and GDP chain price indexes. These also have a sequential stage-of-processing feature, with the PPI finished goods preceding both the CPI and the GDP price indexes in the production chain. The PPI finished goods and the CPI commodities indexes have the most volatile price movements, and the CPI commodities and services and the GDP price indexes have the least volatile prices. One reason for the lower volatility in the latter two indexes is that they include services, and services in general are more insulated than materials from supply shocks.

Figures 11.2 and 11.3 do not, on visual inspection, suggest lead and lag patterns among the various price indexes. One reason is that the figures are based on annual movements, but leads and lags typically occur in shorter monthly and quarterly periods. Another reason is that leads and lags may not be apparent visually, but they show up in statistical analyses.

The results of three such analyses are summarized here. The first two have

Figure 11.3 **Producer Prices, Consumer Prices, and Gross Domestic Product Prices: 1980–96**

Annual percent change

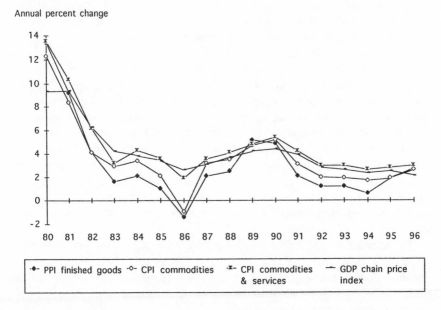

-•- PPI finished goods -○- CPI commodities   -×- CPI commodities   — GDP chain price
                                         & services   index

Note: Based on U.S. Bureau of Labor Statistics data.

generally negative conclusions about the significance of crude materials prices on overall inflation, and are covered first.[19] They indicate that crude materials prices were a better predictor of the CPI in the 1970s and early 1980s than from the mid-1980s through the mid-1990s. Crude prices were also a better predictor of overall inflation in the short-run of less than one year than over multiyear periods. In addition, the PPI for finished goods diminished in its predictive power of future movements in the CPI over the period.

A sample of reasons suggested in one or the other of the above studies that may explain part of the declining importance of crude materials price movements on overall inflation is noted here. One is the lessened use of crude materials as an inflation hedge because financial futures and Treasury bonds are better hedges against inflation, which means that crude prices are less an indicator of inflationary expectations than they are of factors specific to the materials markets. Another is that preemptive monetary policies by the Federal Reserve taken in advance to restrain economic growth and inflation when crude materials prices rose sharply have dampened the transmission of crude prices through the rest of the economy. But if this is true, it sounds like question-begging that would be very difficult to substantiate empirically. Another possible reason is that crude materials account for a smaller proportion of the items produced in the economy, while engineering products, electronics, plastics, and services have become more important. This trend has been apparent for a long time, however, and unless a critical mass of the noncrude materials items was reached, or there was a sharp acceleration in the trend toward noncrude materials items, its influence on the declining importance of crude materials is questionable.

A third study, still in the research phase at the time of this writing in the spring of 1997, contains some positive evidence.[20] Consistent with Figures 11.2 and 11.3, time-series models show price movement relationships among the three PPI stages of processing, and between the PPI finished goods and the CPI. This research recognizes that while the stage-of-processing theory implies that the products flow systematically forward from crude materials to intermediate materials to finished goods, such a unidirectional movement does not occur in practice. For example, sometimes a crude material skips the intermediate material stage and moves directly to the finished good stage, and sometimes an intermediate material or finished good moves backward to a previous stage. The models do suggest that most of the influence on prices is in the forward direction.

The stage of processing approach for inflation analysis requires more development for it to be useful in a systematic assessment of the transmission of inflation. In the interim, partial analyses of the transmission may add a limited dimension for assessing the propagation of inflation. The analyst should keep abreast of further research in this area.

INFLATION AND CAPACITY UTILIZATION

Capacity utilization (CU) measures the proportion of industrial structures and equipment that is used in producing industrial output. The structures and equipment are the indicator of capacity. For example, if a factory with the structures and equipment capacity to produce 1,000 cans of paint a month actually produces 800 cans a month, its CU is 80 percent and its unutilized capacity is 20 percent.

The Federal Reserve Board provides monthly CU measures for the manufacturing, mining, and electric and gas utilities industries. The capacity measures are integrated with the Federal Reserve's industrial production index. The data are available for manufacturing industries beginning with 1948 and for mining and utilities beginning with 1967.

Theoretically, the direction and level of CU rates indicate the degree of inflationary pressure in the economy. A rising CU tends to reduce unit costs of production for a time, as the existing capacity produces a larger volume of goods. The cost advantage of the larger volume (increasing returns to scale) continues until CU reaches a level at which further increases in production raise unit costs (decreasing returns to scale) because of machinery breakdowns, increasing use of older and less efficient equipment, hiring of less productive workers as unemployment falls, and laxness by managements in holding down costs (referred to as X-inefficiency).

The specific CU point at which the turnaround occurs on costs, and consequently affects inflation, varies among industries and is hard to quantify precisely. At this threshold, increasing production and rising production costs foster higher prices, and decreasing production and costs foster stable or declining prices. Analogously, rising production costs spur companies to reduce costs by increasing capacity through new investment in structures and equipment, and relatively low and falling CURs reduce business incentives to expand capacity (replacements of run-down and outmoded capacity account for greater shares of structures and equipment investment during such periods), as discussed in Chapter 5.

Capacity Utilization Methodology

The CU measure is the percentage that the industrial production index is of industrial structures and equipment capacity in the manufacturing, mining, and electric and gas utilities industries. The industrial production index is the numerator, industrial capacity is the denominator, and the ratio is multiplied by 100.

$$\text{Capacity utilization} = \frac{\text{Industrial production index}}{\text{Industrial capacity}} \times 100$$

The industrial production index (IPI) measures the output of the manufacturing, mining, and electric and gas utilities industries. The monthly output data are based on direct data on production volume adjusted for inflation, and indirect data on production worker hours or electric kilowatt-hour consumption in the various component industries, depending on the available information for each industry. The indirect labor and electricity data are converted to production based on projections of historical trends on labor productivity and of technological trends in the usage of electricity in the various industries. Annual revisions to the IPI incorporate a greater proportion of direct production data than the monthly data. The various component industries are combined into the index by weights associated with each industry's value added in the five-year economic censuses.

An industry's capacity is measured by its capital structures and equipment facilities that are operated on a schedule of the typical working day and week. The capacity measures assume an eight-hour day and five-day working week for most industries, though these are higher for some industries such as steel, petroleum refining, and utilities, that maintain production around the clock. The capacity measures for manufacturing and gas utilities are developed mainly through an indirect estimating procedure based on a Census Bureau survey of capacity utilization in manufacturing and the cumulative dollar investments in structures and equipment adjusted for inflation and depreciation.[21] For a limited number of manufacturing industries, more direct measures of capacity are used, such as weighted combinations of gas engines, transmissions and axles, and brakes for motor vehicles, and physical quantity data for the primary processing industries of steel, nonferrous metals, paper, petroleum refining, and chemicals. Electric utility capacity is based on kilowatt generating capacity adjusted for reserve capacity needed for outages and peak summer and winter usage. Mining industry capacity is based on some direct measures, and where these are not available, the capacity levels are inferred from long-term production trends derived by connecting the production expansion peaks of business cycles.

Capacity rises at a relatively steady rate with no cyclical ups and downs because in any period, capacity is composed mainly of existing facilities, with only marginal net changes made for the addition of new investment and deduction of depreciated facilities. The overall CU for all industries usually ranges from 75 to 85 percent, toward and around the upper end during expansions and toward and around the lower end during recessions. The range of CURs for individual industries varies from this overall average.

The overall CU typically does not approach or exceed 100 percent. The major exception is high mobilization during wars, when industry undergoes a widespread conversion to two and three eight-hour shifts a day. Because such multiple shifts are not considered typical capacity levels that can be sustained over long periods in peacetime, they do not result in an upward adjustment in the estimated capacity levels. Thus, the CU theoretically may reach the 100 percent range. But industry would probably operate at this level only during a full-scale war, and perhaps not even then. For example, the peak manufacturing CU in the Korean and Vietnam wars were 92 percent and then only for a few months. There are no estimates for World War II because CU measures were not developed until 1948. It remains unclear whether even a full-scale war would raise the CURs to the 100 percent range.

Measurement Problems

Production capacity is an elusive concept to define and measure. Theoretically, a business' ultimate capacity is the output it could produce if it operated seven days a week, twenty-four hours a day, with allowance for maintenance of existing equipment, shortages of materials, and other downtime. This level of operation is referred to as "engineering capacity." Other than in wartime, it is realistic only for industries with continuing process operations in which it is more efficient to operate around the clock. "Practical capacity" refers to the usual operations schedule that is realistically maintained on a continuing basis. These vary among industries from single and multiple eight-hour shifts over a five-day week to continuous operations seven days a week, as noted above. Practical capacity is the implied definition in the CU measures.

Another continuing problem with any statistical measure of capacity is whether plants that are closed down in recessions are considered permanently removed from production, or if this capacity is considered "found" and available again in expansions. While the Federal Reserve uses consistency checks with alternative data and statistical procedures to modify aberrant movements in the capacity figures, a considerable amount of indirect estimating is associated with the preparation of the capacity figures. Finally, the capacity figures do not include imports, which are an important source of added supply in some industries and which in effect increase capacity.

In sum, the capacity measures have basic limitations both in their definitions and quantification. Therefore, measures of capacity and of CU should be considered broad orders of magnitude.

Trends in the Capacity Utilization and Inflation Relationship

The relationship between the CU and overall inflation in the economy is assessed here for the CU in all manufacturing industries. Manufacturing accounted for 17.3 percent of the gross domestic product (GDP) in 1994, and the other components of the CU measure totaled 4.1 percent of the GDP (mining was 1.3 percent and electric and gas utilities 2.8 percent). The analysis focuses on manufacturing because the production of manufactured goods incorporates purchases of mineral products and electric and gas energy.

Figure 11.4 shows the relationship between the CU for all manufacturing industries and the PPI for industrial commodities from 1984 to 1996. The white diamonds that slope upward to the right are the long-term average for all years. It signifies a direct relationship between the CU and prices, with the CU and the PPI moving in the same upward or downward direction. This is consistent with the theoretical discussion of the relationship at the beginning of the section. At the same time, the individual years are widely dispersed around the long-term line, which means that the relationship is not rigorous from year to year.

This relationship between the CU and the PPI for industrial commodities was also calculated for the 1967–96, 1980–96, and 1983–96 periods. But the one in Figure 11.4 for 1984–96 had the closest movements between the CU and the PPI. Other calculations for the 1984–96 period between the CU and the PPI for finished goods, the CU and the CPI, and the CU and the GDP price index had weaker relationships than that in the figure. Of these, the PPI for finished goods had by far the best relationship. The GDP price index had the worst, as the CU and the GDP price index moved in opposite directions.

For some industries, however, an inverse relationship between the CUR and price changes may be more the norm than the exception. It is conceivable that in some cases equipment does not break down any more often at high operating rates than at low rates and indeed it may even perform better when continuously

Figure 11.4 **Capacity Utilization in Manufacturing versus the Producer Price Industrial Commodities Index: 1984–96**

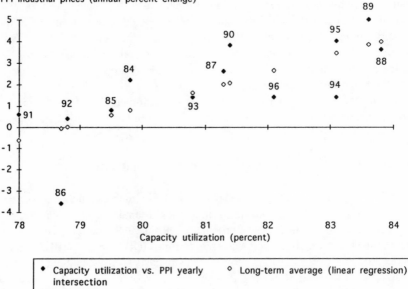

Note: Based on Federal Reserve Board and U.S. Bureau of Labor Statistics data.

in use. Similarly, hiring less productive workers when unemployment is low may not be very much of a problem in basic processing industries, such as textiles, paper, chemicals, and petroleum refining, where output is typically expanded by using more raw materials and running the equipment longer rather than by hiring more labor. Thus, at least in basic processing industries, an inverse CU-price relationship may be realistic.

An econometric study by Kenneth Emery and Chih-Ping Chang of the CU-inflation relationship found that the previously noted threshold CU, above which inflation accelerates and below which it decelerates, is about 82 percent for the total of all manufacturing industries.[22] The study also found a better relationship between the CU and the PPI than between the CU and the CPI, consistent with the above calculations. Nevertheless, the study found a deterioration in the CU-inflation relationship in the 1983–96 period compared with the pre-1983 period, contrary to the above calculations. A possible reason for the deterioration cited in the study is the more aggressive monetary policies taken by the Federal Reserve in the 1980s and 1990s than previously to prevent inflation from accelerating when the CU is considered to be at or above the threshold. But as in the previous section on the PPI stage-of-processing inflation analysis associated with sharp rises in crude materials prices, this attribution of forward-looking Federal Reserve policy sounds like question-begging that would be very difficult to substantiate empirically.

In relating the CU to inflation, the analyst should recognize the limitations of the measurement of capacity, and the lack of a rigorous year-to-year relationship between the CU and inflation. In addition, estimates of the threshold CU below 84–85 percent as a trigger for accelerating or decelerating inflation appear to be low. This suggests that a sustained higher CU than generally prevails would be necessary for the economy to be inflation prone.

DOMESTIC INFLATION AND IMPORTS

Imported goods and services provide additional choices for U.S. households, businesses, and governments in the specification, quality, and price of items purchased. Imports also are a surrogate additional industrial capacity when there is a shortage of some items. This section focuses on the effect of imports of commodities (goods) on domestic inflation. Commodities and goods are synonymous and distinct from services, with the nomenclature difference arising from their use in the statistical measures of the U.S. Bureau of Labor Statistics and the U.S. Bureau of Economic Analysis.[23]

Figure 11.5 shows the movements of four price indexes that compare the price movements of imports and domestic commodities from 1991 to 1996. The four price indexes are: imports of commodities from the import price indexes prepared by the BLS; imports of goods based on the gross domestic product (GDP); production of domestic goods based on the GDP; and the total of domestic and imported commodities based on the CPI. The GDP price measures use the price movements for individual commodities from the CPI, PPI, and import and export price indexes in adjusting the GDP for inflation. The resulting price indexes derived from the GDP inflation adjustment procedure differ from the CPI, PPI, and import and export price indexes because the GDP price indexes use a different weighting structure.

The prices of imported commodities were more volatile that the prices of domestic and all commodities during the six-year period. Over the entire period, the imported commodities had an accelerated rate of inflation, while the domestic and the domestic plus import commodities had a stable to decelerating rate of inflation. The import-domestic differential movements are due to differing proportions of various types of goods imported and all goods purchased.

The effect of imports on domestic inflation cannot be determined from the comparisons in Figure 11.5. In exceptional situations where imported items have a significant role in the U.S. economy and the prices of those items change sharply, such as oil, a broad gauge of their effects can be estimated. In the case of oil, economywide price changes both including and excluding energy are

Figure 11.5 **Price Movements of Imported, Domestic, and All Commodities: 1991–96**

Percent change

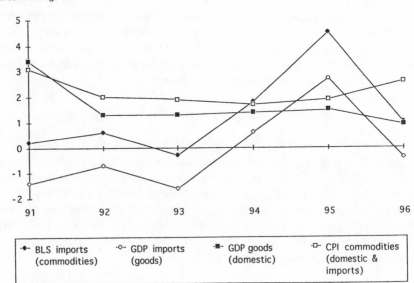

Note: Based on U.S. Bureau of Labor Statistics and U.S. Bureau of Economic Analysis data.

regularly published in the various BLS price measures, and so oil's overall effect is readily apparent.[24]

Theoretically, imports would be expected to lessen inflation in the United States through the increasing competition they bring to American markets. But the extent to which this occurs is not known.

On the topic of the effect of changes in the value of the dollar on the U.S. inflation rate, the issue hinges on the extent of the change in the value of the dollar and the extent to which it is reflected in the price of imported goods (Chapter 6 discusses the value of the dollar). In an analysis of the relationship of changes in the value of the dollar to the CPI inflation rate over the 1973–95 period, Roberto Chang found that changes in the value of the dollar have a relatively small effect on inflation.[25] For example, a sizable decline in the value of the dollar of 10 percent leads to an increase in the CPI of 0.76 percent in the first year following the shock. Assuming an initial inflation of 3 percent, the first year after the dollar decline would raise the rate to 3.02 percent (3 x 1.0076). Subsequent increases of 0.96 percent in the second year, 0.45 percent in the third year, and 0.21 percent in the fourth year would have similarly small inflationary increases (of course, the percentages are interesting for their low magnitude, not for the specific numbers). The study shows a much smaller effect of a rise in the value of the dollar lowering inflation. Chang explains the relatively small effect of a dollar decline on inflation as due to the fact that foreign firms exporting to the United States price their products in light of the competitive prices in U.S. markets. Thus, following a decline in the dollar, the firms consider making price changes in their products in part to maintain their market share (maintain current prices), and in part to maintain profit margins (raise prices). This limits the extent of price change following a dollar change, and results in part of the dollar decline being absorbed by lower profits. It is referred to as "pricing to market," and is contrary to the "law of one price," which presumes that firms charge the same price for the same item in all countries.

In an earlier study, Wing Woo came to a similar conclusion regarding the importance to foreign firms exporting to the United States of pricing their products to be competitive in U.S. markets. Thus, a primary factor determining prices of foreign goods was the aim of foreign exporters to maintain their market share in pricing actions following a change in the value of the dollar.[26] Woo also noted that changes in the value of the dollar can affect inflation through their effect on demand, as the markets for items produced by U.S. export and import competing firms are influenced by fluctuations in the dollar.

In evaluating the effects of imports and the value of the dollar on inflation, the analyst should focus on large changes in prices over sustained periods. With the notable exception of oil prices, the effects of changes in the value of the dollar and import prices tend to have a small effect on inflation for short periods.

MISERY INDEX

In national elections from the 1970s to the 1990s, the CPI has been part of the debate between candidates because of its inclusion in a number called the misery index. The misery index is the sum of the CPI inflation rate and the unemployment rate, and it has been used in election campaigns as a summary measure of the pocketbook issue. Because high rates of inflation and unemployment are undesirable, economic well-being and the misery index are inversely related. Thus, the nation is better off when the misery index is low than when it is high, and the incumbent party will gain from a low index and be at a disadvantage from a high one.

The misery index is a rough guide to how voters perceive their economic well-being. But it has several limitations. It gives equal weight to unemployment and inflation, which may be an accurate reflection of the public's perceptions only when the two components are at certain levels. It excludes employment, which may be rising while unemployment also is rising, as discussed in Chapter 9. And it does not distinguish whether the index level is particularly high or low except in relation to past periods. Because of its use in campaigns, it is interesting to compare the experience of the index with the outcome of presidential elections.

Figure 11.6 **Misery Index in Presidential Election and Immediately Preceding Years: 1947–48 to 1995–96**

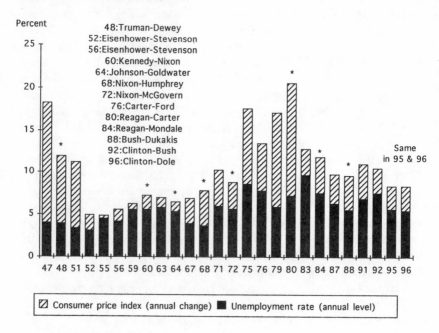

| ☑ Consumer price index (annual change) | ■ Unemployment rate (annual level) |

Note: Asterisk indicates that the winning presidential candidate had the advantage of the misery index movement.

Figure 11.6 shows the misery index in the thirteen presidential election years from 1948 to 1996, and in each of the years preceding the election year. The preceding adjacent years are included as an indication of the recent economic record of the incumbent party, which may be best remembered by the voters. In eight of the thirteen elections, the party won when the recent movement in the misery index favored it. For example, the incumbent party benefited if the index declined between the pre-election year and the election year. This pattern did not occur in the 1952, 1956, 1976, and 1992 elections, when the misery index favored the loser. In the 1996 election, the misery index did not change from 1995, so it favored neither the incumbent nor the challenger.

The misery index is a highly simplified view of pocketbook issues. It also does not reflect the intrinsic level of the index, other pocketbook issues such as income, other domestic and international issues, or the personalities of the candidates. The pocketbook issue is important, but elections are won on a combination of factors. While the misery index may suggest which candidate has an advantage because of the economic environment, it does not necessarily presage the outcome of the election.

REVIEW QUESTIONS

- What is the nature of price movements during periods of accelerating inflation, hyperinflation, disinflation, zero inflation, and deflation?
- Why is the weighting structure important for a price index? Give an example.
- How would the CPI have to change to be a cost-of-living index?
- How are issues of quality measurement used in statements that the CPI overstates or understates inflation?
- What is the effect of the following quality and market price changes on the CPI?

Quality Characteristics and Market Price	CPI Price		
	No change	Increase	Decrease
A loaf of bread is made smaller and the price is unchanged.			
Airbags are made standard equipment on a new car and the price of the car is increased by the cost of the airbags.			
An apartment building is renovated by dividing each four-room apartment renting for $800 a month into two two-room apartments each renting for $600 a month. The renovation cost is $100 a month for each two-room apartment.			

- What are the problematic aspects of the relationship between capacity utilization and inflation?
- What is the analytic interest in the stage-of-processing PPIs?
- What are the general circumstances when import prices have a noticeable effect on inflation?
- What factors limit the extent to which changes in the value of the dollar affect inflation?
- Although the misery index gives equal weight to inflation and unemployment, inflation directly affects many more people than unemployment. What is a rationale for giving equal weight to each?

Extra Credit

- Suppose you were writing a business contract calling for payments over the next several years to be indexed to a major inflation gauge. What measure would you choose? Why?

NOTES

1. Daniel Yergin, *The Prize: The Epic Quest for Oil, Money, and Power* (Simon and Schuster, 1991), pp. 522–25, 636–38, 718–21, 746–51, 758–64.

2. Robert J. Gordon, *Macroeconomics,* 6th ed. (HarperCollins, 1993), pp. 284–85.

3. The survey data are collected quarterly and annually. The frequent collection provides the potential to update the weights more often than the current ten-year intervals.

4. Patrick C. Jackman, "The CPI as a Cost of Living Index," paper presented at the 65th annual conference of the Western Economic Association, San Diego, June 29–July 3, 1990.

5. Bureau of Labor Statistics, U.S. Department of Labor, *Handbook of Methods,* April 1997, ch. 17. This provides a detailed description of the CPI methodology.

6. Strictly speaking, changes in the size or number of an item are a change in quantity.

7. Use of the word "hedonic" reflects its root meaning of pleasure. The characteristics of a product in a hedonic price index are assessed for the pleasure, or utility, they give the buyer. In addition, the hedonic price index includes the effect of changes in the cost of production, as such costs are incorporated in the price of the product.

8. Paul R. Liegey Jr., "Apparel price indexes: effects of hedonic adjustment," *Monthly Labor Review,* May 1994.

9. Brent R. Moulton and Karin Moses, "Addressing the Quality Change Issue in the Consumer Price Index," *Brookings Papers on Economic Activity* 1. Forthcoming.

10. David C. Swanson and Joseph Pavalone, "Variance Estimates for Changes in the Consumer Price Index," *CPI Detailed Report,* U.S. Bureau of Labor Statistics, April 1996, p. 10.

11. Katherine Abraham, "Measurement Issues in the Consumer Price Index," report to the Joint Economic Committee, U.S. Congress, June 1997. See also Moulton and Moses, "Addressing Quality Change Issues."

12. Advisory Commission to Study the Consumer Price Index, *Toward a More Accurate Measure of the Cost of Living,* final report to the Senate Finance Committee, December 4, 1996.

13. See note 11.

14. Dean Baker, *Getting Prices Right: A Methodologically Consistent Consumer Price Index* (Economic Policy Institute, 1996), April 12; and Dean Baker, "The Overstated CPI—Can It Really be True?" *Challenge,* September-October 1996.

15. Committee on National Statistics, National Research Council, *Measuring Poverty: A New Approach* (National Academy Press, 1995), p. 26.

16. Bureau of the Census, U.S. Department of Commerce, *Poverty in the United States: 1995,* September 1996, p. C–8.

17. While antitrust programs of the U.S. Department of Justice and the Federal Trade Commission are aimed at preventing and eliminating anti-competitive industry practices that tend to raise prices, the effect of these programs on the overall price level is difficult to ascertain. Enforcement of the antitrust laws also changes over time with the political party that has the presidency, as Democratic presidents pursue a more active antitrust program than Republican presidents.

18. Because the inflation rates are calculated from similar phases of the business cycle in which the final years of the comparison—1948, 1959, 1969, 1979, 1989, and 1996—are years of economic expansion, they provide a consistent representation of long-term trends; calculating the rates from terminal periods that include both expansion and recession years would distort the averages (see Chapter 1 under Calculating and Presenting Growth Rates).

19. S. Brock Blomberg and Ethan S. Harris, "The Commodity-Consumer Price Connection: Fact or Fable?" *Economic Policy Review,* Federal Reserve Bank of New York, October 1995. See also Fred Furlong and Robert Ingenito, "Commodity Prices and Inflation," *Economic Review,* Federal Reserve Bank of San Francisco, no. 2 (1996).

20. Tae-Hwy Lee and Stuart Scott, "Investigating Inflation Transmission by Stages of Processing," U.S. Bureau of Labor Statistics, Office of Research and Evaluation, January 2, 1997. Mimeo. See also Lee and Scott, "Transmission of Producer Prices Through Stages of Processing," *Proceedings of the Section on Survey Research Methods,* American Statistical Association, pp. 110–119.

21. Carol Corrado, Charles Gilbert, and Richard Raddock, "Industrial Production and Capacity Utilization: Historical Revision and Recent Developments," *Federal Reserve Bulletin,* February 1997.

22. Kenneth M. Emery and Chih-Ping Chang, "Is There a Stable Relationship Between Capacity Utilization and Inflation?" *Economic Review,* Federal Reserve Bank of Dallas, First quarter 1997.

23. The U.S. Bureau of Labor Statistics uses "commodities" in its price index measures. The U.S. Bureau of Economic Analysis uses "goods" in its gross domestic product price measures.

24. The core rate of inflation excludes both oil and food prices, as noted earlier in the chapter.

25. Roberto Chang, "Is a Weak Dollar Inflationary?" *Economic Review,* Federal Reserve Bank of Atlanta, September/October 1995.

26. Wing T. Woo, "Exchange Rates and the Prices of Nonfood, Nonfuel Products," *Brookings Papers on Economic Activity* 2 (1984).

 12
FINANCE

Money is a lubricant for the economy. It allows a greater specialization of production and division of labor and thus higher productivity and better living conditions than is possible in a barter economy. Money also has a life of its own in financial markets, which affects the economy. These financial aspects of money are the subject of this chapter.

Monetary policy refers to Federal Reserve (FR) System actions that affect bank reserves, the money supply, and interest rates. The FR influences the money supply by affecting the levels of bank reserves available for loans and consequently impacting interest rates on loans to households, businesses, and governments. Monetary policies aim at moderating extreme cyclical fluctuations of high inflation during expansions and high unemployment during recessions, with the goal of achieving steadier economic growth, high employment, and low inflation over the long run. Chapter 2 gives an overall perspective how the FR implements monetary policies.

Fiscal policy consists of the spending and taxation actions taken on the federal government budget by the Congress and the President. Fiscal policy impacts the economy through changes in the size and direction of the federal government budget (Chapter 2). Monetary policy is more easily implemented than fiscal policy because it is geared solely to influencing the economy, whereas fiscal policy is derived secondarily as the outcome of spending programs and tax laws to meet the nation's civilian and defense needs in the most efficient and equitable manner. Monetary policy is also more flexible because it can be modified quickly and often. By contrast, fiscal policy responds more slowly to changing economic conditions because of the lengthy legislative process involved in changing spending programs and tax laws.

This chapter focuses on the money supply and interest rates in relation to economic growth (Chapter 3), employment (Chapter 8), unemployment (Chapter 9), and inflation (Chapter 11). The appendix summarizes the organization and independence of the FR system.

MONEY SUPPLY

The money supply measures certain financial assets held by households, businesses, nonprofit organizations, and state and local governments that are available for consumer, business, and government spending. The money supply is used, along with other economic indicators, by the FR to determine monetary policies.

In preparing the money supply measures, the FR provides three alternative definitions—M1, M2, and M3—that range in coverage of financial assets from M1 as the most limited to M3 as the broadest. For example, M1 includes only currency, demand (checking) deposits, interest-bearing deposits that are used for writing checks (e.g., NOW accounts), and nonbank travelers' checks. By contrast, M3 includes all of these plus savings and time deposits, money market deposits and money market mutual funds, Eurodollars, and more. The money supply excludes such financial assets as corporate stocks, commercial and government bonds, and life insurance. The FR publishes all the money supply measures weekly.

The various assets included in the three measures differ in terms of liquidity and FR influence over their movements. Liquidity is the ease with which money can be withdrawn from accounts or obtained from the sale of assets without the risk of losing value. The FR influence over the movements of the three money supply measures reflects the extent to which the various assets are subject to the FR regulation of reserve requirements for commercial banks and other depository institutions. M1 is the most liquid and theoretically subject to the most FR influence; M2 and M3 are increasingly less liquid and less subject to FR influence.[1]

Distinctions in terms of liquidity are based on assessments of the risks of particular assets losing value if converted to cash. For example, nonbank travelers' checks function as currency; demand deposits often require minimum balances below which penalty fees are paid; saving deposits may forfeit some interest payments if withdrawn before certain dates; and money market securities are subject to current market interest rates, which impose a greater risk regarding the future value of these assets. M1 is the most liquid of the money supply measures, while M2 and M3 are increasingly less liquid because they include progressively greater proportions of assets that are based on current market rates.

The money supply differs from other economic indicators in this book in a basic way: it is the only indicator on which a governmental authority acts solely and directly to affect its performance. The federal budget deficit is acted on directly, but the federal budget is not solely associated with influencing the economy, as noted above. The other indicators reflect economic activity but are not active instruments in economic policy. Even when incomes policies of voluntary price and wage guidelines or mandatory price and wage controls are in effect, the consumer price index and wage rate indicators, while they record the

Table 12.1

Money Supply Measures (billions of dollars)

	December 1996
M1	**1,081.0**
Currency (excludes bank-owned cash in bank vaults)	395.2
Demand (checking) deposits	402.5
Other checkable deposits (e.g., NOW accounts)	274.8
Nonbank travelers' checks (e.g., American Express)	8.6
M2	**3,833.1**
M1	1,081.0
Small time deposits (less than $100,000)	944.1
Savings deposits, including money market deposit accounts	1,271.0
Money market mutual funds (retail: minimum initial investments less than $50,000)	536.6
M3	**4,927.1**
M2	3,833.1
Large time deposits ($100,000 and more)	489.6
Overnight and term Eurodollars	112.6
Money market mutual funds (institutions: minimum initial investments $50,000 or more)	299.3
Overnight and term repurchase agreements	192.5

Source: Federal Reserve Board.

Note: The sum of the components do not equal the totals because certain adjustments are made at the total level to avoid double-counting. For example, deposits of one bank held by another are excluded, as are assets held by money market mutual funds in other components of M2 and M3.

impact of those policies, are not direct instruments used in achieving the price and wage goals.

The money supply is an intermediate economic indicator, in contrast to ultimate indicators such as the gross domestic product, unemployment, or the consumer price index. The money supply is of policy interest because it influences interest rates. Interest rates are the price of money, and thus the level and movement of interest rates affect the quantity of loans and the ultimate indicators.

Table 12.1 shows the components of the M1, M2, and M3 measures of the money supply. Each successive measure takes the previous one as a base and adds new elements. The differences in the dollar levels of the alternative measures are substantial, most notably between M1 and M2. As of December 1996, M2 was 3.5 times as large as M1, and M3 exceeded M2 by 29 percent.

Money Supply and Economic Growth

The money supply in part reflects the decisions of households, businesses, nonprofit organizations, and state and local governments to hold their assets in certain financial forms—currency, checking accounts, savings accounts, money market deposit accounts, money market mutual funds, time deposits, Eurodollars, and so on. The money supply is also influenced by FR monetary policies.

In economic theory, the amount of money is related to spending and the resultant economic growth, employment, and inflation. A larger money supply means more spending, and a smaller money supply means less spending. The FR affects the supply of money by expanding or restraining the amount of commercial bank reserves available for loans, and in turn the amount of bank reserves affects interest rates.[2]

There is an assumed short-run inverse relationship between bank reserves and interest rates—more bank reserves lead to lower interest rates, and fewer bank reserves result in higher interest rates. As more reserves become available, banks, finance companies, and other lending institutions increasingly compete to extend credit, tending to lead to lower interest rates. In turn, lower interest rates induce households to borrow money for consumer items and housing mortgages and prompt businesses to borrow money for inventories and structures and equipment investment. Because these loans become checking accounts for borrowers, the money supply increases. The opposite occurs when fewer reserves are available, which tend to raise interest rates and lower borrowing, and consequently lower the money supply.

Schematically, these relationships appear as:

Higher growth and employment

Reserves>Interest rates>Money supply>Spending

Higher inflation

Theoretically, there is a direct relationship between money supply growth rates on the one hand and economic growth, employment, and inflation on the other. But there is much debate over the strength of the relationship, and the relationship is neither simple nor close. There are clearly time lags, and the lags are variable and difficult to quantify with precision. Estimates range from less than one year to about two years because other factors affect the economy—for example, opportunity costs of alternative outlets for money, the federal deficit, the value of the dollar, oil prices, inflationary expectations, productivity. Monetary growth is more closely related with inflation over the long run.

These nonmonetary conditions also sometimes override the expected relationship between bank reserves and the money supply noted above. During periods of high economic growth and employment increases along with low levels of unemployment, rapid growth in the money supply may be perceived by lenders as overstimulating the economy and causing further price increases. When lenders do perceive that greater monetary growth will lead to greater inflation, they attach an "inflation premium" to interest rates. The inflation premium could result in interest rates rising, rather than falling, in response to greater monetary growth. Lenders attach an inflation premium to interest rates to keep the purchasing power of their incomes from deteriorating due to inflation when the loan is repaid. A similar pattern of nonmonetary factors weighing heavily may occur during recessions and periods of high unemployment when, despite lower interest rates, households and businesses do not increase their borrowing and spending because of declining incomes.

The limited power of FR policies in the face of these nonmonetary factors is suggested by the use of the colloquial expressions "pulling the string" and "pushing the string" to describe FR policies. Generally, the FR is considered to be more effective at slowing economic growth by raising interest rates (pulling the string) than at quickening economic growth by lowering interest rates (pushing the string).

Money Supply Targets and Their Implementation

The Full Employment and Balanced Growth Act of 1978 (the Humphrey-Hawkins Act) established goals for reducing unemployment and inflation (Chapter 2). The act also requires the FR to report to Congress twice a year, in February and July, on its objectives and plans for growth rates of the money supply during the calendar year.[3] In these reports to Congress, the FR provides target ranges for the growth of M1, M2, and M3. However, the FR does not always provide targets for all of the money supply measures. For example, from 1987 to 1997, no target was given for M1 in reports to Congress because of its higher sensitivity to interest rates and problems in understanding its behavior relative to income and interest rates.

The target ranges are set to provide the amount of money estimated to be necessary to accommodate what the FR considers to be a desirable and realistic path for economic growth, employment, and inflation. Through its effect on bank reserves, the FR seeks to influence a panoply of economic functions, starting with short-term credit costs, in a continental, postindustrial economy that is enormous, complex, increasingly open to international influences, and highly variable by region. But monetary policy, although capable of being finely tuned from day to day, is a crude device for achieving all the good things the American public wants and tends to expect the government to bring about: jobs, high wages, profits, price stability, predictability. Over the years, FR policies have centered on combating inflation, with the long-run goal of "price stability," which is zero inflation in the overall price level (Chapter 11). The FR view is that with price stability undergirding the economy, the natural generative forces of American life bring about jobs, high wages, profits, and so forth.

The target ranges typically allow the FR considerable discretion in modifying growth rates in the money supply as economic trends and the demand for money evolve through the year. For example, in the February 1997 report, the ranges for 1997 are 1 to 5 percent for M2 and 2 to 6 percent for M3. The Humphrey-Hawkins Act treats these targets as guides instead of requiring that they be met, as long as reasons for not achieving them are reported to Congress. However, because the target ranges are so wide, they appear to be of limited use. Writing in 1997, Michael Akhtar notes that the target ranges have not been reliable guides for monetary policy for several years.[4]

The FR uses three tools to influence the money supply: open-market operations, the discount rate, and reserve requirements.[5] All three tools can be used to affect commercial bank reserves, interest rates, the volume of bank loans, and the money supply.

Open-market operations are the purchase and sale of U.S. Treasury federal government debt securities by the FR in the secondary market of previously issued securities. Since commercial banks invest in federal securities as a source of income and nonbank investors in federal securities maintain bank checking accounts, bank reserves are increased when the FR buys and decreased when it sells federal securities. These operations can be carried out daily, if needed, and are the FR's primary means of influencing bank reserves on a current basis. Open-market operations are reflected in the movement of federal funds interest rates, which in turn indicate whether the thrust of current monetary policies is aimed at stimulating or restraining economic activity (federal funds are discussed below).

The FR uses open-market operations to influence the federal funds interest rate. The *federal funds rate* is a monetary policy operating target for short-term interest rates. Federal funds is the rate charged for loans between banks.[6] These typically are for overnight loans that allow banks to meet reserve requirements, although there are "term" federal funds with maturities from a few days to over one year (the average is less than six months). Because banks do not receive interest on their reserve accounts with the FR, the federal funds market has dual incentives. Banks typically keep their reserves at the minimum required, but they sometimes fall below the minimum, which causes the need to borrow, while banks holding reserves above the minimum requirement gain interest by lending the surplus. The name "federal funds" reflects the transfer of these funds at FR Banks.

The federal funds interest rate on interbank loans is the clearest indicator of current FR monetary policy. The FR's open-market operations (typically conducted a few days a week), which raise or lower bank reserves and thus the availability of bank credit for loans, virtually determine movements in the federal funds rate, as well as the need for banks to borrow to meet their reserve requirements. In addition, interest rates on commercial short-term securities such as certificates of deposit and commercial paper reflect movements in the federal funds rate. The federal funds rate should not be confused with the FR discount rate noted below.

The *discount rate* is the interest rate that the twelve regional FR Banks charge commercial banks in their regions for loans (the Appendix covers the FR organizational structure). A lower discount rate encourages banks to borrow from the FR, which raises bank reserves. Commercial banks typically obtain such loans to meet short-term liquidity needs when other sources of funds are unavailable. Banks may also need longer-term loans (referred to as extended credit) when they have more serious liquidity or management difficulties that can be resolved only over protracted periods. When necessary, the FR changes the discount rate to bring it in line with other short-term interest rates or to signal a change in FR policy on the growth rate of the money supply. The FR restricts borrowing from the "discount window" for the emergency-type purposes noted above in order to prevent banks from using it as a general source of low-interest funds. The symbolic importance of the discount rate exceeds its importance as a price of money actually borrowed.

Reserve requirements are the legally required reserves that each commercial bank, thrift institution, and credit union must maintain with the FR Bank in its region in proportion to its demand deposits and NOW accounts. Since the Depository Institutions Deregulation and Monetary Control Act of 1980, commercial banks that are members of the FR system, as well as nonmember banks, are subject to the reserve requirements. The direct purpose of reserve requirements is to ensure that banks maintain sufficient liquidity to conduct daily operations such as clearing checks and meeting the ongoing needs of customers. These reserves also make it possible to implement monetary policies in conjunction with open-market operations.

If there were no reserve requirements, the FR would have a less effective fulcrum for inducing banks to expand or contract loans. Because commercial banks, thrift institutions, and credit unions have their own demands for reserves for their business operations, the FR probably would have to model these financial institutions' demands for reserves to its monetary policy open-market operations and federal funds rates. This would result in less certain monetary targets because the financial institutions' demands for reserves are more difficult to ascertain than the FR imposed reserve requirements which are known. Such a situation would lead to a greater volatility of interest rates and impair the FR's effectiveness in conducting monetary policies, as noted by Gordon Sellon and Stuart Weiner.[7] Thus, open-market operations would be less effective because there would be no regulatory limit on the volume of money and loans that the banking system could create.

The FR may change reserve requirements within certain legally prescribed limits, but because even small changes can significantly affect banks' liquidity, the requirements are changed infrequently, and then typically open-market operations are undertaken to ensure no net change in bank reserves.[8] Reserve requirements have been used to counteract developments in particular financial markets—such as varying international interest rates that cause money to flow between the United States and other nations in a way that hinders the implementation of domestic monetary policies—or as a signal that the FR is changing its policies toward expansion or restraint.

Reserve requirements are not used to maintain the financial solvency of banks, however. This is done by the banking regulatory agencies—the FR for state-chartered FR member banks, Comptroller of the Currency (U.S. Department of the Treasury) for nationally chartered banks, and Federal Deposit Insurance Corporation for state-chartered nonmember banks that have FDIC insurance—in their supervision of bank operations.[9] The supervision includes ensuring that banks meet capital requirements, which specify the levels of bank owners' equity investment as a percentage of total bank assets. Proposals have been made to reorganize the banking regulatory system that, if enacted in legislation, would change the supervisory responsibilities of the existing three agencies and/or create a new agency.

Reserve requirements also put an upper limit on the ultimate increase in the money supply resulting from bank loans. When a bank gives a customer a loan, it increases the customer's checking deposits by the amount of the loan. Because checking deposits are part of the money supply, the loan increases the money supply. The expansion of the money supply from when the customer first uses the loan to buy a car, pay school tuition, or purchase other goods and services multiplies several times as the car dealer and the school deposit their receipts in their respective banks, and those banks in turn extend loans with the new deposits, and so on.[10] Since the relending and respending occur in successive time periods, it may be several years before the cumulative ultimate expansion of the money supply from a single loan is reached.

Over the long run, independent of changes in the demand for money during cyclical expansions and recessions, an increase in the money supply is needed to accommodate the gradual growth of the population and business activity. This continuing increment is put into the economy by the FR's purchase of Treasury securities in open-market operations.

Monthly data for the money supply measures are based on reports from samples of large and small commercial banks, savings and loan associations, mutual savings banks, credit unions, and brokers and dealers. Because the weekly data are based on fewer reports, they should be used with caution. They fluctuate considerably from week to week and are sometimes substantially revised based on the more complete information underlying the monthly measures.

Money Supply, Economic Growth, and Inflation

Relationships between growth in the money supply and economic growth, as measured by the gross domestic product (GDP), are theoretically most consistent for the GDP in current dollars because money supply measures are in current dollars and thus relate to actual price levels (Chapter 3 covers economic growth). As for which of the three money supply measures is most closely related to the GDP movements, theoretical arguments could probably be made in support of any one of them.

In the comparisons shown here, the change in the money supply in one year is assumed to affect the GDP growth rates six months later. It is based on annual growth rates for the money supply calculated from the fourth quarter of one year

Figure 12.1 **Money Supply (M1) versus GDP in Current Dollars: 1960–96**

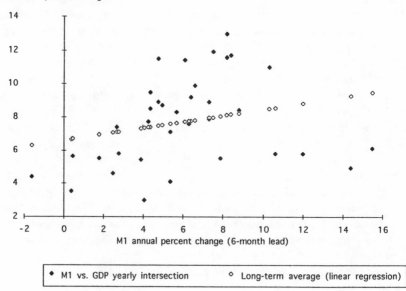

Note: Based on Federal Reserve Board and U.S. Bureau of Economic Analysis data. See text for meaning of 6-month M1 lead.

to the fourth quarter of the next year, and the annual growth rates for the GDP are based on the growth in one subsequent calendar year. For example, money supply growth from the fourth quarter of 1994 to the fourth quarter of 1995 is matched with GDP growth from calendar 1995 to calendar 1996.

Figure 12.1 shows M1 in relation to the GDP in current dollars, and Figures 12.2 and 12.3 compare M1 movements to the GDP adjusted for inflation (real GDP), and inflation as measured by the GDP chain price index (Chapter 11 covers inflation). The points representing each year show the money supply growth rate in the initial year and the GDP measure in the following year. For example, 1960, which is the first year shown in the figures, represents the change in the money supply in 1960 and the change in the GDP in 1961. Over the long run, the closest relationship in each figure appears as an upward-sloping line to the right. Thus, an increase or slowdown in the rate of money supply growth would be associated with a similar movement in the GDP and inflation. The closest comparison is with GDP in current dollars (Figure 12.1). But it is not stable or predictable from year to year. The upward-sloping line to the right (of white diamonds) represents the long-term average relationship. Because of the wide dispersion of the years around the long-term line, there would be a

Figure 12.2 **Money Supply (M1) versus Real GDP: 1960–96** (in chained 1992 dollars)

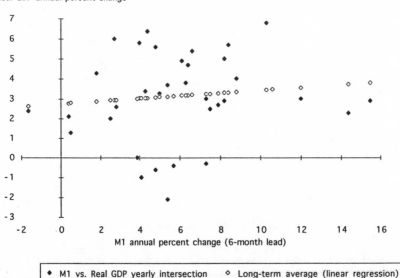

Note: Based on Federal Reserve Board and U.S. Bureau of Economic Analysis data. See text for meaning of 6-month M1 lead.

large margin of error in using it to predict GDP in any particular year.

The M1 relationships with real GNP and inflation (Figures 12.2 and 12.3) are both less consistent than that with GDP in current dollars (Figure 12.1), although M1 corresponds more to inflation than to real GDP. Overall, using the money supply to determine current-dollar GDP, real GDP, or inflation is problematic. Similar comparisons with longer lead times between the change in M1 and GDP and inflation, and between M2 and M3 and GDP and inflation also showed weak relationships.

In assessing movements of the money supply measures as a gauge of future economic growth and inflation, the analyst should consider the money supply as a clue only for GDP in current dollars. The money supply by itself is a poor predictor of future short-term movements of real GDP or inflation.

Money Supply Targets and Velocity

The money supply targets used by the FR in conducting monetary policy discussed previously are based on an expectation of the demand for money in

Figure 12.3 **Money Supply (M1) versus GDP Chain Price Index: 1960–96**

GDP price index annual percent change

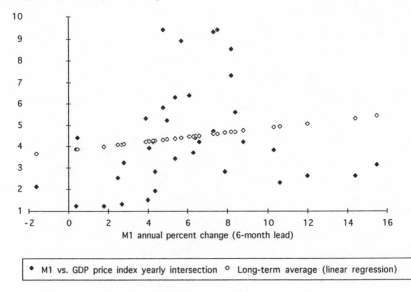

M1 annual percent change (6-month lead)

| ◆ M1 vs. GDP price index yearly intersection   ○ Long-term average (linear regression) |

Note: Based on Federal Reserve Board and U.S. Bureau of Economic Analysis data. See text for meaning of 6-month M1 lead.

relation to economic growth. One simple measure of this relationship is the ratio of the GDP to the money supply. This ratio is called the velocity of money and indicates the relative extent to which households, businesses, nonprofit organizations, and state and local governments hold financial assets (it also may be thought of as the turnover of money). Velocity is inversely related to the public's desire to hold money. If the GDP grows faster than the money supply, velocity increases; if the money supply increases faster than the GDP, velocity decreases. Velocity is a behavioral relationship of the public's tendency to hold financial assets in the most liquid forms, such as low-interest or non-interest-bearing assets, because the public perceives a need for the money in the near future and wants it readily available, or because it does not want to risk a loss in capital value. The future need may be for consumer and business spending, investments in anticipation of higher interest rates, and so forth.

Figures 12.4a, 12.4b, and 12.4c show trends from 1959 to 1996 of velocity for M1, M2, and M3, respectively. Each year is represented by the fourth quarter of the year—1959:4, 1960:4, and so on. Movements of the three measures are quite different. M1 velocity rose fairly steadily from a turnover ratio of 4 in the early 1960s to 7 in the early 1980s and then fluctuated with increasing

Figure 12.4a **Money Supply (M1) Velocity: 1959–96**

Ratio

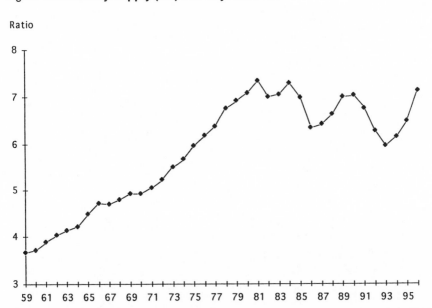

Note: Velocity is current-dollar GDP divided by M1. Each year represents the fourth quarter.

volatility during the 1980s and 1990s. M2 fluctuated within a turnover ratio of 1.6 and 1.7 in the 1960s and 1970s, rose to 1.8 in the 1980s and also was more volatile during the decade, and rose fairly steadily to a ratio of 2 in the mid-1990s. M3 showed a long-term decline, although with several interruptions, in the turnover ratio from 1.7 in the early 1960s to 1.3 in the mid-1980s, and then rose with two interruptions to 1.6 by the mid-1990s. This general volatility reflects the fluid reactions of households and businesses to changing patterns of economic growth, inflation, and interest rates. It also results from the development of new financial instruments such as interest-bearing NOW accounts and money market funds, and the solvency problems of financial institutions including failures of savings and loan associations and commercial banks.

Movements in velocity are difficult to predict. Consequently, money supply targets are subject to the uncertainty of the movement of velocity. For example, if the GDP growth rate turns out to be close to the rate assumed when the money supply targets were projected, the money supply will exceed the target if velocity is much lower than anticipated. Analogously, the money supply will be lower than the target if velocity is much higher than expected. This occurs even with the wide upper and lower limits set by the FR for its money supply targets.

Figure 12.4b **Money Supply (M2) Velocity: 1959–96**

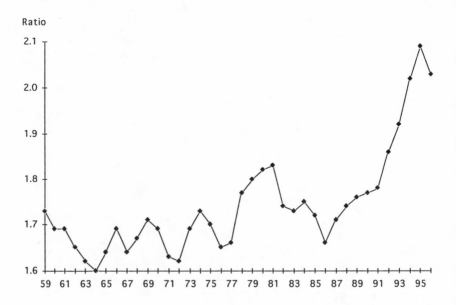

Ratio

Note: Velocity is current-dollar GDP divided by M2. Each year represents the fourth quarter.

The uncertainty of velocity movements points up the difficulty of projecting money supply targets in relation to the GDP. In assessing the likely outcome of money supply targets, the analyst should keep in mind that while the FR can influence the quantity of money, underlying economic factors such as economic growth, unemployment, capacity utilization, the federal deficit, the value of the dollar, oil prices, and inflationary expectations dominate movements in the money supply.

INTEREST RATES

Interest is the price of money. Major elements determining the interest rate on a loan include: (1) competing opportunities for lenders' funds in other loans or investments (referred to as "opportunity cost"); (2) risk of default on the loan; (3) expectation of inflation in discounting the future value of interest payments and repayment of the principal of the loan; and (4) availability of alternative sources of funds for loans from banks and investors (i.e., the supply of loanable funds). There is a direct relationship between the first three elements and the level of interest rates—the greater the opportunity cost, the risk of default, or the expectation of inflation, the higher the interest rate. In contrast, a greater supply of loanable funds tends to lower interest rates, which is an inverse relationship.

Figure 12.4c **Money Supply (M3) Velocity: 1959–96**

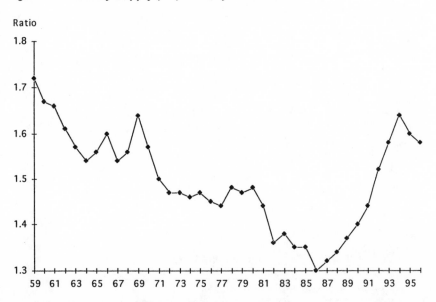

Ratio

Note: Velocity is current-dollar GDP divided by M3. Each year represents the fourth quarter.

Interest Rates and the Money Supply

While influencing the money supply is an important intermediate tool for conducting monetary policy, decisions to borrow and spend are directly affected by interest rates. Households, businesses, and other borrowers think in terms of interest rates because they represent the cost of credit, while money supply movements as such are removed from borrowing decisions. Theoretically, in the short run a speedup in the money supply's growth rate would lower interest rates, and a slowdown in the money supply's growth would raise interest rates, as indicated previously.

Figure 12.5 shows the relationships for 1960–96 of changes in M1 and interest rates. The interest rates are yields on U.S. Treasury securities with a three-year remaining maturity.[11] The three-year rate is used to reflect intermediate-term borrowing for investments. The comparison is based on annual changes in the money supply from the fourth quarter of one year to the fourth quarter of the following year, and annual changes in interest rates in the subsequent calendar year. Thus, the money supply changes lead the interest changes by six months.

The figure shows a slight direct relationship between the money supply and interest rates, with the long-term line sloping upward to the right. The relation-

Figure 12.5 **Money Supply (M1) versus Interest Rates: 1960–96**

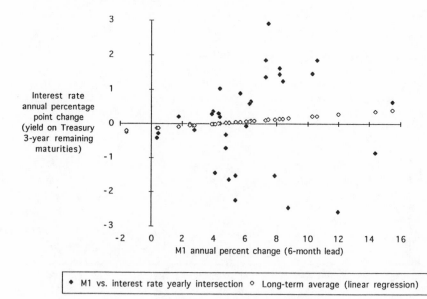

Note: Based on Federal Reserve Board and U.S. Department of the Treasury data. See text for meaning of 6-month M1 lead.

ship is tenuous at best, however, as the individual yearly points are widely dispersed around the average line in a randomlike pattern.

One of the factors affecting the slight direct relationship between the money supply and interest rates is the risk of inflation. When inflationary expectations rise, lenders and borrowers raise interest rates above what they would be when lower inflation is expected. This "inflation premium" is intended to protect the purchasing power of the loan when it is repaid, as noted previously. Inflationary psychology thus reverses the expected relationship between money supply growth and interest rates. In this situation, an acceleration of money supply growth is associated with fueling inflation by making money more readily available for borrowing and spending. The resulting rate of economic growth, higher than the economy can sustain without causing an upward spiraling of inflation, leads to higher interest rates as lenders act to compensate for expected higher inflation. In short, an easing of monetary policy, which the credit markets perceive as inflationary, may be counterproductive and produce higher interest rates.

In assessing the impact of the relationship between interest rates and the money supply, the analyst should review both the changing demand for money by borrowers and the inflationary expectations of lenders. This includes shifts in spending plans by households and business borrowers, and shifts in lenders' perceptions of future price movements. The money supply by itself is no predictor of interest rates.

Real Interest Rates and Economic Growth

Real interest rates, defined as the market rate minus expected inflation, represent the cost of borrowing adjusted for lenders' expectations of future inflation. Real interest rates rise when lenders are concerned that inflation will accelerate and they decline when inflation is expected to recede, due to the imposition and removal of "inflation premiums" on interest rates discussed previously. Higher real interest tends to retard borrowing and economic growth, while lower real interest tends to stimulate borrowing and growth. For this reason, inflation is not likely to lead to higher, sustained growth.

Figure 12.6 shows trends in real interest rates and the gross domestic product adjusted for inflation (real GDP) during 1960–96. Real interest rates are calculated as the yield on Treasury securities with three-year remaining maturities less the current inflation rate represented by the GDP chain price index.

Real interest rates in the 1960s were around 2 percent, declined in the 1970s to under 2 percent, and were even negative in 1974 and 1975. Real interest rates were exceptionally low in the 1970s, even though inflation and nominal interest rates were high and accelerating. One explanation is that lenders assumed that the high inflation was only temporary, and therefore nominal interest rates would be sufficiently high to compensate for any future loss in purchasing power arising from inflation when interest payments and the principal of the loan became due.

By contrast, real interest rates were much higher in the 1980s than in the previous decades. The sharp increase in the early 1980s peaked at 8 percent in 1984, declined to 4 percent by the end of the decade, and bottomed at 2 percent in 1993. Real interest rose again to 4 percent in the late 1990s. Thus, while real interest in the mid- and late 1990s is much below the highs of the 1980s, it is noticeably above the levels of the 1960s and 1970s. This may reflect a belief in the 1990s that the U.S. economy is inflation-prone, even though inflation in the 1990s has been much lower than in the preceding two decades. The high inflation of the 1970s, despite having decelerated sharply in the 1980s and slowing still further in the 1990s, seems to have left a lingering psychological memory into the late 1990s.[12]

Economic growth has declined continuously from the peak rates of the 1960s in each of the following decades through the 1990s. But the year-to-year relationship between real interest rates and economic growth as measured by the real GDP is weak. High economic growth in the 1960s was associated with low interest rates, lower economic growth in the 1970s was associated with lower interest rates, lower economic growth in the 1980s was associated with higher interest rates, and lower economic growth in the 1990s is associated with rising interest rates.

Figure 12.6 **Real Interest Rate versus Real GDP: 1960–96**

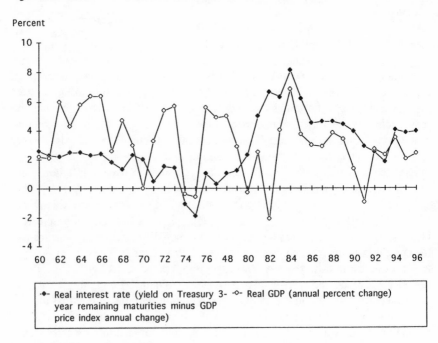

Percent

Note: Based on U.S. Department of the Treasury and U.S. Bureau of Economic Analysis data.

Establishing a linkage between real interest rates and economic growth requires that both the level as well as the movement of interest rates be taken into account. What is the break-even type threshold of real interest rates that is suggestive of future high or low rates of economic growth? The author is aware of no such threshold that has been developed from economic analysis.

In assessing the relationship between real interest rates and the real GDP, the analyst should keep abreast of research that relates the level of real interest rates to economic growth.

Interest Rate Yield Curve

The various interest rates charged on different kinds of debt instruments are influenced by several factors. They include the maturity period of the debt (i.e., the length of time before repayment is due), the relative risk of default by borrowers, and the differing tax rates assessed on interest from commercial and government securities.

The differential interest rates on short-term and long-term debt instruments reflect distinctions in liquidity as well as expectations regarding the future course of inflation. In terms of liquidity, short-term rates are typically lower than long-term rates because short-term debt instruments can be sold for cash more quickly and with less risk of a significant capital loss on the initial amount of the loan than is the case for long-term debt. Short-term rates also tend to be lower because of the expectation that inflation will continue or even accelerate in the future. These interest rate differentials are often depicted with a yield curve that shows interest rates rising as the maturity of the debt lengthens.

While long-term interest rates are typically higher than short-term rates, the distinctions vary considerably over time as noted in the following examples of annual averages from 1953 to 1996. Yields on U.S. Treasury securities with remaining maturities of three and ten years were actually higher than those on new issues of Treasury three-month and six-month bills in 1973, 1974, and 1979. The ten-year yield was lower than the two bill rates and the three-year yield in 1966, and the six-month bill and the ten-year bond yields were lower than the three-month bill yield in 1980 and 1981. Also, the spread between short-term and long-term interest rates usually varies within 1 to 2 percentage points, but spreads of only 0.5 percentage point and less occurred during 1962–69 and in 1989. Additional instances of this reversal of the general pattern undoubtedly occur in shorter monthly periods than the one-year averages cited here.

Expectations about future interest rates drive the yield curve. For example, when short-term rates are expected to rise in the future, the yield curve will rise more steeply than usual. Such a steeply rising curve typically occurs when a recession is perceived to be bottoming out and the anticipated recovery and subsequent expansion are expected to provoke greater demand for loans and concomitantly higher long-term interest rates. By contrast, a flatter yield curve typically occurs during an inflationary period when the FR tightens credit to curb the inflation. The yield curve declines when short-term interest rates are expected to fall in the future. The expectation of slower economic growth or recession reduces demand for loans, leading to lower long-term interest rates. Figure 12.7 shows illustrative rising and declining yield curves.

This model of rising and falling yield curves is not unanimously accepted, however, as Henry Kaufman points out.[13] Some analysts say that the focus on the importance of short-term interest rates is misguided and more attention should be paid to the long-term rates. Others claim that because lenders tend to specialize in either short-term or long-term loans, the interest rates charged on the two kinds of debt in fact have little relation to each other.

Interest rate spreads on yield curves are used in the leading indicators and experimental recession indexes covered in Chapter 13. Yield curves that signal the likelihood of a future recession are also noted by Arturo Estrella and Frederick Mishkin.[14] For example, based on data from the first quarter of 1960 to the

Figure 12.7 **Illustrative Yield Curves**

Interest rate

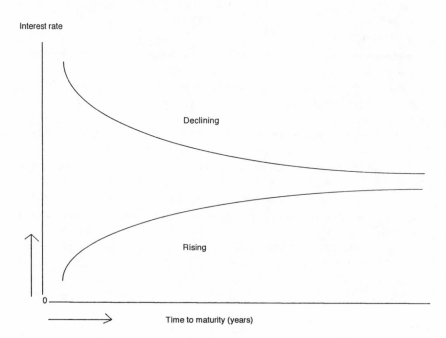

Time to maturity (years)

first quarter of 1995, they conclude that when the spread of the ten-year Treasury bond yield minus the three-month Treasury bill yield is 0.76 percentage point in one quarter, there is a 10 percent probability that the economy will be in a recession four quarters later, but when the spread is −2.40 percentage points, there is a 90 percent probability of a recession occurring one year later.

In assessing the relationship between the yield curve and future movements of the economy, the analyst should treat the yield curve as confirming or rejecting other analyses of economic growth and inflation.

Interest Rates and the Stock Market

Investor portfolios often include some combination of fixed-income securities and common stocks. Fixed-income securities, such as bonds and mortgages, are loans generally at which interest is paid at intervals, such as every six months, while other fixed-income securities such as U.S. Treasury bills and zero-coupon bonds yield an interest income when the securities mature and the borrower repays the principal of the loan. They reflect the interaction of the demand for money by borrowers, the supply of money by lenders, and current and anticipated inflation rates, as noted previously.

Common stocks are more speculative investments in the equity ownership of

Figure 12.8 **Corporate Earnings/Price and Dividend/Price Ratios and Treasury Three-Year Constant Maturities Yield: 1955–96**

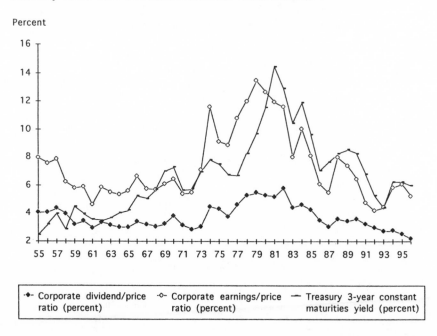

Percent

	Corporate dividend/price ratio (percent)	Corporate earnings/price ratio (percent)	Treasury 3-year constant maturities yield (percent)

Note: Based on Standard and Poor's Corporation and U.S. Department of the Treasury data.

corporations. Common stocks provide income from dividends, plus capital gains or losses depending on the difference in the price of the stock between the time it is bought and when it is sold. Dividends to stockholders reflect the earnings of the company, with companies on average paying dividends of 40–60 percent of corporate profits after taxes in the 1990s.[15] Capital gains and losses reflect expected future earnings and the discounted future value of the company, which involves speculative assessments of the future growth of the company and how other investors are likely to respond to expectations of the company's growth.

In financial markets, there is a continuing interaction among interest rates, corporate earnings and dividends, and stock market prices, as investors move funds between fixed-income securities and stocks to maximize their profits. The earnings/price ratio and the dividend/price ratio of various company stocks, together with interest rates, represent different rates of returns of major investment outlets that investors compare in deciding where to put their money.

Figure 12.8 shows the movements of corporate earnings, dividends, and interest rates during 1955–96. The earnings and dividend data are the ratio of earnings and dividends to the price of the stocks based on the Standard and Poor's

Figure 12.9 **Corporate Earnings/Price Ratio versus U.S. Treasury Three-Year Constant Maturities Yield: 1955–96**

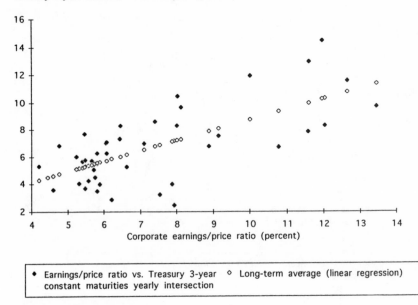

Treasury 3-year constant maturities yield (percent)

Corporate earnings/price ratio (percent)

| • Earnings/price ratio vs. Treasury 3-year constant maturities yearly intersection | ○ Long-term average (linear regression) |

Note: Based on Standard and Poor's Corporation and U.S. Department of the Treasury data.

composite index of 500 stocks on the New York Stock Exchange, the Nasdaq, and the AMEX. The interest rates are based on U.S. Treasury securities with remaining maturities of three years. The figure indicates a closer relationship between corporate earnings and interest rates, both in terms of yearly movements and the spread in the levels, than with corporate dividends from the 1960s to the !990s. The dividend/price ratio has more stable year-to-year movements than the earnings and interest rate data.

Figure 12.9 shows the relationship between the corporate earnings/price ratio and the three-year constant maturity interest rates during 1955–96. Each black diamond represents the intersection of the corporate earnings/price ratio and the interest rate for a year, and the line of white diamonds is the long-term average. The long-term line slopes upward to the right, which indicates a direct relationship. As earnings increase, interest rates increase, and as earnings decline, so do interest rates. But although consistent with the theory that higher earnings are associated with a growing economy that requires more borrowing and consequently leads to higher interest rates, the relationship is rough. The individual

Figure 12.10 **Corporate Dividend/Price Ratio versus U.S. Treasury Three-Year Constant Maturities Yield: 1955–96**

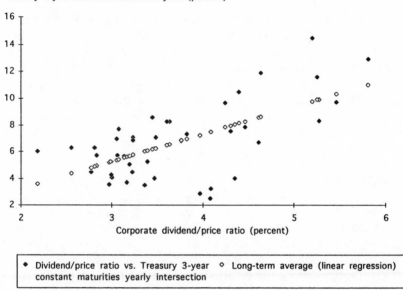

Treasury 3-year constant maturities yield (percent)

Corporate dividend/price ratio (percent)

● Dividend/price ratio vs. Treasury 3-year constant maturities yearly intersection	○ Long-term average (linear regression)

Note: Based on Standard and Poor's Corporation and U.S. Department of the Treasury data.

yearly points are widely dispersed around the long-term line, which means earnings and interest rates diverge widely in their year-to-year movements.

Figure 12.10 shows the relationship between the corporate dividend/price ratio and interest rates during 1955–96. It has similar direct relationships and a wide dispersion around the long-term average line as Figure 12.9.

Because the interactions between the stock market and interest rates vary widely in their year-to-year movements, the analyst should consider the long-term direct relationship as only a tendency for interest rates and the stock market to parallel each other.

APPENDIX: FEDERAL RESERVE ORGANIZATION AND INDEPENDENCE

The Federal Reserve System is headed by a seven-member Board of Governors in Washington, D.C., and twelve regional Federal Reserve Banks located around the country.[16] The seven governors are appointed by the President, subject to confirmation of the Senate, and are permanent members of the Federal

Open Market Committee (FOMC). The FOMC establishes overall monetary policies. The governors' terms are for fourteen years, with one term expiring every two years. This limits a President's ability to "pack" the Board. The chair of the Board's term is four years.

Each FR Bank has a board of nine directors—six are elected by the commercial banks in the region (three represent the member banks and three represent the public) and three public members are appointed by the FR Board. The FR Board designates the chairman and deputy chairman from the three public members it appoints. The FR Bank's board of directors appoints the Bank's president subject to FR Board approval. Five presidents of the FR Banks are members of the FOMC at all times, four on a one-year rotating basis, and the Federal Reserve Bank of New York's president is a permanent member of the FOMC. Thus, the FOMC is composed of twelve members, the seven FR governors and the five presidents of the FR Banks.[17]

The presidents of the FR Banks bring to the FOMC deliberations a special knowledge of the patterns of economic growth in different sections of the country as well as of the economic concerns of each geographic region. Because these regional concerns vary (for example, local areas have different levels of unemployment), they could lead the presidents of the FR Banks to vote on the FOMC from a regional rather than from a national vantage point. But in analyzing the Bank presidents' votes, Geoffrey Tootell concludes that the Bank presidents vote from a national rather than a regional perspective.[18] In addition, because the presidents are representatives of commercial banks, there is a concern that this background leads them to concentrate on fighting inflation more than nonbank representatives would, and thus vote for higher interest rates more often than persons who do not represent commercial banks. In analyses of the voting records of all FOMC members, Geoffrey Tootell concludes there is no significant difference between the voting records of the FR Bank presidents and the FR Board governors once the political party affiliations of the Bank presidents and the Board governors are taken into account.[19] Democrats and Republicans on the Banks and the Board tend to vote in line with their political affiliations, Democrats tending toward lower interest rates than Republicans. However, others believe the voting records show that the FR Bank presidents favor higher interest rates more frequently than the FR Board governors.

The FR Board, the FR Banks, and the FOMC have different monetary policy powers. The FR Board determines reserve requirements, each FR Bank proposes changes in the discount rate in its region subject to FR Board approval, and the FOMC establishes the money supply targets and directs open-market operations. In general, there is considerable interplay between the Board and the Banks (particularly through the FOMC), but the FR Board has greater authority. The Board alone changes reserve requirements (although after consulting with the Banks), the Board must approve changes proposed by the Banks in the discount rate, and the Board's governors represent seven of the twelve members of the FOMC.

Institutionally, the FR Board reports to Congress. It is legally independent of the President. Since the executive branch does not participate in formulating monetary policies and the FR does not participate in formulating fiscal policies, coordination can be a problem. The FR and the President are in fact sometimes at odds, a situation that has been criticized for leading to unbalanced fiscal and monetary policies. Such disagreement usually occurs when unemployment is rising or when unemployment is high and is not declining or is declining only slowly, and the President wants to stimulate employment growth while the FR emphasizes its traditional inclination to hold inflation down.

This leaves Congress as the only branch with direct links to all parties engaged in developing monetary and fiscal policies, the FR for monetary policy and the President for fiscal policy. While congressional review of the FR's annual and semiannual monetary reports could provide a vehicle for coordination between Congress and the FR, in practice this does not occur. Congress does not have the authority to redirect FR policies if it is dissatisfied with them. Congress can only force the FR to report and testify to it. But because Congress feels uneasy, and perhaps even inadequate, in assessing the economic and financial relationships, it does not change the FR charter to enable it to direct the FR to take specific monetary policy actions. Indeed, while individual members of Congress occasionally express their opinions, Congress as a legislative body does not articulate its own view of FR policies. More members express disagreement with FR policies when unemployment is rising, just as the President does, as noted above. Obviously, Congress and the President are more responsive to election prospects than are appointed FR officials. There is also a conspiratorial-type suggestion that Congress deliberately does not intrude in monetary policymaking in order to be freer to criticize FR performance when unemployment and/or inflation are high.

Despite the general principle of FR independence, the FR has been subject to political pressures from Presidents. The most notable ones involved Harry Truman and Richard Nixon, of which there have been several accounts.[20] In both cases, the Presidents advocated low interest rates to stimulate economic growth, and in the case of President Truman also to hold down interest costs on the federal debt. The episode with President Truman led to the "Treasury-Federal Reserve Accord" of 1951, which freed the FR to act independently, and thus enacted a major change in the relationship between the FR and the President. Twenty years later, President Nixon tried to undo the 1951 accord by pressuring Arthur Burns, chairman of the FR at that time, to influence the Federal Open Market Committee to lower interest rates in order to boost the economy and thus help Nixon win reelection in 1972. The effect of Presidential pressure on FR actions is disputed, but that it occurs is indisputable. One view of the effect of such pressure is that when the pressure is public, the FR resists in a show of independence, and the White House effort may be counterproductive.

REVIEW QUESTIONS

- The money supply differs from other economic indicators in the nature of actions taken to affect it. What is the difference?
- What would happen to the effectiveness of open-market operations if reserve requirements were abolished?
- Reserve requirements are used to oversee the financial solvency of banks.
    _____True_____False
- Characterize the relationship between movements in the money supply and those for the GDP in current dollars, real GDP, and prices.
- Why doesn't the generally inverse relationship between the money supply and interest rates hold during periods of inflationary expectations?
- Contrast the monetary policy roles of the discount rate and the federal funds rate.
- How would a threshold-type analysis between the level of real interest rates and economic growth be useful for monetary policymaking?
- How do yield curves suggest future changes in borrowing and economic growth?
- How does the stock market affect interest rates?
- The Federal Reserve is required to report its money supply targets to Congress twice a year. How does this affect Federal Reserve independence in conducting monetary policy?
- How does the independence of the Federal Reserve differ from the independence of the Supreme Court?
- What is the concern about including Federal Reserve Bank presidents on the Federal Reserve Open Market Committee?

Extra Credit

- Why is an inverted yield curve—that is, one showing short-term interest rates higher than long-term rates—a sign of an impending recession?
- In March 1997, the Federal Reserve raised short-term interest rates, while leaving the discount rate unchanged. What does the above statement tell you about the importance of the discount rate as a monetary policy tool? Also, how did the Federal Reserve effect the rise in rates?

NOTES

1. M1 is subject to the greatest FR influence because it has the highest proportion of assets subject to FR reserve requirements. Analogously, M3 is subject to the least FR influence because it has the lowest proportion of assets with reserve requirements—reserve requirements are imposed only on demand (checking) deposits and NOW accounts, and these components are included in all three money supply measures. The effect of FR influence over money supply growth diminished considerably during the 1980s, as hold-

ers of checking accounts, savings deposits, and other financial assets, in seeking the best place for their funds, transferred them from one type of asset to another much more frequently than previously. This greater movement of funds resulted from the lifting of interest rate ceilings on bank deposits under the Depository Institutions Deregulation and Monetary Control Act of 1980, the creation of a variety of new income-producing financial instruments, the increased use of Sweeps in which banks shift customer checking accounts overnight into savings accounts not subject to reserve requirements, and the increased internationalization of the U.S. economy. It also led the FR to discontinue inclusion of M1 targets in its reports to Congress from 1987 to 1997.

2. This tendency for the money supply to be affected by the change in bank reserves is generally true for the mainstay of FR actions through the use of open-market operations. In the occasional case when the FR changes the required reserve ratio, that relationship does not necessarily hold. For example, the money supply will drop with a rise in the required reserve ratio even if bank reserves are unchanged. Open-market operations and reserve requirements are covered in the next section.

3. Full Employment and Balanced Growth Act of 1978, Section 108. See also Board of Governors of the Federal Reserve System, *Purposes and Functions*, 1994, pp. 26–27.

4. M.A. Akhtar, *Understanding Open Market Operations* (Federal Reserve Bank of New York, 1997), p. 28.

5. *Purposes and Functions*, ch. 3.

6. Federal Reserve Bank of Richmond, *Instruments of the Money Market*, 7th ed., 1993, ch. 2. This has a good discussion of federal funds.

7. Gordon H. Sellon Jr. and Stuart E. Weiner, "Monetary Policy without Reserve Requirements: Analytical Issues," *Economic Review*, Federal Reserve Bank of Kansas City, Fourth quarter 1996.

8. Also, frequent changes in a bank's reserve requirements would complicate its financial planning. In addition, reserve requirements that exceed the reserves a bank would voluntarily hold for its business operations impose a cost to banks by the amount of foregone interest, and the FR hesitates to raise reserve requirements because it would increase that cost.

9. Savings banks and savings and loan associations (thrifts) are supervised by the U.S. Office of Thrift Supervision, and credit unions are supervised by the National Credit Union Administration.

10. In this example of how loans create new bank deposits, we use a 10 percent reserve requirement on transaction deposits for banks, thrift institutions, and credit unions (in 1997, the first $4.4 million of transaction deposits had no reserve requirement, deposits of $4.4 to $49.3 million have a 3 percent reserve requirement, and deposits above $49.3 million have a 10 percent reserve requirement). Suppose customer A deposits $10,000 in the Atlantic bank. The Atlantic bank then lends $9,000 to customer B's checking account. Customer B buys a car for the $9,000, and the car dealer deposits the payment in the Pacific bank, which increases the bank's deposits by $9,000. At this point, deposits in the Atlantic bank are reduced by $9,000, resulting in a net increment of $1,000 from customer A's initial $10,000 deposit. The Pacific bank then lends $8,100 of the new deposits of $9,000 it obtained from the car dealer (again allowing a 10 percent reserve) to Customer C. Customer C spends the $8,100 for college tuition, and the college deposits the $8,100 in the Continental bank, which reduces the Pacific bank's net increment in deposits to $900 (9,000–8,100). The chain continues with the Continental bank lending $7,290 (10 percent less than 8,100) to customer D, and so on. The total amount of new deposit creation through this mechanism is the sum of the net increment of deposits that each bank has after its loan is spent by the borrower. Thus, increments to the deposits of the Atlantic and Pacific banks of $1,000 and $900 add $1,900 to the money supply.

This fractional reserve system adds decreasing increments to the money supply in the successive rounds of lending and spending from the initial $10,000 deposit by customer A until the process diminishes to zero. Mathematically, the limit to the increase in the money supply is obtained by dividing the initial deposit by the reserve ratio, in this case $10,000/0.10, which amounts to $100,000. That is, the initial deposit of $10,000 can result in an ultimate increase of $100,000 in the money supply. This is also referred to as the deposit multiplier, which in this case is 10 (100,000/10,000), and in a simple form is obtained by 1/0.10 (i.e., 1/reserve ratio).

11. Joint Economic Committee of Congress, *1980 Supplement to Economic Indicators*, p. 108. These estimates are based on constructing yield curves (interest rates and years to maturity) for the most actively traded Treasury securities, and reading the ten-year interest rate from the curve.

12. Examples of events in the twentieth century that had greater and longer-lasting impacts than the inflation of the 1970s and 1980s are World War I, the Great Depression of the 1930s, World War II, the Korean War, and the Vietnam War. While the inflation of the 1970s and 1980s was not as momentous as the depression and the wars, it continues to have an important psychological effect on the U.S. economy in the late 1990s.

13. Henry Kaufman, *Interest Rates, the Markets, and the New Financial World* (Times Books, 1986), ch. 12.

14. Arturo Estrella and Frederick S. Mishkin, "The Yield Curve as a Predictor of U.S. Recessions," *Current Issues in Economics and Finance*, Federal Reserve Bank of New York, June 1996. The interest rate spreads cited in the text are interesting for the substantial differences in the probability of a future recession, not for the specific numbers.

15. Kevin Cole, Jean Helwege, and David Laster, "Stock Market Valuation Indicators: Is This Time Different?" *Financial Analysts Journal*, May/June 1996, Fig. 4.

16. *Purposes and Functions*, ch. 1.

17. The FR New York Bank president is a permanent member of the FOMC because the New York Bank implements FOMC monetary policy decisions through buying and selling Treasury securities in open-market operations and through buying and selling the U.S. dollar in foreign exchange markets; the foreign exchange interventions are done in cooperation with the U.S. Treasury Department, which has the overall responsibility for U.S. international financial policy. This special role of the New York Bank evolved over time and reflects its geographic location in the center of financial markets and the legacy of the influence of its forceful president, Benjamin Strong, in the 1920s (Greider, *Secrets of the Temple*, pp. 292–93, note 20).

The rotating sequence of the eleven other FR Bank presidents on the FOMC varies slightly. The Cleveland and Chicago FR Bank presidents serve alternately every third year. The FR Bank presidents for the other banks serve alternately every third year from the following three groups: (1) Boston, Philadelphia, Richmond; (2) Atlanta, St. Louis, Dallas; (3) Minneapolis, Kansas City, San Francisco. There is no record of why the Cleveland and Chicago presidents are on the FOMC more frequently than the other nine Bank presidents. This may be because, in the early 1930s before the FOMC was established by law in 1935, Cleveland and Chicago were part of an open-market executive committee of five Federal Reserve Banks (the others were New York, Philadelphia, and Boston), and Chicago was the second-largest city and financial center, and Cleveland represented heavy industrial areas.

In passing the Federal Reserve Act of 1913, Congress left the designation of which cities would have regional FR Banks to a three-member Reserve Bank Organizing Committee, composed of the Secretary of the Treasury, Secretary of Agriculture, and the Comptroller of the Currency (see Roger T. Johnson, *Historical Beginnings . . . The Federal Reserve*, The Federal Reserve Bank of Boston, Revised December 1995, pp. 35–51).

This reflected the political pressure from various constituencies to have a Reserve Bank in their district, which may not have been possible to resolve legislatively. When the Committee's recommendations were questioned as being politically motivated, the House of Representatives held hearings in 1914, and the recommendations were upheld. In an interesting analogy, Congress took a similar tack on the military base base closings in the 1990s, when it set up a commission to recommend specific base closings that Congress could only accept or reject as a whole, thus making the closings politically feasible by absolving Congress from the ire of particular constituencies. Despite the reliance on the Reserve Bank Organizing Committee, there were several allegations that politics had a role in which cities were recommended to have Reserve Banks, resulting in the House hearings noted above (see Roger Johnson, *Historical Beginnings*, pp. 49–51). For example, Missouri, a relatively small state, is the only state with two FR Banks, St. Louis and Kansas City. But when the Federal Reserve Act was passed in 1913, the Speaker of the House of Representatives, Champ Clark, was from Missouri, and Senator James Reed, an influential Senator, was from Kansas City; also, David Huston, the Secretary of Agriculture and a member of the Reserve Bank Organizing Committee, was from St. Louis. Other examples of suspected political influence are that Cleveland won out over Cincinnati and Pittsburgh because Newton Baker, the Secretary of War and a prominent member of President Woodrow Wilson's cabinet, was from Cleveland; and that Richmond won out over Baltimore because of the influence of Representative Carter Glass, who was from Virginia, and because John Williams, the Comptroller of the Currency and a member of the Reserve Bank Organizing Committee, was from Richmond.

18. Geoffrey M.B. Tootell, "Regional Economic Conditions and the FOMC Votes of District Presidents," *New England Economic Review,* March/April 1991.

19. Geoffrey M.B. Tootell, "Appointment Procedures and FOMC Voting Behavior," *Southern Economic Journal,* July 1996.

20. A. Jerome Clifford, *The Independence of the Federal Reserve System* (University of Pennsylvania Press, 1965), ch. 8. See also William Greider, *Secrets of the Temple: How the Federal Reserve Runs the Country* (Simon and Schuster, 1987), ch. 10; Donald F. Kettl, *Leadership at the Fed* (Yale University Press, 1986), chs. 3 and 5; and William Safire, *Before the Fall: An Inside View of the Pre-Watergate White House* (Doubleday, 1975), pp. 491–96.

13
LEADING INDICATOR SYSTEM

The leading indicator system is based on the concept that each phase of the business cycle contains the seeds of the following phase. The four phases of the business cycle of rising and falling economic growth are recovery, expansion, recession, and contraction (discussed in Chapter 1). By focusing on the factors operating in each phase, the leading indicator system provides a basis for monitoring the tendency to move from one phase to the next. The system assesses the strengths and weaknesses in the economy as clues to a quickening or slowing of future rates of economic growth, as well as to cyclical turning points in moving from the upward expansion to the downward recession, and from the recession to the upward recovery, but it does not provide specific forecasts. But an experimental model of the system forecasts the probability that the economy will be in a recession six months later.

The Conference Board publishes the leading indicator system in its monthly report, *Business Cycle Indicators*. James Stock and Mark Watson publish monthly experimental recession indexes.

OVERVIEW

Development of the leading indicator system evolved over a quarter of a century. In 1937 Secretary of the Treasury Henry Morgenthau Jr. requested Wesley Mitchell to compile a list of statistical series to observe for clues as to when the recession that began in 1937 would turn up into a recovery, which Mitchell did in collaboration with Arthur Burns. In 1950 Geoffrey Moore revised this list and added a new set of indicators to observe when an expansion is likely to turn down into a recession. And in 1961 Julius Shiskin developed the leading, coincident, and lagging composite indexes that are the framework of the leading indicator system today.[1]

The terms "leading," "coincident," and "lagging" refer to the timing of the turning points of the indexes relative to those of the business cycle. The leading index turns down before a general recession begins and turns up before the recovery from the recession begins. The coincident index moves in tandem with the cyclical movements of the overall economy, tending to coincide with the designations of expansions and recessions discussed in Chapter 1. The lagging index turns down after the beginning of a recession and turns up after the beginning of a recovery.

The system is based on Wesley Mitchell's theory that expectations of future profits are the motivating force in the economy.[2] When business executives believe their sales and profits will rise, companies expand production of goods and services and investment in new structures and equipment, but when they believe profits will decline, they reduce production and investment. These actions generate the recovery, expansion, recession, and contraction phases of the business cycle. The leading indicator system treats the future course of profits in two alternative perspectives: (1) businesses' expectations of future sales (leading index), and (2) the differential movements between current production (coincident index) and production costs (lagging index).

The system has been criticized for being excessively empirical and lacking a theoretical framework. Reference is often made to a 1947 article by Tjalling Koopmans that criticized the work by Mitchell and Burns in general and particularly attacked their 1946 book, *Measuring Business Cycles*.[3] The author disagrees with these criticisms and argues below that the system is grounded in economic theory.

THE PROCESS OF CYCLICAL CHANGE

For background, it is useful to summarize the cyclical phenomena considered to be the major elements underlying the leading indicator system. To illustrate, assume as the cyclical starting point the beginning of the recovery from the low point of the previous recession; this is referred to as the recovery. In this initial stage, an impetus for increasing production starts an upward movement. Sales increase as households begin purchasing durable goods they had deferred during the recession. Unit costs of production decline because the increasing volume of sales is spread over the fixed depreciation and maintenance costs of existing structures and equipment, as well as over the lowered workforce and other services resulting from the cutbacks of nonessential costs in the preceding recession. The result is that profits, which are sales minus costs, increase.

As the momentum spreads and employment and household spending increase, business executives become more optimistic about future sales and order more goods for inventories and invest in new structures and equipment to increase and modernize productive capacity. This is heightened by the increased number of new businesses that start up in anticipation of continued growing markets and higher profits, which in turn stimulates more production, hiring, and spending. When production rises above the high point of the previous cyclical expansion, the recovery turns into the expansion phase of the cyclical upturn.

At some point, however, the upward momentum slows. Sales of some items are no longer as brisk because households' needs have changed, and higher prices cause households to defer purchases. Unsold inventories of goods accumulate, leading to reduced prices to sell them, and to reduced orders for new goods to replace them, and thus lower future production. But these goods had been produced at high costs, as the high industrial capacity utilization during the expansion led to an increasing use of outmoded and less efficient equipment, hiring of less efficient workers as unemployment rates fell to low levels, and obtaining loans at high interest rates when the overall demand for money was strong. The high production costs lead businesses to try to maintain prices in order to limit reductions in profit margins, but the resistance to lowering prices in turn leads to lower sales. The combination of lower sales and higher production costs reduces profits enough to dampen incentives for investing in new structures and equipment capacity. The slowdown in sales leads to lower production, and the consequent lower employment, incomes, and spending.

The slowdown has a snowballing effect, analogous to the upward spiral in the earlier stages of the expansion, as households and businesses retrench in their spending. The high point of the expansion has been reached. There is less incentive to take out additional loans, which would bolster spending, because thanks to lower incomes, existing loans have become a greater burden to repay. Production and employment are further reduced, bringing on a recession. Increasing numbers of businesses close down during the recession, and existing businesses cut costs by maintaining lower inventories and reducing employment. If production declines during the recession below the low point of the previous cyclical recession, the recession turns into the contraction phase of cyclical downturn. Technically, the 1981–82 recession turned into a contraction, as the coincident index at the low point of the recession in the fall of 1982 was below the low point of the previous recession in the summer of 1980. But this was so minimal that it hardly qualifies as a contraction. In fact, the last occurrence of a contraction was during the Great Depression of the 1930s, when production was clearly below the previous recession low in 1927 (see Chapter 1 under Determining Business Cycle Phases).

The depressed level of production ultimately runs its course as households who have deferred spending because of the economic uncertainty begin to replace their older goods and buy new housing at the lower recession-induced interest rates. This turnaround in sales encourages businesses to order more goods for inventories, thus stimulating production, and the stage is set for the recovery phase, which completes the cycle.

While this is a highly simplified version of cyclical economic movements, it depicts the basic rationale of the leading indicator system. But each business cycle has its unique characteristics due to variations in inflation, unemployment, population growth, development of new products, soundness of the banking system, competition from abroad, and other factors.

Because each business cycle is unique, the upturn and downturn of any particular cycle are not fully replicated in any other cycle. Therefore, in assessing economic relationships based on past data, the analyst should be alert to similarities and differences between the current and previous economic environments.

Duration of Cyclical Expansions and Recessions

While recessions have been less frequent since the end of World War II than previously, they have not gone away. The continuing appearance of recessions has raised the question about whether there is a greater likelihood of a recession occurring the longer an expansion continues. Research on this by Francis Diebold, Glenn Rudenbusch, and Daniel Sichel concludes that before World War II there was a greater chance of a recession occurring the longer an expansion was in progress. After World War II, however, there is no indication of a linkage between the length of an expansion and the onset of a recession.[4]

THE PRIMARY ROLE OF PROFITS

The leading indicator system is based on the idea that profits are the driving force in the private enterprise economy. Business decisions on production, prices, employment, and investment are understood in relation to profits—both the trends of past profits and the perception of future profits. Thus, changing expectations of profits affect the direction and pace of economic growth.

The system combines several component economic indicators into a composite leading index, a composite coincident index, and a composite lagging index. The following discussion capsulizes the three composite indexes and the rationale for each of the components.[5]

The composite leading index indicates business perceptions of future profits. It represents businesses' anticipation of future economic developments, and the response in actions and plans to those expectations. The ten component economic indicators of the leading index are:

1. *Average weekly hours, manufacturing.* Because of uncertainty in the economic outlook, employers are more likely to adjust the hours of previously hired workers before hiring new workers at signs the recession is ending, or laying off workers at signs the expansion is weakening.

2. *Initial claims for unemployment insurance.* Increases or decreases in unemployment indicate business expectations of the demand for labor.

3. *Manufacturers' new orders, consumer goods and materials* (constant dollars). Business commitments to buy items indicate future levels of production.

4. *Vendor performance, slower deliveries diffusion index.* Delivery time reflects the strength of demand, brisk when the time from the placement of the

order to delivery is long because of the large backlog of orders, and weak when the delivery time is short.

5. *Manufacturers' new orders, nondefense capital goods industries* (constant dollars). Business commitments in the volatile cyclical industries that fluctuate considerably between expansions and recessions.

6. *New private housing units authorized by local building permits.* Permits provide advance indication of housing construction, which is cyclically sensitive to changes in interest rates and expected changes in employment.

7. *Stock prices, 500 common stocks.* Stock prices reflect investor expectations of economic growth and profits, and thus future investment and household spending. High stock prices make it easier for businesses to raise funds for structures and equipment investment and other ventures by selling new stock to the public (equity financing), which entails no required payback to the buyer of the value of the stock or the payment of dividends. By contrast, low stock prices make it more likely that businesses will obtain funds from the public by selling bonds—that is, debt financing, in which the principal is repaid and there are specified interest payments. Stock prices also affect household wealth, and in turn future consumer spending. Stockholders perceive they have more to spend when stock prices, and thus their wealth, are rising than when they are falling. Stock market prices also reflect speculation, insider trading, and program trading, however, which are not associated with underlying economic factors. When the stock market is dominated by these speculative-type actions, its usefulness as an economic indicator is diminished.

8. *Money supply, M2* (constant dollars). The amount of financial liquid assets generated by the interplay of investments, savings, borrowing, and lending affects the purchasing power available for business and household transactions, such as buying materials, hiring labor, investing in structures and equipment, and buying consumer goods.

9. *Interest rate spread, ten-year Treasury bonds less federal funds.* The interest rate spread is associated with the stance of monetary policy. A wider spread indicates a looser monetary policy tending toward lower interest rates, and a narrower or negative spread indicates a tighter monetary policy tending toward higher interest rates.

10. *Consumer expectations.* Household attitudes on the outlook for the economy and their own financial well-being give clues to future household spending. In a sense, expectations are self-fulfilling.

The coincident index measures various aspects of production that reflect the current pace of economic output. It indicates whether the economy is growing or declining, and thus is the primary gauge of expansion and recession periods. The four component economic indicators of the coincident index are as follows:

1. *Employees on nonagricultural payrolls.* Represents the labor inputs in producing goods and services.

2. *Personal income less transfer payments* (constant dollars). Real income earned by labor and investors reflects the resources used in producing the nation's output.

3. *Industrial production.* Because manufacturing, mining, and gas and electric utilities tend to be the more cyclically volatile industries, current production levels in these industries are a good indicator of the cyclical elements in the economy.

4. *Manufacturing and trade sales* (constant dollars). Movement of goods within the economy between manufacturing plants, from manufacturers to wholesalers, from wholesalers to retailers, and from retailers to households and businesses traces the flows of goods in production and from production to distribution.

The lagging index represents production costs and inventory and debt burdens that may encourage or retard economic growth. A slow increase or a decline in the lagging index is conducive to economic growth, while a rapid increase in the lagging index is conducive to a recession. The lagging index also confirms that a cyclical upturn into a recovery and a cyclical downturn into a recession has occurred. The seven component economic indicators of the lagging index are as follows:

1. *Average duration of unemployment.* This indicator is plotted on an inverted scale, appearing to rise when the average duration of unemployment actually falls. As the labor market strengthens in an expansion, the ranks of the unemployed come to be dominated by people who have just started to look for work. Unlike the long-term unemployed, they may not jump at the first job offer they receive, and so a low average duration of unemployment is associated with rising wage pressures in the economy.

The link between the duration of unemployment and production costs is that persons unemployed for long periods are assumed to have less marketable skills than those unemployed for short periods. Therefore, recruiting and training costs vary directly with changes in the number of long-term unemployed persons, rising as the long-term unemployed increases and declining as the long-term unemployed decreases.

2. *Inventories divided by sales (ratio), manufacturing and trade* (constant dollars). Inventories are a major cost factor for businesses. The higher inventories are relative to sales, the more expensive they are to hold, because they entail borrowed money, which results in interest costs, or because they tie up company funds.

3. *Labor cost per unit of output, manufacturing* (monthly change). Labor costs in relation to production affect profits, which in turn influence decisions to expand or contract production, employment, and investment.

4. *Average prime rate charged by banks.* Interest rates charged for business loans indicate the cost of borrowing, which affects profits and the willingness to borrow.

5. *Commercial and industrial loans outstanding* (constant dollars). The interest burden on existing loans is higher, and the availability of money for new loans is lower, the greater the level of outstanding loans.

6. *Consumer installment credit outstanding divided by personal income (ratio).* The debt burden of consumers suggests they are likely to take on more loans when the ratio is low and thus increase spending and to repay existing loans when the ratio is high and thus decrease spending.

7. *Consumer price index for services,* (monthly change). Prices of services reflect price pressures stemming from production costs in labor-intensive industries.

In assessing monthly changes in the leading, coincident, and lagging composite indexes, the analyst should consider whether the movements represent those of most of the component indicators or if they result from relatively large movements of a small number of the component indicators. The movements of the composites are more significant when most of the components move in a similar direction than when they are driven by large movements in a small number of components.

LIMITATION FOR FORECASTING

The leading indicator system provides a striking example of how revisions to preliminary data affect analyses of the state of the economy (Chapter 1 has a general discussion of data revisions under Data Accuracy). Based on revised data, the system provides early signals of a cyclical downturn well before the onset of most recessions and of a cyclical upturn that is observable before about half of all recoveries. The problem is that many of the "advance" signals become apparent only years later when the revised data are incorporated into the system. The contemporaneous preliminary data that are available to analysts during the critical months preceding recessions and recoveries often do not provide such early indications of cyclical turning points, as noted by Evan Koenig and Kenneth Emery.[6]

Table 13.1 compares the contemporaneous preliminary data of the leading index to the revised data (as published in 1997) of the leading index for the months preceding the five recessions and recoveries from 1969 to 1991. The preliminary data measures in the table were derived by the author from previously published data when the leading indicator system was conducted by the Bureau of Economic Analysis in the U.S. Department of Commerce (The Conference Board assumed responsibility for the system in December 1995). The preliminary measures are based on taking the data series as they existed on the eve of the peak of each expansion and the eve of the trough of each recession (the leading index data are first available one month after the reference month). For example, data for July 1990, which is the high point of the expansion preceding the recession that began in August 1990, first became available at the

Table 13.1

Leading Composite Index: Advance Indication of Cyclical Turning Points
(months)

	Contemporaneous preliminary data[a]	Revised data[b]
Peak expansion month on the eve of recession		
December 1969	3	8
November 1973	0	9
January 1980	10	15
July 1981	3	3
July 1990	0	6
Trough recession month on the eve of recovery		
November 1970	1	7
March 1975	0	1
July 1980	2	3
November 1982	8	8
March 1991	1	2

[a]Measures derived by author. See text.
[b]Published in *Business Cycle Indicators*.

end of August. In reviewing these data, which were available at the end of August, the author determined that the leading index was level for the preceding eighteen months, with no discernible rising or declining trend. Of the five recessions, the preliminary data gave no advance indication of a downturn in two cases, only three months' notice in two cases, and ten months' notice in one case. In contrast, the revised data, which became available in subsequent years, showed advance indications of six to fifteen months before a downturn in four of the five cases.

The revised data are superior in establishing lead times of at least six months before the onset of a recession because they incorporate economic indicators and statistical methodologies that better represent the economy of the contemporaneous period than the measures used at the time. Major overhauls of the composite indexes occurred at ten- to fifteen-year intervals through the 1980s, but became more frequent in the 1990s. Two types of changes are usually made: (1) the composition of the indexes is changed to replace some data components with new or modified ones, and (2) new formulations of the statistical factors such as weights and standardization factors are introduced. In addition to these basic structural changes, monthly data are continuously revised on a current basis as part of the routine preparation of revised economic data series. Revised data are important for developing historical analytic relationships, but they obviously do not ensure that the subsequent contemporaneous preliminary data will give observable advance signals of cyclical turning points. Because the economy is continually changing and every business cycle is different, indicators selected on the basis of their performance in past cycles do not always provide the same level of performance in future cycles.

The lack of advance indications of cyclical turning points in the preliminary data significantly limits the use of the leading indicator system for economic forecasting. This highlights the need for the analyst to assess rates of change in the composite indexes in addition to their change in direction for clues of future economic movements. Because the leading index, on a contemporaneous basis, may not turn down several months before the onset of a recession, or may not turn up several months before the onset of a recovery, it is important to be watchful of a slowing in the rate of increase during expansions and a slowing in the rate of decrease during recessions.

METHODOLOGY

The leading, coincident, and lagging composite indexes are developed by combining the component economic indicators within each of the three composites into the single aggregate number.[7] The three indexes for each new month are calculated based on the monthly movements of the components. The general concept is similar to that used for preparing the consumer price index, in which the index number weights are kept constant over periods of several years (Chapter 11).

Many economic indicators are evaluated to determine their appropriateness for inclusion in the composite indexes.[8] The overall considerations in selecting them are (1) their theoretical role in the leading, coincident, and lagging process, and (2) how they perform empirically in terms of leading and lagging general business cycles after World War II. The specific criteria used are economic significance (theoretical importance); statistical adequacy (quality of the underlying survey and other statistical data from which they are calculated); timing (consistency in leading, coinciding, or lagging general business cycles); conformity to business cycle directional movements (upward in expansions and downward in recessions); smoothness (extent of erratic increases and decreases that obscure cyclical movements); and currency (promptness of the availability of current data—they must be monthly, not quarterly, series in time for preparing the monthly indexes).

The component data series selected for use are then combined into the three composite indexes using equal weights for each component economic indicator. Equal weights, in which all component indicators have the same importance, are assigned to all components because research indicated that differential weights used in previous versions did not materially affect movements of the composite indexes.[9] A modification is made to ensure that components with relatively large upward and downward movements do not dominate the index. This is achieved by using differentiated "standardization factors" for each component indicator of the leading and lagging composite indexes so that the volatility of the monthly movements is the same as the volatility of the coincident composite index. The volatility is the variance of the month-to-month percentage changes in the coincident index.

Inversion of Unemployment Indicators

Economic data that are plotted on charts typically are depicted as reflecting a rising economy when the line moves upward and a declining economy when the line moves downward. These upward and downward movements conform to the directional movements of the upward (expansion) and downward (recession) phases of the business cycle. But for two indicators of the leading indicator system, initial claims for unemployment insurance (leading index) and average duration of unemployment (lagging index), this movement is reversed. For them, a decline indicates a rise in or stimulus to production, as they conform to the business cycle phases in the reverse direction. Consequently, the scales on the vertical axes of their charts are inverted so that, graphically, an increase is shown as declining and a decrease is shown as rising. This makes their directional movements visually consistent with general business cycle movements. They are also inverted when used to calculate the monthly movements of the leading and lagging composite indexes, so that the unemployment numbers do not distort the indexes' movements. If they were not inverted, they would have invalid movements.

ANALYSIS OF CYCLICAL MOVEMENTS

Figure 13.1 shows the movements of the three composite indexes in the cyclical expansions and recessions from 1960 to 1996. The National Bureau of Economic Research is the arbiter in designating the turning points of the general business cycle (Chapter 1). The vertical bars represent recession periods.

The behavior of the three composite indexes is consistent with their theoretical role discussed earlier. The leading index turns down before a recession and up before a recovery. The direction and timing of the coincident index are close to those of the general economy, as the turning points of the coincident index are identical or very close to those in the overall economy. The cyclical turns in the lagging index occur after those in the general economy, except for the case noted below. Because the lagging index is last in the sequence of cyclical movements, it also confirms that a cyclical turn has or has not occurred.

For the leading composite index, the lead time in signaling the onset of a recession varied considerably among individual cycles. In the four recessions from 1960 to 1980, the lead time ranged from eight to fifteen months. The lead time shortened substantially in the recessions of 1981–82 and 1990–91 to three

Figure 13.1 **Leading, Coincident, and Lagging Composite Indexes: 1958–97**
(Index: 1992 = 100)

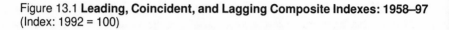

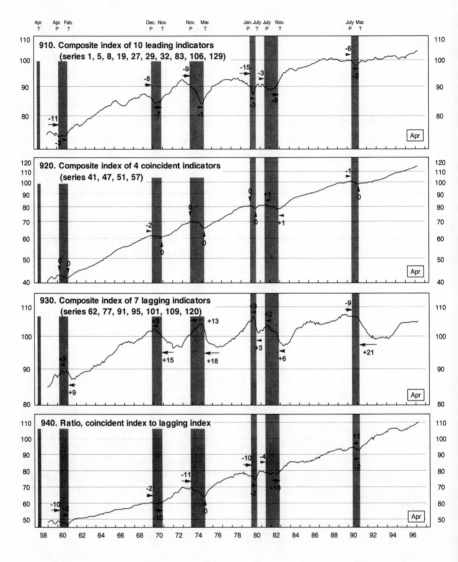

Source: The Conference Board, *Business Cycle Indicators,* April 1997.

Note: Vertical bars are recession periods. Numbers are monthly leads (–) and lags (+) from cyclical turning points.

P = Peak: High point of expansion.

T = Trough: Low point of recession.

and six months, respectively. The lead time at recoveries had smaller, although noticeable, differences among the cycles, ranging from one to eight months.

For the lagging composite index, the cyclical variations were even more stark. The lag time after the onset of a recession also varied considerably among the cycles, ranging from two to thirteen months in the five recessions from the 1960s to the 1980s. But counter to the theory, the lagging index led the onset of the 1990–91 recession by nine months. In fact, the lead of the lagging index exceeded the lead of the leading index by three months in the 1990–91 recession. The lag time at recoveries ranged from three to twenty-one months.

Statistical analysis of the revised composite indexes suggests the following broad pattern of the advance indication of the onset of a recession by the leading index, based on Conference Board Studies.[10] This is the tendency for a decline of 1 to 2 percent in the composite leading index, together with a decline of at least half of the component indictors of the composite for a six-month period, to be a general, although by no means certain, warning of a pending recession.

The above analysis centers on the likelihood of a prospective turning point in the business cycle. There is no assessment of the relationship between the size of a decline in the leading index preceding a recession to the size of the decline in the coincident index during the recession. Similarly, there is no assessment of the relationship between the size of the rise in the leading index during a recession preceding a recovery and the time it takes for the coincident index during the recovery to reach the peak level of the previous expansion, above which the recovery turns into the expansion phase of the business cycle.

The leading indicator system is most relevant for assessing the strengths and weaknesses of the economy in terms of growth rates, but not for forecasting a cyclical downturn into a recession or an upturn into a recovery. Even in the revised measures of the system, there are wide variations both in regard to the anticipatory onset of a recession and a recovery in the composite leading index and in the confirmation that a recession and a recovery began in the lagging composite index. This is accentuated by the still weaker advance signals in the contemporaneous preliminary, as distinct from the later revised, indexes. The system needs more development for it to be useful for signaling cyclical turning points.

Coincident/Lagging Ratio

The coincident index divided by the lagging index is considered by some as an alternative leading index.[11] Theoretically, this ratio is significant because it relates production to costs, providing in effect another view of profits, which is the underlying concept of the leading indicator system. This reflects the fact that profits are the difference between production and costs. For example, if the coincident index (production) increases or decreases at the same rate as the lagging index (costs), there is no change in the profit picture, thus signifying continued economic growth at the current rate. Differential movements in the two indexes suggest other tendencies in the economy, however. If the coincident index increases at a faster rate or decreases at a slower rate than the lagging index, this indicates an increase in profits (since revenues are rising faster than costs) and higher economic growth in the future. But if the coincident index increases at a slower rate or decreases at a faster rate, a decline in profits and lower future economic growth are indicated. Algebraically, the relationship of the coincident/lagging ratio to profits appears as follows:

$$\frac{\text{Coincident}}{\text{Lagging}} = \frac{\text{Production}}{\text{Costs}} = \text{Profit rate}$$

Figure 13.1 shows that the coincident/lagging ratio had monthly leads similar to those of the leading composite index before three of the six recessions from the 1960s to the 1990s—1960–61, 1973–75, and 1981–82. The coincident/lagging ratio leads were several months shorter than those of the leading composite index preceding the 1969–70 and the 1980 recessions. And contrary to the notion of a leading indicator, the coincident/lagging ratio lagged the onset of the 1990–91 recession by one month. Before the onset of recoveries, the coincident/lagging ratio had leads similar in length to those of the leading composite index.

The coincident/lagging ratio shows noticeable variations in the pattern of lead times for individual cycles, as in the case of the leading composite index. This uniqueness of each cycle limits applying historical relationships to the current phase in any cycle, as noted previously.

An advantage of using the coincident/lagging ratio to predict economic movements is that it is based on different data and a different concept from those in the leading composite index. This independent database, which is internally generated from the leading indicator system, is a check on the leading composite index. In addition, the coincident/lagging ratio suggests a concept of equilibrium between sales and costs in which the economy is considered to be relatively well balanced with no significant excesses or deficiencies in production, incomes, costs, and prices. Yet, this state may never be reached in practice, as adjustments are made continuously to production, prices, wages, and interest rates—all aimed at increasing profits.[12]

Despite these ever-changing relationships, one tendency that may be observed from historical behavior of the coincident/lagging ratio is that the economy is more balanced when the ratio is unchanged at a relatively high level during the expansion period, suggesting that further expansion is likely.[13]

Cyclical patterns of the coincident/lagging ratio vary noticeably from cycle to cycle and from the timing of the leading composite index. In periods when movements of the coincident/lagging ratio and the leading composite index are similar, the analyst should give greater credence to the signals of the leading indicator system than when the two measures have divergent movements.

False Signals

The economy moves unevenly in both cyclical expansions and recessions, slowing down and speeding up as well as declining for short spells in expansions and rising for short spells in recessions. Because of these variations, it is often difficult in the current period to determine if a changing rate of growth or a reversal of direction signifies a fundamental change or a temporary counter-movement from which the previous trend will reappear. Temporary reversals of direction in the leading indicator system—reversals, that is, suggesting a cyclical change that did not follow—are known as "false signals." For example, the leading composite index declined temporarily in 1966, 1984, and 1995. Those downturns suggested possible oncoming recessions, but the movements were subsequently reversed. A slowdown in economic growth as measured by the coincident index followed these downturns, but the declines were limited and did not turn into a recession. Therefore, these downturns were false signals. False signals bring into focus the analytic skills needed in using the leading indicator system as a forecasting tool.

PROBABILITY OF FUTURE RECESSIONS: EXPERIMENTAL INDEXES

As noted previously, the leading indicator system does not forecast when turning points in the business cycle will occur. Nevertheless, James Stock and Mark Watson developed on an experimental basis two monthly recession indexes that predict the likelihood of a recession six months ahead.[14] Their measures are available from the National Bureau of Economic Research (NBER). The forecasts do not necessarily represent the views of other researchers or the directors or officers of the NBER, and they are not a publication of the NBER.

The Stock and Watson recession indexes are based on establishing a leading index and a coincident index that are rigorously linked to each other in terms of their historical relationship. The goal of their system is for the leading index to predict what the coincident index will be at a future date. Based on the historical experience of the indicators, they construct a leading and a coincident index so that the leading index typically leads the coincident index by six months. Using these indexes, they can make statements such as, "The probability that the economy will be in a recession six months from now is X percent."

The coincident index in the experimental recession indexes has the same four components as the coincident index in the leading indicator system, except that the experimental index uses "employee-hours" in place of "employees" in nonagricultural industries.

The component indicators of the experimental leading indexes differ substantially from those in the leading indicator system. The system's leading composite index has ten domestic components, three of which are financial. One experimental leading index has seven components, three of which are financial, and thus has a substantially greater representation of financial variables than the system's leading composite index. This experimental leading index also includes an international item and an employment item related to slack work, neither of which is in the leading composite index. The component items of the experimental leading index are as follows:

1. New private housing building permits
2. Unfilled orders for durable goods manufacturers (constant dollars)
3. International nominal exchange rates between the United States and the United Kingdom, West Germany, France, Italy, and Japan, trade weighted
4. Workers employed part-time due to slack work in nonagricultural industries
5. Ten-year Treasury bond interest rate (constant maturity)
6. Interest rate spread between six-month commercial paper and six-month Treasury bills
7. Yield curve difference between ten-year Treasury bonds and one-year Treasury bonds (constant maturity)

An alternative experimental recession index is based on forecasts of seven nonfinancial leading indicators. Three are the same as those in the above experimental leading index with financial indicators: housing building permits, manufacturers' unfilled orders, and foreign exchange rates. The four other indicators are a help-wanted index (which is a substitute for the slack-work indicator), average weekly hours in manufacturing, vendor performance (percentage of companies receiving slow deliveries), and capacity utilization in manufacturing.

The coincident and leading indexes underlie the preparation of the two experimental recession indexes. The weights of the coincident composite index are derived from a statistical model that estimates the co-movement in time series. The weights of the leading composite index are derived from a statistical model in which the weights are chosen so that the resultant composite index is an "optimal" predictor of six-month-ahead movements in the coincident index.

The two experimental recession indexes' estimates of the probability of a future recession are based on forecasts of overall economic activity six months ahead. These six-month forecasts, which are updated every month, reflect the expected movements of each of the seven component indicators of the experimental financial and nonfinancial leading indexes, based on statistical analysis.

The probability that the economy will be in a recession six months ahead is derived from a comparison of the expected future movements of the experimental leading and coincident indexes with their behavior in previous expansions and recessions. This technique is referred to as statistical pattern recognition, in which the data set matches, or is in a class of, prespecified patterns.

The experimental recession indexes did a poor job of predicting the recession that began in August 1990. For example, as late as September 1990 (based on

August data), the recession index that included the financial indicators had a 3 percent probability that the economy would be in a recession in February 1991, while the probability for the index excluding financial variables was still only 24 percent.

The low probability of both recession indexes in the 1990–91 recession mirrors the previously noted failure of the leading indicator system to provide advance indication of the onset of the 1990 and previous recessions. The higher probability of a recession in the experimental recession index excluding financial variables reflects the fact that monetary policy preceding the 1990–91 recession generally was neutral, rather than restrictive. For example, the federal funds rate on interbank loans, which is a good indicator of Federal Reserve monetary policies, declined during the last half of 1989 and was level during the first half of 1990 (Chapter 12 covers federal funds). Mark Watson notes that financial variables in the recession index were modestly optimistic.[15] This differs from the tight monetary policies that typically occurred before previous recessions, and which in statistical analyses of previous time periods retrospectively led to the recession index that includes financial variables performing better than the nonfinancial recession index. However, despite this reversal in the performance of the two recession indexes, even the nonfinancial index did not perform well in predicting the 1990–91 recession or in identifying the recession after it began.

In the winter of 1997, neither experimental recession index indicated an impending recession, and one showed much less of a chance than the other. Based on January 1997 data, the recession index including financial indicators had a probability of 1 percent that the economy would be in a recession in July 1997, and the recession index containing only nonfinancial indicators had a probability of 29 percent that the economy would be in a recession in July 1997. This difference between the two recession indexes in which the index including financial indicators has a lower probability of recession than the index excluding financial indicators is similar to the pattern preceding the 1990–91 recession noted above. It suggests that Federal Reserve monetary policies in the 1990s are not as restrictive as they were in previous decades (Chapters 2 and 12 cover monetary policies).

The experimental indexes are a promising development in the field of leading economic indicators and in probability economic forecasting, but they need more research to improve their forecasting capability. This research should focus on improving the forecasting power of the experimental indexes using contemporaneous preliminary data.

REVIEW QUESTIONS

- The leading indicator system is based on two main ideas: (1) the current phase of the business cycle contains the seeds of the next phase, and (2) profits are the prime mover of the economy. Describe the role of profits as the economy moves from expansion to recession to recovery to expansion.

- How do data revisions affect the usefulness of the leading indicator system?
- What is the conceptual difference between the leading index and the ratio of the coincident index to the lagging index?
- In reporting on the leading index, newspaper articles sometimes state that a decline in the index for three consecutive months signals a coming recession. What is wrong with this interpretation?
- During an expansion, assume that for several months the leading index turns down but the coincident/lagging ratio continues to rise. What does this suggest for future economic growth?
- What causes false signals in the leading indicator system?
- What do the experimental recession indexes contribute to the leading indicator system?

Extra Credit

- Why is the lead time of the leading index before a recession typically longer than the lead time before a recovery?
- The gross domestic product adjusted for inflation (real GDP) is the most comprehensive measure of the current health of the economy. Why, then, do we need the index of coincident indicators, in addition to GDP data?
- Why are income transfers, such as Social Security and unemployment insurance benefit payments, excluded from the income component of the coincident index?

NOTES

1. Geoffrey H. Moore, *Business Cycles, Inflation, and Forecasting.* 2d ed. (Ballinger, 1983), ch. 24. The history is recounted in this book. There are three milestone publications of the development. See also Wesley C. Mitchell and Arthur F. Burns, *Statistical Indicators of Cyclical Revivals,* Bulletin 69 (National Bureau of Economic Research, 1938), reprinted in National Bureau of Economic Research, *Business Cycle Indicators,* ed. Geoffrey H. Moore, 1961; Geoffrey H. Moore, *Statistical Indicators of Cyclical Revivals and Recessions,* Occasional Paper 31 (National Bureau of Economic Research, 1950); and Julius Shiskin, *Signals of Recession and Recovery,* Occasional Paper 77 (National Bureau of Economic Research, 1961).
2. Wesley C. Mitchell, *Business Cycles: The Problem and Its Setting* (National Bureau of Economic Research, 1927), pp. 105–7.
3. Tjalling C. Koopmans, "Measurement without Theory," *Review of Economics and Statistics,* August 1947.
4. Francis X. Diebold, Glenn D. Rudenbusch, and Daniel E. Sichel. "Further Evi-

dence on Business-Cycle Duration Dependence," *Business Cycles, Indicators, and Forecasting,* ed. James H. Stock and Mark W. Watson (University of Chicago Press, 1993).

5. The itemization draws significantly on work by Feliks Tamm. See Feliks Tamm, "An Introduction to the System of Coincident, Leading and Lagging Indexes." Bureau of Economic Analysis, U.S. Department of Commerce, 1984. Mimeo.

6. Evan F. Koenig, and Kenneth M. Emery, "Misleading Indicators? Using the Composite Leading Indicators to Predict Cyclical Turning Points," *Economic Review,* Federal Reserve Bank of Dallas, July 1991.

7. The Conference Board, "Details of the Revisions of the Composite Indexes," *Business Cycle Indicators,* December 1996. This describes the methodology of the three composite indexes.

8. Marie P. Hertzberg and Barry A. Beckman. "Business Cycle Indicators: Revised Composite Indexes," *Survey of Current Business,* January 1989.

9. The Conference Board, *Business Cycle Indicators.* All months, 1997, p. 2.

10. See note 7.

11. Geoffrey H. Moore, "Generating Leading Indicators from Lagging Indicators," *Western Economic Journal,* June 1969.

12. Mitchell, *Business Cycles.*

13. Tamm, "System of Coincident, Leading, and Lagging Indexes," p. 12.

14. James H. Stock and Mark W. Watson, "A Procedure for Predicting Recessions with Leading Indicators: Econometric Issues and Recent Experience," in *Business Cycles, Indicators, and Forecasting.*

15. Mark W. Watson, "Using Econometric Models to Predict Recessions," *Economic Perspectives,* Federal Reserve Bank of Chicago, November/December 1991.

REFERENCES

Abraham, Katherine. 1997. "Measurement Issues in the Consumer Price Index." Report to the Joint Economic Committee, U.S. Congress. June.

Adams, Larry T. 1985. "Changing employment patterns of organized workers." *Monthly Labor Review*. February.

Advisory Commission to Study the Consumer Price Index. 1996. *Toward a More Accurate Measure of the Cost of Living.* Final Report to the Senate Finance Committee. December 4.

Akerlof, George A., William T. Dickens, and George L. Perry. 1996. "The Macroeconomics of Low Inflation." *Brookings Papers on Economic Activity* 1.

Akhtar, M.A. 1997. *Understanding Open Market Operations.* Federal Reserve Bank of New York, p. 28.

Baker, Dean. 1996. *Getting Prices Right: A Methodologically Consistent Consumer Price Index.* Economic Policy Institute. April 12.

_____. 1996. "The Overstated CPI—Can It Really Be True?" *Challenge.* September-October.

Baumol, William J., Sue Anne Blackman, and Edward N. Wolff. 1989. *Productivity and American Leadership: The Long View.* MIT Press, ch. 13.

Becker, Eugene H. 1984. "Self-employed workers: an update to 1983." *Monthly Labor Review.* July.

Berry, John B., and Pierre Thomas. 1996. "Fed Requests Probe to Find Source of Leak." *Washington Post.* September 23, p. A1.

Blomberg, S. Brock, and Ethan S. Harris. 1995. "The Commodity-Consumer Price Connection: Fact or Fable?" *Economic Policy Review.* Federal Reserve Bank of New York. October.

Board of Governors of the Federal Reserve System. 1994. *Purposes and Functions.*

Bregger, John E. 1996. "Measuring self-employment in the United States." *Monthly Labor Review.* January/February.

Bregger, John E., and Steven E. Haugen. 1995. "BLS introduces new range of alternative unemployment measures." *Monthly Labor Review.* October.

Browne, Lynn Elaine, with Joshua Gleason. 1996. "The Saving Mystery, or Where Did the Money Go?" *New England Economic Review.* Federal Reserve Bank of Boston. September/October.

Bureau of the Census, U.S. Department of Commerce. 1996. *Poverty in the United States: 1995.* September.

Bureau of Economic Analysis, U.S. Department of Commerce. 1996. "Improved Estimates of the National Income and Product Accounts for 1959–95: Results of the Comprehensive Revision." *Survey of Current Business.* January/February.

Bureau of International Labor Affairs, U.S. Department of Labor. 1992. *The Underground Economy in the United States*. September.

Bureau of Labor Statistics, U.S. Department of Labor. 1993. *Labor Composition and U.S. Productivity Growth*. Bulletin 2426. October.

———. 1996. "Multifactor Productivity Trends, 1994." *News Release*. January 17.

———. 1997. *Handbook of Methods*. April.

Canner, Glenn B., Charles A. Luckett, and Thomas A. Durkin. 1990. "Mortgage Financing." *Federal Reserve Bulletin*. August.

Chang, Roberto. 1995. "Is a Weak Dollar Inflationary?" *Economic Review*. Federal Reserve Bank of Atlanta. September/October.

Committee on National Statistics, National Research Council. 1995. *Measuring Poverty: A New Approach*. National Academy Press.

Clifford, A. Jerome. 1965. *The Independence of the Federal Reserve System*. University of Pennsylvania Press.

Cole, Kevin, Jean Helwege, and David Laster. 1996. "Stock Market Valuation Indicators: Is This Time Different?" *Financial Analysts Journal*. May/June. Figure 4.

Conference Board, The. 1996. "Details of the Revisions of the Composite Indexes." *Business Cycle Indicators*. December.

Congressional Budget Office, Congress of the United States. 1997. *The Economic and Budget Outlook: Fiscal Years 1998–2007*. January.

Corrado, Carol, Charles Gilbert, and Richard Raddock. 1997. "Industrial Production and Capacity Utilization: Historical Revision and Recent Developments." *Federal Reserve Bulletin*. February.

Coughlin, Cletus C., and Kees Koedijk. 1990. "What Do We Know About the Long-Run Real Exchange Rate?" *Review*. Federal Reserve Bank of St. Louis. January/February.

Darby, Michael R. 1984. "The U.S. Productivity Slowdown: A Case of Statistical Myopia." *American Economic Review*. June.

de Leeuw, Frank, and Thomas M. Holloway. 1983. "Cyclical Adjustment of the Federal Budget and Federal Debt." *Survey of Current Business*. December.

Denison, Edward F. 1985. *Trends in Economic Growth, 1929–82*. Brookings Institution.

Diebold, Francis X., Glenn D. Rudenbusch, and Daniel E. Sichel. 1993. "Further Evidence on Business-Cycle Duration Dependence." *Business Cycles, Indicators, and Forecasting*, ed. James H. Stock and Mark W. Watson. University of Chicago Press.

Duncan, Joseph W., and Andrew C. Gross. 1995. *Statistics for the 21st Century: Proposals for Improving Statistics for Better Decision Making*. Irwin Professional Publishing.

Economic Report of the President. 1997. Government Printing Office. February.

Eisner, Robert. 1996. *The Misunderstood Economy: What Counts and How to Count It*. Harvard Business School Press.

Emery, Kenneth M., and Chih-Ping Chang. 1997. "Is There a Stable Relationship Between Capacity Utilization and Inflation?" *Economic Review*. Federal Reserve Bank of Dallas. First quarter.

Estrella, Arturo, and Frederick S. Mishkin. 1996. "The Yield Curve as a Predictor of U.S. Recessions." *Current Issues in Economics and Finance*. Federal Reserve Bank of New York. June.

Fahim-Nader, Mahnaz, and William J. Zeile. 1996. "Foreign Direct Investment in the United States: New Investment in 1995 and Affiliate Operations in 1994." *Survey of Current Business*. July.

Federal Reserve Bank of Richmond. 1993. *Instruments of the Money Market*. 7th ed.

Flaim, Paul O. 1990. "Population changes, the baby boom, and the unemployment rate." *Monthly Labor Review*. August.

Friedman, Benjamin M. 1988. *Day of Reckoning: The Consequences of American Economic Policy under Reagan and After.* Random House.

Fulco, Lawrence J. 1994. "Strong post-recession gain in productivity contributes to slow growth in labor costs." *Monthly Labor Review.* December.

Furlong, Fred, and Robert Ingenito. 1996. "Commodity Prices and Inflation." *Economic Review.* Federal Reserve Bank of San Francisco, no. 2.

Gokhale, Jagadeesh, Laurence J. Kotlikoff, and John Sabelhaus. 1996. "Understanding the Postwar Decline in U.S. Saving: A Cohort Analysis." *Brookings Papers on Economic Activity* 1.

Goldstein, Morris, and Mohsin S. Khan. 1985. "Income and Price Effects in Foreign Trade." *Handbook of International Economics,* ed. R.W. Jones and P.B. Kenen. Vol. 2. Elsevier Science Publishing.

Gordon, Robert J. 1993. *Macroeconomics.* 6th ed. HarperCollins.

Kuttner, Robert. 1984. *The Economic Illusion: False Choices between Prosperity and Social Justice.* Houghton Mifflin.

Greider, William. 1987. *Secrets of the Temple: How the Federal Reserve Runs the Country.* Simon and Schuster.

Hershey, Robert D. Jr. 1992. "This Just In: Recession Ended 21 Months Ago." *New York Times.* December 23.

Hertzberg, Marie P., and Barry A. Beckman. 1989. "Business Cycle Indicators: Revised Composite Indexes." *Survey of Current Business.* January.

Houseman, Susan N. 1997. "New Institute Survey on Flexible Staffing Arrangements." *Employment Research.* W. E. Upjohn Institute for Employment Research. Spring.

Internal Revenue Service, U.S. Department of the Treasury. 1996. *Federal Compliance Research: Individual Income Tax Gap Estimates for 1985, 1988, and 1992.* April.

Jablonski, Mary, Kent Kunze, and Phyllis Flohr Otto. 1990. "Hours at work: a new base for BLS productivity measures." *Monthly Labor Review.* February.

Jackman, Patrick C. 1990. "The CPI as a Cost of Living Index." Paper presented at the 65th annual conference of the Western Economic Association, San Diego. June 29–July 3.

Johnson, Roger T. Revised 1995. *Historical Beginnings . . . The Federal Reserve.* Federal Reserve Bank of Boston. December.

Joint Center of Housing Studies of Harvard University. 1996. *The State of the Nation's Housing.*

Joint Economic Committee of Congress. *1980 Supplement to Economic Indicators.*

Kaufman, Henry. 1986. *Interest Rates, the Markets, and the New Financial World.* Times Books.

Kettl, Donald F. 1986. *Leadership at the Fed.* Yale University Press.

Koenig, Evan F., and Kenneth M. Emery. 1991. "Misleading Indicators? Using the Composite Leading Indicators to Predict Cyclical Turning Points." *Economic Review.* Federal Reserve Bank of Dallas. July.

Koopmans, Tjalling C. 1947. "Measurement without Theory." *Review of Economics and Statistics.* August.

Korns, Alexander. 1979. "Cyclical Fluctuations in the Difference between the Payroll and Household Measures of Employment." *Survey of Current Business.* May.

Korten, David C. 1995. *When Corporations Rule the World.* Kumarian Press and Berrett-Koehler Publishers.

Kozicki, Sharon. 1997. "The Productivity Slowdown: Diverging Trends in the Manufacturing and Service Sectors." *Economic Review.* Federal Reserve Bank of Kansas City. First quarter.

Landefeld, Steven J., and Robert P. Parker. 1995. "Preview of the Comprehensive Revision of the National Income and Product Accounts: BEA's New Featured Measures of Output and Prices." *Survey of Current Business*. July.

Laster, David, Paul Bennett, and In Sun Geoum. 1997. "Rational Bias in Macroeconomic Forecasts." *Staff Reports*. No. 21. Federal Reserve Bank of New York. March.

Lebergott, Stanley. 1986. "Discussion." *Journal of Economic History*. June.

Lee, Tae-Hwy, and Stuart Scott. 1997. "Investigating Inflation Transmission by Stages of Processing." Mimeo. U.S. Bureau of Labor Statistics, Office of Research and Evaluation. January 2.

————. 1996. "Transmission of Producer Prices Through Stages of Processing." *Proceedings of the Section on Survey Research Methods*. American Statistical Association.

Leibenstein, Harvey. 1966. "Allocative Efficiency vs. 'X-Efficiency'." *American Economic Review*. June.

Liegey, Paul R. Jr. 1994. "Apparel price indexes: effects of hedonic adjustment." *Monthly Labor Review*. May.

Lindsey, Lawrence B. 1996. "Statement Before the Committee on Banking and Financial Services of the U.S. House of Representatives." *Federal Reserve Bulletin*. November.

Mark, Jerome A. 1987. "Technological change and employment: some results from BLS research." *Monthly Labor Review*. April.

Mark, Jerome A., William H. Waldorf, et al. 1983. *Trends in Multifactor Productivity*. Bureau of Labor Statistics, U.S. Department of Labor. Bulletin 2178. September.

Marrinan, Jane. 1989. "Exchange Rate Determination: Sorting Out Theory and Evidence." *New England Economic Review*. Federal Reserve Bank of Boston. November/December.

Mataloni, Raymond J. Jr., and Mahnaz Fahim-Nader. 1996. "Operations of U.S. Multinational Companies: Preliminary Results From the 1994 Benchmark Survey." *Survey of Current Business*. December.

McCarthy, Jonathan. 1997. "Debt, Delinquencies, and Consumer Spending." *Current Issues in Economics and Finance*. Federal Reserve Bank of New York. February.

McDonald, Richard J. 1984. "The 'underground economy' and BLS statistical data." *Monthly Labor Review*. January.

McNees, Stephen K. 1987. "Forecasting Cyclical Turning Points: The Record in the Past Three Recessions." *New England Economic Review*. Federal Reserve Bank of Boston. March/April.

————. 1990. "Man vs. Model? The Role of Judgment in Forecasting." *New England Economic Review*. Federal Reserve Bank of Boston. July/August.

————. 1992. "How Large Are Economic Forecast Errors?" *New England Economic Review*. Federal Reserve Bank of Boston. July/August.

————. 1992. "The Uses and Abuses of 'Consensus' Forecasts." *Journal of Forecasting*, no. 8.

————. 1995. "An Assessment of the 'Official' Economic Forecasts." *New England Economic Review*. Federal Reserve Bank of Boston. July/August.

Mitchell, Wesley C. 1927. *Business Cycles: The Problem and Its Setting*. National Bureau of Economic Research.

Mitchell, Wesley C., and Arthur F. Burns. 1938. *Statistical Indicators of Cyclical Revivals*. Bulletin 69. National Bureau of Economic Research. Reprinted in National Bureau of Economic Research. *Business Cycle Indicators*, ed. Geoffrey H. Moore. 1961.

Moore, Geoffrey H. 1950. *Statistical Indicators of Cyclical Revivals and Recessions*. Occasional Paper 31. National Bureau of Economic Research.

————. 1969. "Generating Leading Indicators from Lagging Indicators." *Western Economic Journal*. June.

————. 1983. *Business Cycles, Inflation and Forecasting*. 2d ed. Ballinger.

Morris, Charles S. 1984. "The Productivity 'Slowdown': A Sectoral Analysis." *Economic Review*. Federal Reserve Bank of Kansas City. April.

Moulton, Brent R., and Karin Moses. 1997. "Addressing the Quality Change Issue in the Consumer Price Index." *Brookings Papers on Economic Activity* 1. Forthcoming.

National Association of Home Builders of the United States. 1995. *Home Builders Forecast*. December.

Niemira, Michael P., and Philip A. Klein. 1994. *Forecasting Financial and Economic Cycles*. Wiley.

Office of Management and Budget, Executive Office of the President. 1985. "Statistical Policy Directive No. 3: Compilation, Release, and Evaluation of Principal Economic Indicators." *Federal Register*. September 25.

———. 1996. *Statistical Programs of the United States Government: Fiscal Year 1997*.

——— 1997. "1997 North American Industry Classification System—1987 Standard Industrial Classification Replacement." *Federal Register*. April 9.

Okun, Arthur M. 1962. "Potential GNP: Its Measurement and Significance." *Proceedings of the Business and Economic Statistics Section*. American Statistical Association. Reprinted, with slight changes, in Arthur M. Okun. 1970. *The Political Economy of Prosperity*.

Phillips, A.W. 1958. "The Relation between Unemployment and the Rate of Change of Money Wage Rates in the United Kingdom, 1861–1957." *Economica*. November.

Pindyck, Robert S., and Daniel L. Rubinfeld. 1995. *Microeconomics*. 3d ed. Prentice-Hall.

Polivka, Anne E. 1996. "Contingent and alternative work arrangements, defined." *Monthly Labor Review*. October.

Renshaw, Edward. 1991. *Challenge*. March/April.

Romer, Christina D. 1986. "Spurious Volatility in Historical Unemployment Data." *Journal of Political Economy*. February.

———. 1986 "New Estimates of Prewar Gross National Product and Unemployment." *Journal of Economic History*. June.

———. 1986. "Is the Stabilization of the Postwar Economy a Figment of the Data?" *American Economic Review*. June.

Safire, William. 1975. *Before the Fall: An Inside View of the Pre-Watergate White House*. Doubleday.

Scherer, F.M. 1980. *Industrial Market Structure and Economic Performance*. 2d ed. Rand McNally.

Sellon, Gordon H. Jr., and Stuart E. Weiner. 1996. "Monetary Policy without Reserve Requirements: Analytical Issues." *Economic Review*. Federal Reserve Bank of Kansas City. Fourth quarter.

Shapiro, Matthew D. 1996. "Macroeconomic Implications of Variation in the Workweek of Capital." *Brookings Papers on Economic Activity* 2.

Shiskin, Julius. 1961. *Signals of Recession and Recovery*. Occasional Paper 77. National Bureau of Economic Research.

Sichel, Daniel E. 1997. *The Computer Revolution: An Economic Perspective*. The Brookings Institution.

Steinberg, Edward. 1990. "The Cycle of Discouraged Workers." *The Margin*. September/October.

Stinson, John F. Jr. 1983. "Comparison of Nonagricultural Employment Estimates from Two Surveys." *Employment and Earnings*. March.

Stock, James H., and Mark W. Watson. 1993. "A Procedure for Predicting Recessions with Leading Indicators: Econometric Issues and Recent Experience." *Business Cycles, Indicators, and Forecasting*, ed. by James H. Stock and Mark W. Watson. University of Chicago Press.

Swanson, David C., and Joseph Pavalone. 1996. "Variance Estimates for Changes in the Consumer Price Index." *CPI Detailed Report.* U.S. Bureau of Labor Statistics. April.

Tamm, Feliks. 1984. "An Introduction to the System of Coincident, Leading and Lagging Indexes." Mimeo. Bureau of Economic Analysis, U.S. Department of Commerce.

Tootell, Geoffrey M.B. 1991. "Regional Economic Conditions and the FOMC Votes of District Presidents." *New England Economic Review.* March/April.

———. 1994. "Restructuring, the NAIRU, and the Phillips Curve." *New England Economic Review.* Federal Reserve Bank of Boston. September/October.

———. 1996. "Appointment Procedures and FOMC Voting Behavior." *Southern Economic Journal.* July.

Watson, Mark W. 1991. "Using Econometric Models to Predict Recessions." *Economic Perspectives.* Federal Reserve Bank of Chicago. November/December.

Weiner, Stuart. E. 1995. "Challenges to the Natural Rate Framework." *Economic Review.* Federal Reserve Bank of Kansas City. Second Quarter.

Weir, David R. 1986. "The Reliability of Historical Macroeconomic Data for Comparing Cyclical Stability." *Journal of Economic History.* June.

Woo, Wing T. 1984. "Exchange Rates and the Prices of Nonfood, Nonfuel Products." *Brookings Papers on Economic Activity* 2.

Yergin, Daniel. 1991. *The Prize: The Epic Quest for Oil, Money, and Power.* Simon and Schuster.

Young, Allan H. 1993. "Reliability and Accuracy of the Quarterly Estimates of GDP." *Survey of Current Business.* October.

Zarnowitz, Victor. 1984. "The Accuracy of Individual and Group Forecasts from Business Outlook Studies." *Journal of Forecasting.* January-March. Reprinted in Victor Zarnowitz. 1992. *Business Cycles: Theory, History, Indicators, and Forecasting.* University of Chicago Press, ch. 15.

———. 1992. *Business Cycles: Theory, History, Indicators, and Forecasting.* University of Chicago Press.

Zarnowitz, Victor, and Phillip Braun. 1993. "Twenty-two Years of the NBER-ASA Quarterly Economic Outlook Surveys: Aspects and Comparisons of Forecasting Performance." *Business Cycles, Indicators, and Forecasting,* ed. by James H. Stock and Mark W. Watson.

Zeile, William J. 1993. "Merchandise Trade of U.S. Affiliates of Foreign Companies." *Survey of Current Business.* October.

INDEX

American Bankruptcy Institute, 124
Anti-inflation policies, 50
"Automatic stabilizers," 54–55*f*, 56–57
Autoregressive integrated moving average
  (ARIMA), 67, 70

Baby boom, 211, 214
Balance of payments, 147
  and external debt, 159–64, 165*n7*, 176
  and foreign investment, 160*f*, 161*f*-62
  and foreign trade, 150, 156, 158–59*f*,
    160*f*, 161*f*
Balanced budget multiplier, 54, 58
Bank credit:
  and inflation premium, 61, 276, 284, 287
  and monetary policy, 51, 53, 59–62, 277
  and money supply, 279
Banking regulatory system, 278–79
Bankruptcy, 124
Bonds, 15, 63
  See also Debt instruments
Box-Jenkins, 67
Bureau of Economic Analysis (BEA):
  and balance of payments, 147
  data collection by, 34, 36
  and GDP, 32, 78, 81, 87, 128, 240
  and household income/expenditure, 111
  and income per capita, 196
  and leading indicator system, 306
Bureau of Labor Statistics (BLS):
  and business GDP, 105
  and Consumer Price Index (CPI), 243,
    246, 249, 250

Bureau of Labor Statistics *(continued)*
  data collection by, 34, 36, 182
  and employment cost index, 198
  and establishment survey, 185, 195
  and export/import price index, 154, 158
  and measures of inflation, 240
  and underground economy, 32–33
  and unemployment, 206
Bureau of the Census:
  and capacity utilization, 261
  and consumer purchases, 243
  and Current Population survey, 185, 208
  data collection by, 34, 36
  and manufactured goods, 137
Burns, Arthur, 300
Business cycles, 50–51, 301–03
  analysis of, 309–13
  and business profits, 129*f*, 130*f*, 132*f*,
    133*f*
  characteristics of, 3–14, 50
    volatility, 138
  and consumer behavior, 116*f*
  and consumer price index, 255*t*
  and economic growth, 6, 9–10*t*, 53
  and foreign trade, 151–52*f*, 153*f*
  and GDP, 116*f*, 119*f*, 120*f*, 129*f*, 131
  and housing, 139*f*
  and leading composite index, 307*t*
  and nonresidential investment, 129*f*,
    130*f*, 132*f*, 133*f*
  See also Expansions; Recessions
Business sector:
  foreign-owned firms in, 160, 165*n6*

325

Norman Frumkin is an economics writer. He has worked for the federal government and industry. He has a long-standing interest in the use of statistics for economic analysis and forecasting. He was a staff member of the Advisory Committee on Gross National Product Data Improvement, sponsored by the U.S. Department of Commerce. The committee's report, *Report of the Advisory Committee on Gross National Product Data Improvement,* is referred to as the Creamer Report, for Daniel Creamer who chaired the committee and was the staff director. Mr. Frumkin taught a course on interpreting economic trends at the Graduate School, U.S. Department of Agriculture, which was the stimulus for the first edition of *Tracking America's Economy.* He is also the author of *Guide to Economic Indicators,* published by M.E. Sharpe.